Between North and South

William Wilkins Glenn (1824–1876). *Courtesy of Mrs. Frank H. Merrill and the Ann Arrundell County Historical Society.*

Between North and South

A Maryland Journalist Views the Civil War

The Narrative of William Wilkins Glenn 1861-1869

Edited with Notes and Glossary

by

Bayly Ellen Marks *and* Mark Norton Schatz

Rutherford • Madison • Teaneck
Fairleigh Dickinson University Press
London: Associated University Presses

Associated University Presses, Inc.
Cranbury, New Jersey 08512

Associated University Presses
108 New Bond Street
London W1Y OQX, England

Library of Congress Cataloging in Publication Data

Glenn, William Wilkins, 1824–1876.
Between North and South.

Bibliography: p.
Includes index.
1. United States—History—Civil War, 1861–1865— Personal narratives. 2. Glenn, William Wilkins, 1824–1876. I. Marks, Bayly Ellen. II. Schatz, Mark Norton. III. Title.
E458.8.G57 973.7'82 74-4981
ISBN 0-8386-1581-3

Also by Bayly Ellen Marks:

Maryland Tax List of 1783, Baltimore County, Harford County

Guide to the Microfilm Edition of the Robert Goodloe Harper Family Papers, Maryland Historical Society

Guide to the Microfilm Edition of the David Bailie Warden Papers, Maryland Historical Society

Hilton Heritage

PRINTED IN THE UNITED STATES OF AMERICA

CONTENTS

ACKNOWLEDGMENTS

The original manuscript of the narrative of William Wilkins Glenn is in the custody of the Maryland Historical Society and the editors wish to express especial thanks to Mr. P. William Filby, Director of the Society, for his assistance and encouragement in the preparation of this volume. The staff of the Maryland Historical Society extended a courtesy and expertise that exceeded even their traditionally high standards of cooperation. In this regard, particular thanks are given to Mary K. Meyer, genealogical librarian, and to Nancy G. Boles, former manuscript curator.

The staffs of the Enoch Pratt Library in Baltimore and the National Archives in Washington, D.C., were uniformly helpful, and any attempt to single out individual kindnesses would slight some who do not deserve to be overlooked by absent-minded historians. A noteworthy exception, however, must be Elmer O. Parker, of the Old Military Records Division in the National Archives, who bore up bravely under the imposition of old friendship and rendered the thorough professional service that is synonymous with his reputation.

The technical heroics of Eskil Ohlson in obtaining the photograph of William Wilkins Glenn's portrait that serves as the frontispiece of this volume only increase a longstanding debt of friendship.

Any acknowledgment would be incomplete indeed that did not mention Mrs. Frank H. Merrill, a grand lady whose knowledge of the Glenn family in general is exceeded only by her understanding of and devotion to William Wilkins Glenn in particular. For many years

Mrs. Merrill has given unstintingly from her vast storehouse of Glenn lore with an enthusiasm enriched by her graciousness.

A BRIEF BIOGRAPHICAL SKETCH OF WILLIAM WILKINS GLENN

William Wilkins Glenn was born in Baltimore, Maryland, on July 20, 1824. He was the second child and eldest son of John Glenn and Henrietta Wilkins. His father, who eventually became a judge on the United States District Court, established one of the most lucrative law practices in the city's history. Building upon a foundation laid in turn by his father, Judge Elias Glenn, John Glenn successfully aspired to a position of eminent financial power and substantial political influence.

Described by John C. Calhoun as one of the most intelligent and respectable citizens of Baltimore, a business partner of Reverdy Johnson, related by ties of marriage and friendship to the powerful Perine family, successor to much of the legal practice of William Wirt, Judge John Glenn moved in an ever-widening circle of the prominent and powerful on both the local and national scene.

As the scion of such wealth and social prominence, William Wilkins Glenn traveled the fringes of grand events, on familiar terms with the great and near-great as well. Of uncertain health, sensitive to a fault in mind and spirit, he was educated in private schools at home and briefly attended William and Mary College before graduating from St. Mary's College in Baltimore in 1841.

Glenn then embarked on a commercial career, serving an apprenticeship in the counting room of a local import house. In 1844 his extensive foreign travels began with a voyage to South America as supercargo on a trading vessel. He visited Montevideo, Uruguay (then in the throes of civil war), and Buenos Aires, Argentina.

After his return to America Glenn expanded his financial interests, forming a partnership with Richard Lemmon in an iron brokerage enterprise. Interspersing his local business and social activities with additional travel in the 1840s, Glenn visited New Orleans as well as the fashionable spas of Virginia and New York. Five feet nine inches tall, with dark brown hair, the blue-eyed Glenn was an attractive man whose family's wealth and position assured him entrée into any circle of the social elite.

The year 1848 saw the first of Glenn's European sojourns. The ill health of his mother and also of two of his sisters, and especially the failing eyesight of his brother John, resulted in a journey to the health resorts of Austria with their celebrated "water cures." In 1851 Glenn returned to Austria, again with his brother John, in a vain attempt to arrest the latter's encroaching blindness. These travels included extensive tours of Germany, Italy, Poland, France, and England, and visits to Berlin, Vienna (then under siege), Prague, Cracow, Paris, and London.

The death of Judge John Glenn in 1853 affected the pattern of William Wilkins Glenn's life for years to come. As an executor of his father's will the duty of managing a vast and complex estate descended upon him and he was never again free from the obligations to his mother and family that he felt this responsibility entailed. The Glenn estate consisted of extensive real estate holdings, ground rents, valuable personal property, and a diversity of stocks and bonds. Included in the property holdings was the 1,000-acre country estate of "Hilton" located in the Catonsville area of Baltimore County. By judicious management Glenn expanded the capital base of the estate and ultimately saw it valued at several millions of dollars.

In 1857 William Wilkins Glenn married Ellen Mark Smith of Philadelphia. They had four children, two sons living to maturity.

With the advent of the Civil War, Glenn purchased controlling interest in Baltimore's *Daily Exchange* newspaper in the hope of influencing public opinion in Maryland. Pro-Southern and anti-administration in its views, the editorial policy of the paper resulted in Glenn's arrest on September 14, 1861, his confinement in Fort McHenry, and the suppression of his newspaper. Unlike other political prisoners arrested during this period, Glenn was allowed to remain at Fort McHenry rather than being sent to a prison out of state. This special treatment, coupled with the fact that he took no oath of allegiance and signed no parole, gives some indication of his influence and the prestige of his friends.

Glenn was released from Fort McHenry on December 2, 1861. He then began an active campaign of aid to the Southern cause, circumspectly threading a path between his dangerous political activities and his obligations to his family as administrator of his father's estate. His subversive activities on behalf of the Confederacy centered largely around the smuggling of persons "underground" into the South. Prominent visitors, especially visiting Englishmen, sought his services and eventually this activity forced him to flee the state in July, 1863. The prior death of his wife in May of that year possibly made his exile more bearable.

Arriving in England, Glenn gravitated to a social circle of his liking among the nobility and landed gentry. After visiting France, he returned to America in 1864 and, again being subject to arrest in Maryland, spent much of the remainder of the war in the North.

In the postwar period Glenn continued his journalistic activities and the financial supervision of his family's fortune. Another European tour followed and in 1872 Glenn sold his newspaper interests and concentrated heavily on silver mining in Colorado and Idaho. He traveled extensively in the West, then, burdened by the pressures of difficult mining operations and frustrating legal entanglements, his health broke down and he returned to Baltimore. He died of Bright's disease at his home on the northeast corner of Charles and Madison streets on June 24, 1876.

William Wilkins Glenn was a man of diverse talents and varied interests. A student of the law, an accomplished writer, and a perceptive poet, he successfully blended a realistic business career with the social and artistic graces. Frequently frustrated, often depressed, reserved to the point of snobbery and stubborn in his dislikes, he was nonetheless a warm and loyal friend keenly interested in the affairs of those around him and sympathetic to their needs. His ability to balance a restless spirit against the necessities of his obligations lends a poignancy to his life that is perhaps best reflected in the circumstances of his death. After an illness marked with great pain, he approached his end with a calm detachment and a mind unimpaired to the last.

The narrative of William Wilkins Glenn that follows was written by him for possible publication. The acridity of his comments doubtless precluded a public airing in his own lifetime, and the rigidity of his personality would not allow compromise with his stated views. This narrative, as well as the circumstances of his life, would seem to rate him a justifiable place among the prominent Baltimoreans of his day and mark him as a valuable commentator on the people and events of those stirring times.

Between North and South

The Narrative of William Wilkins Glenn 1861-1869

EDITOR'S NOTE: Glenn had a curious style in recording dates that may have been somewhat common practice (for he uses it in his letters as well as in his journal), but that may cause some puzzlement in the reader. He uses—often, not invariably—a ditto mark to indicate variously *st* in 1st (1"), *d* in 2d (2"), and *th* in 4th (4"), in a kind of shorthand. His often erratic punctuation and occasional misspellings have also been preserved here.

THE NARRATIVE
OF
WILLIAM WILKINS GLENN
1861–1869

No. 1

Of all my acquaintances there were certainly none in Maryland that had the faintest conception of the terrible revolution that was shortly to convulse the country.* I myself had seen enough in 1856 when Fremont was a candidate for the Presidency, to convince me that the election of Lincoln in 1860 would assuredly be the prelude to great political disturbances and to much financial trouble—and as early as the Spring of 1860, I began to close up all my building contracts, being largely engaged in improving the property of our Estate, and to decline to enter into new ones. It was fortunate for me that I did. After the nomination by the Republicans their party grew stronger and Lincoln was elected President.**

After the Southern States had seceded and formed a new Union the actual state of feeling in Maryland was difficult to get at. Many of the staunchest supporters of the South at a later period were then

* Standard textual material on the Lincoln administration and the military and diplomatic conduct of the Civil War has been largely omitted.

** Lincoln's vote in Maryland in 1860 was 2,294. Douglas received 5,873 votes, Bell of the Constitutional Union Party 41,777, and Breckinridge of the Southern Democrats 42,497. Seventy percent of Maryland's electorate cast ballots in this election.

really Union men. They were not prepared for the crisis & did not accept the fact that the real question was not between South and Union—but between South and North. Many of them too were opposed to slavery and some of them who had been Whigs all their lives, could not free themselves from the fetters of old political association and felt naturally inclined to oppose any party which called itself Democratic. Besides this even the Secessionists *per se* were too timid to attempt to act without Virginia, and Virginia clung to the Union.

There was not only no leader of a Southern party in Baltimore at that time, but there was no newspaper to advocate the [?] cause. The Daily Exchange was the paper to which every [?] looked, but it was very non committal and indeed seemed [?] inclined to espouse the cause of the Union. At that time Mr. Wm. H. Norris was one of the extremest men we had. His office was next to mine. He had been a friend of my father's and had known me all my life. We saw a great deal of each other and grieved together over the course of Maryland and deplored the want of a newspaper and the course of the Exchange. We heard too that Charley Kerr had sold his interest to Fitzhugh and that Frank Howard was about to sell his, thus leaving the paper entirely in the hands of a Northern sympathizer.

Saturday Jany 19" 1861. I dropped into S. T. Wallis' office as was usual on my way down.* Frank Howard was sitting in a chair very gloomy. He had as I afterwards found out actually agreed to conclude the sale of his portion of the paper to which he had devoted a great deal of his time and in which he had sunk a good deal of his money. Besides this he had a great fancy for the occupation. "Bill", said he, suddenly looking up "You are always ready for anything, buy my interest in the Exchange." His only idea then was to get a little better bargain out of me than he could out of Fitzhugh. "Confound your interest," said I "What do I want with it. I'll buy Fitzhugh's". "Will you" asked he, after a moments hesitation. "I think it can be arranged". He then made a statement and proposed that I should come and examine the books. But I told him, I would take his word and that if the arrangement was to be made it should be made at once as time was pressing and the paper was already losing some of its Southern subscribers. The only assurance I required

* Severn T. Wallis had his law office at 37 St. Paul Street in Baltimore. All references to Baltimore addresses come from the Baltimore City Directories, 1860 and 1864. The street numbers were changed in the 1880s. No directories were published from 1861 to 1863.

was that he, Howard should remain with me on the paper, as I felt by no means equal to the task of conducting a newspaper, as I would wish to see one conducted in which I was interested. As I left Wallis asked me to return and dine, which I did. We had a long talk he being very desirous of knowing more of my views on politics and slavery, in both of which he feared that Howard & I might be too antagonistic to work together agreeably and I wishing to get from [?] a frank opinion as to whether he considered this new undertaking [?] a very foolish one or not. Appreciating as I did thoroughly the very decided literary capacity of both Wallis & Howard, I naturally felt great modesty about associating myself with them. I had taken too, apparently, so little interest in public affairs heretofore, that I felt as if I would appear ridiculous in undertaking what more prominent men should have done. So I talked of the matter with Wallis as a business matter—altho the truth was business had nothing to do with it. The paper had always lost money and continued to lose money until it was stopped by our arrest. I bought my large interest, over a half and assumed a mortgage which would more than swamp the whole, solely and entirely for "the Cause". I saw how men hung back and refused to spend money, and I felt that if men of Capital were not willing to risk their money, what was to be expected of the rest of Society.

As soon as the Daily Exchange changed hands, the tone of the paper became decided and firm although by no means extreme and not sufficiently Southern to satisfy those who considered the Union finally dissolved. Frank Howard who assumed the place of Editor in Chief still looked and hoped for reunion. He had his views and notions about Slavery anything but Southern and was very much opposed to the course adopted by South Carolina. Teackle Wallis, who was a wonderfully clever and rapid writer, and sometimes contributed two or three leaders a week gratuitously, had very much the same opinion, and was not at all inclined to back the South up at all hazards. The question of North and South had at that time presented itself to but few men in Maryland. I recollect perfectly well, that Wallis was very anxious to know what were the interests of the State and whether in case of a separation, its development would be most rapid in a Northern and Southern Confederacy. The only two men whose opinion I valued and who were not extreme, who took what I considered a proper view of the situation, and a view which was more than thoroughly borne out by events, were Mr. Gatchell & Govr. Pratt. Mr. Gatchell was at that time one of the Police Commissioners. His companions were Charles Howard,

Hinks & Jno. Davis. Hinks' appointment was a political one & he had no strength of Character. Davis, who had been Clerk of one of the Courts, was put in to satisfy the lower classes that they were properly represented and although a good fellow was perfectly incapable of appreciating the situation. With these men and Mr. Charles Howard, Mr. Gatchell found that he did not altogether agree and being in a minority he yielded to them. His own judgment was however entirely correct. He is one of the few men I have known in life, whose opinions I always think entitled to great consideration. Mr. Wm. H. Norris, better known as Billy Norris, who was not only very Southern but very extreme and who was sadly disappointed at what he called the milk and water trash of the Exchange, after I had become principal owner, went one day to Mr. Gatchell to complain of me and to ask what I could mean after expressing the very decided views I had. Mr. G. sensibly replied "Let the boy alone, Norris. He does the best he can. He has two men with him who are not Southern as he is and he has to yield to them to some extent." And this was the truth. I could not afford to split with Howard or Wallis. I had no experience in Editing a paper and not the Capacity to Edite [*sic*] it as I would wish to see it edited. I was often worried beyond measure that I could never urge them beyond a certain point and now and then I would put in short editorials myself, for the purpose of committing the paper, so that it could not well recede. The other man to whom I alluded was Thomas G. Pratt, formerly Governor. He was right from the beginning, but was never willing to run any risk. He wished to work in secret and push other men forward, but had no fancy to assume the lead of a doubtful Cause. If however the Legislature had appointed a Committee of Safety, as he and others wished, to set aside Govr. Hicks and take the power into their hands, I am satisfied he would have consented to serve as one of them.

Charles H. Pitts would have been a good man if he had been at all interested. But he was not. He was out of sorts generally. He had got too lazy to work and the condition of his finances annoyed him. Besides this he never could forget the abuse that had been heaped upon him the tricks that had been played upon him in old days by the Democrats. The name of Democrat was sufficient to arouse in him a strong sentiment of antagonism, and like many others he did not seem at first to comprehend that this had become a great national question in which all party distinctions were sunk.

Jany 1861. There was held a very large and enthusiastic Union

Mass Meeting at the Maryland Institute Hall. Immediately after this, Mr. Norris, who by the way had always been Whig, and some of the Democrats determined upon a counter meeting. Mr. Norris was however the head and center of the whole movement. Our offices were separated only by a door and we of course saw each other frequently. He communicated his project to me and about half a dozen of us had a meeting at the office of John Thompson Mason, who was then Collector of this Port. It was then determined to have a preliminary meeting of prominent ward democrats, for the purpose of getting an expression of the sentiment of the people. Messages were sent by the Custom House Clerks to about two men from each ward such as Jesse Hunt, who had been Mayor, Vansant, the Hatter, always a prominent ward politician, Peter Mowell, Iron Master, one or two Members of the City Council and men of that Class, of the people and having influence over men by whom they were supported or whom they employed. About twenty five responded to the call & we met again in the Custom House, in Mason's office.* Here we had a long talk and finally Mr. Norris harangued them and endeavored to obtain from them a decided expression of opinion. But it was no use. One and all expressed the same sentiment. "We are for the Union first. If that cannot be saved, then we are for the South." They were all men engaged in business, strongly inclined to regard their own interests and evidently not at all disposed to revolutionizing. Billy Norris was much disappointed, but still it was determined to go on and invitations were issued to a number of gentlemen for the purpose of holding a more formal meeting and taking the final steps necessary for a mass meeting. A list of names was accordingly prepared and I revised them taking particular care that the names of Mr. Sam. W. Smith, Teackle Wallis, Pitts and others, whose presence I deemed absolutely necessary to give a proper tone to the meeting, should be upon the list and that invitations should be sent them. The following day Mr. Norris showed me a series of resolutions which he had prepared. They were certainly of a most extraordinary character, rhapsodical and violent and only calculated to do much more harm than good. On the day of the Meeting I went after Wallis to be sure and have him present and took the trouble to go and dine with Pitts, that he might have no excuse for staying away. I was very much afraid that Norris and his party would take such extreme measures as to drive away many

* John Thompson Mason's office was at 35 St. Paul Street. William Wilkins Glenn's law office was located at 6 North Calvert, between Baltimore and Fayette streets.

of the strongest men, who were not then sufficiently advanced in their views, and thus render the first leading step of the Southern party a total failure. Subsequent events convinced me that the majority of the people of the State were by no means ready for separation. They were opposed to coercion but they clung to the Union. We met again in the same place. Mason took the chair. After a good deal of talk, I moved that a committee of five be appointed to draft resolutions, thinking that I would of course be chairman and that in this way, we would of course modify considerably the objectionable resolutions which Mr. Norris had in his pocket at that time. I was disappointed however. Mason did not even appoint me one of the committee and he did appoint Norris chairman. The committee met of course at Norris' office and being most of them men who yielded to him and who were glad to have someone to think for them, adopted his resolutions as they were. I forget entirely who the men were. Matters having gone this far, the next effort was to get Speakers. Norris made a show of inviting Wallis, whom he evidently did not want, and arranged it so as to keep Wallis out. Senator Hunter was then talked of. But I think he was away from Washington. Benjamin was written to, but he prudently declined for the reason that it was not becoming for a citizen of a State no longer in the Union to urge his views upon citizens of States which had not seceded. Then Wise was thought of and one or two men equally extreme but no one was to be had. I was a good deal in Norris' office with the Committee and I began to fear more & more that the formation of a strong & well supported Southern party was going to prove a failure.

February 1" 1861. I heard this morning that no speakers had been certainly engaged except Charley Gwinn. Matters certainly looked very hopeless. The meeting was to be held next evening. I went to see Charley and said "Charley are you going to speak to those resolutions of Norris'. Can you speak to them". "I cannot speak to them," said he with a half smile, "but I can speak along side of them." After some further talk I went to see Robt. M. McLane. I told him the conditions of things, told him that our whole organization was about to be ruined simply because of these blood and thunder resolutions to which no sensible men would commit themselves, and I begged him to go and see Mr. Norris and see what he could do in the matter. I told him that neither Pitts nor Wallis would undertake to advise him in the matter, intimate as they had always been with him, on account of the great difference of opinion between them and of the extreme irritability which Norris manifested on this subject and the want of consideration with which he treated their opinions. And I added that he was the only man to whom Norris would listen. Finally he replied "Well, if you desire it, I will go and try what can be done." The time was short. He went off almost immediately. The result of his interview was that Norris, who by the way was sadly disappointed at the result of his endeavors to get up what he called a spirited meeting, consented to have his resolutions revised. Bob McLane gave them at once to Charley Gwinn, who was very ready with his pen and he remodeled them the same evening.

February 2nd. I saw McLane and we read over the resolutions. They were rewritten to be sure and in much better taste, but the point & sentiments were the same and I knew we could not get the men we wanted to speak to them. "What is to be done" said McLane. "Oh! said I, now that we have razored Billy Norris, there will be no trouble in cutting down Charley Gwinn. Let us go in and see Wallis." In we went. After a long talk, I went out and after some difficulty succeeded in dragging in Pitts. There we four talked and revised for two hours until I was in despair. Wallis and Pitts would actually agree to say nothing at all decisive. At last I got up and started to leave, when McLane caught me and begged me not to leave him alone with those two men. I staid on and about two o'clock we finally agreed upon the resolutions as they appeared, with the exception of one word. Wallis agreed to speak, so did Pitts and McLane had I think made up his mind to speak any how, if the meeting proved to be at all large and respectable. So at last we were all right as to good speakers. I took the resolutions and started off for the purpose of having them set up in type. I stopped at my Law office for a few moments, during which time Norris stepped in to know what had been done. I gave him the resolutions to read. He was disgusted beyond measure and when he came to the passage which said "if compromises could not be so made as to ensure etc. etc. our sense of right no less than our commercial and political interests will incline us to cast our lot with Virginia and the other slave holding states"—he picked up a pen, dashed it violently across the word "incline" and wrote above it "decide". This I determined to let him settle with his friends. I certainly too agreed with him that it was as little as independent State's rights men, holding our views could say. I knew it suited McLane too & I was very anxious to see Mr. Wallis committed to a more decided policy. I took the resolutions to the Exchange office and had them set up. Wallis & Pitts knew nothing of it until I gave them copies at the Meeting. Pitts was very indignant, and refused to take any part in the meeting. Nothing could induce him to speak. Though loudly called for, he excused himself on the plea of hoarseness. McLane, delighted at the success of the meeting which was large, spoke enthusiastically and talked about meeting the invaders on the banks of the Susquehannah which should run red with their blood. Hence the nickname Bloody Bob which he has since borne. Wallis was called for and to my great gratification fell in with the temper of the Meeting and committed himself thoroughly to the resolutions as altered. The only drawback to the meeting was the appearance of Govr. Lowe. How he got there I never knew. He suddenly appeared, was called for, made a very ranting and extreme speech of a character which tended much more to do harm than good. With this exception everything was most satisfactory and we at last had a respectable party committed to a decided opinion.*

Febry 3rd. I could not but laugh this morning at Sister Mary's remark when I related the foregoing incidents at the breakfast table. "Ah! Yes" said she "don't you see it. Mr. Wallis' unselfish enthusiasm and Mr. Pitts cautious prudence." Sister Mary & the rest of the family indeed rather sided with Mr. Pitts. Sister Mary particularly had a strong dislike of everything which bore the name of Democrat, and was rather inclined to consider me a renegade. I recollect perfectly well, one evening last year, when a large Breckinridge procession was marching up Charles Street and round the Monument. I threw open all the window shutters of our house, on the corner of Charles and Madison Streets, and lighted up all the gas so as to produce quite an illumination. I went out by the Monument to see the effect of it and found to my surprise that my sisters had closed the shutters

* The resolutions adopted at the February 1st mass meeting at the Maryland Institute Hall called upon Marylanders to attend a State Convention on February 15th to take a firm stand on Maryland's position in the sectional crisis. The sixteen resolutions blamed the Federal government for failing to uphold the Constitution and, while expressing devotion to the Constitution and to the Union, called for resistance to any attempt by the Federal government to alter the interpretation of that Union. Although generally supporting the Crittenden Compromise, the farmers of the resolutions hoped that their sense of justice would "decide us to cast our lot with Virginia and the other slave-holding States of this confederacy." The resolutions are entirely sympathetic to the South and opposed to any attempt by the North to force the Southern states into submission. Regarding Governor Hicks's refusal to call a convention, the resolutions state that he "does *not* represent the sentiments of the people of the state." Reiterating their stand against armed coercion of the South, the resolutions urge local citizens to organize to oppose any "employment of military force to coerce by bloody process the seceding States." (Baltimore *Sun,* Feb. 2, 1861.)

& turned down all the superfluous gas—at which I laughed, as it was not my house.* They appeared to be quite annoyed when I announced to them that I had purchased a large interest in the Exchange.

After the meeting at the Institute ward organizations were formed and meetings held from time to time. No where however was there any concerted action or any well digested plan of operation. Commissioners came up from the South to Washington and were refused an audience. But Seward was in constant private communication with them and beguiled them by his assurances into the belief that under no circumstances should the South be attacked and war brought on. The Peace Convention met in Washington and dispersed without effecting anything.** Every one saw that matters were getting worse daily and still nobody in Maryland at least dreamed of the terrible revolution into which we were drifting. What astonished me most was that there were no leaders in Maryland who were willing to take a prominent part or act independently. There was but one opinion. Everyone said "Wait for Virginia. See what she does". Even Mr. Norris & his party who were extreme enough for anything insisted on waiting for Virginia. I argued the matter with him in vain. I assured him that the independent and decided action of any one State would have the same influence upon States, as the manly & determined action of one man had upon his fellow men. I urged that it was plain that if the North could be made to understand the true feeling

* The Washington Monument, designed by Robert Mills, was built between 1815 and 1829 on land donated by John Eager Howard. The monument forms the center of a four-block area crossed by Charles Street running north and south, and Monument Street running east and west. This area is bounded on the south by Centre Street, on the west by Cathedral Street, on the north by Madison Street, and on the east by St. Paul Street. The central section of the area is known as Mount Vernon Place. The Glenn residence, on the northeast corner of Charles and Madison streets, was built in 1859. Part of the estate of Judge John Glenn it was owned by his widow, Henrietta Wilkins Glenn, and after her death in 1891 was sold by the surviving trustees of the Judge's estate to the University Club, which is still located at the Charles and Madison address. The building is of red brick, three stories and a raised basement, with brownstone window frames (these are now painted white). It was expanded at a later date along the Madison Street side.

** The Peace Convention met at Willard's Hall in Washington, D.C., on February 4, 1861, with former President John Tyler as chairman. There were 132 delegates from 21 states. John Thomas Scharf (*History of Maryland,* Vol. III, Hatboro, Pa., 1967) lists Reverdy Johnson, Augustus W. Bradford, William T. Goldsborough, John W. Crisfield and J. Dixon Roman as the Maryland commissioners. A detailed study by Robert Gray Gunderson (*Old Gentlemen's Convention,* University Wisconsin Press, 1961) lists, in addition to the above, John F. Dent and Benjamin C. Howard as delegates. The Convention recommended a thirteenth amendment to the Constitution similar to the Crittenden amendment.

in the Border States and if the Border States would unite and declare that unless sufficient Constitutional guarantees were given to the Seceded States, they would make common cause with them, there certainly would be no war. But he would not listen to me. It was "wait for Virginia. We cannot act until she acts." Virginia did not act then. The North deceived by the attitude of the Border States laughed at the idea of there being much real Southern sympathy in Maryland, declared that "Virginia could not be kicked out of the Union" and ridiculed the notion of Kentucky's attempting to ally herself with the South. In this latter state Crittenden and Guthrie did a great deal of harm to the Southern Cause. Crittenden was old, and as was apt to be the case in the Border States, most of those who were well advanced in life and had grown up with the Union and watched its development with pride, strove hard to preserve it. Crittenden too had introduced his milk & water Peace Resolutions which he had committed himself and by which he hoped to hand his name down to posterity as the Savior of the Country.* Guthrie had large controlling rail road interests which gave him great influence. The large majority of the young men sided with the South. They had the numerical weight but the elderly man had the political control.**

April 11." [*1861*] The administration being secretly determined on war resolved if possible to force the South to strike the first blow. Accordingly a messenger was sent to Col. Anderson, then in command of Fort Sumter, from Washington. Having informed the military authorities at Charleston of the object of his visit, he was allowed to pass, but after his return it was discovered that he had in fact been the bearer of secret information to the effect that the Fort would soon be provisioned by the U.S. Govt. Up to this time great courtesy had been shown to the garrison of the Fort and provisions & vegetables had been constantly sent them from the City. It was however not the intention of the military authorities to allow the U.S. Government to exercise this privilege and as soon as it was known that this was intended and it was understood that Seward's messenger who had been allowed to communicate with the Fort had, by order of his principal, been guilty of a great breach of faith, it

* The full text of Crittenden's resoultions is printed in Scharf, *History of Maryland,* 3:373. Briefly, his compromises would have prohibited slavery north to be secured by "unamendable" Constitutional amendments.
protected slavery south of that line. The objectives of the compromise were to be secured by "unamendable" Constitutional amendments.

** February 24, February 27, and March 14, 1861, follow April 24.

was determined to take Fort Sumter before reinforcements arrived. Today its surrender was demanded.

April 13." Fort Sumter fell, after nearly two days bombardment. There was great excitement in Baltimore. The general feeling however was against the action of South Carolina. Wm. T. Walters made himself very busy in collecting subscriptions for the purpose of firing a salute in honor of the occasion, which was done. This Walters was a large liquor dealer, who had a large trade with New Orleans. He talked loudly, worked pretty well and gave his money as long as it was safe. The moment there was any chance of arrest he left for Europe to spend his time while the war lasted.

April 14". The President made his call for 75,000 men, & called an extra session of Congress for July 4".

April 17". The Virginia Convention passed an Act of Secession by a very small majority, and began at once to assume a defensive attitude.* The Southern men in Maryland assumed a more determined attitude and expressed great indignation at the idea of troops being raised in one state to subjugate another. Still nothing was done. There was no concerted action. The Clubs met more frequently and Mr. Norris addressed them repeatedly urging them to arm and drill.

April 17. This evening there was a meeting at Norris'.** Wallis and Frank Howard both advised me not to go, saying that I only compromised myself by associating myself with so extreme a party. But I decided to go, because, as I told them, I thought one of us ought to know what was going on and because too I thought I had some influence which I had at least exercised for good, in the case of the Maryland Institute meeting. When I got to the house, I found there were just thirteen of us present. I could not help smiling at the ill omen although I little thought that before the summer was over half of us would be in Fort or skulking in the woods. The meeting was in secret. Its object was evidently to organize an armed resistance to the passage of troops through Maryland. Mr. Norris, who I thought was suspicious of me, commenced by saying that as this meeting was a private one, he thought it necessary that the opinions of everyone present should be clearly understood and that he should demand in turn of everyone what were his views & if he was prepared

* The Ordinance of Secession passed the Virginia legislature on April 17, 1861, by a vote of 88 to 55 and was ratified in a general election on May 23, 1861.

** William Norris lived at 92 West Monument Street and had his law office at 79 West Fayette Street in Baltimore.

to go all lengths to carry the State out of the Union. After putting the question to about eight men my turn came. I laughed at the question, said as far as I was concerned, I considered the State virtually out already, and that I thought this preliminary proceeding quite unnecessary among gentlemen. Mr. Harrison uttered the same sentiment and the question was stopped.* Norris then entered into a discussion as to the Constitutional power of the President to call out troops in the Northern States to march into the Southern States. He declared it was clearly unconstitutional and said that J. V. L. McMahon, St. George Teackle and James Mason Campbell, were of the same mind. An effort had been made to get these gentlemen to give a written opinion to that effect. Teackle would not sign until the other two did, Campbell too wanted the others to sign first and McMahon would not sign at all. Norris was indignant at their utter want of manliness. The law he said was clear and Parkin Scott supported him. "Do you" said he, turning to me, "go down and publish it in the Exchange." "I know nothing about it" said I. "If you are clear do you write what you choose and state your point clearly and I will have it inserted." But he would do nothing—nor would Parkin Scott. They referred me to the Statute in question and that was all the satisfaction I could get. About eleven o'clock I left, satisfied that the meeting was a failure, that nothing would be done and that it was useless to wait any longer. I went down to Wallis' office, stated the point to him and we got down a volume of U.S. Laws to examine the Statute. He was quite struck with its force and picked up his pen and wrote a few lines, short but to the point. With these, after we had revised them to satisfy me that they were sufficiently decided, I hurried to the Exchange office, stopped the form from going to Press, had the article double leaded and placed it at the head of the first column.**

* The gentleman mentioned was William G. Harrison. (See entry in glossary.)

** The lead article, page 2, column 1 of the *Exchange* for April 18, 1861, reads as follows:

> We published yesterday, from the *National Intelligencer,* a copy of the second section of the Act of 1795, under which Mr. Lincoln has called out the military by his proclamation. It is as follows:
>
> "Sect. 2 *And be it further enacted* That whenever the laws of the United States shall be opposed or the execution thereof obstructed in any State by combinations too powerful to be suppressed by the ordinary course of judicial proceedings, or by the powers vested in the marshalls by this act, it shall be lawfull for the President of the United States to call forth the militia of such State, or of any other State or States, as may be necessary to suppress such combinations, and to cause the laws to be duly executed, and the use of militia to be called forth may be continued, if necessary, until the expiration of thirty days after the commencement of the next session of Congress."

April 18. The appearance of this short leader in the Exchange telling the people "that the passage of troops through the State could be legally and ought to be resisted" had of course great influence and was much discussed. I could hear however of no organization for resistance of any kind, and as far as I knew, the men who most desired it, and who had done most to encourage it, had abandoned all hope of resistance in despair. Disgusted with the attitude of many people, I had a day or two before prepared a small circular for signature, containing very few words but those few to the point. I had them given to different parties to obtain signatures. One of them I laid on the counter of the Exchange, but signatures were affixed so slowly that I soon found it was no easy matter to make men define their position.

April 19". The Mob attacked the Massachusetts troops as they were going through Pratt Street. Everyone was taken by surprise. I do not believe there was any organization of any kind and in the beginning the only weapons of the assailants were bricks and stones.*

The exigency, with a view to which Mr. Lincoln has exercised the power conferred on him, and which is the limit of such power, accordingly, is defined in the proclamation, as follows:

By the President of the United States

A PROCLAMATION

Whereas The laws of the United States have been for some time past, and now are opposed, and the execution thereof obstructed in the States of South Carolina, Georgia, Alabama, Florida, Mississippi, Louisiana and Texas by combinations too powerful to be suppressed by the ordinary course of judicial proceedings, or by the powers vested in the Marshall, by law, now therefore, I, ABRAHAM LINCOLN, *President of the United States,* by the virtue of the power in me vested by the courts and the laws, have thought fit to call forth, and thereby do call forth, the militia of the several states of the Union, to the aggregate number of *Seventy five thousand,* in order to suppress said combinations and to cause the laws to be duly executed.

It is, therefore, perfectly clear, that under the Constitution and the Laws of the Union, the militia thus called forth can only be to "suppress" combinations, "and cause the laws to be duly executed" in the particular States enumerated in the Proclamation. There has been no official allegation of "combinations," or actual or anticipated resistance to the laws in the District of Columbia, or in any State or Territory of the Union, except in the Confederate States so named, and any use of the militia, in the District, or in any other State or place, except the States so named, for any purpose whatsoever, is, and will be, a plain and palpable usurpation, of the grossest and most dangerous character, which may lawfully, and ought to be resisted. It is, moreover, the right and duty of the militia, so called forth, to refuse to serve except in the States in the Proclamation named, for by serving they incur all the risks and consequences to which usurped and arbitrary power is subject, in a free government.

* Various books on Maryland history list the riot casualties at twelve citizens and four soldiers killed, and thirty-six soldiers and an unknown number of

The news spread like wildfire through the town. The indignation and enthusiasm were unbounded and by night there was no need of circulars for signature nor for private organizations. The whole people seemed to be of one mind. A meeting was hastily called and assembled in Monument Square. Wallis spoke among others. Everyone was for resistance. Columbus O'Donnell was on the stand & applauded Wallis very decidedly. Hundreds, I may say, of men who twelve months [ago] were most extreme Union men were now all Southern. Harvey, I recollect was parading with a double barrelled gun. Men volunteered by scores and organized themselves into companies. Govr. Hicks was in town. He was frightened to death & wanted to go to the Fort to place himself under the protection of its guns.* He sought refuge in Mayor Brown's residence and passed the night there. Fearing an attack on the city it was determined by the Police Commissioners to cut off communication with the city by the destruction of the rail road bridges. Marshal Kane went to Brown's to consult him & they determined to get the assent of Hicks. He had gone to bed. The two went into his room and told him that the threatened danger to the city necessitated such a step. They asked his advice. He did not wish to give it. He rolled and groaned. Brown insisted and declared he would not act without explicit orders from him. Hicks twisted the sheet over his head rolled over agst. the wall and moaned rather than exclaimed "Oh! Yes. Go and do it."

April 20". Brown came to Wallis' office and told him what had happened. "Did you get it in writing"? asked W. "No" said Brown. "Well, replied W. depend upon it he will lie out of it"—and lie out of he did eventually. Nothing could be done then, for Hicks had gotten up before daylight, sneaked out of the house without the knowledge of any of the family and taken the early train to Annapolis. This morning the rail road bridges were burned.

April 21". Lincoln telegraphed to Mayor Brown & Govr. Hicks to come to Washington. Hicks was not here. Brown went taking with him Wallis, Dobbin & John C. Brune. They had a lonk talk with Lincoln and urged upon him the folly of attempting to march troops through a town in such a state as Baltimore was. Genl. Scott was called in. Finally, by his advice, it was determined not to send any

citizens injured. Mayor George William Brown describes the riot and gives his version of the position of Maryland in the Civil War in *Baltimore and the Nineteenth of April, 1861* (Baltimore, 1887).

* Fort McHenry, commanding the entrance to Baltimore Harbor on Whetstone Point between the northwest and middle branches of the Patapsco River, is now a National Shrine.

more troops through and that the troops which had moved down from Pennsylvania and were encamped a few miles north of Baltimore should be ordered back to Harrisburgh. Lincoln gave the necessary orders to Major Belger in presence of the gentlemen from Baltimore. Major Belger afterwards informed Wallis that as he went out of the room Seward privately directed him not to obey the orders, but to instruct the Commanding officer to retain the troops where they were.

While everything was in this state of confusion, Maryland was in no condition to act. Hicks had withstood every effort made to call a convention and even steadfastly refused to call together the Legislature. Doctor Rd. S. Steuart was in Baltimore. He followed Hicks to Annapolis & forced him to convene the Legislature. I am satisfied he would have shot him if he had refused.

The resignation of army and navy officers increased very rapidly once the call for 75,000 men.

April 22d. Baltimore happened not to be represented in the Legislature. It became necessary to elect delegates. Norris was very anxious to have thoroughly Southern men nominated. So was Walters. Norris was confined to his house. Walters & I went round to the Mayor's office. We got together several men, among whom was Wallis & tried to agree on a ticket.* Ben Presstman was among them, but there was no doing anything with him. He thought he knew better than anybody else and we gave up the attempt. I tried very hard during the day to get together a sufficient number of gentlemen to effect our object. No one seemed to know exactly what they wished & finally Mr. Norris refused to have anything more to do with the matter. There was no help then but to leave the nominations to the Democratic Convention which was to meet for the purpose in Fayette St. below Calvert. Walters & I agreed to be there and to use our influence to control the nominations.

In the evening we went there & found the men who met there in general very well disposed. Our object was to get good men irrespective of party, who represented different interests in as well as districts of the city. There were some men there who came to argue their own nominations. Old Mr. Kyle was quite anxious for the nomination. The assassination of his gallant son, by the roughs at

* According to Scharf, *History of Maryland,* only one ticket was presented, that of the States Rights Party. The candidates were John C. Brune, Ross Winans, Henry M. Warfield, J. Hanson Thomas, T. Parkin Scott, H. M. Morfitt, S. Teackle Wallis, Charles H. Pitts, William G. Harrison and Lawrence Sangston. They received 9,244 votes.

the polls, sometime previously, entitled him he thought to this compliment. I was requested to enquire about the character of some man, I forget who and I went to Lawrence Sangston, to ask him. Sangston did not know much of him, but replied "that he was very willing to receive the nomination for himself." I was rather amused at his want of delicacy and being quite satisfied of his unfitness for the place, I told the story. His name however was started in this way & he was nominated. As the meeting was organized I left, not desiring to associate myself with a meeting exclusively democratic & composed chiefly of old democrats. They made however for the greater part, excellent nominations.

April 23d. "South" issued its first number. This paper was put into operation by Billy Norris & his friends for whom the Exchange was not sufficiently extreme. Tom Hall, formerly of the Exchange was employed to edit it.

Today the 7" Regiment of N. York & some Massachusetts troops, arrived in Annapolis on their way to "defend the Capitol". Portions of the track between Annapolis & the Junction had been torn up. They were obliged to march as far as the Washington Rail Road.* If they had been attacked they would easily have been cut to pieces and as many of the young men were mounted, armed and organized I am satisfied they would have been attacked, had it not been for the counsel of Govr. Pratt who advised them to keep quiet.

April 24. Annapolis being in possession of U.S. troops, it was deemed unsafe for the Legislature to meet there. Governor Hicks by proclamation convened them at Frederick.

Feb. 24". [*1861*] Lincoln arrived in Washington, having dodged from Harrisburgh to Philadelphia, leaving his family behind him —and travelling thence to Washington in a Scotch cap & cloak in disguise.

* Massachusetts troops under the command of Brigadier General Benjamin F. Butler arrived off Annapolis during the night of April 20, 1861. They had sailed down the Chesapeake Bay from Perryville on the Susquehanna River. These troops were supplemented by New York troops under the command of Colonel Marshall Lefferts. Annapolis was occupied on April 22nd, and the Annapolis and Elkridge Railroad was speedily secured. The Annapolis and Elkridge was the only rail line connecting Annapolis with Washington, D.C. It ran some twenty miles from the state capital along the south shore of the Severn River to Annapolis Junction, approximately eighteen miles from Baltimore, where it joined the Washington Branch of the Baltimore and Ohio Railroad. Northern troops reached the critical Annapolis Junction on April 24th. The inhabitants of Annapolis and the surrounding area were considered hostile to the Union but, despite several false alarms, the Northern troops were not attacked.

Feby 27. Peace Conference in Washington adjourned.

Mch 14. [*1861*] Southern Commissioners in Washington demand recognition.

Apl 29". [*1861*] Mails begin to assume regularity and telegraphic communication again opened between Washington and the North. During the few days succeeding the 19" April, communication with Philadelphia was to a great extent cut off. There was no travel except by stage. Some days it was impossible to obtain a single New York Newspaper. In New York they were absolutely ignorant of what was occuring in Baltimore.

May 14". [*1861*] By this time order was perfectly restored and troops were gradually being quartered in and around Baltimore. To day Ross Winans Member of the L. was arrested on his way down from Frederick where the Legislature was in session.*

May 21. N. Carolina seceded. Vote unanimous.

June 2d. [*1861*] Chief Justice Taney delivered his opinion in the District Court of the United States upon the Habeas Corpus—exparte John Merryman. The court was crowded. Great indignation was expressed against the Administration. Andrew Ridgely was very decided in his views and was willing to form one of a posse comitatus to proceed to the Fort, demand the prisoner and sustain the majesty of the law. The Administration had however determined to support its authority by the sword. Events, as in all revolutions, had progressed with wonderful rapidity. Col. W. W. Morris, afterwards

* On May 5th Butler's troops occupied Relay on the Patapsco River, a key junction on the Baltimore and Ohio Railroad. On May 13th they entered Baltimore, took possession of Federal Hill, and began the Federal occupation of the city.

The Legislature, meeting at Frederick, adjourned on May 14th. Ross Winans, a Southern sympathizer and inventor of a "steam cannon," was arrested and removed from a train at Relay in the presence of Governor Hicks and several other legislators. John Merryman, a state militia officer, was arrested on May 25th for his part in burning railroad bridges following the April 19th riot. Winans was held only briefly. Merriman, however, became the subject of a writ of *habeas corpus* issued by Chief Justice Taney which the Federal authorities refused to honor on the grounds that President Lincoln had authorized the suspension of such writs. Taney's reply in the celebrated case *Ex Parte Merryman* extended his position that the President could not suspend writs of *habeas corpus*. Dr. Jean Baker in *The Politics of Continuity* (Baltimore, 1973) discusses the importance of the Merryman case and concludes that it "has become a legal backwater, with little relation to the application or development of habeas corpus . . ." (p. 60). The case, however, supplied the Democrats with political ammunition, for they could depict themselves as persecuted by the administration

Genl. Morris and for a long time in command at Fort McHenry, told me afterwards that it was he who had taken the initiative step in suspending the writ of Habeas Corpus. It was during May I think. A youth was enlisted & mustered in at the Fort. Being under age a writ of Habeas Corpus was issued and the Deputy Sheriff went to the Fort to serve it on Morris. Col. Morris refused him admittance.* He told me that there was a very animated discussion at a cabinet meeting next day on the subject. Several of the Cabinet were very much opposed to this stretch of military authority and Genl. Scott who was present was very much opposed to the violation of the majesty of the law. Whether Morris was reprimanded or not he never would tell me. The boy was given up a day or two after, but Morris always prided himself on having set the example which was so soon after followed by the administration.

June 8". Democrats had been very busy in nominating for Congress. The election was to come off next week. Bob McLane was very anxious to go to Congress & had maneuvered so as to get the nomination. He had not yet accepted it. I was afraid he would—so went to him and told him, that Henry May had determined to run as an Independent Candidate, that the great object in view was to defeat Winter Davis & that it was necessary for his opponents to unite on one man. Under these circumstances I told McLane the Exchange could not support him. He did withdraw his name.

June 13". Election. May elected. Winter Davis defeated.

June 17". Battle of Great Bethel.

June 27. Arrest of Marshal Kane. Police Board suspended. John R. Kenly appointed Provost Marshal. Commencement of searches of Houses for arms.

July 1. [1861] At 2 A.M. the houses of the different members of the Police Board were surrounded. They were carried off before day break to Fort McHenry—Howard, Gatchell, Hinks & Davis.

July 2d. News came this morning of Dick Thomas' famous exploit of capturing the steamer St. Nicholas. A few days before he walked into Wallis' office took a seat & began to converse. His cousin John Thomas, came in and joined in the conversation. Presently Richard said "Well, if neither of you know me I think I am safe"— & he

* According to Scharf, *History of Maryland,* 3:429: "Major Morris was, on the 4th of May, served with a writ of *habeas corpus,* by Judge William F. Giles, of the United States District Court, for the purpose of releasing from the United States service an enlisted soldier, named John George Mullen, who had petitioned for release on the ground of minority."

moved back his wig from his forehead, when they recognized him. He told them they should shortly hear from him. He went on board the St. Nicholas disguised as a French lady. He jabbered French most profusely and made great confusion. He took supper with the ladies & made quite a scene at the supper table. Afterwards he took possession of the Steamer with his accomplices made several prizes and carried them all up the Rappahanock.*

July 4. We had for sometime headed our telegraphic column in the Exchange "Federal Telegrams". There had been numerous engagements in Western Virginia, Missouri & along the Potomac the accounts of which were much falsified. Today I had put under the heading of "Federal Telegrams"—"Accuracy not vouched for". This appeared for some time afterwards.

July 5". Hinks caved in. He was unwell and made that a pretense. He gave a parole. The truth is he was worthless.

July 18. McDowell advances on Bull Run and his attack is repulsed.

July 21. Battle of Bull Run. Complete rout of Federals.

July 24. Washington still at mercy of Confederates. Maryland open to them. They are anxiously looked for but do not appear. We learned afterwards that Davis refused to allow the army to follow up the victory in opposition to the advice of Johnston and Beauregard. This was incorrect. Many stories have been told of the blind confidence of the Federal leaders in their ability to deal the rebellion a crushing blow in this battle. Among other preparations they had made were several wagon loads of irons and hand cuffs. They had bought all that were to be had in Baltimore & Philadelphia certainly and had purchased largely from other places. They evidently expected to treat not a few rebels as felons.

Aug 5. [1861] Today the Joint Committee on Federal Relations made the celebrated report on the Memorial of the Police Commissioners, prepared by Mr. Wallis, protesting against military usurpation and calling upon the people of the country to take warning and to come to the rescue of free institutions.**

* The capture of the Washington, Alexandria and Georgetown Steam Packet Line steamer *St. Nicholas* under Capt. Jacob Kirwan occurred June 28, 1861, off Point Lookout at the extreme southern end of St. Mary's County, Maryland, where Potomac River meets the Chesapeake Bay.

** The full text of the Police Commissioner's Report and the resolution of the Joint Committee on Federal Relations of the Maryland Legislature can be found in the Baltimore *Sun,* August 6, 1861, p. 2 col. 2.

Another report had been made by the same committee on the 9" May which, while it declared the war unconstitutional and recommended the recognition of the Confederate States, declared it inexpedient to call a State Convention or to organize and arm the Militia and recommended the people of the State to abstain from violent interference with troops in transit through State territory or quartered upon it.

This was in reality all that the Legislature did, and I must confess that I to the last was very dissatisfied with its proceedings. The tone of to day's report was the one thing that satisfied me and I expressed that satisfaction to my satisfaction in the Exchange. But here everything stopped. Within a short period the State was under Martial law and of 25,000 copies of the Report, nearly 15,000 were seized & destroyed before they could be distributed.

There really was not a man of any prominence in the State, who was equal to the Crisis. Governor Pratt's views were more to my mind than any other man's and he could have carried a strong party with him. But he would not come forward. He put himself in communication with other men, advised them & urged his views, while he himself staid in the background & would not appear. He would not even go to Frederick to exert his influence upon the Members. He and those with him desired the passage of a Bill to arm the Militia and the appointment of a Military Committee to assume control of the forces of the State independent of the Governor. Had such a committee been appointed he would have served upon it. But nothing was done. An advance of the Southern army was confidently expected. There was a strong revolutionary feeling throughout the State and hundreds of young men were ready to join Joe Johnston as soon as he appeared at the Annapolis Junction prior to an attack upon Washington. It was afterwards well known that this was Johnston's plan, but that it was opposed by Davis. There was no attempt at individual organization or State Revolution, because that was thought inexpedient. A letter from Benjamin to P—, advised him expressly "not to make such an attempt then, for they will be unable then to give the necessary assistance; but that all that was necessary for the present was to keep up a decided feeling in the State, so as to require the presence there of at least 20,000 Federal troops, which would thus be kept from Virginia." Events progressed rapidly and each day resistance became more difficult.

September 13. [1861] I arose, breakfasted & went to my office. I soon heard the rumor of arrests. The Legislature was to meet in a day or two. All the Baltimore members had been dragged from their beds late in the night.* Tom Hall, Editor of the South and Frank Howard as Chief Editor of Exchange were also arrested. The Members of a Legislature which had refused to arm the State and had advised non resistance were imprisoned on the Charge of planning the secession of the State. So much for the middle course. What folly in a revolution! These men were all taken to Fort McHenry. I found John Thomas, took my carriage and drove down. Many of my friends opposed my going and declared I would be arrested. They were sadly frightened. My reply was "that if they wanted me, they would take me anyhow." In the fort we saw Col. Morris—in comman—but were allowed no communication with the prisoners, except a few words at a distance. We conveyed them some money through Morris.

I learned today how extreme was the fright of the Federals after the defeat at Bull Run. Col. Morris had everything in readiness after the news came, kept a force under arms all night had the furnace heated and kept shot red hot, in order to bombard the town in case of a rising.

I returned home late and after dinner went to the Exchange office. I did feel very pugnacious and in this humor wrote the leader for next morning. Neilson the foreman said to me after it went upstairs "If you put this in, it will be the last Editorial you will write." "Never mind that," I replied; "do you put it in."**

Sep 14. I was privately informed that I was to be arrested. I could easily have gotten away, but it was a point with me. The Administra-

* Those arrested on September 13, 1861, included: Mayor George W. Brown, Baltimore City members of the House of Delegates Ross Winans, Severn Teackle Wallis, Henry M. Morfitt, Charles H. Pitts, William G. Harrison, J. Hanson Thomas, T. Parkin Scott, Lawrence Sangston; Congressman Henry May; State Senator Dr. A. A. Lynch; and Baltimore County Delegates Robert Denison and Leonard K. Quinlan.

** The lead Editorial in the *Exchange* on September 14, 1861, reads as follows:

> Although we have been cut off, by the recent arrests, from most valuable editorial assistance, and the Power that has crippled us already may be called into exercise to crush us out entirely so long as the blow remains suspended we shall not hesitate to uphold the cause we have espoused, let the Consequences be what they may. The Tenure of power is, at best, but temporary. Of power grossly abused, the limits are sharply defined, for men who respect themselves will not long endure what, by concerted action, they can shake off. But principles are eternal. Tyranny cannot change them, nor can legions of bayonets weaken, in the least degree, their inherent vitality. Whatever others may do, we shall stand by them to the last.
>
> Now, let us see whether the people will strengthen our hands for the work that is before us.

This was the last issue of the *Exchange*.

tion evidently wanted to stop the paper, without having the odium of directly suppressing it. It thought by the arrest of Frank Howard to frighten me. Now after I had committed myself I was allowed the chance of escape. Even my brother urged me to go; but stir I would not. I determined to force the Government to have recourse to military power if they wished to muzzle free speech in Maryland. After dinner, McPhail came to the house with a small force and took me off. I was allowed time to get my trunk. It was very hard parting with my wife and sisters. This kind of thing was new to us then and they had no idea what was in store for me.

I was driven to Fort McHenry and locked up in a room furnished with one table, a chair, a blanket & some straw. It had evidently been used by other prisoners and had not been cleaned out. All the other prisoners had been sent off during the day, to make room for others, for the wholesale arrests which were afterwards so common, were just being inaugurated. Late in the evening I received some bedding from home.

Sept 15". Solitary. Visited by Pr. Marshal who inspected me and took a proper description of my person.*

Sep 16". Visited by Genl. Dix, whose Head Quarters were then at Fort, although he was in command of the Department, who informed that my wife would be permitted to visit me. I was transferred to a room on the ground floor. This evening political prisoners began to come in. They had been mostly seized upon the boats, as they came to Baltimore, from the lower counties on their way to Frederick. They took their misfortunes differently. Some were despondent, one or two got drunk; most of them were thinking of the best way of getting free. Jim Maxwell had his fiddle & was very jolly. When the pinch came, it was he who showed the most pluck of this batch. As a general rule they were like the guests which were bidden to the marriage feast. One had his farm, another his merchandise & they got back to them as soon as possible. As they came in fifteen or twenty men were huddled together in the guard room. Half a dozen were crammed in with me. My room was about 12 x 14.

Sep 17". Had an interview with General Dix. I informed him that business was sadly disorganized, that many men with families were thrown out of employment and that the stoppage of the Exchange might cause much distress among the employees of the office. Business

* The Provost Marshal's office was filled by a civilian, Mr. George R. Dodge, who was appointed by General Banks on July 10, 1861, and served until October 1861.

in fact was at the time utterly stagnant. I told him too that the men in our employ were not selected for their political opinions and that I had never proscribed anyone on that account. I hoped then that he would not interfere with the reissue of the paper by the men in the office; that I desired to allow them to publish a paper without any editorials whatever, containing a mere summary of news and that the profits realized should go exclusively to them. I assured him moreover that neither Howard nor myself would write anything more until we could write as we chose, as we did not feel inclined to submit to the censorship of the Press. Fortunately for us, we had retained Warren as Commercial Editor of the Exchange. He was a thorough Yankee. Sherwood, who did our press work, because we could not get it done elsewhere was a Black Republican and Carter our lead man, who afterwards behaved very well, had only a short time previous, when I had threatened to stop the Exchange, because of the money I was losing and of the little public spirit manifested by men who were supposed to be its warm supporters, applied at the Custom House for a clerkship under the new Administration—at a time too when no Southern man cared to go near the building.* All this had its effect. When I was first arrested, I was of the opinion that the stoppage of the Exchange for a few weeks would have a telling effect upon the people of Maryland. Indeed Wallis and Howard both thought so. We had several times before discussed the probabilities of our arrest and what was the best course to pursue as to our interests in the paper in case either Howard or myself or both were arrested. We quite agreed as to the propriety of a temporary stoppage in the latter event. Three days convinced me how wrong we were. The people had been advised not to resist foolishly before and they showed no desire to revolutionize now that the last crowning blow was given to their liberties. Govr. Pratt had advised the men of the counties privately not to attack the New York troops on their way from Annapolis to Washington, and the Legislature had advised the citizens of the State not to come in conflict with the military forces of the United States. When I reflect upon it, I think it was very natural for the people not to come to the rescue of those men who had told them that it was inexpedient to resist. I saw too that after the first little flare—it was not a flame—of indignation had subsided, the chief anxiety of the subscribers to the paper, would be to know where they were to get the News—for which there was a

* The Baltimore Custom House was located on the northwest corner of Gay and Lombard streets. The building, erected in 1852, was torn down and replaced by the present Custom House in 1901.

great craving—very naturally—and that in ten days most of them would send for some other paper and the Exchange would become a thing of the past. I was satisfied that the sooner a new paper was issued the better. Everyone would see and understand from the type, & advertisements, that it was the old thing in another shape. The only thing I did was to control the name. I insisted on calling it the "News-sheet", as a sort of token to the people of Maryland, to keep fresh in their memory the fact that their press was muzzled and that the publication of anything more than a simple News Sheet was not permitted.

Sep 19". Today the first copy of the paper was issued under the name of the Times. Neilson, our foreman in the composing room, now that he appeared as principal instead of sub, began to assume magnificent proportions. He did not wish to run a paper with no name, a mere offshoot of a former publication. So he must needs issue the new paper as The Times. As soon as I heard of it, I sent him word very shortly to obey my instructions or to shut up shop.

Sep 24. Today the paper appeared under its proper title "The News Sheet".

October. [*1861*] By the first of this month I was, strange to say, tolerably comfortable in my prison quarters. I had received from home bedding and books, I was allowed provisions of liquors and my wife came to see me frequently. A few other friends were allowed to come from time to time. Other prisoners were detained at Fort McHenry only for a short time. They were allowed no comforts and as soon as a sufficient number had accumulated to warrant the expense, a steamboat was ordered down and they were shipped to some larger Fort. I never knew to what influences I owed my first detention. Afterwards Morris kept me there himself.

This man was rather a strange compound. His military views & his predictions as to the character and length of the War, showed decided capacity. On other matters he sometimes displayed unpardonable ignorance. At times he was a perfect brute; then again he would be kind and good natured. He often manifested a strong friendship & was willing to serve you, while at the same time his love of trickery so predominated that it was a real pleasure for him to catch a friend in a trap. He would call up prisoners and use every argument to induce them to forsake their opinions and take the oath of Allegiance and the moment it was done he would turn from them in contempt and speak of them most disparagingly. When quite young he had become engaged in a liaison with the woman who afterwards became his wife. Whether he or she was most to blame I never knew. He was stationed at that time in Delaware. The population of the country then was small, vice was less common & the tone of morality among the men was much higher than it is now. A charge of seduction was made against Morris and he was court martialed for "conduct unbecoming an officer and a gentleman." Hon. J. A. Bayard was at that time a young lawyer & was employed by Morris to defend him. He took the ground that though the conduct might be unbecoming a gentleman, there was nothing unmilitary in the offence & that it did not come within the jurisdiction of the Military Courts. Morris was acquitted but was compelled to marry the woman. He was a great card player and used to win largely from his junior officers. He was known in Florida as Black Bill a name which stuck to him ever afterwards. Officers who served with him there told me seriously that at one time there was a proposition made to make him a monthly allowance by subscription in order to induce him not to play. When pay day came he was always sure to have nearly all the money of those officers who would play with him. Frequently they were in debt to him. Nor were these the only stories against him.

During my first ten days imprisonment I was kept closely confined to my room. I was only allowed to leave it for a few moments each day under guard. My room I swept & cleaned myself—as I was forced in fact to do during the greater part of my stay there. At the end of ten days Morris came in to my room with an absurdly stringent parole, giving me permission to walk about in the little chicken coop of a garrison and prohibiting me from speaking to any of the men or talking on political subjects to anyone whatever without his permission. He had no idea I would sign it. Genl. Dix had sent down a much simpler form. Morris had amended it. I laughed when I read it & said to him "Colonel my health is suffering here & I must walk about. I cannot well corrupt anyone here and you certainly know I have no desire to talk to them." I then picked up a pen and signed the paper. I then asked him if he would take a drink to which he gave a cheerful affirmative reply. The water was so bad, I could not drink it. I had some bottles of Seltzer Water in the room. "Colonel" said I "will you take plain or Seltzer Water with your brandy." "Seltzer" said he "What's that"? "Let me show you" said I and as I poured the water in the brandy and it sparkled up like champagne, he took it tossed it off, smacked his lips and evidently wished for more. From that day he was a constant visitor. He commenced by being fond of my liquor. He soon began to like my society. He had around him a parcel of Volunteer officers whom he hated. The fact that I would hold as little intercourse as possible with them rather pleased him. There was from the beginning great jealousy on the part of the old army officers at the appointment of civilians. He like too the perfectly independent and fearless manner in which I talked and the resolution I showed. I took care too from time to time to send him presents of Whiskey which proved very acceptable. Crittenden had sent father in from Kentucky in 1846 a barrel of Bourbon Whiskey. This Whiskey he sent as very fine. I had put it after five or six years in demijohns. It had not improved and as I had never liked Corn Whiskey, I had left it untouched, as not good enough for my friends. Crittenden was now a great card. I thought of the Whiskey, had some bottled & sent down labelled "Crittenden 1846". Morris used to call it the Crittenden Compromise. It had quite a reputation among these men, who knew no better. I kept him supplied with it. It was not the only time I used it advantageously.

After I had been paroled to walk about, Genl. Dix stopped me one day in the yard to have a talk. He endeavored in a soft way to get my views on the oath of allegiance. I gave him my opinion so plainly that he never mentioned the subject again. Some time after a parole was suggested, but it was one I could not think of. When I was first imprisoned, I would have given a simple parole not to leave the city or to report daily to Head Quarters, during any specified time. Later I declined even that.

I corresponded a good deal with my friends in Fort Warren. They had been sent first to Fortress Monroe, then to Fort Lafayette & finally to Fort Warren. Morris used to read all the letters I sent & received. I used to tell him, it would be very improving to his style. Sometimes I would tell him a letter was private & I did not wish him to read it. He always passed them for me. He manifested on all occasions perfect confidence in my word. There was one other man besides myself in whom he manifested even greater confidence. I allude to John H. Thomas, Wallis' law partner. He appeared to be very fond of him & was always glad to see him. It was evident however that he had the greatest desire to have John in his clutches. He once got upon a scent he thought and persued it vigorously for some weeks. He promised me to tell me about it some day, after it had failed & he knew that John & myself suspected him. But he never made good his promise.

October. [*1861*] To day Henry Johnston was brought in, with his countryhouse porter. The Johnstons had had some large transactions with Simon Cameron & Cameron had given them a pass to cross the lines. Henry had been several times to Richmond and had made a great deal of money, dealing largely in Southern Exchange and Bonds at a period when few people were allowed that privilege. He had lately gone through with this man servant in whom he had great confidence, but fearing himself to go to Richmond he had stopped at Winchester & sent this man on to Richmond to communicate with his bankers there. On returning through the lines, the two were seized by Seward's order. Johnston's friends telegraphed at once to Cameron, who instantly ordered his release. Seward heard of it & countermanded it. The two squabbled and Henry & his man Friday were sent to the Fort.

When they reached the Fort they were flung into the guard house, a small room probably 15 x 20, with barred door & grated windows. It was then empty. I have often seen it crammed for several days or more. The door was always locked at sun down, when a large tub was shoved in to them. This was the only extra convenience allowed them. When the door was opened in the morning the smell that came from this badly ventilated room was enough to make a well man sick. It was a shocking place to put a decent man into and I went at once to Morris to remonstrate, but he was in such a bad temper that I thought it best not to approach him. Next day I saw him again; but he was still very crossgrained & I merely said that "I hoped he would not keep a gentleman shut up in such a place long", to which I received no satisfactory answer. I felt sorry for Henry. He was not in there for patriotic motives and he did not take it kindly. I could see him, in the afternoon, as I walked about the parade ground, looking at me through the bars, grinding his teeth.

The following morning Ellen* came down with quite a lot of provisions. Among them was a basket of grapes from the grapery. I picked out a bunch of Palestine Grapes, the bunches of which are very curious. This was over 15 inches long. I was quite sure Morris had never seen them before. I went with these into his office, held them up before his eyes and asked him to take them down to Mrs. Morris with my compliments. His eyes sparkled. In ten minutes he came trotting over to my room. After we had taken a drink, I again remonstrated with him about Henry J. "Ah! Yes," said he, "Why

* Ellen Mark Smith (1832–1863) married William Wilkins Glenn on October 29, 1857, in Philadelphia. They had a son, John Mark Glenn, in 1858; their daughter, Mathilda Wikoff Glenn, had died on July 15, 1861, when she was 8 months old. Another daughter, Ellen, was born on March 14, 1862. See also Glenn's narrative entry for "Jany 1863."

has he not given his parole"? "Boy" said I, "have you suggested either to him or to me that he could have a parole?" "Come along then said he, let us go pay him a visit". In ten minutes, Henry was paroled & I had him transferred to my room where he staid for more than two weeks. During that time his family were allowed to see him daily. As soon as Seward & Cameron had settled their little difference Henry was released.

The adjoining room to the guard house was almost a cell. It was so small and so close. In it was Dick Thomas—alias Zarvona. He was under strict guard. His companion Col. Alexander had escaped some time before, he & Zarvona evidently having bribed the guard. Morris was of course furious. He considered it as a sort of personal disgrace to himself. Z. refused to give any parole & was very strictly guarded. There was a hole in the wall between his room & the guard room for a stove pipe. Two days after Henry J.'s arrival, Z. tossed a note through this. J.'s man got it & brought it to me. As we were under parole not to communicate with him here the correspondence stopped. I learned afterwards that Thomas soon after managed to obtain a key to the cell. He would doubtless have tried to escape had he not been transferred to Fort Lafayette, before he found a favorable opportunity.

Nov 10". [1861] Today Mary Low accompanied Ellen to the Fort. She had no difficulty in getting in. All I had to do was to tell old Morris that there was a handsome woman about and he would send her a pass in order to get a look at her. He was very fond of a fine looking woman, was always happy to escort them around the ramparts and to hand them into carriages. His great delight was to get his hands on them if only for an instant. He had not the slightest delicacy or refinement. Mrs. Low had been for some time in England with her husband Andrew Low of Savannah. They had gone over to England before the war broke out. They had returned by way of Canada, from whence they had gone to Cincinnatti [*sic*]. There Low made several efforts to get passes to go through the lines, he being anxious to get home & she being particularly desirous of getting back to her young children, which she had left with her mother, Mrs. Stiles. Failing in his attempts, he had taken his tickets for Washington intending to apply directly to Seward, when to his surprise he was arrested. He was carried directly through to Fort Warren. His wife travelled through with him as far as Harrisburgh, where she was literally turned adrift in the streets, with her luggage, without friend or acquaintance. She took the train for Baltimore, called a hack at the Depot and ordered him to drive to our house. She staid with us about three months we being unable to get a pass for her. At last I accidentally heard of a plain man whom Seward would like to oblige. He had connections who were glad to serve the Lows and by his efforts she was finally enabled to get through.

I never knew why Low was arrested; nor did he. I suspect it was brought about by his connection with Green his former partner who was a conceited and very talkative man. The total stoppage of shipments of cotton had determined Low to close up his old business and in Liverpool he had a full settlement with Green. After this he said to Green "that their business relations had required a certain degree of intimacy between them, but that even that was unpleasant, and that as there was now no further necessity for it, for the future he desired that they might be total strangers". When Low took passage for America he found Green was coming out in the same steamer. Anxious to avoid each other, Low came out in the Canada steamer, while Green went to Boston. Green was arrested soon after his arrival. He was also taken to Fort Warren where he and Low arrived almost at the same time and were put in the same room.

Nov 16". News came today of the seizure of Mason & Slidell on board the Trent. The Commercial Advertiser, an afternoon New York paper was the first comment upon it, as I recollect, and did so in a sensible manner. The morning papers of the day following took a very different view of the matter and applauded Wilkes roundly. In a few days there was but one sentiment expressed throughout the country. State Assemblies endorsed Capt Wilkes, Congress sustained him. The unanimity of the people was perfect, their enthusiasm unbounded and their determination was thorough. Morris insisted that Wilkes had made one mistake & that was in not hanging them at once to the Yard arm of the Trent. "Men," said he, "never get a chance like that but once in their lives & Wilkes has lost his." He laughed at the idea of surrendering the prisoners. So did everybody. I told him that the people were insane but that Seward was not and "the result of this," said I "will be that England will make a peremptory demand for these gentlemen & then you will see the most disgraceful back down upon the part of this Administration, the world ever saw. Even I will blush for a nation of which I once was a citizen". He laughed at me.

*Jany 1" 1862.** News came today of the surrender of Mason & Slidell and their attachés. England did make a very peremptory

* January 1, 1862 is out of sequence.

demand. Capt Kennedy, R.N. who was then stationed at Halifax, afterwards told me that he had had the despatches copied and that the instructions to Lord Lyons were "to make a peremptory demand for the Trent passengers held in confinement, and, if they were not given up within three days, after demand made, to demand his passports & leave the country." The admiral at Halifax was further instructed, he said, to consider this as declaration of war and to commence hostilities at once, in whatever quarter he thought proper, without awaiting further instructions. Capt Hewitt was at New York with the Rinaldo. After waiting for two days he began to entertain a cheerful hope of seeing active service. On the third day he went to work to put his vessel in war trim; but in the afternoon news came that Seward had complied with the demand. He waited almost to the last moment allowed him.

——— Today I took leave of my wife, being notified that I was to leave for Fort Lafayette next morning. I sent home my books & little traps that I had gotten together to make myself comfortable and made my final preparations for a much more disagreeable imprisonment. I had been offered two or three paroles which I had refused. Morris had told me that he had interested himself in me and gave me to understand that I would probably be released. Yesterday I was offered a very simple parole which I declined. Genl. Dix then wrote to my wife and gave her to understand that my fate was in my own hands. He thought that because she was a Philadelphia woman & had a brother in the Federal army that an appeal to her would have great influence. I was very sorry for her, for she was not strong, and though she showed a great deal of Character throughout and endured a great deal of physical pain to get to see me often, without complaining, I knew these things told upon her. While she was in the Fort to day, Morris again came to me with a parole. When I refused to sign it, he told me to come to his office. I went there. He told me to sit down at his desk and write whatever I chose and he would release me. I told him I would write nothing and walked away. He came over to my room soon after and appealed to Ellen. He asked her what she thought of a man who would not give a parole. "Col Morris, she replied, I know Mr. Glenn is right, and if he were to give a parole he thinks he ought not to give, I should never speak to him again". "Hie-tie-tity," said Morris & walked away. Ellen bad me good bye bravely. Late in the afternoon, Morris came to me again. "Now," said he, "Glenn, you are a good fellow and I like you very much. You have been here some time and we are friends. Take my advice, give a parole, go home, keep quiet and when this war is over we will meet again as friends & renew our intercourse with pleasure". I made no reply. "You need not think, he went on, that you are going to Fort Warren where all your friends are and where Col Dimick the officer in command is a gentleman. You are going to Fort Lafayette, where you will be under a man who is known to be very severe, you will be put in a casement with half a dozen others, probably not fit associates for you, you will have no comforts and you will be treated like a dog." I was rather indignant at this. Col Burke had the reputation of being a thorough brute and the sufferings of the prisoners at Fort Lafayette were sometimes terrible and at all times great. I turned sharply to him and said "Don't you think, said I, I have thought of all that Johnny." "You have, said he, & you won't give a parole." "Col. Morris," replied I, "I'll hang first". "You d—d rebel," exclaimed he and turned on his heel.

——— This morning I made my final toilet in my old quarters. I was only awaiting the arrival of the boat in which we were to embark. I had been shown the list of prisoners with the charges against them. Zarvona's name was at the head. Mine came second. There was no charge against me. I was styled W. W. Glenn, Editor Exchange. I was scarcely dressed when sister Anne came down in the carriage. Morris came in and told me I was ordered to report to Genl. Dix. At first, I did not wish to go. I told I was tired of talking. But he told me I had better go, as he thought I would be released. I gave a parole to return at ten o'clock if not released by Genl. Dix and left. At my office I found Bowie Davis and Judge Crain. These two went with me and we had an interview with Dix. Dix proposed a parole. I told him I knew no difference between that and an oath of Allegiance. At last he said "Very well"! go home when I want you, I'll send for you". And I went. I was perfectly satisfied afterwards that Morris had authority and instructions to release me, but he thought it would be a smart thing to get a parole out of me. This kind of dealing too suited his nature. He would lay a trap for his dearest friend.*

Febry 14" 1862. Low arrived today, having at last obtained a parole from Fort Warren to come to Baltimore. His wife had gone South without him, having gotten a pass only a short time before. Andrew Low was in reality an Englishman. He had served as a young

* For documents relating to William W. Glenn's imprisonment and parole see Appendices A and B.

private in an artillery company in the Florida War & had soon after been naturalized. Since then however he had not exercised the rights of citizenship. He preferred his English nationality and had his children by his first wife in England being educated.

Soon after Low came, a visitor was announced one evening after dark. I went forward into the library. He introduced himself as Capt. Schultz. He said he had heard a gread deal of my annoyances, that he sympathized with me, that he was desirous of aiding me etc. I knew Low was supposed to be living with us as his wife had been, and I immediately began to suspect that he took me for Low. However I let him talk on. He told me that he was a great friend of Seward's, that Seward staid with him, when he came to New York, that Fred was a good fellow & that they all plaid whist together frequently. I then recollected that a man of this name, who had been a river Captain on the Hudson had been sent out last year by Seward to do some dirty work in England. I was sure this was the scoundrel. Presently he made a remark which showed plainly that he thought he was talking to Low. "Pardon me" said I "Captain, you are talking to the wrong man, evidently. I too have been for some time in prison and I have suffered much harsh treatment, but my name is Glenn." He jumped up and exclaimed "And are you not Mr. Low". No! said I. "I've not another word to say," said he Not another word. I am off." "Stop" said I Captain" We may as well understand each other. Mr. Low is a particular friend of mine. He is anxious to get South to his wife and family. He can go South on parole. That will not do. He will only go South when he obtains the privilege of effecting an Exchange. Now you are a friend of Mr. Seward's. He wants to oblige you. Do you arrange this matter for Low, and I will pay handsomely for it". "Mr. Glenn, said he, stretching himself & rising from his seat "You are a gentleman I see you understand business". Shortly after he left promising to see me the next day or the day after at latest.

In the morning I went to Low & told him what had happened. I had expressly kept Schultz from obtaining an interview with Low, because I knew pretty well that Schultz would surely swindle him. Low had been a very successful Cotton Merchant and by his prudence and business capacity had amassed a large fortune. He had been for a long time accustomed to large transactions and had had the good fortune not to be thrown much into communication with common men of ordinary capacity and small views who mistook cunning for cleverness. He did not believe in the natural rascality of lower natives and even when he suspected men he could not bring himself to distrust their "sacred" pledges. Thinking I had the matter well in train and not feeling authorized to go any further without consulting Low, I told him next morning what had happened. He told me Schultz was a dirty fellow and expressly forbade me from doing anything more. Schultz telegraphed me to come to Washington. I did not go. We had some correspondence & there the matter dropped. A few days after, Schultz, determined not to lose his prey, came up to Baltimore & managed to obtain an interview with Low. He abused me a good deal for behaving, as he said, uncourteously, talked a great deal of his sympathy with Low and of his influence at Washington and finally induced Low to trust his case to him. When I heard it, I foresaw the result and I begged Low not to pay the rascal one penny, but to wait first till he got to City Point, then to write to me & I would settle with Schultz. This he promised. In a day or two Schultz came up with the necessary papers from Seward. All was arranged except payment. Low told him I would settle as soon as I had news of his safe arrival at City Point. Schultz, putting on an air of offended virtue, walked up to Low, laid his hand on his shoulder and said in a tone of earnest entreaty "My dear Mr. Low, please to believe that I am a gentleman". Low could not stand this. He gave in and proceeded to write a check. "Will you please let me have it in two checks" said Schultz in his blandest tones. Low gave him two checks for $500 each—one of which no doubt went to Fred Seward. These were Fred's perquisites. Seward's friendship was great for Schultz but he had great consideration for his son.

Low next day went to Fortress Monroe, to learn that all Exchanges were stopped—& to be ordered back. This was the last he heard of Schultz. He lost his money and his friend. When he left Baltimore he also directed his agents in New York to settle with Evarts who had been employed by them in the first instance. Evarts sent in a bill of $1500 which was paid. I had instructed Schultz when I first saw him to enquire particularly at Washington, if Evarts really had done anything for Low. I knew he had done nothing for Mrs. Low & that her pass was obtained solely by other influences than his. Evarts had done nothing except to talk with Seward and urge Low's case, when he was at Washington on other business. Low was thus swindled out of $2500—which he paid very foolishly. He got through a long time after by accident. Bob Magraw was at Washington & found Stanton in a good humor. Stanton expressed his desire to oblige him. He immediately asked for an Exchange for his brother Harry, who was still under parole & suggested Low as a good Exchange. Stanton consented & Magraw induced him to sign the necessary order before he left him.

While Low was here, Russell of the London Times, spent a week in Baltimore. He was at the Eutaw House. One evening Low & I went to see him. Russell had never seen Vallandigham, who was then quite a card. He expressed a desire to make his acquaintance. V. happened to be in the house. I went off, found and brought him to Russell's room. Russell's obsequious and cringing behavior astonished Low & myself. We had heard of the toadyism of middle class Englishmen to birth or distinction, but we were not prepared for this exhibition. Russell was very clever, very entertaining & full of humorous anecdote. In writing Battle painting [?] was his speciality. In this sort of description he was unsurpassed. He was not a deep thinker nor an able talker. In his Military experiences he had been thrown in with many English officers. Not a few of them dubbed him "a clever snob". He had also friends among them. Trollope spoke always warmly of him, & declared that he was a man of honest & independent views, who left America because he was unwilling to write from America as Delane of the Times instructed him.

Trollope was also here. He staid at Guy's where Low stopped and Low and I saw him very frequently and intimately. He was exceeding Republican and believed in the great history of Democratic institutions. He was a very different class of man of Russell, and without being conceited put a proper estimate upon himself. He was always willing to yield to others the place that the accidents of society entitled them to, but he was never subservient. I thought him a most excellent specimen of his class and had a great regard for him.

He and I worried Low a great deal about a joke of Thackeray's. Thackeray when in Savannah had staid at Low's house & was very fond of him. He spoke of Low beautifully in the Roundabout papers while Low was in Fort Warren.* After he heard of his release he wrote to Russell "How is my dear old Buffa–lo". Low was rather a thick set, heavy, sober faced man. We thought the *mot* capital both as pun and description. Low could not see it and it worried him so, we at last abandoned what we considered a very happy nickname.

Vallandingham [*sic*], to whom I alluded, was at this time fre-

* William Makepeace Thackery, *Roundabout Papers* (1st ed., 8 vols., London, 1863) in a section entitled "On Half a Loaf" discusses the *Trent* affair and the seizure of the Southern Commissioners: ". . . one of the best friends I had in America–the most hospitable, kindly, amiable of men—from which I had there received the warmest welcome and the most delightful hospitability—was a prisoner in Fort Warren, on charges to which his life perhaps might be risked."

quently in Baltimore. He was one of the few men in Congress, who believed strongly in the success of the South and not only wished the South to succeed but spoke pretty openly for a politician. He was a connection of J. V. L. McMahon's and came over to see him. He liked besides the little ovations he received here. McMahon was very Southern, though he had not the manhood to speak out. This may have been partly due to the fact that he was sick and blind and partly to his old habit of never undertaking a cause in which he was not sure to succeed. He had a number of visitors at his rooms in the Eutaw House and small levees when Vallandingham came up. V. who afterwards dodged so much told me at this time that the desire of his party and of himself, in the West was to see the South recognized, to enter into the Southern Confederacy and to admit the Middle States if they desired to come; but never again to have any political connection with the New England States. He told me more than once, when I put the question to him squarely that in the success of the South lay the only hope for the preservation of Republican liberty on this continent. These I always believed were his real sentiments. It was hard to tell however. He varied them like all of our politicians to suit his own purposes and to further selfish ends whenever he thought it necessary. There are exceptions doubtless, but in my experience, I have rarely found a man who had been much in political life and had served more than one term in Congress, who was not a political prostitute. The lobby system, by which members of Congress could at all times be got at, the open bribery and the indirect influences were very demoralizing. The desire for reelection and the necessity of making oneself popular with the crowd, did the rest.

By the summer of 1862, it became evident that there was little chance of interference on the part of England. Up to this time every Southerner had believed that it was utterly impossible for England to restrain from recognition, if her people were still alive to sentiments of justice and honor or if her statesmen had sufficient capacity to forsee the consequences inevitable upon non recognition. Every Southerner thought it immensely the interest of England to make a friend and Ally of the South. Now it became plain that England's policy was to make the most money possible out of both parties, at the present, to keep aloof from war and to let the future take care of itself. About this time Vallandingham began very decidedly to trim. There were to be nominations both for the Senatorship from his State and for a seat in the House from his district. I forget which came first. V. thought it best to have two strings to his bow. He played a pretty Southern game until the first nomination was made. He lost it. Then he became a strong Union Man. It was during this period that he made the speech in New Jersey, I think in Feb 1863, in which he said "There is a party formed upon the basis of recognition of the independence of the South. Gentlemen, I abhor that party". This did not do. He lost the second nomination. His only chance now lay in the Governorship. He became very Southern again, was arrested, tried and banished South. He went through the South to Wilmington, shipped there & was very near being captured by a Yankee Cruiser. He used to tell a very good story of the coolness he showed on this occassion, & of the ruse that was practiced by his advice. I saw one of the officers of the vessel afterwards in London. He said that V.'s condition was pitiable, during the danger & that he went below and hid himself in the cabin. The Captain when he saw how critical was his condition, ran up the British flag, ordered his crew to put on some blue English Jackets and bore down upon the steamer. They passed close to each other, hailed and bore away.

I had a very amusing evidence in the Spring of 1863 of the manner in which the mails were tampered with. I knew perfectly well that my letters were opened—& I never sealed them, but fastened them with gum, so as to have them opened without tearing the envelope. On one or two occasions they were returned to me, but with some simple endorsement on the cover, as a flimsy excuse for the act. After V. had made the New Jersey speech just alluded to, his Maryland friends were very indignant. Unwilling to condemn him unheard, I wrote to him, directing my letter to the New York Hotel where I knew he was going, quoting the extract referred to and saying "You are reported as having said this. Your friends here are anxious to know what you did say." I then added that "I was sorry to see the contemptible record which the New York democrats were making for themselves". The letter was very short. In a very few days it was returned me, in an official envelope, without any remark whatever. My envelope had been torn off & thrown away.

On a former occasion a Prussian officer arrived in New York, bringing with him letters from an old friend Capt Hubert von Böhn of the Prussian engineers. It was early in 1862 when experienced officers were very scarce. A Colonelcy was offered him soon after he reached New York and without waiting to enquire into the rights of the struggle, he accepted the Commission. Ordered to Washington, he enclosed me the letter of introduction, regretting that he could not then deliver it in person & promising to call at the very first leisure moment.* I pictured to myself a Yankee Colonel in full uniform ringing at our bell and applying for admission. In order to prevent any *contre temps* I at once wrote to him, explaining the situation in Maryland & telling him "that our doors from the outbreak of the war had been closed to all wearing the Federal livery & were now more firmly closed than ever. I added that should the time come when he saw fit to lay aside the uniform I should always be glad to see a friend of von Böhn's". In a short time the letter was returned to me through the Post Office, in an Official Envelope, with some endorsement, I forget what, on my Envelope. The Colonel must have seen the letter, for I never heard of him afterwards.

Feb 18" 1862. Today we had the full news of the capture of Fort Donelson. Of course there was great excitement among the loyal citizens of the North and in Baltimore, where loyalty was at a much higher premium, than in the Northern cities, on account of its scarity, there was a great display of flags. All the newspapers but the News Sheet ran out their colors. A party of roughs went into the News Sheet office and ordered the flag to be put out. Carpenter & Carter were there. They knew I would object & so came to see me. Carpenter proposed to go & see Dix. He told Genl. Dix there was no general order to that effect and he did not propose to submit to the dictation of a mob. Genl. Dix finally agreed to send a police guard round there for protection. He did send two policemen, who staid at the corner until near one o'clock, when they left declaring that they would not stay any longer to protect such a d—d secession hole. Carpenter & Carter left too, leaving the office in charge of no one. John, the office boy, was at the counter. Meanwhile fearing trouble, I had gone up home & got my revolver. The last flag that had appeared from this building was the flag of Maryland. On the 19" April 1861, the United States flag had been pretty generally discarded and we, as many others did, had mounted a small state flag. When I got to the office, finding John alone, I told him to keep quiet and if they wanted to pull the office down to let them pull. I staid with him. Soon after the roughs came in again and asked why the flag was not out. Then they took a small toy flag and nailed it to the awning post in front of the door. A little before two o'clock McPhail, Asst. Pr. Marshal came in and told John that if the flag was not put out he could not prevent trouble and said significantly that he would

* The letter of introduction from von Bohm is in the Glenn Papers, MS 1017, Maryland Historical Society. The name of the officer introduced is not mentioned.

give him till three o'clock. John came to me. I said "John the News sheet nominally & its profits really belong to Carter & Neilson. Therefore I do not like to take control. But the Materials and the subscription list actually belong to me. Now if you hang out no flag, the paper *may* be stopped by Government or by the roughs. If you hang out a flag the paper *will* be stopped by me beyond a doubt." "What shall I do then?" "Keep quiet and let them pull." He kept quiet. I staid with him till after the alloted time. I left then for nearly an hour & then returned. There was no trouble. The roughs seeing we were determined did not proceed to extremities. Carpenter & Carter returned about six o'clock.

May 17" 1862. Many of our people had become very despondent. Blunders had been committed in the West & the Federals had gained much territory there. McClellan had changed his base, had massed a large army on the Virginia Peninsula and was threatening Richmond. Not a few thought it would fall. It was sad to see how few had pluck enough to trust their friends; for the pluck that makes you trust yourself teaches you to trust your friends. At the club this evening everyone seemed in despair. The question seemed to be when would McClellan be in Richmond. Wm. Henry Hoffman was the croaker of the party. He made one or two bets when I offered to bet him that the Southern army would be in front of Washington before the Northern army was in Richmond. The men present were astonished at me. Some cried "good for Glenn". H. took the bet. I won it.

April 1862. About this time, I was spending the evening out when a footstep approached my chair from behind and a hand was laid upon me. I turned and saw Dr. R. S. Steuart. He has been concealed for more than six months. His neighbors are so bitter against him that he dare not go home, and he committed himself so decidedly on the 19" April & is known to be so decided a Southerner, that it is more than likely he would be thrown into a Fort. He goes about from place to place, sometimes staying in one county, sometimes in another and then passing a few days in the city. He never shows in the day time & is cautious who sees him at any time. He has several negroes in his confidence at different places. Not long ago he went down home to spend the day. He rode through the woods and passed over his Estate to his house by day time. After spending the day with his family, he resisted all the entreaties of his wife and left her at dusk. He had not been gone a great while, before the house was surrounded by cavalry. An overseer from a neighboring plantation had been at one of the tobacco houses as Dr. S. rode by and had gone into Annapolis some 12 miles off to give the information. The troops sent to apprehend Dr. S. fortunately waited till after dark in hopes of surprising their prey more certainly. The house was thoroughly searched but without success. It was then closely guarded for the night. About two o'clock Mrs. S. a frail and delicate lady, stole down stairs in her slippers. At a side door she found a guard asleep. She stepped past him cautiously, walked nearly half a mile to the quarters, waked one of the slaves and sent him off to his master's sleeping place, which she knew, to tell him what had happened. In the morning the officer in charge tried to learn the whereabouts of Dr. S. from the house servants. He took up the waiter, a trusty fellow, levelled a musket at him & threatened to shoot him if he refused to disclose what he knew. His threats were useless.

Dr. Robinson was also concealed in this manner for a long time & had some narrow escapes. Once while staying at Ramsay McHenry's, some detectives who got wind of his whereabouts, went to Belair & waited there until Mrs. McHenry came into the town.* They then followed her closely, hoping by this means to get to the house unobserved or rather without attracting attention, going in her company. Mrs. McHenry was in despair, for she had her suspicions. Fortunately as they neared the gate, the road forked. The detectives, thinking the two branches came together again, whipped up, took the left road & endeavored to pass her. Mrs. McH. whipped up too & thus gained a little start & succeeded in getting through the gate & shutting it behind her. Dr. R. was signalled & made his escape in time.

Mr. W. H. Norris was obliged to dodge about for a long time. It was very funny to see him as you approached his retreat, always on the *qui vive* as he was, warily watching every vehicle, horseman or foot passenger who came towards the house. He remained concealed in this way until he was allowed to come to town to see his wife. She had been seized in a brutal manner & carried off to the Old Capitol Prison. Her confinement there & rough usage had made her very ill. Having nothing really against her she was released.** Norris soon after went South. He has been in one or two battles, always volunteering where there is a fight & the last I heard of

* Ramsay McHenry, son of Daniel McHenry, was unmarried. His mother was Sophia Hall Ramsay McHenry (1794–1874), who lived with him on their estate, "Monmouth," near Emmorton in Harford County.

** Mary Norris (Mrs. William Norris) was arrested on March 3, 1862, for correspondence with disloyal persons and with Col. Zarvona in code. She was kept at Old Capitol Prison and discharged March 18, 1862.

him, had a horse killed under him. She followed him. Both went underground.

March 28" 1862. Elias Glenn left me, determined to go South. The depression that affected the despondent people had no influence on him. He thought he ought to go and he went.

Dr. Wm. M. Gwin has been gone one or two days. He had already made the attempt to go through underground. He had gone down the bay in a small schooner and had been shipwrecked. These small bay craft at one time carried a great many men and a large amount of contraband. They loaded openly and went boldly over to Fort McHenry, to be searched if necessary. They were never detained until after some months the trick was found out. Important despatches used to be sent this way. They wd. be put in a tin case, enveloped in lead. This was tied to a string and suffered to drop over the side of the vessel. In case of danger, the string was cut or broken at the last moment. Gwin refused to try the route again and was very anxious to find a different one. This was difficult at the time as the Potomac was closely guarded, but as the route selected for Elias promised to be the safest, we determined on that. Gwin was very tall & his full suit of gray hair, brushed back off his forehead, gave him quite a remarkable look. He very much resembled the pictures of General Jackson—of whom he was a great pet and protegé and whose natural son he was always reputed to be. He promised to dye his hair and to take as little luggage as possible. He was to go on to Media in Penna, where his daughter Cary was at school & then to start from there, thus attracting less notice, than if he came from Baltimore. When the day for starting approached, I went to his home and found to my surprise three reasonably large trunks nearly packed. Great Heavens said I Dr. Gwin "do you expect to go through with a coach & four". I talked in vain. Mrs. G. would send a trunk to her daughter Lucy then in Richmond. "Then, said I, if you will take these trunks, at least you must not take them with you. I will send two by express as far as Wilmington". I sent these trunks off, but the only good I accomplished was to suggest the possibility of taking another trunk, which was afterwards packed without my knowledge. So he took four instead of three. Besides this he took with him an enormous broad brimmed plantation hat, in a paper box, with his name printed in full in large letters on the side. His two trunks sent by express reached Wilmington. He went to Media, returned to Wilmington and sent his luggage up to B's where he was to stay the night. B. was not at home. When he did come in, the first thing that attracted his attention was this great paper box, with this name printed in full, lying on the floor at the end of the passage where everybody could see it who opened the door. He seized it & went into the library where he found Gwin quite at his ease. "Good God, said he, Doctor, have you no consideration for your own safety or other people's. Don't you know the risk you run and I run if it is known that you are in my house, on such an errand". With that he proceeded to tear up and burn the paper box. The hat Gwin refused to relinquish. He preferred to abandon the one he was wearing. He refused too to dye his hair. His folly proved his salvation. Next morning his pile of luggage was sent to the station & placed upon the platform, ready to be shipped on the Delaware road, after the Balto. & Phild. trains had passed. The police had gotten wind of this route and two detective were on the spot, for the first time, to arrest all suspicious characters and to examine luggage. Gwin's huge pile disarmed suspicion. They seated themselves on his trunks. He walked away and seated himself in the Delaware car, which was switched off. There he waited quietly, for nearly half an hour smoking his pipe. The detectives saw what they supposed to be a venerable old quaker, with grey hair & a broad brim and did not molest him. He started safely. At the terminus of the road there was another guard. This had been provided for. Gwin got off the train about four or five miles from the terminus. Here he hired a conveyance and started to reach the bay. His extraordinary appearance & his numerous trunks which were piled one on top of another on the hinder part of the vehicle, so that they could be seen at a distance of several miles in this flat country attracted a great deal of attention. Where he stopped he talked so much & so mysteriously about the Senate and foreign countries that the rumor got afloat that it was Yancy,* who had recently returned from Europe & was now on his way South. The man who was to meet him and be his pilot evidently got frightened and refused to come near him. He was left at the mercy of friends to make his way as best he could to the Eastern Shore of Virginia. As he neared this he stopped for a day at a country tavern. While he was walking up & down on the porch, a stranger who had probably seen him at Washington, approached and said "I believe this is Dr. Gwin." "No sir! What put that in your head Sir. And what business, is it of yours Sir, who I am". Gwin could be very rough. He had learned this from old Jackson, who was very proud of the roughness he could summon up, when occasion required. "I beg your pardon," said the man, humbly and rather frightened. "I thought you were Dr. Gwin and that you wanted

* Alabama secessionist leader William L. Yancy (1814–1863).

to get across and that I could help you Sir." "Come along, Sir, come along then, said Gwin, taking him by the arm, come along to my room and let us talk about it." They succeeded in getting a boat & Gwin crossed over the bay. He staid in the Confederacy till 1863, when he went out from Wilmington to Paris—taking his daughter Lucy with him—& joins his wife & daughter Carry abroad.

Gov. Morehead of Kentucky was in Baltimore at the same time & talked a great deal of going South. He talked a great deal indeed of everything, of his experiences in Fort Lafayette & Fort Warren among other things. Sometimes he talked a great deal too much, for he was wretchedly imprudent. He frightened Mrs. Gwin awfully the day after Dr. G. left by joking with her openly at Barnum's public table about his departure. Dr. G. was by no means beyond reach & Mrs. G. was very fearful of arrest. I had told him what route Dr. G. had taken under a promise of secrecy, he having begged me to point him out a safe route that he might go himself. In less than four hours after I had told him, he was discussing the matter with Mrs. Gwin. Soon after this he went to Canada & there got in with a Yankee who had a patent for making saltpetre out of shavings. This fellow persuaded him that it was a valuable invention for the South & Morehead without knowing anything more of him, actually gave him the warmest & most confidential letter to me. Fortunately I was on my guard & soon discovered that the fellow was not willing to put his invention to a fair test and that he did not care who bought it so that he got well paid. I take for granted it was worthless for I never heard more of it. Many of Govr. Morehead's experiences were very interesting, especially those relating to his intercourse with the Southern Peace Commissioners during their stay at Washington and his conversations with Lincoln.* When he told what he had seen or heard he wrote pleasantly enough. He was a man of no power of thought and only one of the thousands which our sovereign people had setup to worship. He was a calf but not a golden one. In this respect the uneducated Israelites did better than we.

Feb. 5" 1862. Today Jesse D. Bright was expelled from the Senate. The ostensible reason was a letter of introduction given by him to some man, with a patent for fire arms, who was on his way to Richmond. The letter was to Mr. Benjamin & was written some time before the commencement of hostilities and at a time when nothing was thought of any correspondence with leading personages in the

* The Confederate Peace Commissioners, appointed February 25, 1861, were A. B. Roman, Martin I. Crawford, and John Forsyth.

South. I recollect perfectly well that we sent a reporter from the Exchange to Montgomery Alabama, while the first General Assembly was in session and that we were very anxious to obtain the contract for the Confederate Government printing, so little did we at that time anticipate the terrible war that soon after broke out. This letter however was not the real cause of Bright's expulsion. It was made a pretense, it being the only charge that could be made against him. The Republican members of the Senate determined to expel him because he steadfastly opposed the war; and the war had become the settled policy of the Administration. The Republican Senators had a caucus and determined that if Bright would only consent not to make any factious opposition to the war they would let him remain, but that if he refused they would expel him. To his shame be it said they induced James Alfred Pearce, senator from the Eastern Shore of Maryland* a Southerner born to be the bearer of this dishonorable proposal. But we were not altogether surprised at it. Pearce had always been known as an utterly selfish [*sic*] and as one who would neither risk his comfort or liberty for friend or country. Bright gave him for answer that he had never voted a cent nor a man for the War and he never would. Pearce actually attempted to persuade him to do as his opponents proposed. Bright stood firm & was expelled. Many of us thought that he would be immediately sent off to a Fort; but he was unmolested.

After he left Washington he came over to Baltimore and spent several months, during which time he received many letters from the West, almost all of which remained unanswered. Late in the summer he went out to Indiana, so as to see his friends and to be there when the nominations for the autumn elections were made. There was a strong Democratic party in Indiana, who desired Union with the South, and also a large number of Democrats entertaining these views in Illinois and in the Southern part of Ohio. Bright naturally expected that his friends in Indiana would send him back to the Senate for the remainder of his term, only a few months, as an endorsement of his policy. And this was their desire. When the Democratic Caucus met to consider and adopt a platform they drew up a very fair set of peace resolutions, but at the end they spoilt all by annexing a resolution with some absurd nonsense in it about carrying on the war under the Constitution. This Bright objected to. He assured them that if they would leave it out, they would carry the State, while if they insisted on putting it in at least 16,000

* Maryland Senators were chosen alternately from the Eastern and Western Shores during the first half of the nineteenth century.

voters in the State would stay away from the polls. He was overruled. The platform was adopted and Bright was offered the nomination for the Senate for the short term, provided he would endorse the platform. His friends said "This is decided upon by the party and you ought to acquiesce in it". He refused and lost the nomination. When he told me this afterwards, he told me that at least 16,000 Democrats staid away from the polls, refusing to vote for war in any shape no matter how constitutional it could be made to appear and that the Democratic ticket—which was carried was elected in fact by the votes of Republicans who talked war loudly, but who in reality wanted peace & thought this was the true meaning of the Democratic resolutions.

Turpin who expected to get the nomination for the House of Representatives from his district, was quite as disappointed as Bright was at the platform adopted. He was in Colfax's district, the strongest Republican district in the State & knew that he would be beaten by Colfax under any state of circumstances. He refused to endorse the resolutions, but went home, adopted an independent platform and stumped his district thoroughly so as to let his constituents understand thoroughly what his views were. He told them that he would advocate 1" a cessation of hostilities 2d. recognition of the Southern Confederacy 3d. Union of the Western States with the South. 4" Union also with the Middle States if they desired 5" No Union under any consideration with any of the New England States. 6". Opposition to the payment of one dollar of the war debt or of one cent of interest upon it. He polled a much larger vote than he expected and ran Colfax very closely.

This sentiment certainly prevailed very largely in the west, even as late as the autumn of 1864. Why the Western States continued to support the Government & to supply men, I never could understand. It is hard to say what Democratic Institutions and great prosperity have to do with demoralizing a people and making them utterly worthless, but certain it is that in the Free States where Democracy has born its worst fruits, scarcely one leading man of high moral courage has been found. I am quite prepared [to] believe that nothing could be more disgraceful, as a general thing, than the private history of politicians and prominent [persons] in all revolutions, could it be gotten at. Desire of place, fear of loss of liberty or property, greed of gain all develop the worst portions of men's natures in such crises; but I hardly think any record could be so disgraceful and as wanting in redeeming traits as the record of most of our Enlightened Democrats—perhaps I should say Democratic Republicans.

Feb 22d 1862. Jeffn. Davis first Inaugural.

Mch 10" 1862. McClellan moves on Manassas to find it evacuated and many of the bristling cannon made of logs of wood painted black.

May 4" [1862]. McClellan who had moved his army to the Peninsula, after making regular approaches to Yorktown finds it evacuated.

May 5. Battle of Williamsburgh. James Sewall was with his family at a farm house in the rear of Williamsburgh, which Genl. Keyes used as his head quarters. Sewall & his wife gave a very astonishing account of Keyes. They said that in the beginning of the battle, of which he never saw anything, he would mount his horse, ride down the lane a short distance and then come tearing back. As the troops became engaged he did not even go this near to the field of operations but walked up and down the porch exclaiming every time he heard the roar of artillery "Great God! how it rattles". They were amused beyond measure, notwithstanding their troubles. Keyes aides were continually galloping up receiving & taking orders. The Sewalls had a farm near Fortress Monroe. Their house was plundered & their property stripped. Mrs. Sewall had inherited the China presented to Wm. Pinckney, while Ambassador at the Court of Versailles. This was all stolen as well as the China her husband inherited. They buried the family silver. The hiding place was discovered and this was stolen too. Strange to say in less than two years, these people were too glad to get a pass from one of the Generals to go back & work their farm with stolen negroes and soon after one of the girls engaged herself to a Yankee officer. There may be wisdom in yielding to the force of circumstances, but it certainly is a sad commentary on the weakness of poor human nature.

May 8". Merrimac destroyed. The greatest loss the South has so far sustained & sacrificed through mismanagement, which never could have happened had not Buchanan been wounded. He I believe was wounded too while endeavoring to save the men from the ship (Congress?) that he had run down. The luck which the South had from first to last with its Navy, was unparalleled. Everything turned out unfortunately.

May 30. Battle of 7 Pines. Joe Johnston wounded—which results in appointment of Genl. Lee.

No. 2

May 26. The destruction of the Merrimac, the surrender of Norfolk & of the Peninsula & the investment of Richmond has caused great despondency among the Southerners of Baltimore. Accurate information was of course difficult to be had and it was believed by many that the South would not be able to withstand the tremendous pressure brought to bear upon it. I who still believed in an advance of the southern forces kept myself in the *qui vie* and the moment I received news this morning of the defeat of Banks and the total route [*sic*] of his army, which had been driven helter skelter across the Potomac, above Harpers Ferry, I left my office and went home to make my preparations for leaving the city and placing myself in a position where I could keep open a communication with the Southern Army in case of an advance. As a general thing the courage displayed by the North has not been of an elevated character. Theirs has been merely the brute courage of the bully developed and strengthened by successes. At a later period of the war when Lee was in Pennsylvania, the other Northern states were bitterly complained for their want of enthusiasm and the tardy manner in which they forwarded troops. New York was ready to make the best terms she could. In 1864 when Sherman was progressing slowly in the West the peace sentiment promised to prove triumphant in the autumn elections, the democrats proposed to adopt a decided peace platform & expected confidently to sweep the country. Government credit was at a low ebb. Sherman gained decided successes and the Democratic Convention adopted a modified platform, which their nominee, McClellan, refused to abide by. He declared himself a Union War man and was supported by the party. Further successes apparently killed the peace feeling entirely and Government credit, in face of protracted war & promised foreign complications was better than at any previous period of the revolution.

On this single occasion however the signal defeat did not humble them in our city. To be sure Banks was routed but that was a small mater. McClellan was thundering at the gates of Richmond & was soon to be in possession of that city. As soon as news came that Banks had crossed the Potomac the greatest excitement prevailed in town. An extra demonstration of loyalty was made. Flags were hung out in all directions, throngs crowded the streets, the roughs moved around in squads and it was dangerous for a known Southerner to walk along the thoroughfares. I had not gone far up town before

I heard that they had taken possession of the Maryland Club.* I immediately changed my programme and endeavored to assemble a a party of gentlemen to resist Mob Violence. This I found very difficult to effect. I then proceeded to the Club, which had been abandoned by the roughs, at the remonstrances of Mr. Johnathan Meredith, after roaming about the building for a short time. The town was in a terrible state. I knew that the Military authorities were not at all inclined to protect "disloyal" men and I anticipated further trouble. I represented to the men in the Club, that later in the day the roughs would probably return in force and that as this Club was particularly obnoxious to them, they would commence by an attack upon it; that in the heat of excitement they would then probably go to Hanson Thomas, then to our house, then to Robt. McLane's, then to Genl. Howard's & so on,** making no particular distinction of persons but attacking those houses they came to first, of persons at all obnoxious to them. I begged them to arm themselves, come to the Club & make their defense there and I assured them that if resistance was made, the military authorities would then certainly interfere and prevent further strife. But one man present, Jas. H. Barney, was willing to adopt this course. Fortunately for us, later in the day Genl. Wool thought that the excitement had had sufficient sway, that the Southerners had been sufficiently insulted & took steps to prevent any outbreak. I did succeed, by nightfall, in getting together a party of gentlemen who met at our house. We discussed the propriety of organization for defense against the Mob and appointed a committee to report plans. When we broke up, as we left, we found two extra policemen at the door, who apparently took note of all the men as they passed. Next day the town became quite quiet and the committee after one meeting did nothing more.

From that time, until I left for Canada in July 1863, there were always two policemen on duty at our corner.

June 24". [*1862*] Exchanges of prisoners were taking place. Men released from the North were allowed to come to Baltimore travelling alone under parole to report to [*sic*] themselves to the Military auth-

* The Maryland Club, founded in 1857, was located at the northwest corner of Franklin and Cathedral streets in Baltimore, two blocks south and one block west of the Washington Monument. It later moved to Charles and Eager streets, and is there today.

** Dr. John Hanson Thomas lived on the southwest corner of Mount Vernon and Washington Places, Robert McLane at 154 North Charles Street, and Benjamin Chew Howard at 39 Mulberry Street.

orities here. Among the many I saw from Fort Warren was Austin Smith, son of Govr. Smith of Virginia, a brave & gallant fellow. He was soon afterwards killed in the seven days battles before Richmond. Victor [von] Sheliha also came along. He was a Prussian & had been in service abroad. He was a thorough engineer, had been engaged on the defenses of Nashville before its evacuation and later in the war superintended the completion of the defenses of Mobile, where he was stationed for a long time. Today he returned from Richmond, by flag of truce, not having been able to effect a special exchange as he had anticipated. He brought me the news that Stonewall Jackson, instead of being in the valley, threatening Maryland, as was still supposed by the Federal Government, was within one days march of Richmond expecting to unite with Lee and make a combined attack on McClellan. I insisted on his not mentioning it to a soul & that he was imprudent even in telling it to me. As soon as the first news of the battle commenced I told the story at the Club, where until then great despondency had prevailed. The effect was most inspiriting.

*May 30.** Battle of Seven Pines. Johnston wounded. Lee takes command.

June 15. Bernal introduced me to Lord Ed. St. Maur at the Club. He had a letter to me from Russell. I soon found that he had come over with the desire of going south, but everybody had told him the difficulties were so great and that there was so much risk of being caught that he had abandoned his project. He was quite young, just of age and had a great dread of having his name in the newspapers as being caught in the act of violating the orders of this Government—on account of his father's position in the English Cabinet. He was quite Northern too and really not very anxious to undertake the enterprise. After I had a talk with him, I represented the matter in so different a light that he determined to go. I had some time since determined that the only hope of a speedy termination to the war lay in foreign recognition or in the breaking down of the currency. I still thought the former was the most likely event and I determined to devote myself to giving intelligent Englishmen every facility for acquainting themselves thoroughly with the true condition of Southern affairs and the spirit of the Southern people. I had an additional reason for sending over Lord Edward. He was decidedly Northern and it might prove useful to make so intelligent a convert.

* The entry for May 30 duplicates a prior entry; Glenn's entry for June 15 is out of sequence.

We went up to Doughoregan Manor to spend a day with John Carroll and perfect our plans after which Lord Edward went to Washington to call on Lord Lyons.

Lord Lyons of course attempted to dissuade him from carrying out his project, and went as far as to tell Lord Edward that if he was caught and thrown into prison, he need expect no aid from him as Minister. Lord Lyons from the beginning did every thing he could to prevent the slightest offense being given to the Federal Government. It was wonderful to see how a gentleman could be so abjectly submissive as he was. He made later several remonstrances to me through his attachés and suggested to me that I was not only doing a very imprudent thing in facilitating the underground passage of Englishmen, but that I was running great risk myself. As this was my business and not his, I of course paid no attention to it.

Lord Edward returned to Baltimore. Facilities were abundant. He got into a Steamboat, landed on the Patuxent, met some Confederate officers who were over for clothes and was landed in Virginia the same evening. Here his real difficulties commenced. However after getting on some distance he reached the railroad to Richmond. Gov. Letcher was about starting for Richmond in a special train. Lord Edward made application to the Governor, who gave him a passage and treated him most civilly there and afterwards in Richmond. He had the good luck to see the seven days battles and on his return was sent through by flag of truce to McClellan's head quarters. Arrived there he immediately entered into a discussion with the first officers he saw as to the merits of the strife, condemned the conduct of the North and expressed himself surprised that men could be found to engage in the task of conquering a gallant people who only desired their freedom. This was considered rather impertinent & was reported to McClellan, who immediately sent him back to Richmond, as he came. He then ran the blockade again crossed the Potomac, went to Washington & passed on to Baltimore, where he made direct for our house being afraid to go to a public hotel. I was much amused at his enthusiasm. "I was Northern" said he "when I went over, but I came back a thorough Southerner—thorough". In a few days he went to Canada & when he afterwards reached home wrote a capital article for the October number of Blackwood.

Aug. [1862] Frank Lawley came to Baltimore bringing me a letter from Russell. Lt Col. G. J. Wolseley came down from Canada bringing me a letter from Lord Edward St. Maur. With him was D. [*sic*] Muir Inspector General. A few days after their arrival

Septr. [*1862*] Genl Lee crossed into Maryland, took possession of Frederick & detached a considerable force to take Harper's Ferry. We were all wild with excitement. The military authorities in Baltimore appeared to have lost their heads. There was no protective force any where and no pickets upon the roads. A mounted Corporal's guard could have raided where it chose and communications with the Confederate Army were not only open but easy. Lawley and I drove out to Hilton. Next morning we started in a buggey wagon, drove across to the Libery road and there prepared for a fresh start for Frederick* when we heard that Genl Lee had fallen back towards Hagerstown and that McClellan was advancing. This changed our plans and we of course returned. Two days afterwards when there was no necessity for it, pickets were placed upon the roads in every direction. Lawley and I started for Hilton after dusk and were not allowed to proceed more than four miles. There nothing could induce the guard to let me go by, although I reassured the Lieut in command that I lived but three miles off, and that my wife & family expected me. Fortunately I had an old pass in my pocket from Genl W. W. Morris, passing me to and from Fort McHenry. The officer was a volunteer, young and ignorant, and I so imposed upon him and bullied that he not only passed me but Lawley too. We met another picket further up and another at our own gate, who had been stationed there specially, because they said "there were d—d rebels lived in there". A few days later

Septr 20". After the battle of Antietam. *Sep 16* Lawley determined to take the usual route, through the lower counties. Wolseley concluded to go with him. This route had got to be the safest. The contraband traffic carried on in small boats which sailed boldly from the Baltimore wharves had been put an end to. Passenger could no longer expect safely to pass by the Fort and the cutters in small oyster boats, under the pretext of going across to the Eastern shore. The Patuxent Steamers had been stopped** and communication by water with the lower part of the State was difficult. Conveyances & safe drivers were hard to find. Public houses along the road were few and

* The Liberty Road, seven miles north of Catonsville, was an alternate route to Frederick. Glenn and Lawley reached it via Rolling Road, which runs from Liberty Road to Elkridge Landing past Glenn's estate, "Hilton." The Frederick Turnpike, which passed through Catonsville, was the major east-west thoroughfare in Maryland and was thus likely to be heavily patrolled.

** The Baltimore City Directory for 1861 shows no steamers sailing for the Patuxent, but the 1864 Directory notes that the *George Weems* and the *Planter* will resume service to that river.

far apart. Provided with a private rockaway and a good pair of horses, Dr. Steuart acted as coachman and the trio started together. They put up at private houses the first two nights, when the Dr. forwarded them to Piscataway and returned. At Piscataway they were in great danger. They had scarcely arrived when a company of cavalry dashed into the little town on a search for contraband goods. They had hardly time to send their little baggage out into the cabbage patch when the troop pulled up at the hotel door. Fortunately they were not molested. Soon after they were able to send their baggage some distance down the road by hand to a convenient spot where they picked it up afterwards as they went by in their empty and unsuspicious looking vehicle. After this they had great trouble for Dr. S. had actually turned them adrift without telling them whom to apply to for assistance. At Leonardtown they succeeded in making necessary arrangements with the hotel keeper and started to persue their journey. Unfortunately when near the river they fell in with th Captain of a Gunboat. Lawley succeeded in persuading him that they were on their way to Washington, when the fellow became amazingly civil and it was with the greatest difficulty they could induce him to allow them to decline his very pressing invitation to take passage with him to Washington, where he was going to start for next day. A second trial was more successful. They crossed in safety and after much trouble succeeded in reaching Richmond. From thence they proceeded rapidly to Winchester where the main army then was.

One of the first persons they met there was Kirby. He was actually invited to join a riding expedition with them. They declined to meet him. This fellow had some time before come down from Canada & had spent some time in Baltimore where he had succeeded in ingratiating himself in the good opinion of many people as an ardent friend of the South. I scarcely knew him and felt prejudiced against, although he was received very generally. I had good reason to suspect afterwards that he was playing the spy, and the day before Lawley left, as we went into Guy's hotel to lunch, I saw the fellow who had just come to Baltimore, seated at a table. He rose to speak. I declined to give my hand and told my reasons why. He soon after left town, passed up through the Federal lines & crossed to Winchester by that route. He was admitted into the Confederate lines and received by the officers. But from the day these gentlemen declined to meet him. he was watched and after some months was arrested in Richmond, when on the eve of his departure. Plans and memoranda were found in his trunk sufficient to convict him, but the Southern Cabinet forbore to execute him. After a long confinement he was sent North.

August 2nd. [*1862*] Today the George Washington & Mary Weems were seized.* These boats were on the Patuxent route. The owners had been several times notified not to carry contraband goods, as it was suspected that a large amount of freight was sent by this route to the lower counties, from whence it was run across the Potomac. The owners had replied that they had no knowledge of any such route and begged that an officer might be sent to overlook all the freight that was shipped at Baltimore. This was not done. Genl. Wool was at this time absent for a few days and Genl. Morris being next in command took his place. He thought this a grand opportunity to exercise authority and laid his plans accordingly. On Saturday morning just as the Mary Washington was about starting a company of soldiers came aboard, and the steamboat was carried over to Fort McHenry. Here all the passengers who declined to take the oath of Allegiance were thrown into prison. Every place else being full, the church was appropriated to their use. The cargo was overhauled and everything capable of being used South was confiscated. I had gone down to Fair Haven for a few days & expected to come up Saturday. The George Washington was expected there at ten o'clock on its way down. Two o'clock came & there was still no sign of the Baltimore boat. Govr. Pratt & the rest of our party felt satisfied that something was wrong and declined to leave. I determined to trust to my influence with Morris & started by the George Weems when it came along, about half past two.** About six o'clock as we neared North Point, the Mary Washington hove in sight. An officer hailed us from the deck, the boat bore down upon us, the two ran alongside of one another and a company of soldiers preceded by half a dozen detectives came quickly aboard. The Mary Washington then proceeded on her way. All the gang ways of the George Weems were immediately taken possession of & guarded. The men passengers were orderd back to the upper cabin, the women to the lower one. In a few minutes I saw the Colonel in command propound some questions to a little girl and I immediately said to the men around me "The Col. is proposing

* The *George Washington* of the Maryland & Virginia Steamboat Company is mentioned in records of 1829 and 1840. There is no *Mary Weems.* The *Mary Washington* of the Weems Line, built in 1854, was in regular service between Baltimore and Fairhaven, Anne Arundel County, until abandoned in 1888.

** The *George Weems* of the Weems Line was built in Baltimore in 1858 and was in the Patuxent, Fairhaven, Baltimore service until she burned in 1869. In 1861 she sailed for Fairhaven every Saturday and Wednesday.

the oath of allegiance to that little child our turn is to come. Decide what you will do". Detectives then came back & searched all the passengers on two or three of whom were found Confederate paper and letters. I then walked forward first. My name & residence were demanded & taken down. I was asked if I would take the oath. "Of course not" was my reply. I was ordered to stand aside & placed under guard. Most of the passengers stood firm and joined me. Some few, who half an hour before had been most ardent Southerners became suddenly quite loyal, some wanted to know what the oath was, some man wanted to consult his wife first who was in the cabin below. The boat was finally taken to Fort McHenry where those of [us] under guard were marched on shore, through a crowd of soldiers, who jeered and hooted as we passed, into the garrison. There a report was made to General Morris and we were ordered to fall in & march to our prison. At this moment I stepped out of the ranks and said "Colonel, I wish to speak to General Morris." He recognized me as the leader and said "What is the mistake in your case". "None at all," replied I "that I know of, but General Morris is a friend of mine and I wish him to know that I am here". I then handed him my card, an engraved card which seemed to inspire the fellow, a New York volunteer, with some degree of respect. He took it in and came back with orders to show me on to head quarters. I walked in very easily, went up to the General, held out my hand and said "How are you General". He looked up into my face with a curious expression. He evidently thought he had caught me fairly this time and was rather pleased. At last he said "What the devil brought you here"? I replied "that I had gone down to Fair Haven three days ago with a party of friends, that I had had a bad run at Whist and that I had quit them & come up apparently in bad company, judging from my present condition." I laughed quietly at my little joke, when he said "Is that all." "That is all," said I. "Colonel" said he "march those other prisoners off; I will look after Mr. Glenn." The Colonel left. I stood aside for one moment, when I saw that the General was still undecided; so I said to him "General, where is Mrs. Morris. I have not seen her for some time, I think I will go down and take tea with her." He looked up and smiled and said "Wait a little & I will go with you." I did wait. We did go down. I staid at his house two or three hours, still I felt a prisoner. Finally about ten o'clock he asked me "How I proposed to go home". I answered him quickly, as if my visit had been a premeditated one "that I had intended to walk up." "Well" said he, "here is an ambulance about to go up, you had better go in it" and I did.

The other prisoners were wretchedly treated. In the church there was nothing but bare boards, there being no cushions to the pews. The prisoners had no blankets. I sent comforts to some of them and Mrs. Morris was very kind to one who was quite ill. Two days after I was down there and saw the same Colonel come up to the guard. "Guard said he, how are the prisoners coming on". "Pretty well," was the answer, "they have 17 Blankets and want about as many more". They have already said he, 17 too many" and walked off. Some of these gentlemen were afterwards sent to Fort Delaware and kept in duress for three months. There was no charge against them.

June 26–July 1". Seven days battles in front of Richmond. known as McClellans great "change of base."

Aug 14. [*1862*] The News Sheet was seized today. Carpenter (the Editor), Neilson who had been chief compositor on the Exchange and Sultzer, the Clip, were thrown into Fort McHenry. Genl. Morris with his usual cunning had tried to implicate me. He cross questioned these men closely to know if I was not in some way interested in and responsible for the conduct of the paper under its present name. He learned nothing. I saw him shortly afterwards. When I told him what sort of a man Sultzer was & what his part of the work was, Genl. M. discharged him as not being worth feeding. Neilson hung out bravely for a time and dreamed of glory and martyrdom. But he soon caved in and made terms *about*

Sep 5. [*1862*] Carpenter stood out like a man. He was afterwards sent to Fort Delaware and was kept in prison for two or three months. The charges against him were "general disloyalty".

Wooden sheds had been put up for these men, divided into small rooms in each of which were two or three plank bunks. At a later period when the crowd of prisoners was great they were huddled together in the big stable and in its loft. When the prisoners of war came through for Exchange I have seen the stalls filled with men many sick some wounded, but all uncared for.

John Thompson Mason was in the Fort at this time. He had been one of the most violent Southern men we had. He was very gloomy. His wife came to see him several times and rather bullied him, I thought, into standing up for his rights. Like most of the prisoners, however, he made some terms.

Aug. Frank Vizitelly "Hartist and Hauthor", of the Illustrated London News came to Baltimore to go South. He had been for a long time with the Federal army, obeying instructions I presume. I suppose he was now going South according to orders. He gave a very different reason for it. He said that he had been in company at Memphis and had heard a noble hearted girl say that she would rather be the woman of a Southern soldier fighting bravely for his cause, than the wife of any man—no matter who—who was not in arms. V. was so struck with this he said that tears came into his eyes and he would go to the land where such noble sentiments were common. He was a magnificent and most amusing liar. His tales of his campaigns with Garibaldi were beyond compare. He never was quite charming till he was half drunk. Then he would sing and talk till morning. The West River boat was still running.* He went in it & from there across to the Potomac. He had a photograph of mine and a letter from me which I afterwards heard were displayed rather publicly on several occasions. It was a great piece of luck, I was not informed on. When I afterwards saw him he gave me a brilliant account of the battle of Fredericksburgh, all of which he had witnessed. Capt. Phillips, Guards, who was there and did see the fight laughed at V. & said he kept himself in a very safe place all day. V.'s business was sketching, not fighting. A year later he went to England. He proposed to write a book. Sketching was his profession, but composition was his forte. He was great by his pencil, he would be glorious by his pen. Poor fellow! I think he must have written one article as a sample for a magazine which was not accepted. His style was too stilted and flowery. I waited in vain for article & book. I saw neither and soon heard that V. had relinquished his aspirations to "hautorship" and returned to sketching. His h's were most amusing sometimes.

October 6". [1862] Today the "Gazette" was issued. It was of course the Times, the News Sheet, the Exchange, under another name. Carpenter, he being the most obnoxious as the Editor, who by his summaries managed to inspire a cheerful hope in the hearts of the public, was left off the staff. That was the only change. And this was only for a few months.

Septr. News today of the brutal arrest of Judge Carmichael at [Easton, Maryland].**

* The West River boats of the Individual Enterprise Line were the *Kent, Champion* and *Pioneer*.

** For information on the Carmichael Case see Apendix C. According to the Baltimore *Sun* of May 29, 1862, McPhail had with him policemen John L. Bishop, William H. Cassell, Easton Horner, and James Pryor "of his force." Policeman Bishop appears in the 1859 Baltimore City Directory. Arrested with

The whole details were most shocking. He was perfectly upright & manly and determined to do his duty as an officer of the law and not of the Government. Some soldiers and police officers were sent over to arrest him. They entered the Court while it was in session. They knocked him over the head with the butt of a pistol and dragged him bleeding and senseless out of the room. Few occurrences more infamous have ever occurred. He was brought up to Fort McHenry.

On receipt of the news I immediately endeavored to call a meeting of the bar, for the purpose of protesting against the perpetration of such an outrage. Jonathan Meredith, who I knew, though a Union Man had once been hightoned & plucky, was the first I applied. His answer was that Southern men had begun this in Kentucky. I went to Andrew Ridgely. He said such things must be expected in a civil war. I came to the conclusion that nothing was to be hoped for from Union Men. Those who denied their sister states the right of Self Government were not easily shocked at acts of oppression perpetrated upon the persons of their political opponents. Nor were these men violent "Union Shriekers" "Loyal leaguers". I took them for moderate men & thought the natural instincts of gentlemen would influence them. From them I turned to our own men. Fred. Frick was willing to do anything. Geo. Gill had to go to his farm. Another could not come. We got finally a small meeting together at Fredk. Brune's. Old Judge Chambers was there. The result of it in fact, was a sort of suggestion that the sooner Judge Carmichael gave a parole and got out of prison, the better. This he finally did, after some time. Those men in Fort Warren, who still held out, expressed their surprise greatly at his accepting any terms after such an outrage. As it turned out it was just as well. Who is any better off?

Septr. 22. President issues his Emancipation proclamation.

W. Winder Pollock, arrived in New York from the Pacific. Like many navy officers he had stuck by his Flag. It was a sort of faith to them. They knew nothing of States rights or Central Government. They had a flag & they would not forsake it. It was the same case with James Harwood. He came home, about 12 mos. before. He would stick by his flag. He was home for several months before he made up his mind that to fight for a flag was an idea, while to fight for a cause was a principal [*sic*]. When he got that far he went South.

Judge Carmichael were prosecutor J. W. Powell, crier of the Court Alexis E. Pascault, and citizen William Nabb. Powell's full name was Isaac Canon Wright Powell.

As soon as I heard Pollock was in New York I went on and joined him. We spent three days together, never alluding to the subject we both had most at heart. I knew that he had refused to take active service agst the South and that he had staid as long as he could in the Pacific. Indeed he was marked on the Navy List as not "mentioned for promotion"—which was of course on acct. of his sentiments. The only remark that was made was once as we passed down Broadway. I saw a Virginian, who was still in the Navy, sitting at the window of the St. Denis Hotel. "I pity that man" said I. "When this war is over he will have no friends at home and the very men of the North for whom he has fought will despise him as a traitor". As we returned to Baltimore, when we entered Maryland, he saw for the first time the guards of soldiers along the line of the road. It made his blood tingle. In a few days he went across the lower Potomac. He got through without difficulty.

The underground routes varied constantly. When all communication was entirely stopped on the lower Potomac, it would be opened on the upper—and then again from the Eastern shore. Sometimes the travel was very dangerous and the the treatment to those caught very rough. I recollect on one occasion, a young lady, who was a governess in a private family in St. Mary's County, crossed over from Virginia to return to her home. She was seen, by the Commander of the Gunboat who overhauled the boat, putting something in her bosom. The boat was hailed and hauled alongside. The officer ordered her on deck. She replied that he might have the civility to hang over a companion way. This was done and she came upon deck. The officer immediately seized her and thrust his hands in her bosom for the papers he said were concealed there. He did not ask for them. He then said that he did not believe she was a woman at all. She replied that "she thought his own indecent act had already convinced him of that". His answer was "that he had known many a man with as large breasts as she had" and in spite of her entreaties took her down into the cabin for further examination. The brute was afterwards Killed.

The treatment of ladies in many instances was disgraceful. Mrs. —— neé Phenix, who was seized near Washington and examined in the Balto. Custom House declared that she thought the women who examined her, were certainly men in disguise, so disgustingly minute was their search of her person and so marked was the delight they manifested in the exercise of their vocation. —Capt. Wynne of the Grenadiers and Capt. Phillips of the same corps, came to Baltimore. They were very anxious to go through. I took at first very little interest in the matter. I did not think that either of them were men to influence public opinion or take even the trouble to write out their experiences for publication. The routes too were almost closed. However after staying here a week they left in the Eastern Shore boat* and went as far as Kent Island, where there was a depot for Northern deserters & for contraband goods.** They sailed from there in a small boat. There was little wind and quite a fog, in consequence of which they nearly ran into a gunboat. When quite close to her the Capt. boldly came to & dropped anchor. This saved him. In the night he slipped his cable and drifted back with the flood tide. They afterwards landed in St. Mary's County, crossed a narrow neck of land, and started in a row boat to cross the Potomac. As they neared the right bank Phillips, an Oxford boatman, recognized the sweep of a barge. He could not however persuade the men in charge that he was right. In a short time a man of war barge came in sight carrying a strong light in the prow, with which the horizon was from time to time swept. Fortunately they were close in shore. They all lay down in the boat & luckily escaped detection. Afterwards they got on well to Richmond, where they were received as English officers always are received. Phillips was fortunate enough to be with General Lee's staff at the battles near Fredericksburg.

After spending several weeks there they started to return & got as far as Leesburg. Here they separated. Phillips took the important letters, which he had foolishly undertaken to bring through, and went alone to Pt. of Rocks, where he deliberately crossed. He had gotten on so very luckily so far that he forgot all the cautions he had received. On reaching the Maryland side he walked up to the guard & on being stopped said he was on his way to Washington. The orders being strict not to allow any one to pass, he requested to see the Officer of the day, & was told the Corporal of the Guard was all that was necessary. After an interview with him, he was allowed to pass. A train soon after came by and he came to Baltimore. He had a letter from Benjamin to Gladstone in his boots. Also letters for the London Times from Lawley and for the Illustrated News from Vizitelly. All except Vizitelly's letter & sketch were despatched immediately. That I took home to look at.

Wynn followed about six hours after & also passed the pickets. Unfortunately no train was due for some hours and he went to the

* The Kent Island boats were the *Cecil,* Capt. William T. Rice, the *Balloon* of the Eastern Shore Steamboat Company, the *Hugh Jenkins,* and the *Chester* of Slaughter's Line.

** A Federal depot was at Queenstown, on the Chester River, opposite the northern portion of Kent Island. An atlas shows a steamboat landing near Queenstown in the 1870s.

tavern. Here some suspicion was excited & he was sent for by the General. His baggage was searched & cards & notes were found from Longstreet J. E. B. Stuart & others. Many of the things bore Phillips name. Wynne led them to believe that P. was behind. The river was accordingly picketed for some distance up & down and the Genl. —an Irish one—swore that he would have Capt. Phillips if he had to picket the shores of the St. Lawrence. Towards the end of the day he found that P. had gone on and then forwarded Wynne to Baltimore. So far things did not look badly. Wynne's only trouble was the insult he had received. An illustrated book was found among his effects containing colored cuts of the different Confederate Uniforms. It was published by one Winn in Richmond.* When this was found out Wynne was charged with being a tailor travelling under false colors. Sunday night, about 12 o'c, Phillips who had been spending the evening with me, had gone back to Guy's, returned & told me that Wynne was at Guy's a prisoner, eating his supper. We went down. Phillips stopped over the way in the shade. I went in & found that Wynne had been carried off to Prison, no one knew where. I went to Phillips' room, got his brushes & combs & a few light traps and left. He went back with me & staid all night. Next morning after breakfast, I took him round to the Club, as being so public that he would certainly not be molested there. Wynne had been taken to the watch house where he was found by Constable, the Provost Marshal, who saw, he said, by his boots that he was a gentleman. When he found that he belonged to the Guards he was very civil, as Englishmen generally are to their betters. In the morning Constable released Wynne on his parole for the day and went to Washington to see about his case. We waited till the late train was near at hand & Constable not arriving, Phillips left for New York. He got into the cars, a ticket was purchased for him, his bag was checked & he got to New York where he remained some days under an assumed name. He was lucky to get off. Constable came into Baltimore as he went out, with positive orders to arrest Phillips, who for some reason was supposed to be the more important man of the two. I had an interview with Constable & Wynne at Guy's. C. told me that the matter was graver than he thought it was, that it was known Capt. P. was in town and that he would be arrested. I laughed and told him "if that was all, he need not be uneasy as Phillips had left for Canada." Next morning, I came out of my door, with Vizitelly's picture in my hand and a little note book of Phillips in my pocket. I noticed two extra men at the corner in addition to those always

* Richmond, Virginia, publisher Charles H. Wynne had his plant at Main and 14th streets in 1860.

stationed there, but it did not excite my astonishment and I passed by them. Half an hour after my brother who had been staying in town all night also went out. He was immediately seized. Knowing nothing of Phillips he was astonished and told the men they could not know who he was. He was he said Mr. Jno. G. He thought they wanted me. "Oh Yes, said one of them, we know who you are perfectly well. You are Capt. Phillips"—and his Scotch cap confirmed them in this conjecture. As he was about being carried off, he told them that as they declined to take his testimony perhaps they would take a negro's testimony. Thomas* was called from the front door —and afterwards Henry, the coachman,** was called from the side door round the corner. Both told the same tale and John was released. The negroes were highly delighted "at having got Massa John off". They were not then as important as they are now. These detectives I afterwards learned had been sent to the house with orders to arrest any one besides me coming out. They had learned at Guy's that Phillips had gone off with me.

After a few days Wynne was lodged in the Old Capitol. There no one took the slightest notice of him. Lord Lyons & all his legation left him alone although one of them, Malet, was a brother of an intimate friend of Wynne's. I wrote him and sent him $50—and after some time, although I knew the business was a risky one, for people had been more than once arrested there for refusing to take the oath, which was demanded of them before they were allowed to go in, I went down to see him. Wood, the Keeper, allowed me an interview. He was very civil to Wynne and permitted him to have a room to himself. He saw he was a gentleman and he had money. I was the first person who had been near and he felt bitterly the neglect of the Legation. Shortly after I sent him some books and some plum cake, among other things. He had been in several weeks when he heard that Lord Lyons was negotiating his release, but he determined if possible to effect his escape and thus not only to get free but to do so without being under any obligation to Lord Lyons. By the aid of a common breakfast knife he cut out a panel in a side door in his room. The door was old fashioned and the panel was large. At

* Thomas was probably a free Negro, since the 1860 census does not list any slaves belonging to William Wilkins Glenn, and Thomas does not appear on the slave inventory of Judge Glenn's estate in 1853 nor in the executor's inventory in 1864.

** Henry was a Glenn slave, born c. 1826. He remained with the Glenns as a coachman until at least 1876. See Baltimore County Inventories, Liber NH 68, folio 532, Hall of Records, Annapolis, Maryland, and the Glenn Papers, MS 1017, Maryland Historical Society.

night he slipped the panel out and passed into a vacant room. From this he found communication by which he passed to the fourth story and on to the roof. Here he reconnoitered for some time, but found he could not succeed in reaching the lightning rod. He returned to his room before day break, made a paste of bread & the cake I had sent him and with this made his panel apparently fast. He wheeled his bed against the door. Next night he again made the same trip, but was forced to abandon the lightning rod. He determined to try the chimney, but thought it would be folly to attempt this in the light colored clothes he wore, as the soot would betray him, even if he got safely through. He returned to his room & passed a second very anxious day. He feared that the next room might be occupied & also that Lord Lyons might get him released, which he was not just now anxious for. The third night, having put on a suit of dark clothes he again made a venture. The room was empty. The way was clear. But the roof was covered with snow & so slippery that he could not reach the chimney. He was in despair. He went back to his vacant room again & found the passage door open. The night was a fearful one & strange to say the Guards had been withdrawn from the cold passages through the house. With his boots round his neck he crept down to the second floor. Here he found a door open & entered the room a vacant room. The window was easily raised. He passed through, let himself down & dropped noiselessly. The roof was slight and he found himself in a porch. Proceeding to the end of this he let himself down. His feet touched the top of a fence. It was the fence which separated the yard from the street. He balanced himself on the top of it. Beneath him the guard passed to & fro within a few feet. His heart thumped so he feared that the guard must hear it. After a little breathing time, he dropped in the snow, waited till the guard passed him again and then crept across the street. It was still an hour before daybreak. He put on his boots and went to a pot house where he got a cup of coffee and awaited the hour for the Baltimore train to start. When the time came he went to the depot purchased a ticket & was stopped at the ticket gate as a deserter. Surely he looked like one. He was as rough as a man could be & looked as if he had never made a toilet; but it was a great insult to mistake a Guardsman for a Yankee—& worse for a Yankee deserter. He was searched. Nothing but his precious knife, with which he carved his way to freedom, was found. He was released. The train started and he was free.

It was a little past eight o'clock. I was seated at the breakfast table. Thomas came in saying "deres a gentleman down in the kitchen". "A gentleman! and how did he get there?" "Comed in de backway, Sir." I saw from Thomas' smile, there was something curious on hand. He was quite intelligent and on several occasions had shown himself a faithful negro. "And who is it, Thomas?" "Dat dare Capt. Wynne Sir". I went down. There was Wynne, wet & shivering. I brought him up, dried him and fed him and took him at once up to N's. He was very uneasy about Wood. Now said he "they are in my room. They know I am gone. They are after me." He would have taken the Northern C. Rail Road* at once but I would not let him go so soon & without any baggage. In less than half an hour I had my wagon out and after taking some turns round streets to throw George, the Coachman,** off my track, I picked Wynne up & drove him out to P's. We were just in time. Wood was furious when he found Wynne had escaped. He had treated Wynne with unusual consideration and he looked upon Wynne's escape as a violation of hospitality. It was proving a bad thing for him. He received a severe reprimand & was near losing his place. He went to the Baltimore train at once. He reached here in less than an hour after Wynne had left. He said "I know where he is. He is at Glenn's and if he is not at his house in town, he is at his house in the country". But he was too late.

Lawrence was at that time here. I got a passport for him by his permission from the Br. Consul, gave it to Wynne, furnished him with a carpet bag and change of clothes and after a few days, when the pursuit was probably gone in the wrong direction, started him through Pennsylvania by rail to Ohio, where he crossed by an out of the way route into Canada. I wrote to Wood afterwards begging him to send me the clothes & traps "which Capt. Wynne had left in the hurry of his departure." Wood considered this adding insult to injury. Phillips trunk I forwarded him a few days after he left—not directly, of course, for I was narrowly watched.

Decr. 1862. Lord Hartington & Col. Leslie had already been in Baltimore.*** They wanted to go South, but could find no one to take charge of them. Leslie was a very good fellow, fond of sport and

* The Northern Central Railroad ran from Baltimore to Harrisburg, Pa. Its Baltimore Depot was at Calvert and Centre streets.

** George was a Glenn slave, born c. 1820. He is referred to in the following excerpt from a letter of Mary Glenn to William Wilkins Glenn, November 8, 1863: "George did not go off with the rest of the ———, but I was quite sure I had told you of his stealing your carpets, & hams & quilts of Mother's. He is in jail and is to be sent to service to the E. Shore if anyone will take him." Glenn Papers, MS 1017, Maryland Historical Society.

*** Some authorities identify Hartington's companion as Colonel William Leslie toddy, who did not care a rap for any political questions which did not affect him personally. Hartington was apparently very heavy and uninterested. Besides he was Northern decidedly. I did not think it worth the risk to further their views. Now they came back after a long tour in the West, showed much more interest and were better informed. They were very anxious to get South. I was again applied to and thinking that as they were both in Parliament and as they would return to England with their Southern views fresh upon them, it might, in case of a division, make a difference of two votes. One Sunday morning they sent their bags to my house. I was afraid to start from Guy's. Poinsett Pringle, a bright & noble boy, was here at the same time. The three breakfasted with me & afterwards went to the stable and started in my rockaway for Howard County. About fifteen miles from town they were met by a scout who took them to D's house. Here they bought horses and met their guide Shipley.* They crossed the Potomac not far from Leesburg, kept to the North of that town & got to Richmond. After some time, they attempted to run out from Charleston but failed. They returned to Richmond & crossed the Lower Potomac. Two boats started together. They were pursued and Hartington & Leslie saved themselves by hard pulling. They abandoned their boat as they touched shore and heard it fired into almost immediately. They came back with their views much altered and as thoroughly Southern as any Englishman could be who was not afraid of the North.

*Nov 28" 1862.*** The political prisoners who still remained at Fort Warren, had finally received their release and today arrived in Baltimore. There were but twelve or fourteen of them, all of the hundreds who were arrested, having made some compromise with the Government. There were a few instances where men were released without oath or parole, but they were very rare. My own was the only case of a Marylander, I recollect. There were a number of friends to welcome them home, after their long absence. They were much affected by the warm reception they received which was

(see glossary entry), member of Parliament and chairman of the Commons Committee in Military Affairs. (Ella Lonn, *Foreigners in the Confederacy,* Gloucester, Mass., 1965. p. 356, 358). An interesting vignette of "Harty-tarty" is given by Anita Leslie, *The Marlborough House Set,* (New York, 1973), p. 50 ff. Leslie claims that Hartington's American visit was intended to abate his passionate affair with Catherine "Skittles" Walters (see Glenn's narrative entry for January 1" 1864) and that he was accompanied by Charles Powell Leslie.

* Shipley is variously designated "E. M." or "P. M." Shipley. Edwin M. Shipley of Carroll County, Maryland, was known for his Southern sympathies.

** The date sequence is reversed.

quite unexpected by them, as they had an idea that they were being forgotten by their friends. And indeed they had been by many. "Out of sight out of mind." Besides the time had gone by when the resistance of a few men, unsupported as they were by any portion of the community, could be of any use. Their resistance to the despotism which had been established was become a personal matter. They preserved their own self respect by their conduct and that of other people. Still I saw that kind of resistance was so perfectly useless that I should have thought as well of them if they had agreed six months before to give a simple military parole, which did not affect their opinions nor their state action. Sister & Mary* were at the depot and brought Wallis up in the carriage.

These gentlemen were very much fêted and entertained for some time. They were in excellent spirits and had high hopes of being able to restore a better tone to the State. They could not understand that the Administration had released them simply because it was indifferent to the little influence they could exercise. They imagined that they had triumphed over the Government. One of the first things proposed was the reissue of the Exchange. Both Frank Howard & Wallis desired to start it on the first of January. I objected to this. I was satisfied it was too soon, but thought that the time was fast approaching and that we might safely count upon the freedom of the press being sufficiently restored by April. As I could not agree with my chums I proposed to go to New York and see if we would be sustained there by the Democratic party. I had no objection to risking my liberty and my capital, provided I could do good. I had no idea of making a useless and foolish sacrifice. I did not wish to ally myself with the Democratic party, but I wished to have its support. I went to New York to see the men connected with the Press there. The principal man was S. L. M. Barlow. He was the chief controller of the World. I had never seen him before though I had heard of him at Washington. Before I talked with him half an hour I came to the conclusion he was the most overated man I ever met. He was bright and entertaining and a man of taste. He had been successful in business. As a thinker he was superficial and utterly incapable of appreciating the terrible nature of the crisis in which the country was plunged. He could not then be persuaded that the South was in earnest and firmly believed that the Southern people would be glad to come back under proper guarantees. Neither he nor anyone else were willing to pledge themselves to stand by us,

* "Sister & Mary" refers to Anne and Mary Glenn.

if we were arrested and our paper broken up. Barlow expressed the sentiment of all when he said that New York could not make common cause with Maryland, that New York had as much as it could do to take care of itself, and that no matter how strictly we might confine the discussions in the Exchange to purely constitutional subjects, they could not undertake to promise to resist any illegal violence or military coercion the Administration might see fit to practice upon us. "In fact" said he "Maryland is a disloyal state. What we say here about liberty, is patriotism. When you say it there it is treason". And so the matter dropped. Liberty had no friends in the North. There was a struggle for place— a desire for party success—but that was all. The contest in the North from the beginning was the contest of pothouse politicians. There was scarcely a single man who did not yield to the pressure when it became popular.

I had with me at this time the manuscript of Frank Howard's "Fourteen Months in American Bastille".* I went around among publishers and endeavored to get it published. No one was willing to run the risk. I brought it home. It was soon after gotten out & gotten off secretly by Kelly & Pitt. It took so well that a second edition was published. The publishers were not molested then. After two months or more the balance of the Edition unsold was seized and one of the firm was thrown into prison. Howard was not molested. Up to the time I write this, Feb 1865, no one of these Fort Warren prisoners has ever been molested or interfered with. To be sure they have been very prudent and given no cause for suspicion.

April 1863. Williamson, carriage maker,** was in Baltimore on his way to New York for the purpose of purchasing material for ambulances and wagons. The Iron boxes and hubs and rims which required long seasoning were entirely wanting in the South. He had a contract with the War Department, who agreed to pay all costs, expenses & Insurance and to give tobacco or cotton, in exchange, with a permit to ship. As the Insurance costing about 33% carried nearly the whole risk there could be no loss. With enterprise the cotton & tobacco gotten out paid large profits. Williamson was so very indiscreet that I declined to have anything to do with him. He had nobody to back him here and went on to New York. The goods when purchased were shipped in schooners which cleared for Washington. When on the Virginia coast, a signal was run up in front of

* Frank Howard, *Fourteen months in an American Bastile* (Baltimore: Kelly, Hedian & Piet, 1863). The Maryland Historical Society lists three editions.

** Glenn possibly refers to Angus Williamson, who was a coachmaker at 56 German Street in Baltimore.

the sails, so that it could not be seen from the bay side. Scouts from the signal corps were on shore for the purpose of answering the signal. If not answered the vessel sailed on towards the Potomac until the return signal was given. The vessel then ran into shore, the cargo was unladen and a number of wagons and a guard were on hand to take charge of the property.

Harry Brogden of the signal corps was in town on business for a week at the same time. Soon afterwards George Lemmon was here for some days. They used to come and go almost at pleasure. Young Sotheron,* on furlough, used to walk about the streets as if he were at home. I remonstrated with him and told him he ran great risk of being taken up as a spy.

It was astonishing to me that more harm did not result from the perfectly loose manner in which Marylanders behaved. Matters of the greatest importance and often very compromising were talked of with the greatest publicity. Still they never seemed to get to the ears of the Federals, so unanimous was the feeling of the native born Marylanders and so distinct was the devision between them and the Yankees. Genl. Dix had a proper appreciation of this. When some one asked him how he could send a letter South, he replied "Go, ask any little girl you see in the street in Baltimore" and he was right.

I have always thought that Maryland in fact aided the Southern cause, in the position which she occupied, than as a member of the Confederacy. In the first place she furnished in volunteers not far short of 30,000 to the Southern Army, more than South Carolina furnished before the conscription. South Carolina was in the Confederacy fighting to defend her own property. Maryland was not defending herself. The way to protect her property was to keep quiet and submit. Her sons were fighting for a principle and for South Carolina's property. Besides this the perfect free masonry which prevaded in Maryland enabled scouts to go and come as they pleased and to obtain information with the greatest possible ease. If the Federal army had made Pennsylvania its grand base instead of Maryland not one scout could have moved around there where one hundred moved around in Maryland. It was the position of Maryland which made the information from Washington so acces[s]-ible. The seat of Government was in fact in the enemy's country. All private information passed over wires erected in a hostile State. The

* Two Sothrons served in the 1st Maryland Infantry of the Confederate army. Webster H. Sothron was a private in Company H, and Marshall Sothron a private in Company I. Both survived the war. They were the sons of Col. John H. Sothron of "The Plains," St. Marys County, Maryland.

government uses cyphers but they are soon found out and few despatches pass over the wires which are not taken off by drop wires and forwarded if necessary to Richmond. The officials in Washington are surrounded by Southern friends. A great deal leaks out this way. Many of them, apparently loyal, are southern at heart and serve the South for a little love & more money. There are informants, in every department, some of them high in office. A scout of General Lee's who was on here a few days ago, came for the purpose of obtaining information from some of these men. All this never could have happened had Maryland been in the Confederacy.

Jany 1863. G. A. Lawrence, author of Guy Livingstone came here. He brought me letters from Ernest Clay (afterwards Seymer) of the Legation. He represented himself as on his way South, seeking the position of voluntary aide to some noted General. He simply lied. He was sent out here by Algernon Bentinck, of the London Morning Post, to write for pay. Bentinck gave him at least £200. to start with. He had an excellent outfit and proposed to travel to Richmond with his luggage as he would travel to New York. He had an immense pair of cavalry boots which he refused to part with under any considerations. I told him "Lawrence, you can't take these things. You can take quinine. It is used in the lower counties for Medicine. You can take saltpetre it is used for curing hams. But these boots are never used. They are clearly contraband. No vessel that sails from Baltimore would take them aboard. They would endanger confiscation of the cargo. No person will drive you to the Potomac, if you take these boots along. You can try the stage from Washington if you like, but if you are found with these boots on, they are a sure ticket to the Old Capitol". He would stick by his boots. They were a fine pair. He was proud of them. The lower route was quite open when he came. He trifled about until it was closed. I then proposed to him to go as Hartington & Leslie went, and I bought for him a capital horse, which he named Falcon. He never saw him but once & then only at a distance. He makes a grand story about it in "Border & Bastile". It is useless to go into the details of this man's follies and weaknesses. He made a great display, talked foolishly, compromised his best friends and had really not the slightest desire to get South. He got an outfit of saddle, holster & pistol in Baltimore. He made a grand display of them to attract attention. He had half a dozen chances to go South and neglected them all and after the most bloody talk, gave his pistol away on the banks of the Upper Potomac lest he should "be tempted, if attacked, to shoot some one". He finally, after escaping every danger, in spite of himself and after getting through all the picket lines and entering Confederate territory rode, directly into the garden of a man named whose house he was expressly cautioned to avoid, by taking a circutious route, as this man was the only one he had to fear on the route. He got cornered at a low fence, which he did not try to leap and surrendered to one man with a double barrel gun and a pistol. He tells in Border & Bastille an immense story of a home guard and minié rifles— all a fabrication. He had squandered all his money in Baltimore, could get no more there and doubted the experiment of reaching Richmond penniless. When he was caught he had about his person, a letter from me to an agent of mine near Cumberland. There was nothing in the letter. Still as he did not use it in Cumberland, it was no longer of use to him. He kept it as a passport in Richmond. It was taken on him and from this time began my serious troubles. In a few days he was lodged in the Old Capitol. An examination was entered into & every effort was made to implicate me. My friends of the Washington legation notified me in time, but my wife was then about to be confined and I had to take my chances.*

I was however unmolested. A few days after Mrs. Atwood came to Baltimore. She was a ward of Genl. Geo. Williamson's. She had once been a play actress I afterwards learned. She and Genl. Williamson had left Canada not a great while before and had been seized & thrown into Fort Lafayette, on the charge of communicating with the South. She had obtained her release on the ground of English Citizenship. She was very mysterious, asked a great many questions about my position & my trustworthiness and expressed a desire to see me, to convey to me a private message. After some days I went to see her. I saw at a glance that she was not a lady. We entered into conversation. She asked me many questions & finally expressed her astonishment at the fact that I could not correspond directly with Canada & offered to give me an address by which my letters could be safely sent through the mail. I thanked her, & said "I had no longer any correspondence. She then told me with great mystery that in the Old Capitol, she had seen a man named Shipley who begged her to tell me "to look out". Shipley was the man who was captured with Lawrence as a guide. I told her I knew many men of the same description named Shipley & therefore could not tell if I knew this particular one or not and that as for the advice "I did not need it—there were many ways of opposing the Government without

* Ellen Smith Glenn's last child, William Lindsay Glenn, was born on April 22, 1863. She died on May 9, 1863.

doing it covertly and thus uselessly rendering your neck liable to the halter and your property to confiscation—and that I preferred to fight my fight in a way which did not render it necessary for me to look out". We soon after parted. I was satisfied she was a spy, sent up for the especial purpose of entrapping me. Lawrence soon after obtained his release and was glad enough to shake the American dust from his shoes. He went to England, wrote Border & Bastille, compromised me dreadfully under the thin disguise of Mentor and John Carroll openly, that the world might know he had been a guest at Doughoregan Manor. He was utterly without moral character and a great blower. It was tiresome to hear him talk of his exploits. When however he got into a small circle of literary men, among whom he was first, he could be most charming for a few hours, on the light literature of the day. His memory was capital. He could repeat his own verses by the page and they were even better than his prose. His Legend of Fraquhair [*sic*] is as good a ballad, to my mind, as I ever read.

February 1863. There were few general entertainments this winter. Society was almost entirely Southern—and every annoyance was given to those who attempted to encourage gaiety. The Union Shriekers who knew they would not be allowed to share in the amusements of the Southerners gave information that the parties, which were apparently given for social amusement, were in fact treasonable gatherings. The Assembly Room* was decorated with flags and the Assemblies were consequently broken up, as this kept away the Southerners. A few young people quietly met once a week to dance the German Cotillion. General Schenck determined to stop this because his daughters, who were here, were not invited. He sent his aide one evening and a small guard to inspect the premises. They entered the room uninvited took a look & were speedily asked out. They said they came to see if there was any treasonable demonstration there, but finding none they left quietly. Still these annoyances were excessively disagreeable. There was difficulty in some of the Methodist Churches, the Union portion of the Congregations insisting on putting the flag around the pulpit.

May. [*1863*] Battles of the Wilderness and lamentable news of the death of Stonewall Jackson. This was more than the loss of an army to the South. A curious accident happened to two of Lawley's letters to the London Times describing these battles and Jackson's death.

* The Assembly Rooms were on the northeast corner of Lombard and Hanover streets in Baltimore, and had been erected in 1851.

The underground route was very thoroughly closed. Few went or came. Lawley paid high but found messengers difficult to be had. He entrusted this package of letters to a young man who lived near Leonardtown. Unfortunately he was arrested in that place by an officer who hired a light wagon and drove him, as a prisoner towards Washington. The wagon was exchanged afterwards and sent back to L'town. On the following Sunday the wagon was hired for a drive to church. After church was over, the seats were found to be very warm from exposure to the Sun and were turned over. In doing this, a package of letters fell upon the floor of the wagon. It was addressed to C. Smith Montgomery—a name assumed by Mackay in New York. Beyond this there was nothing else, not even New York. The gentleman who found them, tore off the envelope. He found another addressed simply "Gosling & Sharpe, Bankers". Not knowing that these Bankers resided in London, he again tore open the envelope & found another with the name Mowbray Morris written upon. This gave him no clue & he opened this envelope as he had done the others. He found the letters signed F. L. Having no trace whatever of the authorship or ownership he proceeded to read them. They were found so interesting that he showed them to friends and they were circulated from house to house for several days. Finally they fell into the hands of Judge Ford. He saw them at a friend's house read them and asked what was to be done with them. "Burn them" was the answer "no one wants them". "But," said the Judge, "they are evidently intended for some English paper. Why not try and find out for whom they are intended." "What can I do. How can I find out," was the reply. "Give them to me" said F. and he took them. Shortly after he came to Baltimore. He met some friends at Barnums and told the story. On asking their advice they said "Take them to Bill Glenn. If they are English, he will know all about them". The same day, he brought them to my house. "Do you know anything about this? asked he. "I know said I, that this is Lawley's handwriting." And who is Mowbray Morris? "He is the business man of the London Times." The letters went safely over by next steamer.

May Fitzgeral [*sic*] Ross came along. He was very anxious to ride a raid with J. E. B. Steuart. He had been the beau sabreur of Heidelberg in his day, had fought his hundred duels and was now a captain in the Austrian Hussars. He insisted on taking his uniform & sword with him. He refused to travel without it. So much luggage was quite out of the way, but as underground travel was so nearly closed, I told him to try it, as the very boldness of the thing at such a time would disarm suspicion. There had been a convention in Baltimore.* Several Eastern Shore gentlemen were about returning home. He left with them, arrived safely in Princess Ann & after a few days crossed the bay and reached Richmond. His uniform was however a nuisance. He had no chance to wear it. He tried it one day and as I prophecied, nearly flung a whole division into confusion. They had never seen such a sight & their curiosity was not to be restrained. Ross staid a long time in the South. He took with him a photograph of a particular friend to Mr. Benjamin and another to Burton Harrison, Mr. Davis' private secretary. These were his letters. He wrote an account of what he saw for Blackwood, in January & February 1865.

June 1863. Lee crossed into Maryland, going as before into the western and most narrow portion of the State, where considerable Union feeling prevailed and where he could expect to receive but few reinforcements. Hundreds in the State were ready to join him but they were miles off, without organization & without arms. He crossed into Pennsylvania and reached Pennsylvania before he gave us the slightest intimation as to his plans. From Gettysburg he sent down for a trusty person to be sent to confer with him. But this was too late. The whole country was in an uproar. New York was ready to open its arms and receive Genl. Lee. The State refused to send troops to defend Pennsylvania. New Jersey voted troops and then recalled them. Philadelphia was in a panic of fear. The condition of things in Baltimore surpassed belief. The military authorities were frightened out of their lives and the most ridiculous defenses were erected. Negroes of every kind were impressed, so much so that the markets were entirely broken up for a day or two, absurd little forts were erected about in spots, around in the city, many of which were commanded by hills close by,** and about one half of the city—the

* The Baltimore *Sun* mentions three statewide conventions in April and May, 1863: the convention of the African Methodist Episcopal Church on April 18 continued into early May, the Maryland Tract Society met on April 14, and the assembly of the Protestant Episcopal Church for the Diocese of Maryland met May 28.

** An 1863 military map of Baltimore County in possession of the Maryland Historical Society shows several army encampments in the Baltimore area. Camp Cheesborough was near the Mt. Clare station of the Baltimore and Ohio Railroad. Fort Dix guarded that railroad where is crossed the Patapsco River at Relay south of Baltimore. Fort Federal Hill over looked Baltimore harbor from across the Northwest Branch of the Patapsco River. Camp Belger was near Mount Hope in the northwestern sector of the City, Camp Bradford was near Governor Bradford's home at Charles Street and Lake Avenue, and Fort Marshall in east Baltimore guarded the Baltimore, Wilmington and Philadelphia Railroad near the present Patterson Park, most populous part—was fortified with tobacco hogsheads and sugar hogsheads—the latter being empty & filled with dirt. The whole thing was ridiculous. These barricades were guarded by citizens, most of whom would have run away from a Confederate pop gun.

June 30. Tonight the most tremendous efforts were made to induce the Union people to rally to the protection. Fire Rockets were shot up a few miles north of the city. Signals were made from the top of the Washington Monument. Alarm bells were rung, and every means was resorted to alarm the people into resistance to their foe. But the people seemed to take Lee's approach very easy. I walked down the Street to see if the brave fellows would rally. I heard one say to another "Don't talk to me. Just remember how the d—'d rebels rallied on the 19" of April". And he was right. That was a rally. The streets were patrolled—the barricades were guarded and no one was allowed to pass them after 11 o'c. A large row of hogsheads was placed across Charles St. below our door. The front door was out of the lines. The side door fortunately was in them.

July 1. [1863] I awoke to find Martial law declared. It had in fact prevailed for a long time. I was satisfied it was time to be off. I did not know it until after I left the house and then had no time to go back. I went to my office, found my clerk Mr. Hardy and told him that I had some important payments to arrange for, which I would do in the street. I made an appointment to meet him at 12 o'c. I chose the most public corner in the City knowing that that would be the last place the detectives would expect to find me. I had hardly gone off, before a detective came & asked for John. He saw John who promised to go to the Marshall's office. Soon after they sent to my office, but I was not to be found. I sent word by Hardy to my people that I was gone, and at noon started to leave town. All the railroads were guarded. Pickets were on all the carriage roads. You could not possibly get out without a pass. Strict orders had been issued forbidding anyone to leave. I quietly took the Passenger Cars out Baltimore street and rode as far as the toll gate. There I saw the first line of pickets just ahead and I got out. I walked up the small cross road some distance to the Cemetery there, went down to the back of it, and got across the falls there, as best I could.* The

* The Passenger Rail Road Depot was at Baltimore and Smallwood streets. The tollgate of the Calverton Turnpike was at Calverton Avenue and Franklin Street, and the Catonsville Depot at Frederick Road and Baltimore Street in the western portion of Baltimore City. Western Cemetery is bounded by Edmondson Avenue on the north, Longwood Road on the east, and the Baltimore and Potomac Rail Road (now Penn-Central), and Gwynn's Falls to the south and west.

water fortunately was tolerably low. I then struck across the fields and finally brought up at Frick's, reeking with perspiration and fagged out.* Here I dined. At dusk I got a wagon & drove over, through Catonsville, to Hilton.** Here I soon got the muskets and cartridges out of the house and out of their hiding places and effectively concealed them. I ordered my horse to be all ready for an early start, expecting to be with Genl. Lee in less than 48 hours, and spent the evening quietly with my sister. I told John's wife*** about his arrest, but laughed at the idea of his having any trouble, as he was blind and as they really had no charges against him. With me it was very different. I knew perfectly well from the British Legation that Seward and Stanton were both very annoyed at my supposed communications with the South and that the letter, found on Lawrence, although it proved nothing had excited their suspicion still more. What had made me particularly watchful was the fact that Percy Anderson had come up to Baltimore only a few days before and had begged me to be careful, as I could have no idea how bitter the authorities in Washington were against me. I thought therefore that as soon as it was found that I had gotten out of the way, John would be released without further ado.

The family retired at an early hour, after bidding me good bye. Mrs. Harwood begged me to leave that night, but I laughed & said I only waited till four in the morning when I would be off. Fortunately I sat up late. I thought I would write some account of the condition of things in Baltimore for publication in the N.Y. Daily News. I knew they never would be published in Baltimore. I had just finished at midnight & was reading over what I had written when I heard the dash of cavalry. I turned down the light as I heard them dash round the house. I could not leave without telling the girls. I rushed upstairs & knocked at their doors. They were frightened and delayed for some time before they opened. I told them it was no use for me to try and protect them and left them. This lost me much time. I had not a moment to pick up either hat or shoes. I had been writing in loose slippers. When I got down stairs every door & window was guarded and the officers were banging at the door.

* William F. Frick's home, "Hill Top," was off the Frederick Road in the vicinity of Irvington, to the west of the city line.

** The 1,000 acre "Hilton" estate bordered the Patapsco River from the vicinity of the flour mill at Orange Grove to the Thistle Cotton Mill at Ilchester, a heavily wooded and rugged piece of property now the "Hilton" district of the Patapsco State Park and the Catonsville Community College.

*** John Glenn's wife was Anna Corey Smith (1827–1894), sister of Mrs. William Wilkins Glenn.

"Hilton"—the Glenn estate near Catonsville, Baltimore County, Maryland. The photograph shows the mansion house much as it would have appeared in Civil War times, before extensive twentieth-century renovations. The estate is now the site of the Catonsville Community College. *Collection of J. Hurst Purnell, courtesy of the Catonsville Community College.*

They were so sure they had me that they did not kick it open. Henry, the House servant was too frightened to hurry and this gave me a little time. Finding no avenue of escape I became desperate and was on the point of opening the kitchen door, in which I then was, and making a dash with a brick for my only offensive weapon. Fortunately, I slid the bolt gently to peep out. The door opened onto a sort of verandah, which they appeared to have taken as a portion of the house, although it was bright moonlight. As I got into the air I breathed more freely. I crept along to the end of the lattice work, by the Carriage road. A few feet on my right was a mounted guard. A few feet on my left was another. By this time Henry had gotten to the front door. The officer commanding was questioning him with a pistol at his head, as I afterwards learned. This accounted for his nervous stammering. I could hear portions of the conversation. "Where is your master?" said the Captain. "Gone to town, Sir." "You lie you scoundrel." "Deed & deed Sir Massa John went to town this morning." "Damn your Master John, where is your Master Wilkins?" "He's in de house!" "All right men," cried the Captain, "damn him shoot him if he runs." At this I thought it was time to go. I had no idea of trying a fort again, as I knew this time it would be for the war. I preferred to risk the chance of a bullet. By good luck a small cloud just then obscured the moon. I saw it would pass in a moment. Quick as thought, I covered up every particle of white I had about me, knelt down and crawled deliberately out between the pickets. About twenty feet brought me to the lattice work of the wood house. Here I was again in the shade. I crept along here a few feet till I reached the open door. I passed under the tail of the pickets horse. I crept in the door and straightened myself up, thinking I at last was safe. But I was on the contrary in the greatest danger. The house dog had died & the negroes had tied a pup there who did not know me. Just as I got safely in the wood-house, the puppy sprang at me, barking furiously. It was a funny scene. I could not kick him. I dared not speak loudly. I could only make faces at him in the half moonlight and whisper to him to keep quiet. I crept on and he barked. Suddenly he stopped. He saw there was something he could not understand and he gave it up. The guards fortunately did not notice him. They must have thought he was barking at them. I got upon the grass and rolled down the hill about fifty yards. Then I rose and ran like a good fellow, cleared the branch and taking a long circuit through fields & woods reached a small tenant house, habited by Joe our cattle man. I got from him a blanket, arranged a signal with him and slept among the rocks in the woods—as much as the insects would let me sleep.

July 2d. At dawn I gave Joe instructions, and borrowing from him a huge pair of boots, I trudged on to another tenants about a mile off. Here I got some breakfast and waited in the woods. Joe went to the house and found it guarded. His pail of milk passed him in. He did not as usual give the milk to the black servants but saw Bridget and whispered to her to bring a coat, hat, hdkf, pair of socks & my pistol if it was to be found, for me up to the cabbage patch. Soon after he left Bridget came down with these things under her petticoat. The guard allowed her to pass to get cabbages. The patch was directly in sight. She went up, stooped down, cut her cabbage & returned quietly to the house. Shortly after Joe picked up the things she had dropped and brought them off to me, with my horse, which had not been disturbed in the stable. Joe and Patrick scouted along the falls to find a safe place to cross, when I rode down, rode across & made my way by back roads & across country to Carrolls—Doughoregan Manor—where I spent the day & slept.

I afterwards learned that the Captain of the troop had upon entering the house seen Mrs. John Glenn, of whom he enquired where I was. "He was here", she replied he came out to inform me of my husband's arrest & took tea here. Since then I have not seen him."

"Oh," said he, "we'll find him". And to work they went. My people were of course frightfully uneasy, having no idea that I had effected my escape and Bridget, expecting to see me tumble down the chimney, a victim of the bullets fired up, said more than once "Oh! Mrs. Glenn he had better come down". As fast as one room was searched my sister would go in & after putting out the lights, creep up to any suspected hiding place & whisper "Are you here. Are you here?" After an hour, they became more easy. I was not forth coming. For the same reason the officer in charge was more excited. He swore he would have me and at dawn went off for more troops.

July 3d. I left at 5 A.M. and rode down to Mr. Hugh Harrison near Ellicott Mills, where I breakfasted.* I sent a note in by his son, asking mother to send me some clothes out to Lexington—Williamson's—on the Reisterstown Road & giving them the first news of my whereabouts. After breakfast I rode over to Sam Brown's where I

* Glenn came in the Frederick Turnpike from "Doughoregan" to the home of the Rev. Hugh Harrison, then rector of St. John's Church at the intersection of the Turnpike and the Old Frederick Road.

lunched and in the afternoon rode on by Blunt's, intending to make my way over to James McHenry's. On the road I met a man with the News Sheet in his hand. This was a sort of a flag. A man with the News sheet or by whatever name it went, was safe. None but a rebel would handle it. I entered into conversation & finding my supposition confirmed, I proposed as he resided near by, to go to his for a little while. "My name is Glenn" said I. "I am making my way out of the State." "Are you Mr. Glenn of the Daily Exchange." "I am." Oh! do come up to my house. We shall be too glad to see you". This happened on another occasion & of course was gratifying. Later in the afternoon, I rode on and as I passed Roslyn gate, met Genl. Howard & Miss Jane returning from a ride. I went home with them, feeling a little uneasy however, as a Dutchman, whom I had not seen, overheard me at the gate, while I was telling of my escape. Miss Jane H. good naturedly rode over to Lexington & got the bundle I had ordered sent there.* I got a clean shirt, a comb and a tooth brush & was happy. In the evening I read till past midnight and then being too uneasy to sleep in the house, took a shawl and slept in the woods.

Mrs. John Glenn, I afterwards learned, in accordance with my suggestions, went to town early this morning to apply to General Schenck for John's release. He knew her well. As a civilian he had been counsel for her sister, Mrs. Backers [?], for a long time and was in the habit of staying at Mr. Backer's [?] house. Here he had frequently seen Mrs. G. as a young lady. Schenck refused even to grant her an audience. He would not see nor speak to her. He would not give her a pass to leave the city again, although she represented that she had left a very young infant at Hilton,** who would have no sustenance till she returned home. He was obdurate & behaved like a brute. Late in the day she succeeded in obtaining a pass from one of the young aide de camps who knew her very well. John was locked up in the Gilmor House prison. His case was worse than I thought it. Some of his good friends had gone to Fish, then Provost

* From Harrison's Glenn traveled north on the Old Frederick Road (Rt. 99) to Samuel Brown's house near the intersection with the Old Court Road. He crossed the Patapsco River from Howard to Baltimore Counties on the Old Court Road near Woodstock, and continued on that road to Atwood Blunt's home in Granite near the Granite Quarry. From Blunt's he continued on Old Court crossing the Liberty Road, to "Sudbrooke," James McHenry's home near the intersection of Old Court and Reisterstown Roads, c. nine miles northwest of Baltimore. General Benjamin Chew Howard's "Roslyn" was the nearest neighbor, and George W. Williamson's estate "Lexington" was a mile east, on the other side of Pikesville.

** The infant was two-month-old William Lindsay Glenn.

Martial [*sic*] and represented to him that he had the wrong man; that I was the one he wanted. "No!" replied Fish "Mr. John Glenn is the most plain spoken of the two, though his brother is the more dangerous".

July 4". At early dawn, I got in again at the window and went to bed. The hour for night expeditions was over. In the afternoon the Gilmor boys and the Hoffmans came out from town, having managed to slip out without passes. I rode over to Robert Elder's to supper and slept there all night, fearing to stay two nights in the same place.*

In Baltimore there was a great flag-flying today. Genl. Schenck had recommended it a couple of days before. The Mayor had endorsed the recommendation.** It was rumored about by his men that he would not be responsible for the consequences where the flag was not shown and furthermore that those who did not put out one should at once be sent South. As this threat had already been frequently carried into effect, it intimidated many. There was a general breaking down and an universal rush for flags. On the Eve of the 4" there was not a toy flag scarcely to be had in the city. Mr. Sam Smith gave way & many people followed him. Wilson Cary bought a flag, to have it ready to put out, in case of attack. Mr. Charles Howard did the same. Teackle Wallis did the same. I was astounded. I sent word to my sisters to fly no flag, with one brother in prison and another in the woods. They did not get the message until too late, but had the pluck to act without it. Early in the morning they saw flags flying round them everywhere. Some large some small—some showing conspicuously, some as much out of sight as possible—but nearly every house had a flag. In their neighborhood, Read's I think was the only house without one.*** They were very uneasy, but stood it out. Later in the day they heard of other friends who were firm. Their hearts misgave them when they saw policemen taking down the numbers of those houses which did not display flags, in the afternoon, but they held out bravely, although there was not a man in the house, and went to bed with fear of [*sic*] trembling. They never heard anything more of the matter. The people of

* Glenn turned north on Reisterstown Road to Robert Elder's "Greenspring Farm" (shown on area maps as belonging to George Elder) in the Garrison area, eleven miles northwest of Baltimore.

** John Lee Chapman became *ex officio* mayor following the arrest of Mayor Brown on September 12, 1861. Elected to office in 1862, he served to 1867.

*** William G. Read lived at 224 North Charles Street in Baltimore.

Baltimore had allowed themselves to be bullied and frightened. It was the first unmistakable symption of the lamentable weakness which was afterwards manifested. The people of Maryland, who did not join the Southern Army, were Southern as long as they thought their interests lay with the South. When their fortunes were in danger they were ready to abandon the cause.

July 5. Sunday. Returned to Roslyn. Found Frank Howard there and clubbed fortunes with him, as he too was on his way to join Lee. Rode over to Jim McHenrys to dinner. Entered by the back way. Pickets were stationed in the road at the front door. In the evening I went back to Roslyn expecting to meet Pat Sullivan who was concealed up the road and had promised to come down.

July 6. I now communicated daily with my family by private hand. I had gotten my clothes, a pipe & some tobacco, ready for a campaign. I rode over to McHenrys and staid all night. Pickets still in front of the door.

July 7. Glenn Perine called by. Astonished to see me. Gave me news of home. In the afternoon returned to Roslyn. Heard from town that it was known where Frank & I were, at that my family thought I was very foolish as the search for me was not abandoned. I on the contrary thought I was safest, by being so near to Baltimore, where they wd. not expect to find me and I was waiting too expecting to open communications very soon with the Southern Army. In the evening I became quite uneasy and watched on the Porch until after 3 o'clock. It was near dawn then and I went to bed—determined not to stay there another night.

It was impossible to get any news. Couriers came and went constantly up and down the road, past McHenrys—but little was gleaned from them. They were used and signal stations were formed all along the road, because it was deemed unsafe to trust to telegraph wires. We could only learn that there was a great battle going on and that the Federal army was barely holding its own.

July 8". My fellow refugees, the Gilmors & Hoffmans, who had no particular reasons to be refugees, all took heart & and being over their scare went back to Baltimore. Frank Howard remained. Rode over to Robt. Elder's & slept.

July 9. Returned this morning by country roads. Met two deserters on the road. This afternoon got my buggy wagon from town & Frank

& I started for Bob Denison's.* On the road met Gil Hoffman coming up who brought messages & accounts of the bitter feeling against me. It was evidently not intended that I should escape. My brother was still in prison. Slept at Denison's.

July 10. Alex Brown & Wambersie came over. Also little Milligan. After dinner we drove to Browns—Brooklandwood—& staid all night.

July 11. Wambersie sent up word that Winter Davis was expected at Milligan's. As Milligan's son had seen us we were not easy. We were amused to learn that as Brady had seen us pass by his house he had taken us for suspicious characters and was very uneasy about Alex Brown.** Plaid [*sic*] billiards all day. I was supposed to be hiding in the woods. I had been all along living on the fat of the land & having plenty of company. Frank Sullivan & Lehr came up.

July 12. Sunday. Bob Denison came over. Gil Hoffman drove over from Roslyn. He brought alarming accounts of my danger and said it was deemed foolhardy for me to remain so near home. Poor Alex Brown became frightened. He imagined that Frank & I would be seized and his property would be confiscated for harboring us. Frank Howard determined to go home. It was quite evident that Lee did not intend to advance again, but would return to Virginia. He left me. I drove over to Hampton & from thence to Glen Ellen*** where my arrival after dark, created quite an excitement appearing as I did under an assumed name.

July 13. Steady rain. Borrowed Harry Gilmor's old coat & Bill Gilmor's Hat & started. Drove by Jim Carroll's—thence by Lee's Mill to Brand's, which I reached after dark, well soaked.****

July 14. Mr. Brand went to Belair to reconnoitre. After dinner

* From Robert Elder's Glenn continued across Hillside Road past Robert M. Denison's estate (between the Old Court Road and the Greenspring Railroad).

** G. B. Milligan's "Glencairn" was at the intersection of Hillside and Falls Roads, nine miles north of Baltimore. Samuel Brady's estate was on Greenspring Valley Road opposite the gates of "Brooklandwood." "Brooklinwood" ("Brooklandwood") is north on Falls Road above Valley Road.

*** From "Brooklandwood" he continued to "Hampton," north of Towson, then across fields and private lanes to the adjoining "Glen Ellen," estate of the Gilmors.

**** Crossing the Great Gunpowder River he came to James Carroll's "Summerfield" near Manor and Glen Arm Roads. From there he rode down to Kingsville, crossed into Harford County at Jerusalem Mills (as Lee's Mill, on the Little Gunpowder River, was known), and continued to the Rev. William Brand's at Emmorton. Belair, the county seat of Harford County, is three miles north of Emmorton.

Mr. Otho Scott rode down to see me and to offer me money. After dinner Mr. B. & I drove over to Priestford, where I appeared as Mr. Lindsay. There was company there, among them Miss Wright from Philadelphia who insisted that she knew & thought she had seen me at Cape May—all of which was quite true.

July 15. Brand and Mrs. Neilson drove to Dublin to reconnoitre. Engaged horse.

July 16. Started at 12 ½ A.M. Reached Bridge* at day light, crossed & arrived at Oxford** too late for cars—at 7 o'c. Forced to remain all day. Left at 4 o'c. for Philadelphia, where I stopped at the U.S. Hotel, a second class house. I was afraid to show.

July 17. Learned that the Pennsylvania train north did not start till after 8 o'clock. So instead of going towards Elmira, I took the early train for New York, at 6 o'c. A.M. Besides I thought that as the riots were scarcely over in New York no one would think there of me. Went to St. Denis Hotel.

July 18. Went over to Staten Island to stay with Mackay.

July 19. Galenga came over. He had just arrived. Had letters for me. Wanted to go South, but had not the nerve to undertake it.

July 20 to 24. Went to Travers and staid there or on his yacht the Restless.

July 26. To New York. Breakfast with Gallenga. Went over to Mackay's. Dined. Walked over to Traver's.

July 28. Dick Webster came over for a day's sail. Capital fellow who did much for me afterwards in London.

July 31. To New York. Met Ryder.

Aug. 1. [1863] Ryder, Webster & I went up to Lebannon Springs.

Aug. 3. Drove over to Lenox to see the Archibald's and

Aug. 4. Left for Albany, where I joined Mackay and as his companion reached Suspension Bridge, crossed over to Clifton House and was at last safe.

* There was a bridge across the Susquehanna River between Darlington and Conowingo.

** The Philadelphia and Baltimore Central Railroad junction was at Oxford, Pennsylvania, five miles from the Maryland line. It is now a station on the Penn-Central Railroad. The Pennsylvania Railroad made the New York to Philadelphia connection.

Aug. 5. Met Gov. Dallas, of Hudson Bay. He had travelled down from his head quarters 1800 miles in a canoe manned by about a dozen Indians. They paddled for six days a week more than twelve hours a day. Sometimes the little streams they went through were so narrow that there was barely room enough for the canoe to pass.

There were several politicians here—Sam Medary—of the Crisis—Geo. H. Pendleton and C. C. Vallandingham. These three men were all peace men. Indeed they were almost Southern. They pretended to me to be quite so. Vallandingham had just returned from Nassau. After being banished South by a Military Commission, he had gone directly to Wilmington and run the blockade to Nassau, from whence he came to Halifax and thence over to Canada. The three, with some other friends were now met to arrange for the autumn Campaign in Ohio. Vallandingham was quite sure of the success of the South & was quite jubilant. If the South won the Democrats in the North were all right. That was all he cared for. Govr. Medary and he both confessed to me that the triumph of the South was indispensable to the preservation of liberty in the North. "In fact, then" said I, "you feel as I do, that the South is fighting not only their battle but yours too". "Yes," said Medary without hesitation. Vallandingham quite agreed with him. Still not one of them had the independence and the manliness to come out boldly as peace men and oppose the military usurpation of Lincoln. Vallandingham contented himself with writing letters from the Clifton House. Beyond the Canada border however he would not stir in person. I urged him to go home, to put himself under the protection of judicial authority, to go if necessary to the jail & seek safety for a time behind its walls, but to make the issue at once between the Military & Civil Authorities, for said I "Depend upon it now is your time. If the people will not stand by you now, after this outrage committed through you, on their rights, they will never stand by you. If your party show any strength and determination, as I believe it will, if it has one man to lead them, the Administration will not make the contest. They have never yet made an issue with the people where there was any show of resistance. They trample only on those who submit like cowards. And you can rest assured that if you lose your chance now, you will never again have such an opportunity while the war lasts." It was no use. He and his friends were mere party politicians. They sought popularity and preferment. They had not the manhood to speak honestly their own convictions. With Pendleton I was simply disgusted. He had the associations & education of a gentleman. He was in fact a Southerner. But like almost all the men in this country who had adopted politics as a profession, he had become a mere political prostitute. He bowed to the will of the people. He despised them but they paid him.

August 6". Clifton House was quite filled with Southern refugees and sympathizers. Several blockade runners were there. One or two officers recovering from their wounds. Mrs. Helm wife of the Southern Commissioner at Havana was also there. It was entirely too Southern for the Yankees. Most of them kept themselves to their own side of the river.

A young Englishman by the name of Bagley was here, just on the eve of starting for a western tour. He received news of the sudden death of an aunt which placed him in possession of £20000 per annum. He abandoned his Western trip and started for England.

Aug. 11. Left for Montreal.

Aug. 12. Reached Montreal & stopped at Donegani House.*

Aug. 13. Quartered at Col. Wolseley's. Phillips was a Montreal. Buller was at Chambly.** Crichton & Wm. Earle also of the Grenadiers were capital fellows. Neville, of the Fusiliers, a cousin of Lawley's, was also very good natured—as was Henry Penn, of the Artillery.*** I messed often with the Grenadiers, sometimes with the Fusiliers, Gunners and 16". I was amazed to see what excellent wine many of these messes had. The guards had superb claret and sherry any man might be proud to own. The champagne was of course of the best.

Sept 10". [1863] Left for Quebec.

Sep. 11. Joined Mary Perine and Frederick Brune & his wife who had come on to see John Brune. Spent the day with them and drove out to Falls. In the afternoon found Maj. W. W. Earl—commonly called Johnny Earl—drove with him for a short time to Lord Monck's & afterwards had a capital dinner at the mess of the 17" with excellent Claret and Sherry and a game of Whist afterwards.

John Brune was still in Canada. When the arrests of the Members of the Legislature were made in September 1861, he had managed to escape and make his way to Canada. Here he fell in with the

* The Donegani hotel was located on Notre Dame Street in Montreal, and had an excellent reputation as a first-class hotel.

** Fort Chambly was on the Chambly (Richelieu) River southeast of Montreal.

*** There is no "Henry Penn" listed among the officers of the Royal Artillery in the nineteenth century. Henry James Penson, commissioned in 1856, served on the staff at Aldershot and retired in 1868.

officers of different regiments, with whom he became very popular. He spent his money very freely and lived very fast. His most intimate friends belonged to the 16" and the Gunners. It was quite evident to me that he had no intention whatever of returning home and that he never cared to see Maryland again. His losses at home had been heavy, he had sold out his house & furniture—or rather had it sold out soon after he left—saw no prospect of assuming the position again he had occupied in Baltimore, where he had been in the habit of entertaining frequently and handsomely, and was apparently quite weary of life. He appeared utterly indifferent to his own fate. His brother & wife were shocked to see him so broken.

Sep 12" 1863. Sailed in Jura.

Received letters on board from John who was again at home. He had been sent by Schenck, who manifested great bitterness to our family to Fortress Monroe, on his way South, an order of exile having been passed. No one was allowed to go with him, not even a servant to protect him from accident, although his wife represented to the military authorities that he was nearly blind. Arrived at Fortress Monroe, he was sent to a common jail with some common men. They were fed on bad bread & meat that turned their stomach. A little bad coffee was all that they could really take with any thing like comfort. The little baggage that some of John's companions carried with them was plundered by the soldiers. The whole treatment was horrible. In a few days John was placed on the flag of truce boat, on his way to Richmond. Mulford fortunately knew who he was. Mulford was on duty at Fort McHenry as a Captain while I was imprisoned there. He was a plain man & had been clerk of some small court in New York State. I had been civil to him and he had been quite struck with the very unusual consideration extended to me by Genl. Morris. On learning John's name he was very kind to him. Arrived at City Point, John had an interview with Ould, to whom he introduced himself. Ould had been a college mate of mine at William & Mary College and was a particular friend of C. Q. Tompkins, a connection and great friend of John's. After some talk, John was left on board for a day or two. He did not go on shore. Ould went to Richmond and on his return proposed to John that he should take the oath of allegiance to the Southern Confederacy. This of course John refused, upon which Ould declined to receive him. John was sent back to Fortress Monroe, where he had an interview with Foster, then in command. Foster knew of him very well and sent him back to Baltimore on parole to report to

Schenck and with a letter stating that there appeared to be no charges whatever vs him and that he supposed Genl Schenck would not desire to detain him any longer. Schenck ordered him to be locked up again. By this time the atrocity of this case had excited the indignation of one or two neutral men—men I mean who were all things to all men and who had influence. They made representations to Stanton of the outrageous abuse of power by Schenck in this instance and finally an order came from the Secretary of War, directing him to be discharged. He got back to Hilton after suffering every annoyance & discomfort and even danger, to find that we were in addition heavy losers by his absence. Crops had been neglected. Wheat was damaged and hay was spoiled. In addition to that the farm had been pretty nearly swept by foragers and the best meadow was ruined by the quartering of cavalry horses upon. Not a chicken or a fowl of any kind was left.

I forgot to speak of the Maryland Club. After suffering every possible annoyance, the club was finally closed by Military order and taken possession of in June last. A guard of the 7" New York Regiment was placed there. The men took entire possession, played billiards, drank all the wine and segars they could find—and which they broke open cupboards to find—and even stole the clothes of the servant men, which were left in their sleeping rooms up stairs. The Club was closed because the members did not choose to issue invitations to Officers of the Federal army. That was of course high treason. Every effort was made to charge the members with using it for political purposes, but no politicians and few even who were really staunch patriots belonged to it.

Sept 14. How wonderful are the facilities for travelling today. A lilttle girl is on board, about eleven years old, who is going out alone to her relations in Egypt. Her Uncle is in business there and has sent for her. She was shipped at Quebec under the care of the Stewards. Arrived at Liverpool, she will be transferred to one of the Mediterranean steamers. Yesterday she was in high glee. Today we are at sea and she does not think it so fine.

Sep 15. We took the nortern passage. Lots of ice today from the pack.

Sep 16 & 17. Heavy weather.

Sep 18. Passengers on deck again looking very seedy.

Sep 22d. Ran into Loch Foyle to land passengers for Derry. I could not resist the attraction of green fields. I ran below & proposed to Buller to go ashore. He had been very sick & was glad to get his feet on dry land. In half an hour we landed, I not knowing why I did so or where I was going. It was a curious piece of luck; but this freak of mine did more for me than I could have imagined. It enabled me in a short time to get the entrée in the kind of society I was most glad to see and in which I could best judge of the state of feeling toward the South and the prospect of any change of policy. It turned out that Buller had once acted as Aide to the Earl of Carlisle. When we went to Dublin he went out to the Mardyke [?] Lodge and found Lady Caroline Lascelles there with her daughters. They were cousins of Lord Hartington. I afterwards went out to spend the day and after I had gone they wrote to Hartington that I was in London. Lord Ed. St. Maur was with Hartington at Dunrobin Castle & thus learned I was in England. When he came up to London he hunted me up and I went to his father's, Stover Lodge, with him. Had it not been for this accident, many men I afterwards knew would never have known I was in England. English people are very good people when you know them well, but some of them are very uncertain and as a general rule I do not think it safe for a stranger to tax them in their own country. I never should have told one of them that I was there. They all however behaved most hospitably to me, far more so than I could expect. The only man who behaved like a scrub was Lord Hartington. I had taken trouble for him and run risks for him. I did for him what no one else could do. I met him in London and he asked me to his house, but in such a way that I did not choose to accept it. He neither called on me nor sent a written invitation and there our intercourse ended. What I did for him, I did because it suited me. I expected no pay and did not want it. But if he desired to make any return, I was determined he should make it in good coin—not in base metal. Besides I got on very well without him.

Charley Stirling of the artillery came across me one day and got me into the Army & Navy Club—commonly called the Rag. Soon after Capt Dick Webster, of the foreign office, got me into the Junior United Service, of which they handsomely made me a member during my exile. To get into these clubs was a great compliment & most unusual. I was told that but one other case had been known, which was that of Louis Napolean, years ago. I took for granted this was a mistake. I was taken in on account I was told of my hospitality to English officers and of the efforts I had made to get Phillips & Wynne off at great personal risk. I did not know I had done so much until I reached England. I soon got through other friends into the Traveller's Club, a small club of 600 members composed of nobility and members of the diplomatic corps. Anthony Trollope and Russell pulled me into the Garrick and Maitland Dashwood put my name down for the Raleigh a fast night club. When Mackay came over he got me into the Reform for a month, but I rarely went there.

These clubs were mostly superb affairs. The only trouble about them was that there was only one room in the house where you could smoke. At the Traveller's they had only recently succeeded in getting a smoking room at all. It was the same way in English houses. In few of them were there any conveniences for smoking. Even Anthony Trollope in his snug little house only smoked in an outhouse, beyond the kitchen and at Escrick Park, a superb Establishment, Lord Wenlock had no place for his guests to smoke but a little bath room, which would not hold more than three people at a time—without smoke. With Smoke there was room for nobody. In fact the only place *in* an English house where one is permitted to smoke is *outside* of it.

I was a member of these clubs, except the Reform, until I left London. The Garrick I liked best. Its smoking room was charming. Thackeray frequented it a great deal. Only three nights before his day he came in there suffering a great deal. Russell asked him why he did not undergo a certain operation which would relieve him and assured him that he would find great relief from it and without danger as not more than one man in a hundred died from it. "Ah! said he "I would be that one man. I cannot risk it."—and rising he put up his hands to his head and exclaimed "I feel I have twenty years of life in me yet and I will do something better than I have ever done before." In less than three days he was dead. Those who knew him best saw that he had the tenderest of hearts, that he could not hear a tale of woe without bringing out at once all the money he had about him. His friends were devoted to him. He was very bitter against Society and seemed to have that snobbish hatred of those who outranked him in society, so common to the most intelligent Englishmen who are not in and of the charmed circle. He abused nobility and hated it because he was not of it. This feeling made him say foolish things. His two daughters were very plain. Worse, they were poor. No peer thought of marrying them. There was no such prospect. Still one day when marriage between peers and women of the middle classes was discussed, he said in an excited way "I'd like to catch any peer proposing for my daughter. I'd like them to try it". On another occasion when his daughters had been invited to a Matinée, which was very general, he said as he was cloaking her in the Entry, in a very audible voice, evidently intended to be heard "Yes, poor girl, they invite you out to these morning receptions where all the world goes, but you are not good enough for the smaller circles in the evening". Lady Ulrica Thynne heard this and told me. Some of his noble friends were become quite sick of his captious remarks. The truth was Thackeray himself was invited out, not as Thackeray, but as a lion. It is a great thing in England to have a lion and as long as a man is a lion he can have a run. But he must be a single lion and not have a whelp or any cubs along.

Oct. 20". [1863] Received news of the stoppage of Gazette. Carter was arrested on the 29 Septr and the paper stopped on a general charge of disloyalty. The Rival papers—being loyal—were continually endeavoring to break the paper up.* Carpenter and Neilson disappeared for a time. On Oct 7. the paper was reissued. Carter behaved in a manly manner & I wrote him from England complimenting him. The paper & its men have had a good record from the beginning. It is marvellous that it still goes on.

* Major rival papers in Baltimore in 1863 included the following: Baltimore *American* (still published), Baltimore *Sun* (still published), Baltimore *Patriot,* Baltimore *Clipper, Evening Transcript,* and the *Evening Times.*

No. 3

1863. My experiences in England were certainly very pleasant although it was rather curious how I got to know the persons I did—for I had no letters of introduction and, being just a little doubtful of English hospitality from former experience, had determined to make no calls on anyone. When the Jura touched at Derry, I was so sick of the ship that I went below and proposed to Buller, of the Grenadiers, who was still more sick in every sense of the word, to go ashore. We landed and went to Dublin. I then learned that he had once been Aide de Camp to Lord Carlisle and he went next morning to the Lodge in the Park to see who was there. Soon after a message came for me to come to lunch & spend the day. I found Lady Caroline Lascelles, her three daughters one of whom was the only really handsome woman I saw in England,—Miss Emma I think, afterwards maid of Honor—& Capt. Lascelles. The Earl was away. Lawrence's book, Border & Bastille, was just out. The Lascelles were cousins of Hartingtons and when they found I was the man who had sent him & Leslie through and who was the Mentor of Border & Bastille they were of course much interested in what I had to say. After I left they wrote to Hartington that I was in Europe & was on my way to London. He was spending a week at Dunrobin Castle. He read the note & showed it to Lord Ed. St. Maur who was there at the same time. Lord Edward immediately took pains to find me out and when he came up to London soon after called on me and took me to Stover Lodge to spend a week.

Teddy Wynne, of the Grenadiers, the only man on whom I counted, was in London when I arrived. I wrote him but received no answer. Thinking there was some mistake I called at his house and found him. He was evidently much annoyed and I was much amused at his conduct. He felt that he was under very great obligations & independently of that would have been glad to serve me had it been convenient. But he had only one week more of leave—his time was all filled up & I had arrived at a most inopportune moment. He had quite a little struggle, but self soon prevailed and the only man of whom I expected anything in England utterly failed me. I think he did manage to get me my first invitation to the Traveller's Club, but that I soon arranged through other parties.

At Stover Lodge I met Lord Harry Thynne who had married Lady Ulrica, daughter of the Duke of Somerset. Through him I came to know his mother the Marchioness of Bath & his brother the Marquis of Bath, owner of the magnificent Estate of Longleat. I afterwards staid with Lord Harry at   and shot over his covers; with Lord Bath at Longleat, in a week, when 8 guns killed over 4000 head of game in four days and then stopped because the beaters were tired out and with the Dowager Marchioness at Muntham Court. This gave me the entrée into society which was of most service to me while abroad. Lord Edward St. Maur was always very kind as was the Duchess;* but my meeting with Lord Harry was a piece of good luck worth more than all else put together. When I returned to London Charley Stirling of the Artillery met me in the street and soon after sent me an invitation to the Army & Navy Club, which he had insisted on having and which I received as a very great compliment—not only from the Managers but from Stirling who had merely known me in Baltimore and who was not in the slightest degree indebted to me. Afterwards Dick Webster, Queen's Messenger, who had never known me in Baltimore, pulled me into the Junior United Service of which Club I was made member during my exile. Marstand Dashwood whom I afterwards met got me into the Raleigh Club—and Trollope whom I scarcely thought recollected me, sent me a ticket to the Garrick. So it was all round. Things came upon me in a most unexpected manner—from sources least expected—and with the exception of Lord Edward St. Maur, who behaved like a thoroughbred, of all the very great attention & kindness I received not one iota of it came from those persons from whom I had a right to expect something. Lord Hartington behaved like a cub. He knew that I was abroad & he knew that I had suffered no little persecution for the assistance I had rendered him at his own request. He did not come near me, passed by me the first time he saw me although he recognized me, and though apparently very civil when we next met at the Traveller's Club only gave me a verbal invitation to come to his house Sunday after breakfast. I did not choose to consider that he owed me anything and if he did, I did not choose that he should pay it in bad coin. As he neither called nor sent me a written invitation, here our intercourse stopped. Leslie behaved little better. He evidently felt that he ought to do something for me, but it was very inconvenient and after making several ineffectual attempts and some large but empty promises, he dodged me during the rest of my stay abroad. It was very amusing to see how differently different people behaved. Percy Fielding of the Coldstreams who had married Lady Louisa Thynne, was kind & hospitable to the last although he had never known me here. And of

* Jane Georgianna Seymour, wife of the 12th Duke of Somerset was the mother of Edward St. Maur.

those who had known me Lawley was another exception. He came over in February & entertained me handsomely as best he could, through his brother Lord Wenlock, with whom I spent a week at his splendid Estate, Escrick Park.

With one or two exceptions the men I met in England were Tories and Military men and to a man they sympathized with the South in the present struggle. I met scarcely any Liberals or Whigs. But the sympathy of the men I met was a very barren sympathy. They had no views at all on the subject, they seemed unwilling to meet or incapable of meeting the subject fairly and were content to rest satisfied with the present and to let the future take care of itself. I was utterly astonished at the want of ability in the Tory party. They seemed to have no leader at all. They would not unite under Disraeli and still he had so strong a party that they could do nothing without him. They could not get along with him. They could not do without him. There were no statesmen at all in the party, no one man to exercise that all controlling one-man power which unites and concentrates and then carries everything before it. The Whigs had this in Palmerston. Never was the power of one man greater in England. The reverence—I can call it by no other word—of the Tories for him was wonderful. They had an idea that the Nation could not do without him and on one or two occasions when they would easily have defeated their opponents and brought about a dissolution, if they had put forward their whole strength they seemed appaled at the idea of losing Palmerston. Even Mr. Bentinck, M.P. commonly known at Big Ben and one of the intensest of Tories, said frankly to me at Longleat "What shall we do without Lord Palmerston". Lord Malmesbury gave me a better reason for refusing to bring about a dissolution. "I have had, said he, enough of a Ministry, not supported by a strong majority. If we go before the country and come into power, we shall be too weak to work without the aid of a portion of the Whigs or of the Liberals, upon whom we can never count. I for one will not take a seat in the Cabinet. As it is we are in great force as an opposition and to a great extent control the Government". There was no one in fact who was ready to make issue with the Ministry.

In the beginning of the War the people of England had been very uneasy about the cotton trade. They feared the effect on their trade and commerce, they feared the result of distress and famine and they were uneasy about riots. Fortunately for them the Confederate privateers flung the whole carrying trade into English bottoms, the demand for blockade steamers gave increased activity to the Ship Yards and the sudden scarcity of cotton and rapid rise in its value enabled the owners of Cotton Mills to get off the very large stocks, which had accumulated and which before the war promised ruinous losses, at enormous profits. The operatives were thrown out of work. Many starved, many migrated, more suffered sadly for many months. But the Capitalists fattened as they got rich. Many thousand pounds were subscribed & much relief was given, but nothing like what was needed. England was anxious for some time, but the poor suffered and starved and died & migrated without rioting. And then when it was evident that there were going to be no mobs, the rich people, who had become richer by the event which caused all this sad suffering—which they could easily have prevented by a little manliness in the beginning—piously crossed their hands over their fat stomachs and thanked God that the English people had borne themselves so nobly through so terrible a trial. People praised each other. The newspapers applauded—and the whole was mere mockery.

The most astonishing thing to me was that intelligent people actually seemed to believe that the British Government was preserving a fair neutrality. It was certainly a hard case on the South to close all ports to its prizes—and still people in England appeared to think that this exceptional proceeding was quite customary. They say the Alexandria stopped, they saw unnecessary delays created in obtaining a decision upon the merits of the case, they saw the Crown defeated & still they talked of neutrality. The case of the rams came & they were actually forcibly detained. The Crown saw after the decision in the case of the Alexandria* that it could not detain them. Delay was made under pretense of getting testimony from Egypt. Then some other excuse was made. Finally the case was argued and ready for decision by the Law Lords. The decision was deferred twice once under the pretense that there was not a full bench & another time on account of some holidays—Christmas or Easter I forget which—which occurred opportunely for the Crown. After all the delays when it was decided by the Lords that British Merchants had a right to sell ships, as well as guns and powder, the rams were detained by the Crown & Laird was forced to sell them to the government. Every Englishman swears by the law and the justice meeted out alike to the poor and the rich and by the honest

* The *Alexandria,* gift to the Confederate government from Fraser, Trenholm and Company, was built at Liverpool. She was seized by the British government on April 5, 1863, but released as the result of an appeal in April 1864. She became the merchant ship *Mary,* was seized again in Nassau, and released in May 1865.

impirtiality which is the bulwark of English liberty. Still everyone saw this and still said "We are strictly neutral."

The case of the blockade was still more flagrant. The treaty of Paris was made in 1856.* It was made at a time when steamers were nearly as plenty [*sic*] and as swift as they were when the war broke out. There was no material change in the situation in 1861. The Southern Confederacy expressed its willingness to conform to that treaty. According to its terms the blockade was less than a paper blockade. It was a mere farce. England observed it when the Federal Government attempted to blockade thousands of miles of coast with less than 100 vessels & continued to observe it faithfully until the North after very many months really made it pretty effective. This also was called neutrality.

The truth was that after the Trent affair the British government was terrified at the prospective expense of a war. The Cabinet had no sooner despatched its ultimatum than it regretted it and it was too glad to get out of the scrape. For the balance of the war it determined to and did eat humble pie. There were no doubt several occasions when it was anxious to and would have been glad to recognize if it could have done so without the slightest risk, but that time never actually came. I was assured in England that Palmerstōn had determined to recognize when Lee was in Pennsylvania last summer, if he had gained a victory at Gettysburgh.

The only really sensible man I met, who took a broad view of matters, was Lord Ed. St. Maur; but he was too young to have either position or influence. He could not see that it was the interest of England to have the States reunited, or to have the North hold the South in subjugation. And he could not see why England should be blind to the fact that the South could be the only nation on this side of the water that was really willing to enter into an alliance which while it proved mutually advantageous, would really be a source of great wealth to Great Britain.

Many of the Military men were much more decided than the civilians. But they neither talked nor wrote. They had no influence in the Councils of the Nation. Their business was to fight the battles of the country when the stupid counsellors had got it into trouble and to get it out of trouble as best they could.

There never was however any really strong feeling for the South such as was manifested for Denmark. As soon as the Allied German powers advanced upon Schleswig, the American War declined into

* The Treaty of Paris, to which France and Great Britain were signatory, abolished privateering, exempted neutral goods from capture, and defined blockades.

small print. The feeling was very warm. There was every possible indication of war. About the

January 1" 1864. I came up from Wales with Gallenga, with whom I had been spending a few days. He was just home from America & went up to London to spend a week. The day we arrived he went to the Times office to see Delane. Delane told him that he had just seen Palmerston and that an ultimatum had been sent out to the Allies, telling them that if they crossed the Eider, it would be considered by England as a casus belli, and that he must leave at once for Denmark or he would not be able to get there. So Gallenga was forced to start off next morning. Everyone thought war was imminent. Denmark had been encouraged to resistance in every possible way by England. Wolsely was in England at the time. He was at the Horse Guards frequently and was promised an important position. At last he gave it up in despair and left. "Before I go," said he to me, "I should go to Leicester Square and pull up my coat tails and say to every dirty little German I meet: kick me well—you have a good right. I am a Britisher—and that is all we are fit for now". It was no use to talk so however. England could scarcely be kicked into a war. She has sunk in the estimation of Europe and America into the rank of a second class power. She makes war now on Japan & China where war is profitable & resistance is weak. Everything is reduced to a purely mercantile standard. England will maintain what position she has so long as she can maintain the dignity of yardsticks pint pots and scales. My own idea is that "Noblesse oblige". I don't mean the nobility of four and twenty quarterings, but your own nobility. And that so soon as a man ceases to assist and maintain his own position just so soon is he forgotten and trodden under foot. And what is true of a man is true of a nation. The love of money is the root of all Evil and I am inclined to think that war is much more elevating and enobling than trade. In our own war it certainly seems that those of the Yankees who go to fight are much more high minded than those who stay at home to make money. The former in many instances have been elevated. The latter certainly have become more than ever frightfully demoralized. The English people certainly do not agree with me. Encourage trade, increase profits and make taxation fall lightly and they don't mind being kicked a little. I was very much struck with the fact that Money after all was fast becoming the standard of position in England as it is in America. The old families cling to their genealogies and those that have them not look up to them and envy them. But a man with forty grandfathers makes a very poor show without wealth. The Nobility are quite as anxious to vie with the rich commoners in display as the commoners are to possess their quarterings. And the rich banker who can entertain the largest number of guests in the handsomest style, who has the best preserved covers and the finest stud of horses, can generally command the best company. The Seymours are one of the oldest families. Yet the oldest Duke did nothing his whole life but accumulate, that he might enable some descendant to vie one day with the City men. The present Duke lives as economically as possible. The savings of years he has recently laid out at Bulstrode, which will no doubt be a handsome country residence, near London, where his son may entertain handsomely. At present he spends his country life quietly at Stover Lodge, far down in Devonshire, where he has poorly preserved covers and no stable. When the Nobility three or four hundred years ago went to the city to marry the daughters of rich men, it was not altogether the thing. Now the daughters of banker or brewer are brought into society at once. The Sons get commissions in the Army—and if a man gets together money enough to buy a few thousand acres of land and return a member to parliament he is made a peer of. It is curious however that no nobleman ever educates his son to business. Many young men who would make creditable merchants or bankers never have the opportunity to develop their talents. With the prevailing greed for gain this cannot last much longer. In a few years younger sons will take to the counter as they now do to the army or the law. The standard has been debased, but people are accomodating themselves to it.

What most surprised me perhaps was the state of Morals among the humbler classes of society in and around London, which was a perfect hotbed of vice. There were a great many anecdotes told me by fast men of the loose life in upper classes—and several cases of *crim con* were made public during my stay in England. But I speak not of those who shop in carriages, as all ladies do. I refer to those who walk. Of them, I think it fair to say, that there is scarcely one whom a clever, well looking man cannot with a little address join & enter into conversation with and from whom he cannot obtain a promise to meet him again. In a short time a little flattery a little attention and money are almost sure to win. Many of the women I allude to are fairly educated and possess attractions that would do them credit in any society. Love of dress and a desire to emulate Anonyma and Skittles,* who are permitted and applauded

* Anonyma seems to be a common name for whore used during the Regency

and copied by the English public, pervert their mind. Difference of cast too has its effect. Many of these women feel that they have received an education which unfits them for the society in which they are born and yet know that their birth prevents them from mating well those in a higher sphere. Hence they say they have nothing left but a *liaison*. Such a condition of things exists no doubt to a greater or less extent in all large communities, but in England, and on the continent generally I presume, it is the result, to a great extent, of a state of Society which dooms a number of men to celibacy. There are a great many younger sons of noble families who are put into the fashionable regiments in the Army and who are given expressly to understand that the cost of their commission and a moderate allowance is all that they can expect. These men, totally unfit for business, accepting celibacy as their fate and deeming the probability of contracting a marriage with a wealthy mate as almost hopeless begin their career in debauchery and find great amusement in corrupting young girls. They understand that they are put in the army to die out, giving in return for the purchase of their commission a sort of tacit pledge that they will not lower the family pride by a marriage and a small family of beggar brats. In the garrison towns such men as these demoralize the younger portion of the female community fearfully and girls seduced by the gay uniforms and attentions of those in a higher class fall an easy prey to them. The countenance given by the upper classes too to *liaisons* certainly has a very bad effect. In England a misalliance is not pardoned, but the illegitimate children of people of rank are at least countenanced in society & not unfrequently received. Lord Egremont, the owner of the magnificent Estate of Petworth, had one illegitimate son, who was styled Percy Wyndham. Lord E. purchased him a commission in the Guards, the most exclusive Military organization in England. He left his Estates to him by Will. Some time after Col. Wyndham having carried a contested election & returned a member to Parliament was ennobled under the title of Lord Leconfield.* What can

period. "Skittles" was the nickname of Catherine Walters, a notorious cocotte or celebrated *demi-mondaine,* depending upon one's point of view. Lord Hartington, 8th Duke of Devonshire, at one time formed an attachment with her.

* Glenn seems to have been confused on this point. The Honorable Percy Scawen Wyndham was the third son of the 1st Baron Leconfield (see glossary entries for George and Percy Wyndham). A soldier of fortune named Sir Percy Wyndham commanded New Jersey cavalry in the Union army and was the object of a Confederate bribe attempt. (David Donald, ed., *Inside Lincoln's Cabinet, the Civil War Diaries of Salmon P. Chase* [New York, 1954], pp. 207–8, 316–17.) Sir Percy's colorful career was terminated after the war by the explosion of an aeronautical balloon in India.

be expected of the Morals of a people when the Govt. thus takes illegitimacy under its protection.

Nor was the State of Religion most favorable to the encouragement of purity in morals. The conflict of opinion between the scientific men and geologists of the day and the implicit believers in the Mosaic record had so thoroughly disturbed the minds of many that they scarcely knew what to believe. Many had wandered over to the extremest form of Roman Catholicism. Others had not stopped until they had reached the confines of infidelity. At a lecture given one night by Froude, he was reported to have said that in 70 years time, the story of a God would be an old woman's tale. He denied it to me, but acknowledged that he had used some such an expression as a quotation from a German author. The Colenso trial was being much discussed and his views eagerly adopted by many people, while Dean Stanley, of Oxford, openly taught that the Old Testament was not an inspired record but only a record of an inspired people. I was much amused one evening at a dinner at Capt Gordon Ives of the —— Guards. Seated at the table was a gentleman named Pakenham, who had been educated at Oxford for the Church, but who by the death of two brothers had fallen heir to a handsome Estate in Ireland. During the course of the dinner, something being said about the antiquities of Ireland, he remarked that a very old piece of some petrified wood had been recently taken from the bottom of a Loch or Lake on his Estate. The water of this Lake he said had the peculiar power of petrifying wood which remained in it for any length of time. The piece in question, about six feet long and nearly two feet in diameter had been dug out in sinking for a foundation for a boat house and, being unusually large, had been laid aside as a curiosity. Mr. P., seeing it himself, had had it carried to his lawn for further examination and to his surprise, found after some days, that while the outer portion was thoroughly petrified, the interior was still in a ligneous state and could not only be cut with a knife but would burn. Struck with the fibre of the wood he sent specimens for examination to Professors Owen & Lyell, who both pronounced the wood to be a fern, evidently the growth of Ireland when the country was in a tropical region, and said that according to their estimates they supposed the age of the wood to be about 30,000,000 of years. Ives, who like most soldiers, had not had a college education & was not quite so well up in the Mosaic Record and chronology as Pakenham, at once said "Bless my soul Pakenham that was before the Bible was written".—"Yes," replied P. with a quiet smile "Some Years".

Talking of education reminds me of the Grace before meat and the thanks after dinner used at Christ Church Oxford. Dining there one day with the Dons, as we sat down, he, at the head of the table said "Benedictus benedicat". When the cloth was removed he said "Benedicto benedicatur". Was ever anything more short, simple & perfect. Let the blessed one bless. Let the blessed one be blessed. What could be more expressive & more charming. Thanks are supposed to be given when the cloth is removed. If the cloth is not removed thanks are still given before the fruit. Why is this? Is it that there may be forbidden fruit in the dish?

The man who most interested me in England was Mr. Butterfield, architect of All Saints in Margaret Street and of another fine church,* I forget the name in Gray's Inn.** He was a thorough artist, a firm believer and a most earnest follower. I saw unfortunately very little of him. I was much struck with a remark made by him about books and writing generally. We were talking about Colenso's book. He said that it was very easy for many people to write, even though they had no great power of analysis and thought, and that, thus, much harm was done by them that they could not undo. "Colenso," said he, "is one of these men. I know him personally. I have more than once before this been disturbed by doubts, but I have made up my mind henceforth never to let my convictions be unsettled by the written arguments of a man I do not know." We were talking one day at dinner about the political condition of England, when he asked me what impression was produced upon me as a stranger. I replied that it did not become me to criticise frankly, firstly because I had really seen too little of the people and secondly because it would be ungenerous in me to find faults where I was being treated with so much hospitality. He insisted however on knowing what I considered to be the tendency of the political institutions of the day. I replied "Republicanism". To my great surprise he agreed with me perfectly and said that he wondered that people did not see what he thought was so evident to every reflecting mind.

When the American War broke out it was the general opinion among men of thought that the effect produced upon England would be very beneficial, that the example of America would strengthen the Conservative party and would put a wholesome check upon the radicals. This may have been the momentary effect in the beginning

* The church designed by Butterfield is All Saints near Holborn.

** Gray's Inn is one of London's Inns of Court or law schools. The original buildings, located along Caledonian Road, were largely destroyed in the 1941 air raids.

of the outbreak. It passed away however very rapidly, and so far from regarding the struggle in its proper light, as really a dissolution of the Union, the Radicals of England saw in the apparent unity of the North and in the vast numerical force and financial power developed by the War, a striking proof of the power & cohesive force of Republican Institutions. What the effect may be hereafter it is hard to say—but certainly while I was in England and today the Radicals of that country were and are as wild as the Republicans of America. When the war ends and the North is split up into half a dozen governments or the whole country is governed by a Military despot—for I take for granted one of these two things must happen—the English people may take warning from America and save themselves from the inevitable fate attendant upon unlimited Republicanism. But today they are deaf to all warnings. Long years of peace at home and the love of gain, fostered and encouraged by the Government, have had their natural effect upon the people. Money is gradually becoming the standard in England as it is in America and all that is truly high and noble is becoming debased. There are shrewd bankers, clever merchants and political economists of reputation in the country, but beyond this, the best men seem really to have lost the power of thought and of looking into the future. As far as I could see there were no statesmen whatever in public life. The policy of the Government seemed to be a make shift policy, Ministers provided only for the present, satisfied, if they got safely through their term, to let the future be cared for by those who came after them. The only thing they were really anxious for was place and for this they seemed ready to sacrifice anything and everything. The Tory party, though strong in numbers, was in reality very weak—for it had no unity, no head and very little cleverness. Many of the country members, of whom it was chiefly composed, were good to vote and that was all. They were of the same value precisely as the balls which were dropped in the ballot box. Each counted one. As a Tory party it had really ceased to exist. All the old Tory principles had been or are being rapidly abandoned, and the Tory of today is more liberal than the Radical of a few years back. It is an Opposition and that is all. Were it not for Palmerston, it strikes me, that this party would entirely be broken up. Such is his great popularity and so great is the confidence of everyone in him, that the administration of the Country is pretty much resigned to him & the Cabinet of which he is a member. As soon however as he is out of power the Radicals will appeal to the country for support and in order to get greater strength will promise their constituents an extension of the elective franchise. This is the only means by which they can beat the Conservative party which is in reality very strong in England. I take it for granted that in a few years there must be a new division of parties. The Tories will unite with the conservative wing of the Whigs, forming a conservative party, while the liberal wing will join with the Radicals—and gradually the power will be taken from the hands of the landowners and wielded by the politicians of the manufacturing districts, who will not hesitate to appeal, as they do in America, to the lowest passions of the people, in order to attain their personal ends. This of course must lead to Universal suffrage and that once established the English Nation must run its course as the United States is doing. It really does seem as if Republicanism were a poison which had no cure when once inoculated in the system and which was inevitably bound to run its fatal course. These were the impressions of last spring and are of today. The results of the war may as I say, check this tendency. This war must end one day—and when it does end, the revolution, that exists & that existed for four years & more, must become apparent to the least thoughtful mind. Then the English may still take warning in time. Republics must be limited as well as monarchies. If power is to be placed in the hands of the people it requires more safeguards and more checks than it does in the hands of a ruler—for the ruler has the mob against him and must respect it—while the people has the mob on its side, and against them the few are powerless.

Late in January the hunting was still good in the Middle and lower parts of England & even in Yorkshire. Fields were still reasonably green and galloping was very good on the turf. I was much struck one day, early in January, at seeing a large rose bud on a bush in the open air. It was well formed & just ready to bloom. A day's sunshine would have made a rose of it. I hunted in Essex & Herts* & Wiltshire & Yorkshire and coursed hare over the Downs. I was quite astonished to see the different style of country in different districts and the different fences used for enclosures, and to remark the training of the horses in the various counties. In Essex for instance the fences were entirely hedges & ditches or banks with a small hedge on top & a ditch on each side. These were called doubles. They were big fences to look at, but very easy ones to get over. I recollect the first one I saw. It was a bank full four feet high with a small loose hedge on top, grown I suppose to hold the bank together. On either side was a ditch four feet wide. I gathered my horse together

* Herts is Hertford, a county in the southeastern part of England bounded by London and Essex.

uncertain as to whether we were going to get over safely, and went at it. I found myself in the next field, my horse haven gotten over almost without an effort. He had jumped on top of the bank, placed first his fore then his hind feet on the far side near the top & then launched himself forward. This leap was in reality much easier than the "singles"—consisting of a ditch & a bank or hedge. These had to be cleared in a fly. In the shires* the horses went through the bull finches in a wonderful way and in other parts they economized their ponies perfectly. But a horse trained for one district rarely did well in another. A Yorkshire horse accustomed to fly everything would soon be pumped in Essex and an Essex horse accustomed to doubling would come early to grief in Yorkshire.

It was curious to see how few men out of a field were well up. Out of a field of two hundred not more than twenty would live through a good run. At the first find everyone would rush for the nearest gate or gap and by the time the second gate was gotten through at least half the field would be entirely thrown out so that their getting in again was a matter of pure accident. There were some men who knew the country well in which they hunted, who always managed to be pretty well up and who yet never took a fence. They were almost as clever as two or three old whippers in and earth steppers I saw on different occasions who in their tattered old hunting caps hunted on foot and frequently managed to be in at the death. The men who really rode boldly, always took the first two or three stiff fences and then having shaken off the crowd took the gates & gaps without losing much time. I could hardly believe that there was so much heartlessness exhibited in a sport in which there was so much good feeling manifested—but no mercy or consideration was shown to any one. I was much amused one day at Anthony Trollope with whom I had been staying & who had given me a mount. We were both well up and riding together, when at the bottom of the slope before us we saw an unusual fence, consisting of a ditch, bank and small flight of three rails on top. It was stiffish. Trollope & I slackened our speed, so as to let our horses take it at a moderate pace. Just then a Londoner, who was always in for a chance to show off & who was a little behind, thinking this a good chance for a lead, urged on his horse, swept by and went at the fence full run. The poor animal already nearly pumped had no chance and, not rising sufficiently high, struck the rails with his

* Shires can simply refer to the counties of England, but in this context it probably refers to those ending with the suffix *shire,* which are concentrated in the southern portion of the country.

knees. The panel fortunately gave way, but the horse was thrown heels over head about fifteen feet and the rider was tossed far out into the field. I though he was done for but the ground was soft & he was not even stunned. The knocking off a top rail made the leap much easier for us and Trollope & I took the fence together. The man who had come to grief was standing in the middle of the field filled with mud & looking hopelessly around for his horse. I thought he deserved every man's commisseration. Not so Trollope. "Hallo," cried he. "We are much obliged to you. A d—d good thing you did for us. I don't know what we should have done without you"—and so he rode on and left him.

In the middle & upper counties the hunters are bred very large. It is no uncommon thing to see a hunter 16 hands high of vast power and any amount of go in him. They are very different from American horses.

There were at this time a great many Southerners in London & in England. A number of them lived quietly at Leamington. Those in London and Liverpool were generally engaged in blockade running or some Southern business. They had their friends and associations among the Middle Classes. The upper classes paid little attention to men who had abandoned their country in its hour of need to trade upon its necessities. Mr. Mason, the Commissioner and Capt. Maury were the only two men I knew who, did not avail themselves of opportunities which offered. They were both perfectly pure men and would have received much attention had they been willing to accept. I heard of Capt. Maury's refusing at least one invitation to a ducal house. They both lived in a very quiet and humble manner. Mr. Mason left England during this winter. He received such studied slights from Lord Russell that he finally received orders from his Govt. to abandon his official post. He soon after went to Paris.

Calling one day at his rooms, No. 24 Upper Seymour Street,* I found him in company with rather a handsome woman, rouged and elaborately gotten up. He was about to go off with her on business apparently rather to my surprise. "Don't you know Mrs. Greenhow" said he, upon which he presented me. She caught my name at once, no doubt recollecting that it was to me she and Mrs. Phillips used to send letters from Washington for publication during their surveillance and imprisonment. She begged me to come and see her and gave me her number in Conduit Street,** where she

* Upper Seymour Street is near Hyde Park in the vicinity of the Marble Arch.

** Conduit Street is in the West End between New Bond Street and Regent Street, also near Hyde Park.

was put up in much more splendid style than Mr. Mason indulged in. I immediately guessed who she was and thanked her kindly. Of course I did not go. She was too notorious a character to be seen much with and my object was to keep as much as possible out of the way of people who were probably watched. She was in high feather at this time. When she left Richmond the Govr. had given her an interest in fifteen bales of cotton which she had succeeded in procuring and in getting safely to L'pool. This gave her a pretty fair Capital to start and Bentley the publisher imagining that he would make quite a little fortune by her book, had undertaken to publish it at his own risk, giving her half the profits which he assured her would be very handsome.* He and his friends made great efforts to introduce her into society and she had quite a run as a notability and a curiosity. She very soon found her level. Her great chaperonne was Lady Franklin, who it appears was pretty much a bird of the same feather.

This Lady Franklin during Sir John's life had never lived on decent terms with him. When he was lost in the Arctic expedition, Lady F. suddenly discovered the profoundest affection for her missing husband & spent her life and *half* of his fortune in organizing expeditions for his discovery and relief. She spent about £5000 a year for several years in this manner and about as much more on herself. Finally her son insisted upon his rights. He came into the fortune. Lady F. retired upon her dower and her enthusiasm for Sir John subsided. She gave Mrs. Greenhow much friendly assistance. There were other people who saw what Mrs. G. was and who learned what her position at Washington had been and declined the honor of her acquaintance.

Febry. 1864. Went over to Paris to spend a few days. Stopped at the Grand Hotel which is certainly the grandest and most thoroughly organized Hotel I have ever seen.** For persons living on the lower floors and taking all their meals in the house, it is very expensive, but for those who live higher up and take only breakfast in the house it is as cheap as need be—astonishingly so, when you consider all the advantages of reading room, society, smoking room etc.

Dr. Wm. M. Gwin and his family were living on the Boulevard close by, over the Jockey Club.*** They had superb apartments,

* Rose Greenhow's book, *My Imprisonment and the first Year of abolition rule at Washington,* was published in London in 1863.

** This is probably the Grand Hotel on the Boulevard des Capucines. There was also a Grand Hotel du Louvre on the Rue de Rivoli across from the Louvre.

*** The Jockey Club was located on the Rue Scribe, Boulevard des Capucines.

much more costly than they could afford; but Dr. Gwin had been living at the Hotel de l'Avoisinante and had got the blues. He declared that he must get cheerful lodgings at any cost. While I was there the Emperor sent for him to question him about Mexico. Mrs. Gwin was very anxious for him to make a grand first impression and Gwin himself was greatly pleased at having an opportunity to propose some plans he had in view. He did have a long interview with the Emperor in which he suggested to him, that he would find it impossible to make any thing out of Mexico proper, as the National debt was already so heavy that the taxation which the country could bear would not more than pay the interest and provide for the annual budget. He then added that the way to make Mexico pay was to colonize Sonora; that it was a very rich mining district and could be rendered very profitable at a trifling expense. Gwin's plan was to take 1000 mountain men as a nucllus [*sic*], to establish himself in a rich mining district, to initiate immigration from California, the Atlantic States and Europe, give the immigrants grants of land and form them into a sort of Military organization which would protect Mexico from invasion from its greatest enemy, California. The mines he proposed to work principally by impressed peon or indian labor. Guaymas was to be made a port of entry.* Through this port Sonora was to be supplied with merchandise of all descriptions from France. Gold and metals were to be shipped in return and the French Government was not only to receive large amounts of precious metal but also to establish a new and very profitable trade, for said Gwin "Miners are the most careless and thriftless people in the world. They never wash their clothes but as soon as they are thoroughly dirty & worn toss them off for new ones. Thus they consume much more than any other class of people." The Emperor was evidently pleased with his suggestions. Gwin wrote them all out and had them put in proper French and submitted them. After I left he had an interview with Maximilians Agent and was quite confident of being sent out to Mexico to carry out his scheme.

While I was staying there I was rather astonished and not a little amused at the power Mrs. Greenhow seemed to exercise over some people. When she left Richmond, she had received a permit to ship 15 Bales Cotton. Having no means to procure the Cotton, she persuaded Dr. Gwin, who was then at Wilmington to advance the necessary funds, promising him half profits. On the passage out the vessel was pursued & some cotton thrown overboard. Mrs. G.'s

* Guaymas is the major port city of the western Mexican province of Sonora on the Gulf of California.

portion was assessed at two bales and she received at Nassau 13 Bales. She however beset the Confederate Agent until she actually induced him to give her the original quantity shipped by her, on the ground that President Davis desired that she should have the profit on 15 Bales, the Agent merely stipulating that she should give him the funds necessary to purchase two bales at Wilmington. This sum Gwin also advanced. After she had been some time in London, Dr. G. who was much in want of money, applied several times for his share of the proceeds but ineffectually. Finally he sent over to Ben Ficklin and begged him to see what he could but Ben declared he would rather deal with ten men than face that woman. Finally he rec'd half profits on five bales and I presume eventually got the whole. But at this time Dr. G. was vexed with her, not only on this account but because she had rather abused him in her book which was just published. To my great surprise two days after I reached Paris I found Dr. G. & Mrs. Greenhow on the most friendly terms and she immediately became a visitor to the house. She had written to Dr. G. to come and see her. He had gone determined to talk plainly to her. In a few minutes she had him as mild as a lamb and all was forgiven. "And now" said she "is there any reason why I should not visit Mrs. Gwin and the girls?" None! said he—and she immediately did visit them and established herself there on the most intimate footing. One day she came in in a mysterious manner with a large envelope in her hand displayed so everyone could see it who had any curiosity. I was not paying any attention to her & barely noticed it. She took Dr. G. in a side room, told him that she had at last accomplished what she wished and expected to have an audience with the Emperor, and told him to be sure and tell me not to mention that I had seen this Card from the Chambellain [*sic*] in her hand. This she did for the purpose of letting me know the fact in case it had escaped my notice. Two days after, as I was sitting in the drawing room, in came Mr. Slidell. Gwin & he went into a side room and had a pow-wow. When they came out & Mr. S. had gone, I enquired what he wanted. He came round said Gwin for the purpose of learning what Mrs. G. said about him." Slidell the moment he heard she was to have an audience, was so afraid of the apparent influence of the woman & was so afraid that if he were behind hand with the Emperor in attention to her that she might injure him at Richmond by her letters or on her return home and thus perhaps effect his recall which he by no means desired, that he immediately went and left his card; and although he had declared she should not set his [*sic*] foot in his house or know his family, he sent Mrs. S. to call upon her too. When she went to have her interview Mr. S. sent Eustis, his secretary of Legation, with her to present her. She had them in fact all at her feet.

The Slidells were living very comfortably in Paris. Both Mr. & Mrs. Slidell were eminently calculated for French society and the Emperor, though he was in reality playing false to the Confederacy all the time, showed Mr. S. and his family numerous little personal attentions, for the purpose no doubt of deceiving him, in which he perfectly succeeded. It was evident to everyone now except Mr. Slidell that no faith was to be placed in the Emperor. Mr. Slidell still to chose to believe in him. These little attentions however made Mr. S. position very pleasant. Without being acknowledged as an Ambassador he still had the entreé to all the society he desired. If any of his friends from the South were in Paris, who desired a ticket to the Imperial Balls, they were given in an informal application and persons thus gained admittance who would otherwise have been excluded, they having no Minister to present them. His position was very different from Mr. Mason's in London and vastly more pleasant. Mr. S. too had means. He had Mortged [*sic*] his property in N. Orleans on the commencement of our difficulties to a French house. It was respected by the Federal Govt. and he thus had some means at least abroad. Besides this he no doubt speculated to a considerable extent with Erlanger, afterwards his son in law, in the Confederate Cotton loan.* He must have made a considerable amount as he was not a man to lose an opportunity to turn an "honest penny".

Corcoran was living there in very handsome style, with his son in law Eustis & his daughter in the same house. Mr. Mason was then in Paris. Withers from Mississippi and Winthrop from N. Orleans formerly of Boston and James McCall from Louisiana were also there as refugees, the latter having registered himself as an enemy. These together with Mr. Frank Corbin, an old resident of Paris, formed a little party which met twice a week to play whist in a quiet way. Gwin would not come in. He could not play well and had not the money to lose. I did not see him at these parties once while I was in Paris.

Comdr. Barron, chief of the Confederate Naval Service in Europe, with his staff were living quietly in a very plain manner in a Hotel

* Frank L. Owsley discusses the attempt by the Confederacy to use cotton as a diplomatic weapon in *King Cotton Diplomacy* (Chicago, 1959). The cotton loans, whereby planters exchanged surplus cotton for Confederate bonds, were initiated in 1861. As long as the idea of starving England for cotton was popular, the loans were well subscribed. Owsley notes that after 1861 the popularity of the cotton embargo declined, and with it the loans.

near the Palais Royal.* The difficulties encountered by them in this Department were enormous. Most of their purchases had to be effected in England and the best sailors were recruited there. But so strict was the surveillance kept on the Confederate agents, that they were hampered in every possible way. While I was with Com. Barron, a gentleman came in who had been obliged to flee from England for fear of arrest for violation of neutrality laws. He had perhaps shipped a dozen men for the Confederate Service. In Ireland they were embarking by thousands for the Federal army & Yankee Agents were busy in Ireland & England too recruiting men for imaginary railroads in America. Everyone knew what that meant. Capt. Sinclair was with Comd. Barron waiting for his ship, not yet out and not likely to get out—and the officers detailed for the Iron Clads. Nick Barney relieved from the Florida for his health and Morris who succeeded him—and others all living almost in seclusion, avoiding notice & economising as much as possible. Govr. Morehead of Kentucky was also there very miserable & unhappy. His home is among Western Men. Among Men of Education and cultivated intelligence he soon sank into his proper level. He was a good natured talkative weak minded old gentleman & very tiresome.

Febry 20" 1864. Returned to England. Stopped a day at Brighton & then went over to Muntham Court to spend a week with the Marchoniss of Bath. Visited Petworth while I was in the neighborhood and also called at Mr. Curzon's very handsome estate. I forget the name. He married an heiress, Lady .**

Went to London. Lawley arrived to the astonishment of every body. Col. Neville & Lord Wenlock called on Friday to know what I knew of L. and on Saturday Neville & I dined with Lawley at the St. James Hotel.*** Lawley was sent for by a great many leading men, who were anxious to get his views. The French Emperor sent a special messenger for him. Lawley was of course charmed. He was in high spirits. He expected the coming campaign would prove a triumphant victory and he thought he could put matters in such a light to the Emperor that he would inevitably change his policy. He soon left for Paris.

March 3d. 1864. Mr. Mason, to my surprise, I learned had returned to London & was at his old quarters 24 Up Seymour St.

* The Palais Royal in Paris is off the Place Napoleon above the Louvre.

** Robert Curzon married Emily Wilmot-Horton.

*** The Saint James Hotel, 77 Piccadilly, was one of the first-class West End hotels listed in an 1878 visitors' guide to London.

When I saw him he asked me to order him from home 2 doz Maryland Hams, which he wanted in England to entertain his friends. I asked no questions, but it was evident he was back again to stay. I learned afterwards that Mr Slidell had had some interviews with Drouyn de L'Huys & was quite confident of speedy recognition. Lawley wrote word that he was exceedingly hopeful of good results from his interview with the Emperor. A few days after I saw Mr. Mason Gregory, M.P. came to see me and assured me that it was believed at the foreign office that the French Emperor was about to recognize.

March 5". [*1864*] Dined at Mr. Mason, with Mr. Dudley Mann, Mr. Buchanan, Mr. Williams, Mr. McRae, the Loan Commr. & one or two others. Jas. Buchanan had been Minister to Copenhagen under President Buchanan. He was staying abroad, because he had talked and did talk very foolishly and was afraid of arrest if he returned to America. Williams was a man of different stamp. He was a rough looking customer and thoroughly western, but he had sense and was the Author of a sensible book lately published "The rise and fall of the Model Republic". Both of these men were utterly destitute of elegance and true refinement, but they presented together very fair specimens of the average run of politicians sent out for a four years "broad" to European states of minor commercial importance, as a reward probably for some very clever and successful electioneering dodges. England, France & Russia were generally pretty fairly represented by men of tolerable Education. Ambassadors to other States were selected without any particular regard to capacity. I have two in my mind now, who were men of no small importance at home.

One was Andrew Jackson Donelson. I saw him in Berlin in 1848. He soon found the Drawing Room & drawing room society a nuisance and he had had established for himself a little reception room adjoining where any one who wished to talk with him could find him. Here he sat with his legs over the mantle piece, squirting tobacco juice in the fire, quite undisturbed by the approach of a Secretary of Legation or any one else. Mr. D." said I, one evening, "how do you manage to get along. You do not seem to speak French and I do not hear you talk German". No! said he, No! I did try the d—d language for a few days, until one day, I heard a little boy, whose eye was caught by some object, cry out to another "Was das da"? Was das da said I, Why d—n it all, that's nigger talk in our country & I determined to have nothing more to do with it. Mrs. Donelson & her daughter Mary, who helped to do the honors were fitting companions for such a lord. He was a very good fellow, at home & had sense I believe, but he was out of his sphere.

The other was Hannegan, who succeeded Mr. Donelson at Berlin. In 1849, I think, I went through there with my sister Etta, en route for America. I called at the Legation to have my passport *visé* but not wishing to trouble Mr. H. and not thinking that he would recollect me, I did not ask for him. I was stopping at Meynhard's unter den Linden.* About noon a servant came to my door and informed me that a gentleman desired to see me. I directed him to ask him up to my sitting room. To my surprise up came Mr. Hannegan. He was very good natured & reproached me for not calling on him, saying how glad he would be to return the hospitality shown him at our house, while in the U.S. Senate. After a little while he asked me what I had to do. I replied "nothing". Then, said he, "come along with me. I am just on my way to Potsdam where I am to have a private audience at Sans souci and you shall go along and we will spend the afternoon with the king."** I imagined myself doing things in this truly American fashion and I declined. He would take no refusal. Finally I excused myself on the ground that I had a young sister with me whom I could not possibly leave. "Is that all? said he, rising and clapping me on the shoulder. Bring her along my boy, bring her along". And he would have taken us both along without further ceremony. Still he was a much more presentable man than many others I saw. This day he was unmistakeably tight.

March 9". Went down to Escrick Park for a week. Lord Wenlock had a splendid stable & gave me capital mounts. The hunting was still pretty fair.

March 17. Went up to Oxford for a day or two, where I expected to hear from Mr. Mason who had agreed to go with me to Leamington to spend a week.

March 21. Went up to London. Found Mr. Mason to my astonishment packing up to leave the country. It was quite evident that

* Visitors' guides to Berlin could not be located for the nineteenth century. Unter den Linden, a boulevard lined with hotels and restaurants, ran from the Brandenburg Gate to the Frederick the Great monument.

** The Sanssouci Palace, Potsdam, was built between 1745 and 1747 as the summer residence of Frederick the Great and is a masterpiece of German Rococo.

Bony* had been playing fast and loose and had deceived them once more. Mr. Dudley Mann was quite out with him and declared that in no case was he to be trusted for a moment.

April 1". [*1864*] I had been thinking of leaving England for some time. The accounts from the South had been very encouraging. The Southern people were in high spirits and expected this campaign to be the end of the war. Besides Lee had asserted privately that he could not winter an army again at Richmond. The difficulties of the commissariat had become too great. It was evident that he must either advance or fall back. In great hopes that the Southern army would soon be in Maryland, I determined to hasten home.

Made my adieux. Had a farewell dinner with Mr. C. Hammersly head of Cox & Co., Army Bankers, who kept a charming house and was a capital host—and bade good bye to the De La Rue's. Mr. Wm. De La Rue was one of the most liberal, considerate true hearted men I met abroad. I felt under great obligation to him. His brother Thomas was a man of extensive scientific attainments and they both stood very high in the confidence of the Government, with whom they had large contracts & of the public generally.

Apl 6" 1864. Left London. Spent night at Chester and walked round its curious old walls and through its quaint streets.

Apl 7". Sailed from L'pool in Nova Scotian as Capt. Gordon. I had written from the Junior U.S. Club for my passage. The purser had naturally supposed I belonged to the Army & dubbed me captain. I saw at once that we had a very common set aboard. I looked around and picked out one man I knew to be a gentleman. It turned out to be Capt. Sitwell of the Engineers going out to Canada, to assist in making the necessary surveys for refortifying Quebec and erecting new fortifications between that point and Montreal. I told him my name & asked his confidence.

Apl 8. Fog all day. Making no headway. Found that there were six Yankee captains on board who had had their ships destroyed by the Alabama or had been obliged to dispose of them in the East Indies. I had taken this route to escape observation. Had not bettered myself.

Apl 9". Reached Derry at 5 P.M. Took aboard lots of emigrants. Left in less than a couple of hours.

Apl 10. My Yankee Ship Mates having already discovered the

* Bony is French Emperor Napoleon Bonaparte III.

history of everybody on board were curious to know my story. I made a confidant of a talking Irishman, a Lieut in the 16". He would soon have found me out if I had not. As it was he swore flatly that I was in the Quarter Master's bureau in Montreal where he had seen me often. I kept quiet & had no further trouble. The Yanks amused me greatly by telling me what they intended to do to my country—England—when settling day came.

April 24. Reached Portland at dusk.* No war news as yet. The Federal army has been largely recruited. A Draft of 500,000 men had been ordered by President Lincoln for March 10"—and another call had been made by him on March 15" for 200,000 more. Genl. Grant who was appointed Commander in Chief on March 12" is evidently to have an overwhelming force to crush out the South at one blow.

April 25" 1864. Left for New York.

April 26". Determined to go home. Met Fitzgerald Ross who gave me the most favorable accounts of the enthusiasm of the Southern people. He says the roads are crowded with soldiers trying to get to the front. All they want is to get a chance to finish the war, for they are determined to finish it and that this shall be the last year of the war. The confidence of the people here is even more astonishing. Grant's forces are innumerable and irresistable. It is painful to a degree to be among these people and to listen to them.

April 27". Reached Baltimore in the Morning, after an absence of 10 months. I left one morning saying to my people, "I am too uneasy to sleep another night in this house. I little thought that would be the last they saw of me; but it was. I had no chance to bid them good bye. My friends all tell me that I am mad to come home. There is no law—no protection. Arbitrary force rules. The negro population is in a state of ferment. Few servants can be trusted any longer and it is scarcely possible to get along with decent comfort. Genl. Schenck who was bitter and violent has been removed. Lew Wallace, who is worse, is in his place.

May 1". [1864] Showed publicly & went to Church.

May 2. Left in buggy with Tom Buckler and drove to Ned Jenkin's where I found Govr. Pratt and a party.

* Close economic ties, bound by the Atlantic and St. Lawrence Railway, existed between eastern Canada and Portland, Maine.

May 3. Drove over to Rev. W. F. Brand's in Harford Co.

May 5. Drove to Magnolia & took Cars to Wilmington, where I met Fitzgd. Ross by appointment.

May 6. To Philadelphia & next day to New York.

Stopped in New York for ten days. Grant's army moved across Rapidan on the 3d inst. The papers have been filled with accounts of his brilliant successes though it is evident he has been driven back & forced to form a new base at Fredericksburg.

May 10. Battle of Spottsylvania. Grant has evidently been fearfully handled but still proposes "to fight it out on this line". The excitement in New York is intense. The confidence of the community painful to a Southerner.

May 18. Left for Canada.

May 21. Reached Montreal & drove to Col Wolseley's, where I stopped and dined.

May 22. Drove out to Cote de Neiges to see Mrs. Hopkins.*

May 23. Dined with, the Magruders at Col Wynne's of Grenadiers.

May 24. Went out to spend day at Hopkin's & celebrate Queen's birthday with Mrs H & her lively sister Miss Bucky.

May 25. Lunched with Grenadiers. Dined at Commdr. Magruders with Leo Seymour & Wynne.

May 26. Dined with Col Neville & Col Stephenson at Fuisillers Mess.

May 27. Dined with Phillips at Grenadiers.

May 28. Drove to de La Chine** up to Club House & crossed to Island to spend a couple of days with Sir Fenwick Williams. De Winton & Fox of his staff were there. Buller & De Horsey came over from Club House & dined. Sir Fenwick is very popular as a host. He does the honors well & is fond of entertaining. He has not much military knowledge and does not handle the troops on parade. He rests on his reputation as the hero of Kars.***

* Côte de Neiges is a western suburb of Montreal.

** La Chine (Lachine) is in the curve of the St. Lawrence south of Montreal, now the exit of the Lachine Canal and the Lachine Locks.

*** The Turkish city of Kars was besieged and captured by the Russians in 1855 when it capitulated from starvation.

May 29. Went to La Chine in the Generals barge to Church. Afterward Yachted with him in Wanderer till dinner time.

May 30. Went to Montreal. Dined with Wolseley at Mess of 60". Military men consider the news very unfavorable to Grant. It is very evident they say that he is making as fast as he can for the White House. He has crossed the North Anna & must have a new base for supplies. Of course we know nothing. The papers are filled as usual with lies.

May 31". Left Montreal for New York.

June 3. [*1864*] Reached New York. Matters look very favorably. Grant has crossed the Pamunkey and is evidently making for the James. Nothing particular from home. The house has not been watched. There are no guards at the corner as of old. I shall go home & try what can be done.

June 4". Reached home. Sent word to Wallis. Received a note from him telling me not to leave the house until he saw me, as he thought there was considerable danger. Later in the day he came up to see me. I had unpacked my trunk & had been lying down. He had been in the house but a few moments when the front door bell rang. I went to it myself and found a detective there. They had evidently been on the watch for me since my last presence in Baltimore. I was in my slippers. The fellow would not even let me go upstairs alone to put on shoes. He signalled to another man & in a moment half a dozen more appeared on the scene. They entered the house, keeping me in strict custody, and commenced a search. The first thing picked up was Lucy's photograph album of Southern Generals. The names were written under each. On the front page was a picture of Genl. Lee not yet published in the North. Under it was written "Commander in Chief". The fellow looked at it, turned it round, said "Commander in Chief—Commander in Chief" and then suddenly, as if a bright idea had struck him, cried out "God bless my soul, I believe it is meant for General Lee". The book was confiscated. They then went to my sleeping chamber & dressing room, abandoning apparently the idea of searching the rest of the house, as this was the third or fourth time and as they saw mother & the girls took it very quietly. The Captain in Command made for my trunk & opened it. There was nothing in it. Where are your clothes, he said. "In my bureau." "When do you expect to leave?" "I have just come home". But when do you expect to start again". "I have just returned after an absence of ten month

The townhouse of William Wilkins Glenn, located on the northeast corner of Charles and Madison streets, near the Washington Monument, in Baltimore, Maryland. The house is presently the home of the University Club. *Courtesy of the Enoch Pratt Library, Baltimore.*

& I now propose to stay." He looked incredulous and went into my dressing room where my bureau was. This room underwent a thorough search & I was not a little uneasy. Tompkins, thinking I was in London had drawn on me for $1000 gold. De La Rue thoughtlessly put the draft in a Bankers hand for collection and had it forwarded to Baltimore. It had been presented during my absence in Canada & my brother, knowing that Tompkins would not have drawn unless he needed the money, had actually paid it. I had received news of this in New York & the letter from De La Rue announcing the forwarding of the draft & giving me news of some blockading friends was in my dressing bag, standing on a little couch. There was nothing in these letters, but still enough in the eyes of these men to condemn me. I helped the men to rummage & behaved with the greatest unconcern. Fortunately I had a smaller dressing case on a side table which I opened for them. Finally I had the satisfaction of seeing them leave the room & go into my chamber. "Where" said the Captain "are your papers?" "Everything, I replied, is in these two rooms. You have access to what you choose. In these drawers are papers, I have not seen for a year." On my bed were lying a number of newspaper articles written by me in England. They were corrected in my own handwriting. I was greatly relieved to see one of the men go to the bed, pick them up as waste paper look under them & toss them down again saying "There's nothing here Captain!" Finally I was marched off to the old Negro Jail, now used as the office of the Provost Marshall & was put in one of the rooms on the third story,* without having an idea what was the charge against me. Woolley was off. It was Saturday night. He did not return and finally I persuaded the man in charge to bail me for $5000 until Monday Morning. Wallis who was with me, went my bail & I came home to find my people as was natural very uneasy & much excited.

June 5. Learn that Grant has crossed the Pamunkey. Evidently on his way to the James River. Changing his base, as McClellan did once before and for the same reasons.

Found out tonight accidentally the Charges against me. Woolley had been informed that I came over from England with despatches from Mason & Slidell, and am now on my way back again from Richmond with return despatches.

June 6". Reported at Provost Marshal's. Locked up again and left

* Donovan's Slave Jail, on the southwest corner of Camden and Eutaw streets, was made a jail for prisoners of the Provost Marshal in 1863.

to cool my heels and wait the pleasure of the great man. Finally after several hours, Woolley sent for me. At first he was offensively imperious but he soon assumed a more gentlemanly tone. My perfect frankness had its effect upon him and when I treated the charges against me as perfectly absurd, showing him proof at the same time of my stay in New York & Montreal. he saw he had been misinformed. "You surely, said I, "do not know my position here. I am head of the family. I represent large property in the city and in several counties. I am a member of the bar. I know what is treason and that in committing it I am simply violating the laws of my State and of the United States. In fact I run the risk of having my property confiscated & my neck stretched. To suspect me of coming from Richmond & then stopping in a town & walking about when I cannot go a square without being known is simply to suspect that I am a fool". After some further talk, in which I said that my property was here as was my family and that I intended to remain at home, he took out a paper and wrote a parole. I was on the point of telling him that I would not sign anything, but held my tongue for the moment. He handed me the paper. It was for an indefinite time. I returned it to him and requested him to name a time within which I should be tried for any charges preferred against me. He altered it. We talked on. He was in a good humor & to my great relief, just as I had made up my mind that we would not come to terms about the parole, he tore it up. I told him if he wanted me at anytime to send for me—that one man would do as well as twenty.

Accounts coming in of Battle of Cold Harbor. Grant has lost frightfully in this campaign.

June 8". Lincoln & Andy Johnson nominated yesterday.* Great crowds at Sanitary Fair in Philadelphia. [?] Southerners go there to show their loyalty.**

June 15. News that Grant has crossed his army to Right Bank of James River. Sadly disappointed to find that he has been able to get even his remnant of an army there. Longstreets*** loss was as

* The Union National Convention met at the Front Street Theater in Baltimore on June 7–8, 1864, to nominate Lincoln and Johnson.

** The United States Sanitary Commission was inspired by the British Sanitary Commission of the Crimean War, and was an outgrowth of many women's organizations. It functioned much as the present Red Cross, caring for the wounded, providing lodging for transient soldiers, and attempting to raise the hygenic standards of army camps. Much of the finances were dependent on money raised at fairs.

*** General James Longstreet (1821–1904) was wounded on May 6, 1864, by a Minié ball in the Wilderness.

unfortunate as Stonewall Jackson's. He was moving his corps, after the battle of   to outflank Grant. They were all in the highest possible spirits. Longstreet was heard to say that in six hours there would not be a man of Grant's army left except as a prisoner or a straggler, on the peninsula. His men were fired into by a division of Confederates who mistook them. Longstreet was hit in the neck near the spine. He fell senseless and is in danger. The expedition was stopped. Luck is against us. Luck never forgives and since the failure [the following is crossed out: Davis so obstinately & foolishly refused] to profit by the fortunes of the day, after the Battle of Bull Run, the South seems never to have had such a chance again. Had Stonewall Jackson remained unhurt six hours more what might have been the consequences. If Longstreet could have remained a few hours in command what might have been the result. On such chances does the fate of war turn.

June 16. My troubles appearing over and nobody molesting me, I determined to go down to Fort McHenry & see Genl Morris. He was always glad to see me and the privilege I had of going in there and interceding for and aiding prisoners and seeing them sometimes enabled me often to render great service. Few if any other Southerners had such privileges & I determined to renew my intercourse. Took my son, Johnny, not yet six & drove down with an old pass given me by Morris in my pocket. He was much surprised to see me. "Where the devil did you come from" said he. "From England I replied. We had some further talk. I asked for Mrs. Morris & his daughter and he took me into his office, where he coolly told me that I was his prisoner. "But General Morris," said I, do "you know that I came down here to pay a friendly visit to you and Mrs. Morris". He said that made no matter. Then said I for heaven's sake let me take this boy home to his Grandmother—do not violate all laws of friendship and hospitality by arresting me in this way—let me go home & send for me tomorrow—I shall be at my house." It was all of no avail. Johnny was in the corner crying bitterly. He thought Morris was going to hang me. It had no effect upon him. Morris would not let me go & did not heed Johnny. He charged me with breaking my parole. I told him I had never given any & that he knew it—that he had chosen to tell people I had given a parole, because he was not willing to admit that anyone had gotten out of that Fort without making some terms, and that I had not thought it worthwhile to contradict him. He then charged me with being connected with a man named Richardson* hanged as

* Noah Brooks refers to the following incident after Gettyburg: "As we

a spy in Frederick Co. I assured him I had never heard of such a man. After a long talk I saw that his suspicions were considerably allayed—and I said to him "Genl Morris, you know what I say to you is true, because I tell you so. And you know I would rather lose my head than tell you what was not so". Well, said he, I believe you would. Finally he seemed quite satisfied he had made a mistake and determined to let me go. But because he had said he was ordered to arrest me, he would only turn me over to Genl Wallace. Wallace was in command of the Department & Morris had no business to arrest me anyhow. It was foul play in him as well as uncalled for. I told him that he was giving me great trouble, that the matter would now pass out of his hands & that there was no telling when I should have it settled. I begged him to let me go to Washington & see the President. Nothing would do. Seeing no other chance open, I determined to go to Wallace. This at least enabled me to go back to Baltimore & get Johnny home. Morris however would not trust me alone. He sent me up under guard, sending a written report by an officer and telling the officer to say to General Wallace "that he knew Mr. Glenn well & had implicit confidence in whatever he would say." I got away from the Fort about eight o'clock.

I did not find Wallace until nearly eleven. He was at Moor N. Falls, taking supper. His adjutant Lawrence was there and Woolley also—both of whom were always very civil to me. As soon as Wallace heard my name he was furious. "Damn him, said he make an example of him, send him to jail." And to the common jail he insisted I should go at once. Lawrence & Woolley remonstrated, stating that there was no charge whatever against me, but Wallace at first refused to listen to them and then wanted to know who would be responsible for me. Woolley at once said that he knew me but slightly but that he would be responsible for me, upon which Wallace turned me over to him. I gave him a verbal parole to appear next day.

June 17. Interview with Woolley. No charges whatever. Am inclined to think Morris was drunk yesterday. Dismissed.

galloped along the open spaces which intervened between the city of Frederick and an Army division standing at rest, we descried the body of a man dangling by a noose from a limb of a tree—a ghastly sight. This was a spy, who had been in the Army of the Potomac for several months, peddling maps and singing army songs. On his person had been found, when he was arrested, a number of minute drawings of the fortifications around Washington. . . . He was tried, condemned, and hanged as a spy." Noah Brooks, *Washington, D.C. in Lincoln's Time*. ed. Herbert Mitgang (Chicago: Quadrangle Books, 1971, p. 83). No mention of the incident can be found in the *Official Records*.

June 21. News of another terrific attack by Grant and repulse. Received a notification from Woolley to report once more. Woolley & I were on pretty good terms. I had sent him some Whiskey as a present & been a little civil to him in that way—much to the surprise of some English officers, who did not understand how I could thus openly bribe an officer. I would give them money if they wanted it.

June 22. Interview with Woolley. I told him I was tired of being thus pulled & I might as well tell him plainly that I would make no compromise whatever with the Government and the authorities might persue what course they thought proper. "I may as well tell you then, Genl Wallace's ultimatum," said he. "You are to take the oath or leave the department." This was a great relief to me for I was sure I was in for a Fort again. He then picked up a large bundle of papers & said "Your case has been thoroughly examined and there is no charge against you whatever". At this also I was well pleased, for I knew some English letters had gone wrong, which would have damaged me, if brought to my door. "I told you before Col Woolley," said I, "that there was none against me". He then asked me what personal enemies I had and if I knew who it was that continually brought malicious charges agst me. Of course I did not know. Woolley appeared quite interested on my behalf and almost insisted on my going to see Wallace & stating my case frankly, saying in his way, not meaning to be offensive "I am sure Genl Wallace does not desire to pursue anyone who keeps quiet and keeps his mouth shut. I told him my little boy was too ill for me to go now. I hardly expected him to live—but that I would go as soon as I was in better spirits.

June 23. Little Billy as ill as possible. In bad spirits & out of heart.

June 24. Determined to go and see Wallace. Sent in my card. He received me in a very insolent way, hair brushed back, feet on the table & attempting to look very ferocious. I quietly took a chair, unasked. When he asked me what I wanted, I replied that I did not know that I wanted anything but that I came at the advice & I might say command of Col Woolley. Before I could say anything more he said "Are you willing to take the oath of Allegiance" in a very swaggering way. "Oh said, I "you must pardon me. It is scarcely worth while to discuss that now". At this he waved his hands & declared that he wished to hear nothing more on the subject. It is impossible to describe the vulgar swagger of the fellow. I smiled and said "that I regretted exceedingly that I had disturbed him". He seemed only the more furious that I neither minded him nor lost my temper.

When I was fairly out of his office, I lost no time. I determined not to give him another chance at me. I went home, got my horse and buggy, took a small travelling bag and started for Pennsylvania by country roads. Wagon broke. Slept at blacksmiths at Jerusalem Mills.

June 25. Drove on to Rev. W. F. Brand's.

June 26. Drove to Hamond's [?] to dinner.

June 27. Drove to Oxford & slept.

June 28. Took cars to Wilmington & Philadelphia.

June 29. To N. York. Stopped at N.Y. Hotel. To night received letters from home. As I expected Wallace had sent for me soon after I left his office & had instructed Woolley to write to me a most insolent note, "giving me my choice. Fort McHenry during the War or exile North of New York and a fine of $10000 if I come south of that place." Having no desire to see the original of this production, I determined to quit as soon as possible. Slept very uneasily.

June 30. Up at day break and off to more quiet quarters.

July 1. [*1864*] Having got my trunk and wardrobe, off to Brattelboro.

July 3d. News of sinking of Alabama off Cherbour. Rumors of large southern army threatening Maryland.

July 5. News of evacuation of Kenesaw Mountain by Johnston & advance of Sherman. Disappointed at Johnston's retreats but suppose he has good reason. We can afford to lose territory but we cannot afford to lose men. I have great confidence in Joe Johnston.

July 7". Much excitement evidently in Pennsylvania. A large force has crossed into Maryland.*

* In July 1864, General Jubal Early crossed the Potomac into Maryland, captured Frederick, defeated General Lew Wallace at the Monocacy River in Frederick County, and headed for Washington as part of a plan to capture the capital and free the prisoners at Point Lookout in southern Maryland. The Point Lookout raid never materialized, but the presence of Confederate forces was felt from western Maryland to the shores of the Chesapeake. General McCausland occupied Hagerstown and demanded ransom, while cavalry units held Middletown and nearby Boonsboro.

July 8". Rumors wild. Nobody knows who is leading the army invading Maryland—whether it is Lee with 60000 men or Early with 16000. The Rebs are at Hagerstown.

July 10. Lew Wallace, the counter hopper General has evacuated Frederick. He is no doubt scared "out of his boots". He is a coward and incapable besides of handling an ordinary brigade.

July 11. Wallace has been completely whipped at Monocacy. Excitement intense. This really looks like business & must hurry back to Maryland to take my part. I am not content to let other men fight for the liberty of my state. I must be with them.

July 12". To New York. News of raid round Baltimore and capture of rail road train at Magnolia by Harry Gilmor. Genl. Franklin taken prisoner. Miss Harper, Dulanys and Bessie Perine on board.* Greatest excitement in Baltimore. Tom Buckler is here on his way home. Have persuaded him to stay a day or two. They will certainly seize him if he attempt to return. As soon as we know where Early is, we will go to Elkton, then go to the Water & cross the bay in a boat to H. Stump's, & then get up to B's—where my horse and wagon is. I don't want to be caught or to have to pay that fine of $10,000.

July 13. Cannot make out what is doing in Maryland. Am satisfied that the invading force is immensely overestimated. Tom Buckler & I went aboard Restless with Travers & Louisa & Hatty to take an afternoon's sail & wait for further news. Went up to Oyster Bay & anchored.

July 14". Early seems to have abandoned his attempt on Baltimore. He could have captured it without firing a gun. The greatest panic prevailed last Saturday & Sunday after Wallace's defeat at the Monocacy. The City Council or rather some of its members met and determined to surrender. The Military Authorities prepared to

Troops under General Bradley T. Johnson cut rail connections between Baltimore and Harrisburg, Pennsylvania, and occupied New Windsor in Carroll County as a unit under Colonel Harry Gilmor swept around the northern outskirts of Baltimore. It was during these raids that the homes of Governor Bradford and Montgomery Blair were burned. On July 29th Johnson returned, this time on the way to Chambersburg, Pa. In August additional raids occurred in the Hancock and Hagerstown areas of western Maryland.

* Magnolia Station of the Philadelphia, Wilmington and Baltimore Railroad was 18 miles north of Baltimore in Harford County. Both the train and the railroad bridge over the Gunpower River were burned by Harry Gilmor. According to his *Four Years in the Saddle* (New York, 1866), a Mrs. P. was responsible for the unintentional betrayal of General Franklin's presence.

evacuate. Government stores were taken from warehouse & piled in vacant lots to be fired. Valuables from banks have been removed to steamers. Everyone was busy for two days packing. Police officers seized gentlemen in the street & put them to work. Johnny Morris, Otho Williams Lehr & others were impressed and made to pack & nail up. Citizens were ordered to enroll themselves for the defense of their native town. To their shame be it said there were a good number of gentlemen, calling themselves Southern, who in their fright actually gave in their names.

Still in doubt—sailed over to New Haven.

July 15. Early has been or is in Washington. Appears to have abandoned the rest of Maryland. What can he be after? If he retreats I certainly am not going to join him. Sailed to New London.

July 16". Genl Franklin has escaped. Early has evidently has retired & crossed into Virginia. What all this means I cannot tell. He has absolutely done nothing, but capture a rail road train and burn Govr Bradford's & Mr. Blair's houses.* Sailed to Newport.

News from Georgia not encouraging. Johnston has crossed the Chattahoochie, falling back towards Atlanta. He retreats however slowly, inflicting severe loss on Sherman. Confidence in him is unabated.

July 17. Finding it useless to go back to Maryland, have sent for luggage to New York. I came aboard for an afternoon & am now travelling in Campaigning style—not the proper thing for Newport.

July 18". Made up a Yacht party—Leonard Jerome, Tom Buckler, Travers & myself—with Mrs. Ronalds, Mrs. MacVickar,** Mrs. LeRoy and Miss Lewis. It was apparently a fast party. Emma Meredith & Mr. Warden were also taken aboard, but they were mistakes. Had a very pleasant day and a very easy time of it. We enjoyed ourselves amazingly, all but Miss Meredith, who though young looking, was old enough to be the mother to some of us and pretended to be horrified, though there was nothing at all that anyone

* Governor Bradford's estate, "Montevideo," was on Charles Street and Lake Avenue in Baltimore County. It was burned July 11 in the presence of the governor's wife. Montgomery Blair's house in Silver Spring was also burned, though that of his father, next door, was spared and protected.

** The MacVickar family in New York City was quite prominent. The Rev. John MacVickar (d. 1868) was professor of moral philosophy at Columbia University. His son, Dr. John August MacVickar, who married Charlotte Neilson, practiced medicine until after 1881. Both Henry G. and William H. MacVickar were wine brokers, and are found in New York City directories from 1854 to after 1881.

could take offense at. Tom Buckler was perfectly fascinated with Mrs. Renolds. She is a Yankee girl quite pretty who married a very common man, usually known by the name of Pete, simply because he had money. Pete brought her to New York. She is very clever, very pretty, an accomplished singer and an excellent singer. She soon had two or three rich brokers in her train. Some of them made good turns in Stocks for her. Jerome built her a beautiful marble Opera House over his stable. The girl that no body would call to see two years ago, is now exclusive. She gave a handsome ball last winter, picking her company. She had a little gas jet arranged to light the back of her headdress. Society is wonderfully developed in New York since the war. I think that for immorality it fairly vies with any European Capital.

July 20. Back to Brattleboro. Early's Campaign appears to have been wretchedly mismanaged and has proved a total failure. In its results it is only a grand cattle stealing raid.

July 24. Col Jaquess and Mr. Gilmore have been to Richmond with passes from Lincoln on a peace mission. Lincoln is evidently very anxious for peace. In New York I find the people very dissatisfied. Laboring men tell me that if the Govt. attempts to enforce another draft this winter they will have a riot and that if they do not have a draft riot they will have a bread riot, for they cannot possibly stand the immense price of provisions much longer. If the South can maintain its present attitude the North cannot possibly get through this winter. Want of confidence is becoming so great that it will break down financially.

July 26. Holcomb, Clay & others have had a correspondence about Peace. They have cornered Lincoln who has written in reply a letter "To whom it may concern."

Aug 1". [*1864*] Johnston has been displaced by Davis. Hood succeeded him has attacked Sherman fiercely in Sherman's lines. If the reports be partially true Hood has lost more men in this dash than Joe Johnston did in his Campaign. Wo is me! that Jeff Davis should ruin the Cause by his personal prejudices. A speech of Davis is reported as having been made at Macon. It must be a Yankee manufacture. If Davis made it, it is disgraceful. It is the speech of a whipped hound who has lost his head.

Aug 3d. To New York, to meet mother sister & Johnny who are coming on to spend a few weeks with me, in my exile.

Aug 4". Back to Brattleboro by New Haven.

Aug. 12. To Saratoga. I suppose I am pretty safe now & need not be so careful as I have been, keeping out of public places and living in an obscure town in Vermont.

Aug 18. Had a long talk with Govr Pratt. He and several others were there, from Maryland on their way to Chicago as members of the Convention. I begged Govr Pratt not to go. I told him we had no place in the councils of Yankees. We have nothing left now but our self respect, let us preserve that. The chances are large that McClellan will receive the nomination and ill becomes a Marylander to be one of a Convention which nominates a man who has been the very first to inaugurate arbitrary arrests. Besides what have we to do with the Democrats. Can anything worse happen to this country than to have this struggle temporarily stopped and to have discordant elements patched together again. Lincoln is the man for every true Southerner. The Democrats do not mean Peace. That will only come from exhaustion. The Democrats are more false than the Republicans & have been so from the beginning. Lincoln will divide the North & unite the South. A Democrat will divide the South & unite the North.

Aug 21. To New York.

Aug 22. I met a number of men at New York Hotel from the New England States on their way to Chicago. They are very uneasy indeed about the Western states and fear that the people there are becoming so dissatisfied that they will "secede" and cut loose from the Eastern States.

Sept 4". Everything has been in the greatest turmoil and confusion. McClellan has tossed his whole party overboard, ignored the platform adopted by his Convention and made a new one for himself. He is now more warlike than the Republicans themselves and there is no issue between the two parties. He has no independence whatever & is not fit to occupy a third rate place in any respectable assembly. The whole feeling of the Convention I am assured was for Peace. Vallandingham who was at Chicago was almost worshipped—as the representative of Peace. He was cheered & applauded on all occasions. Members of the Convention told me that through the whole country through which they passed, the feeling of the people appeared to be strongly for peace and they thought that they would carry a peace candidate by a large majority. McClellan's friends however had it cut and dried before they went there and played their cards pretty well, hurrying his nomination through. If there had been one or two good men to take a stand against him, he would have been beaten. Ben Harris spoke plainly & well but he lost his temper.   speech was better, but neither of them were supported. The truth is there never was a peace party in the North, for the reason that there never were men of sufficient moral courage to lead it. This was McClellan's great want. This was why I always distrusted him. Cowardice too often causes falsehood. I found out on the 27" Augt. from a telegraph operator, who had no business to tell, that Marble had first telegraphed to Barlow that the platform was against them. It was plain from this that McClellan was not satisfied to stand out as a Peace Man & next day I told Mr. Bayard—who was then in New York—what my suspicions were. He could not agree with me. I told him to go & see Barlow, which he did and came back very much concerned, for he placed great hopes in McClellan & a peace platform, not that he thought well of McClellan, but that he thought events would control him. Next day most of the members returned from Chicago, who passed through New York. Among them was Govr. Pratt. He could not believe what I told him and declared that if McClellan did not accept the platform in good faith the convention should be called together and another nomination made. He said he would write to the committee himself requesting them to call the convention together. Govr. Weller declared that he would join him and said he would at once write to Pendleton and beg him not to accept until he knew what course McClellan intended to take. Next day Govr Pratt and I went to see Barlow and in the evening met some gentlemen at his house. They were all of one mind. They saw in this Campaign a mere political campaign & proposed to work the machinery in the usual political style. They could not take a broad view of the question. Next day Starke of Oregon & Govr Weller were as violent as possible at the anticipated breach of faith on the part of McClellan. Finally the Committee of Nomination came to New York. Finding out what McClellan proposed they went to his house to have an interview and finally agreed to write a letter to suit his answer which he had prepared. Barlow said to Govr. Seymour "Why not write it now?" and Seymour & another member went in McClellan's office and there wrote such a letter of nomination as would suit him. Next day at the ratification meeting Weller actually spoke as a McClellan and Starke talked as if he were nothing else. The conduct of all these men was disgraceful. They showed themselves to be mere politicians of the lowest stamp. They cared for nothing but party success and were willing to secure that even at the expense of the country. I thought at first that the McClellan letter was the production of McClellan's advisers knowing that he is a weak man. But Barlow assures me I am wrong. He says McC prepared this letter himself and that the only material change made in it was that he had said "in case negotiations were not successful, there was nothing left but the dread arbitrament of war". This both Barlow & Cassidy told him looked too much like a threat. He asked them what they would say. Cassidy replied say "that in this event the responsibility will rest with those who are in arms against the Union". That will do as well answered McClellan, for it means the same thing.

John Morrissey the Pugilist says McClellan aint much for he aint got no combination. He says any man can fight and get knocked down, but that it is a very difficult thing to stand a long time and take a beating & wait for your turn to come. He added "I whipped Heenan because I knowed Heenan hadn't got any combination. He beat me to a jelly & I couldn't see, but I knowed I only had to wait and he would give in and he did. There is times in a man's life when a man has to think—when a great deal of judgment is required. Then you see what a man is. But McClellan he aint got no combination.*

Sept 21. [1864] Lincoln hearing that I preferred him to McClellan sent me a card permitting me to return to Maryland & remain so long as I behaved myself. A great country truly—but I have no idea of Electioneering for him or any body else.

All the Peace men have broken ranks like sheep. They could not bear the idea of being out of the ring. Men who condemned McClellans course without stint now support him. The cry is "We must not split the party". Is there not one man left in the whole Northern States. Ben Wood's paper was very shaky for a day or two, but it is out again in a manly way. He and his paper are exceptions to the rule.

Sept 30. Pendleton's course is the most pitiful of all. The committee fearing he might give them trouble deliberately insulted him by not notifying him of his nomination. He waited but in vain. They took no more notice of him than if he was a dog. At last someone told him that they considered that he had accepted his presence at Chicago as an acceptance of the nomination. This was all fudge for

* John Morrissey defeated John C. Heenan in an eleven-round fight on October 20, 1858. It is recorded that Heenan broke his hand in the first round.

I know that Barlow & McClellan's friends considered him a dead weight and would have paid handsomely to get rid of him. Efforts were made to toss him overboard. But Pendleton was not to be gotten rid of. He too after all is but a politician. He agreed to pocket the snub—and finally wrote to Belmont—Belmont told me so—as Chairman of the Central Committee, telling him that if it was desirable he would come on to New York & speak. He actually put his honor in the hands, I may say, of the very men who were insulting him. He did come on to New York, spoke and denied his former record like a scrub. Belmont was standing near him on the balcony of the N.Y. Hotel while he spoke. I turned round and said "Well you have whipped him in beautifully. He talks Union & War as if he believed nothing else. How did you manage it?" "The best of it, replied Belmont, is that he has done it all of his own accord. No one here has said a word to him". These politicians are all alike. They prostitute themselves for place and then know no shame.

Octr 8". [*1864*] Started for Baltimore, taking under my charge Mrs. Julius Pringle and her daughter Mary. These two women had recently arrived from Europe. They were in great trouble. Mr. Pringle had died a few months previously in Rome. Poinsett Pringle the favorite son had recently been killed in Virginia. The other two sons were both in the army and Mrs. P., who was in a nervous state, was dreading the receipt of bad news from them, the campaign being active. They had staid, for the first few days, at Mrs. LeCin's [?]—a sister of Mrs. P's—but the difference in feeling & the total want of sympathy manifested, rendered residence there unbearable. Poor as they were, they came to the N.Y. Hotel and took one room together. Mrs. P. was determined to get south underground, if a pass could not be obtained. She was so fortunate as to get a pass and the two left this afternoon in the Norfolk Boat, to be sent through the lines and to take their share of the privations of Southern life, after four years residence abroad.

No. 4

1865

Febry 15. The draft which was ordered for today, as I supposed, has not gone into effect. Government has had too much experience of the worthlessness of drafted men to attempt to enforce a conscription, if it can possibly avoid it. Men who enlist voluntarily as substitutes may stay of their own free will. Men who are drafted are sure not to stay if they can help it. In New York there are other reasons why the draft should not be enforced. It is not desirable to irritate the populace. The quota of New York City was fraudulently estimated as complete last autumn, simply because the Administration dared not then enforce the draft. The lower classes were quite ripe for a riot. More than one of the rail roadmen said to me "If the draft is enforced, there will be a riot. If it is not there will be a bread riot". But the successes of Sherman and the insane belief which seized the Northern mind about the inability of a portion of the South to defend itself and the desire of the rest of the people to return into this "blessed Union", gave people confidence in the ability of Government to sustain itself & pay its debt. Gold consequently went down and with it the prices of provisions, while the rates for labor were not diminished. Now however another element is making itself felt. The withdrawal of labor for the past four years from Agricultural pursuits has so largely diminished production that prices are now from two to five times as high as they formerly were. Chickens that formerly cost 62¢ a pair now cost $3.50 and so in proportion, although Gold is only two for one. This must affect the lower classes seriously.

If Sherman march through South Carolina the Administration will feel itself strong enough to enforce the draft. It is very wise not to attempt to enforce what it cannot carry out with ease. I was much struck with Ben Wood's account of the attempt to arrest him, early in the war. His paper, the Daily News, was at that time excluded from the Associated Press. He got the news however by bribing the majority of the telegraph operators between Washington & New York, which game he continued until the Associated Press gave in. When the order for his arrest came over the wires one of the operators sent it to him, before delivering it to the Marshal. Wood immediately sent for two or three roughs, told them what had happened and gave them three days to get their men together, at which time he said he would be back. He then took the train to

Albany. In the Cars was Bob Lincoln, beside whom Wood took a seat. They had a long chat & when they reached Albany went into the Delavan house to lunch. Some one there called Bob out and told him who Wood was and to be careful how he talked to him. Bob reseated himself. Soon after Seward came in & in his company Wood went on towards Canada. Seward made no attempt to detain him. After staying three days at the Clifton House Wood returned. He was not molested. Seward knew it would be impolitic & had telegraphed Cameron "to attend to his business & he would attend to his State". So much for a little nerve. What a different state of things we might have had in Maryland had our men been true to each other and to themselves.

Hon Duncan F. Kenner, C.S. Senator reached New York on Friday last, by the underground route. He sailed on Saturday for Europe, having gone out it is supposed on an important mission. He said that in Blair's last interview with President Davis he told Mr. Davis "that if the South would send Commissioners across the lines, they would be received and nothing should be said about recognition for the present, provided the South would agree to join forces with the North, carry out the Monroe doctrine and drive the French out of Mexico". This is certainly a very different story from Mr. Lincoln's. His letters to Seward published after the failure of negotiations would lead one to believe that it was the South which was most desirous of compromise, but that the North could accept no terms short of unconditional surrender. All this is to hide his real motives, now that he has failed, and to set himself before the people as a staunch and uncompromising champion. People say North that "Old Abe has now made an honest effort for Peace" Honest! God save the mark! What duplicity!

On Sunday, 12" inst, a negro preacher, H. H. Garnett [*sic*] was allowed to preach in the Hall of the House of Representatives. Is he a John the Baptist—and who is to come after him. Shall we have a civilized gorilla next? Last week a negro was admitted to practice in the Supreme Court.* How long before Lincoln will invite them to diplomatic dinners and lead the way to table with a greasy wench hanging on his arm.

Febry 17". It is stated at Washington privately that France is about to demand the recognition of Mexico. If so, Lincoln must either submit to the demand and receive a minister from Maximilian

* John S. Rock was admitted to the bar of the Supreme Court on February 1, 1865. He was sponsored by Senator Charles Sumner of Massachusetts.

or must expect to see Napolean recognize the South. The rumor has been gaining ground very strongly that after the 4" March, France, Austria, Spain and the Papal States intend only to recognize Lincoln as President of the Free States. It is quite possible however that Napoleon may have circulated this report for the purpose of inducing the North to recognize Maximilian. If this happen. he will toss Slidell and all the Southern party, that he had succeeded in fooling, overboard without the slightest hesitation. He is very false and has been from the beginning. As far as I could see, he was in reality much more the cause of the non recognition of the South than Lord Russell's Cabinet. Mr. Dudley Mann told me last year that in 1862, Leopold, King of the Belgians, being thoroughly convinced of the right of the Southern States to secede and form a separate government, entered into a long correspondence with Napoleon upon the subject and received such assurances from him as to lead him to believe that Napoleon was willing and ready to receive Mr. Slidell as Minister from the Confederate States. A personal interview was finally agreed upon and Leopold proceeded to Paris, preceded by Dudley Mann, who went to consult with Mr. Slidell and to arrange all necessary details. These two were so certain of the immediate recognition of the independence of the South, that they wrote to their friends in Maryland that it was no longer a matter of months but of weeks. I saw myself one letter from Dudley Mann to that effect. When Leopold reached Paris, to his very great surprise, Napoleon refused to make any proposition whatever to England about recognition. All that he could be got to do, was to make a proposal to mediate. This suited neither King Leopold nor Mr. Slidell. They assured the Emperor that England would certainly not agree to mediate—that there was no sense in it, that it could lead to nothing and that at best it was like putting one's finger between the hammer and the anvil. The Emperor was firm. The proposition to mediate was made and rejected—as was expected. Here the matter dropped. The Emperor could not be induced to make any other propositions, although he was assured that in all probability Lord Russell would agree to a joint recognition. Napoleon got credit with the world for being friendly to the South and England for being hostile. Napoleon had played his game, Lord Russell had simply held his tongue.

I heard nothing more of recognition until early in 1864. Mr. Mann had given up all hopes of recognition from England and had received orders to leave London finally. He was in Paris. Frank Lawley, brother of Lord Wenlock & at that time Southern Correspondent of the London Times arrived in England from Richmond. Everybody was anxious to learn from him his opinion of the prospects of the South and he was much sought after, in a quiet way, although he did not show publicly, on account of some unsettled "debts of honor". Napoleon, hearing of him & knowing the family, sent over for him & in a few days Lawley left for Paris. He was in high spirits and flattered himself that the new line of argument which he would take would have great influence with the Emperor. The interview took place in due time & was continued for an unusually long time. Lawley left in high spirits, gave a glowing account of the interview to Mr Slidell and assured him that it was very evident that the friendly disposition of the Emperor would soon manifest itself. Within a few days after this it was reported in Paris that Palmerston had said to a French gentleman that "he thought the time was come to recognize the South and that for his part he wished the South was recognized"—a report which by the way was very prevalent in England. Drouyn de l'Huys sent for Slidell, told him that the Emperor had heard this story and that he was very anxious to know if it is true and gave him to understand that if the report was really correct, there was very little doubt but that it would lead to a speedy recognition. Mr. Slidell was quite taken in by the assurance of M. de l'Huys, and the rumor was soon spread that France was about to recognize the South. I was at the time down in Herts hunting. On going up to London, to my great surprise, I found Mr. Mason back again and evidently come to stay. The same day, Gregory (W. H.) M.P. called to see me and told me the rumor was quite true, that it was believed at the Foreign Office and that he had it from Evelyn Ashley private Secretary to Lord Palmerston. I could not be persuaded to place any reliance upon the report. A few days later Drouyn de l'Huys again sent for Mr Slidell and asked him if he had verified the report as to Lord Palmerston's sentiments as made the frenchman before alluded to. Mr. Slidell answered that it was not for him to verify the report and that even if it were verified, that there was no particular use in it; that if the Emperor was really in earnest, his course was a very simple one. He had only to send over a confidential messenger to England and enquire of the Ministry if England would recognize jointly with France. If the proposition is refused, said Mr Slidell, it compromises no one, but it will not be refused. I have every reason to believe that Lord Palmerston will at once accept the proposition, and such is the feeling among the better classes of English society in favor of the South, that I do not believe you will meet much opposition if any from Lord Russell". To this de l'Huys had nothing more to say. Here the matter dropped and in a few days Mr Mason departed from London as quickly and as quietly as he had come. So much for the wily Emperor. Mr. Mason did not trust him. Mr Slidell put more faith in him, but then the Emperor & Empress were both very civil to Mrs Slidell and her two daughters. Mr. Slidell liked his position in Paris very much.

Senator Foote went on the train with me on Tuesday last week to New York, having just come through the lines. He was in company with a federal officer, apparently under guard. He left on the steamer of Saturday the 11" evidently on business for this Government with whom he had some understanding. He saw Mr. G. W. Dobbin, on his way to Baltimore and told him among other things that he had been opposed to the action of the Southern States from the beginning and that he had been desirous of getting up a counter revolution in the South. He is evidently a false villain—bad as well as foolish.

Govr Pratt came up this morning from Annapolis. He gave me an account of his late interview with the President. Tom Pratt, a Lieut in the Marine Corps, was in Fort Fisher, during the bombardment. He was slightly wounded in the foot, taken prisoner & brought to Fortress Monroe. Montgomery Blair obtained permission for Govr. & Mrs Pratt to go down and see him, which they accordingly did. On his return Govr P. went again to Washington to endeavor to obtain Tom's release upon parole. Montgomery Blair assured him it was useless, as he had tried it himself. Notwithstanding this Govr P. went to see the Secretary of the Navy. "I know" said Mr. Welles "that the President wishes to oblige you and I advise you to go & make your application personally". Govr P. did so, found Lincoln in a very good humor and soon obtained all that he wanted and indeed much more than he had hoped for after his interview with Blair. "Now Governor" said Lincoln "let me see, what I can do and how I can do it. I want to oblige you, but the trouble is, if I do this thing, these men around me will raise such a row about it. But never mind, I'll do it" and down he sat, picked up one of the little cards on which he habitually writes his "orders" and wrote an order for the release of Lieut Thomas St. G. Pratt on parole to commit no act of hostility to the U.S. Government and to deliver himself up when required by the President. Gov P. was also required to give his bond for his appearance. After this the two had a long and rather confidential talk. The Governor is much amused, very pleased and tells me he cannot imagine why the President should wish to favor him. I know very well & so I think does the Governor. In 1861, after the riot of the 19" April, when the State was in a great ferment, the 7" Regiment of N. York were landed at Annapolis & proceeded to march to Washington. They were greatly in fear of an attack from volunteer associations of Marylanders along the route, and as they were in a strange country, where the roads were very bad, they could easily have been terribly cut up by small bands of mounted guerillas. Holliday Hicks was then Governor & in Annapolis. He wrote a note to Govr Pratt, begging him to do all he could to suppress an outbreak and prevent bloodshed and State Civil Warfare. Govr. Pratt accordingly did write to his son in law Daniel Clarke of Prince George's, who was Captain, I think, of a volunteer Mounted Company and to several others telling them that an attack on U.S. troops would be dangerous and useless, as Maryland was still a state in the Union and bound to obey the laws of the U States, she having taken no steps either in Convention or by her Legislature, to throw off her allegiance. When Govr Pratt was seized last summer and sent to Fortress Monroe, Mrs. Pratt wrote these facts to Montgomery Blair and stated to him what was probably true "that Govr Pratt had done more than anyone else to prevent an outbreak". "Well" said Blair "if this is correct, this will do more than anything else to free him from arrest and more than counterbalances anything against him". He was released immediately & Lincoln desired an interview. The Govr. went to Washington. "I do not think" said Lincoln, on meeting him that you have suffered any from your imprisonment. On the contrary, I suspect it has improved you a little." "If you think so Mr President replied he "I advise you to get shut up at once, for I swear I never saw a man who wanted a little improvement more than you. And so they laughed, and Old Abe held out his hand and said that though their sentiments were different, that was no reason why they should not exchange views, and they sat down and had a pow-wow.

Feb 18". Mr. Masons letter to A. Coolidge, Boston dated London, Jany 25" was republished in this morning's Daily News. It is very well put and covers the whole ground as to the treatment of the Confederate prisoners in the different Northern forts. There is no doubt that it has been the policy of the present Administration, since the fall of Vicksburg, when Exchanges were stopped, to force prisoners by ill treatment, starvation, and protracted confinement to take the oath of allegiance and to kill as many as possible of those who refused to make terms.

Bernal, Br. Consul, showed me a letter he had received today from Col St. Leger Grenfell, accused of complicity in the attempt to release the prisoners from Fort Johnson, made a few months since, in October I think, of which Grenfell says he was totally ignorant. G. says "they have tried hard to kill me & I have suffered much from solitary confinement in a cell 6 ft by 3½, ill ventilation & bad food. I had the dysentery when I was shut up. Yesterday my Irons were knocked off for the first time." He also said that the story about his willingness & proposal to take service in the Northern Army, was all a farce; that Stanton had offered him a commission but that he had refused it.

This Grenfell is a regular swash-buckler. He has passed his life in warfare, and has seen service in Spain in the Carlos troubles, in Algeria, where I think he held a commissoin under Abu El Kadar, in India & in Italy. He was John Morgan's right hand man & was of great assistance to him, though he had quite an amicable quarrel with him when he got married and assured him, that he Morgan "would never be worth a damn hereafter".*

He was very fond of talking of Morgan's dash & coolness. He told me that on one occasion, while they were out scouting, Morgan became separated from the party and riding alone came suddenly, at a turn in the road, on a picket guard composed of a Corporal & five men. Fortunately they were dismounted. Morgan rode straight to them and cried out in a stern voice "What is the meaning of this? You know d—d well, the regulations are strict and the order requires that at no time should more than one half of a guard be dismounted at one time. Consider yourself under arrest. There! lay down your side arms. Never mind your horses. March! Corporal, let them fall in and start. I will follow you". They fell in & marched off sullenly. Morgan rode up to the Corporal, cocked his pistol and said "I am John Morgan". The next day in camp the Corporal asked permission to enlist. He said he was very much ashamed of himself, that he had been taken completely by surprise and that he could not return to the Federal service.

On another occasion Morgan & Grenfell were riding together, scouting when the [*sic*] came upon a patrole of a Captain & thirty men. "Well, said Grenfell, here is a nice scrape." "Hush", said Morgan & up he rode to the Captain, whom he berated much in the same manner as he had done the Corporal. "Who are you?

* John H. Morgan married his second wife, Miss Martha Ready of Murfreesboro, Tennessee, on Sunday, December 14, 1862, with Bishop Leonidas Polk officiating.

said he, and what regiment do you belong to?" "And pray who are you", asked the Captain, after replying to his interrogatories. Oh! said Morgan, "I'll soon let you see who I am. I am General so & so," mentioning said Grenfell some name, supposed to be that of a Yankee General, which was however perfectly unknown to him & "I've a great notion to put you under arrest. But come along. I am out looking for John Morgan's men & I will picket you about in Squads where you may be of service". Off they marched, Morgan intending to place them where he could capture them in detail. As luck would have it however, they had scarcely proceeded a mile down the road, before they encountered a Federal regiment of Mounted Cavalry. "D—n it," said Grenfell, "it is all up now, anyhow". "Keep quiet," said Morgan and he rode deliberately up to the Colonel in command, told him that he met these men in a disorganized state, that they deserved to be placed under arrest and added that he would turn them over to him, as he Morgan was on a scouting expedition and did not wish to be bothered with them. He then coolly rode down the line, his horse walking, the reins hanging carelessly over his neck & Grenfell following him. As they neared the last rank, "Come along Grenfell" cried Morgan & gathering their horses together, they gave them the spur, put them over a low fence on the side of the road and were lost among the trees, before they heard the sharp crack of the rifles and the noise of the bullets which splintered the barks of the trees.

In June last Grenfell was in Baltimore for a day. He had gone to Richmond to make some application for Morgan, who was then rather in disgrace for having disobeyed orders and gone off on an independent expedition. He saw President Davis, who declined to grant his request. The two had some words and Grenfell, in a huff, threw up his commission and took passage in a Blockade runner for Nassau or Bermuda, I forget which. He found some difficulty there in getting a passage to Halifax and determined to come to New York. The American Consul gave him a passport. He arrived in New York & reported to Genl Dix, who after some consideration, remarked that he would not place him under arrest. This he said knowing that he had a pass from the American Consul, under which he came. Dix added however, that he must go to Washington & report to the Secretary of War. This he did & soon after left for Canada. He always regretted the foolish step he had taken & if he had not been thrown into prison, I have no doubt, he would have managed to get back before this.

February 21". Prisoners for Exchange continue to pass through. Those today are in a most wretched condition. Pale and emaciated they hardly had strength to stand. Some of them had silver sixpences, which they held up & begged for bread. Miss Barney, who saw them, could not stand the sight. They looked she said as if they hardly had strength enough to hold up the little coin, which they must by the way have had by them for a long time. One man a few days since came down the Street with nothing on him but a pair of drawers and a blanket. Blood marked the track of his bare feet. Miss Williamson* appealed to an officer to allow her to give him some clothing, but was rudely refused. Afterwards as they passed Robt. Brent's, Miss Brent,** who was quite a beauty, was more successful. She took the man, gave him some garments and a pair of slippers. On the boat that took them to Fortress Monroe they were huddled together in a distressing manner with very little protection against the cold and driving rain—for the day was as bad as winter days can be.

I send my cousin Sewall Glenn, Prisoner at Fort Delaware, a ten dollar note occasionally. They allow small sums of money to go in from relations and he writes me, that with twenty five cents a day he can escape starvation. I can get no money to his brother Elias Glenn, who is prisoner at Point Lookout although they allowed his mother to send him a small box last week.

There never has been any excuse whatever for the very brutal treatment of the Southern Prisoners in Northern Forts. It has been the result of a systematic attempt to force as many as possible to take the Oath of Allegiance and to kill off as many as possible of those who would not. The winter has been very hard—uncommonly so. The prisoners in all the forts have been poorly clad and naturally required more animal food. They got neither clothing nor food in anything like sufficient quantities. Now that winter is nearly over and Exchanges have again commenced they are a little better off for clothing—the agreement by which Cotton was allowed to come out for the benefit of Prisoners in the North and food & clothing permitted to be sent South, having gone into effect. Genl. Beall who was detailed by the South to attend to this matter, has

* David and Maria Williamson of Baltimore had five daughters: Virginia (d. 1872) and Mary Antoinette (1823–1872)—both nuns; Rebecca (d. 1898), who had married John Mullen in 1864, Julianna (1828–1899), who became Mrs. Jervis Spencer, and Henrietta M. (d. 1887), who became Mrs. Louis Montgomery.

** Robert Brent lived at 93 Cathedral Street, Baltimore. He had five daughters, who are listed in his obituary as Mrs. William Keyser, Mrs. Dunbar Hunt, and the three Misses Brent.

been for some time out on parole and is working hard. He has some good assistants in New York, where by the way, a large quantity of clothing has arrived from England, evidently part of the proceeds of the Confederate Bazaar held in Liverpool. A considerable portion of this at least will find its way to the prisoners notwithstanding the very rough & uncourteous refusal of Seward to the request made by Lord Wharncliffe.

Of all the sins which rest upon the head of Jeff Davis, it does strike me, that the sad wail, which has gone up from the prisons of the North, is perhaps the heaviest. From the outbreak of the War, to the present day, there has been no single act of humanity or common decency which the North has done voluntarily. It has been kicked into everything. Exchanges went on regularly until the fall of Vicksburg. Until then the South had captured the largest number of prisoners. As soon as the North had a considerable majority, Exchanges suddenly stopped and have now only recommenced when the numbers are again nearly equal and when the pressure from the friends of those imprisoned in the South is so great, that the Administration deems it prudent to give in. But for the Capture of the garrison of Vicksburg, that stoppage of Exchanges never would have occurred. The loss of 30,000 men I attribute to Jeff Davis. I do full justice to Davis as a gentleman, as a man of high tone, as a man who in the severest trials has preserved his dignity and who has issued state papers which are models of manly ability. I believe that in the beginning no one in the Country possessed the Confidence of the South in a greater degree than Davis and did more by his simple nomination to strengthen & consolidate the Young Confederacy. Even afterwards the determination with which he pushed the conscription did him great credit. But Davis unfortunately is a man [of] quick temper, strong attachments and bitter prejudices. His wife says laughingly "Mr. Davis has two faults. He is too fond of West Point officers and his first wife's relations".* He has another. He is too fond of exercising sole and entire control. Not satisfied with being great in the Cabinet, he aimed to show himself great in the field. Not content with ruling as the head he desired to control subordinate departments and he surrounded himself generally with men whom he could easily influence and who would submit to him. Mr. Mallory Secretary of the Navy and Memminger Secretary of the Treasury were sad instances of this. If he had tried, Mr. Davis could not have selected two more incompetent men.

* Jefferson Davis's first wife was Sarah Knox Taylor (d. 1835), daughter of General Zachary Taylor.

What has been however the cause of most disaster to the South, on the part of Mr. Davis, is his quarrel with Genl Joe Johnston. Of course we have not the accurate data here they have in the South, but there always has been communication kept up and I believe my information is pretty correct. In 1861 Johnston was at Harpers Ferry. Beauregard was at Manassas. Johnston sent word to Richmond that Patterson was in front of him with a superior force and could at any time outflank him & cut him off. And that he must retreat & take a position where he could communicate with Beauregard. Davis sent back word "to stay where he was". Beauregard sent a similar message with regard to McDowell, who opposed him, and received a similar answer. This request was made by Johnston & Beauregard more than once. Not being satisfied with this Richmond generalship, they kept up constant communication ["with each other" is crossed out] and pledged themselves to support each other. Finally Johnston destroyed Harper's Ferry & fell back to Winchester, contrary to orders but luckily. When there he received orders to evacuate his old position, Davis having received positive information that McDowell was about to attack. Johnston hurried over to the battlefield. Beauregard offered him the command, which Johnston declined to take. Beauregard fought the army until McDowell had so far flanked him as to necessitate an entire change of line and plan. Johnston then took Command, giving to Beauregard command of one of the Wings. In the afternoon as the right wing of McDowell's army, after a long dusty & circuitous march had not only outflanked but almost completely surrounded the Southern army, part of Johnston's forces appeared on the scene of action, came up at a most opportune moment in the very place they were most needed, out flanked the flanking party and flung it into confusion. By a wonderful piece of luck the Battle of Bull Run was won. The rout was total. This victory was entirely owing to Johnston's action, in violation of orders from Davis. [The following paragraph has been crossed out:] The Southern army next morning and indeed during the week following, might have marched unmolested certainly to the Susquehannock. Late in the afternoon Genl Thomas* arrived from Richmond with several thousand reinforcements. He reported to Johnston who directed him to hold himself in readiness to advance the first thing next morning. He saw Beauregard who told him, the army would advance as soon as it could be got in order. When

* The "General Thomas" mentioned here cannot be identified. General Edward Lloyd Thomas was at *Second* Bull Run. As Glenn later crossed out this story, it is probable that there was misinformation involved.

he told Mr Davis that he held himself in readiness to advance, Davis replied "No! we stop hère"—and stop there he did in opposition to his Generals. [The text then continues.]

Some months after that when McClellan was preparing to transport his forces to the Peninsula, Davis ordered Johnston to fall back to protect Richmond. Johnston objected. He said "let McClellan go if he chooses and I will promise you to make such demonstrations here as will call him away soon enough. I will defend Richmond here". It had been a favorite plan with Johnston from the beginning to enter into Maryland, give the citizens a chance to rise and to attack Washington from the Maryland side. This move had been forbidden by Davis. So now, Davis would not listen to Johnstons plan. Johnston went to Richmond & consulted with Lee, who endorsed him. After his return to his army however, Davis became uneasy and sent a peremptory order for him to fall back. He came to Richmond and told Davis that he would obey his orders of course but that he could not undertake to make a fight at York town, where he could be so easily outflanked. Davis agreed not to insist on this. After the army had taken up its new position and affairs had assumed a more favorable aspect, Davis asked Johnston "what he thought of matters now". Oh! replied Johnston, alluding to McClellan "if that grave digger goes to work with spade and shovel instead of pushing on, of course that gives us time".

Afterwards when they fell back to Richmond, Johnston insisted on evacuation. He did not consider his army large enough to hold it and the place was not then strongly fortified. His idea was to wait till he could fight one decisive battle and gain that in the interior where there could be no retreat to gunboats. Davis would not listen to this plan. At the battle of Seven Pines Johnston was wounded. He still insisted that Richmond was at the mercy of McClellan. When however after the Seven days battles McClellan was driven to seek refuge under his gunboats on the James, Davis called to see Johnston and said "Well General, you see they have not taken Richmond yet." "More fools they" replied he "it is because they have not got a general who knows his strength and how to wield it."

After recovering from his wound, Johnston reported himself ready for service. No notice being taken of this, he after a considerable period applied for active service. He was given command of the Western department. When he went out there he found that his command was a nominal one, for Bragg had orders to report to Richmond directly and so had Pemberton. Johnston immediately set himself to work to do the best that he could. Braggs army was thoroughly demoralized. J. gave new tone and life to it, got in deserters and in fact reorganized it—for which he received Braggs warmest thanks. He then went towards Vicksburgh [*sic*]. Grant had moved down the river & was about commencing his march from below. Johnston was now suddenly placed in absolute command, but too late. He sent orders to Pemberton not to fight in detail and not to allow himself to be shut up. Pemberton disobeyed orders, allowed himself to be cut up in detail lost all his light artillery and then shut himself up in Vicksburgh. Grant besieged the place and fortified his own lines strongly in the rear. Johnston did what he could and after nearly three weeks had expired got together 18,000 men and 20 pieces of artillery most of them drawn by oxen. To attack Grant alone he considered hopeless, but he sent orders to Pemberton to fight his way out & promised to cooperate. Pemberton surrendered—and the number of prisoners taken by Grant made the balance largely in favor of the North.

After this Davis, who still insisted on Sticking to Bragg, notwithstanding his very great unpopularity with his army, being obliged to yield to public sentiment sent Johnston out not to replace Bragg, but to enquire into the condition of the army. It was a trying position to place a man. Johnston informed the President that he would make the examination, but should it prove unfavorable to Genl Bragg, he begged the President to understand that under the circumstances he could not accept the command, were Bragg removed. Johnston however reported that he did not think the removal of Bragg was necessary.

Afterwards Johnston was placed in command and in 1864 the campaign of Sherman which ended in the fall of Savannah commenced. When Johnston was in Atlanta Mr. Davis insisted on knowing his plan of campaign and wished to know if he pledged himself to hold Atlanta. Genl. Johnston is a man of few words; always reticent. He did not satisfy Mr. Davis. Davis offered the command to Hardee who declined it. Urgent representations were made to Mr. Davis. He would listen to none of them. He gave the appointment to Hood. The removal of Johnston produced great dissatisfaction. Davis' friends charged that the army was demoralized by the continued retreats of Johnston. It certainly was demoralized, not by his retreats, but by his removal. He tells his own story in a letter written to Louis Washington, which Mr. Washington had with him in Paris. It said.

Macon Augt 13" 1864.

My dear Sir.—I have had the pleasure to receive your friendly letter. The reasons assigned for my removal are "failing to arrest the advance of the enemy to the vicinity of Atlanta, far in the interior of Georgia" and "not expressing confidence that I could defeat or expel him".

After the battles of the Wilderness Genl Lee adopted precisely the course which I followed and gained great glory by it. He fell gack as far as I had done and much more rapidly or rather less slowly. The enemy also penetrated much more deeply and extensively into Virginia than into Georgia. I have never known sensible men to regard confident language as evidence of merit.

Five days before my removal Genl Bragg assured me that he had maintained in Richmond that Sherman's army was stronger than Grant's. It is very certain that Genl Lee's was much larger than mine. Genl Lee's course has satisfied the Government and country and added to his great glory. The relative strength of Sherman's army and mine made the chances of victory, in case we attacked, in his favor. At Dalton he had a fortified pass close in his rear, as a place of refuge in case of mishap. In moving South, he advanced fortifying and therefore always had an entrenched position close behind him. Victory could not have been decisive for us under such circumstances, while defeat would have been ruinous. We therefore kept near him, to take advantage of any exposure of himself that he might make (but he made none of a general character, such as would have justified battle) and repelled his almost daily partial assults with trifling loss; while, he, on all such occasions, suffered heavily. We fell back before him 93 miles about in 72 days. The sum of our losses was about 10000; his we estimated at four times as much, from the opinions of experienced officers, reports of prisoners taken daily and statements of Northern papers. This course continued would have soon so reduced the disparity of numbers, as to have given us the advantage in battle, and if we could have defeated the enemy on this side of the Chattahoochie, his destruction was certain. I therefore thought and still think my plan of operations correct.

We are living here quietly and comfortably in spite of the excessive heat. Give my regards to Whiting and believe me

Yours very truly. J. E. Johnston.

Genl. Hood took command and in less than three days lost more men than Johnston had lost in his whole campaign. Soon after he lost Atlanta. Then he marched into Tennessee and lost all he had gained. He took a magnificent army. He left it a wreck.

Some time after Hood took command, Col Donaldson, A.Q.M. General, I think to Sherman, arrived in Baltimore on leave. He said that when Sherman received the news of the removal of Johnston, the rejoicing at headquarters was great; that up to that time Sherman had lost 50000 men and could never have pursued his march into Georgia had it not been for the continual reinforcements he had received. This corroborates Johnston's statement as to numbers.

Febry 22d. Great rejoicing over the evacuation of Charleston and the raising the flag over Fort Sumter. Flags are waving and loyalty is exultant.

Singularly enough Joe Johnston's official report is published in today's Daily News. It shows clearly that Johnston did not assume the offensive in the beginning, because he was interfered with by President Davis; that he did not attack at Etowah, because Hood and Polk both assured him their troops could not sustain their positions, although Hardee, who had the weakest position spoke with more confidence; that he did not take the offensive on another occasion because Hood did not obey orders and attack by daybreak as he was ordered and that he had evidently made all preparations to hold Atlanta. It is evident from the report that Bragg was with him under false colors, that he asked no questions & demanded no explanations, although he had been sent there by Davis to report. When we take into consideration Johnston's behavior towards Bragg when he was sent into Kentucky on a similar mission, this certainly shows very badly for Bragg. It does not show well either for Davis that he should have selected Bragg for this mission. It struck me at the time that Davis must have been goaded almost to desperation by the attacks constantly made upon him, that he removed Johnston in temper and that he made his speech immediately after at Macon, which showed so thoroughly the difficulties of the Southern and gladdened the Northern heart so much, in the same bad spirit. That speech to me was disreputable.

Johnston's report is admirable. When we think of the noble army he left, excellent in morale, superb in condition, holding at bay a superior army, forcing his adversary to fight his way at heavy disadvantage and then reflect upon the thousands of lives lost since then, of prisoners taken of material gone, of the entire disorganization of the whole force, and of the country thrown open to Sherman and of the prestige acquired by him, equal to many victories, it is indeed the saddest picture of the war. I do always feel inclined to repeat, what I said when Vicksburgh fell, "that the unanimity of the South is shown in the fact that it is fighting this war against the North and against Jeff Davis and that when it gains its independence it will be in spite of Davis".

More prisoners through to day. Some ladies tried to get food [to] them in the morning, but their baskets were taken from them and they stood told that the "damned wretches" should not have a mouthful. Later in the day there was some detention and they halted for a long time in Cathedral Street above Read. As they had no food, strange to say, free communication was allowed. Everyone was so surprised that no one had anything—or rather one tenth of what they wished they had. Sisters fortunately had about $100 worth of clothing ready in that never failing wardrobe of theirs—& being near at hand took it round. Mother sent money and packages of tea. Tobacco that I had ready was cut up and came to hand. Lucy took all her pin money and left herself penniless. Young Turnbull was on his way to pay his tailor's bill, when he fell in with the column. He spent his trust funds on his friends. He got a can bought milk & refilled it eleven times. One of the men said "Tell me your name. You have been so kind" "Turnbull" "Oh! Are you any relation to Aunt Anne" "Only her son," replied He. I know of no one here who has been more indefatigable than Mrs. Turnbull. The death of her son Graham, Lieut of Cavalry, appears to have sanctified the cause more particularly to her. In the different prisons, prisoners were only allowed to receive from relations. They managed however in many instances to find out the names of well disposed friends & write to them as Aunt, Uncle or Cousin. Mrs. T. has thus a large family. Mother sends boxes to grateful nephews she never expects to see.

Today I heard another anecdote of Sheridan. Mrs. Dabney Harrison, who married a son of Rev. Peyton Harrison, having lost her husband in battle lived unprotected in the valley. Being robbed of nearly all she had she determined to go to Sheridan and ask protection for what little was left. She went with a neighbor in a cart drawn by two horses. Sheridan had the horses shot, & the cart destroyed and sent her back with a reprimand.

Tommy Hutchins or rather Mrs Sarah Hutchins I suspect has asked Capt Wiegel, her Jailor to dinner. Mrs. H's punishment was certainly entirely disproportionate to the offence she committed. To attempt to seend a sword to Harry Gilmor and to be so foolish as to entrust it to a negro, who, she might be sure would betray her, was so very silly as to disarm suspicion. No one could sanely argue from this that she was a dangerous character. Some trifling punishment would have been well enough. To send a woman, educated to refined society, to the commonest penitentiary in New England was simply infamous. But still so foolishly had she behaved, in a manner likely to bring trouble upon other people who were really serving the South, that she got less sympathy than would have been expected. As soon as she was arrested, she broke down utterly. She went on her knees and offered to sign any parole or take any oath that was required. She urged that she was "enceinte", which was not so, and on her return from prison while at the New York made a joke of having used this pretense in order to obtain her release. Now she asks her jailor to dinner. I would like to know if she allowed him to make love to her while she was in jail.

Febry 23. The (cur-) dogs of war seem yesterday to have slept. All loyalty was busy in a glorification over the occupation of Fort Sumter.

The use made by the women of Baltimore of the indulgence granted yesterday appears to have enraged the military authorities. Wiegel Dep. Pr. Marshal declares that it requires an army to keep the women of Baltimore away from the prisoners and issued an order this morning forbidding all intercourse. Yesterday there was no regular preparation, but people did the best they could. Some bought oranges, others provided blankets, others gave tobacco & many gave money freely. In anticipation of another opportunity today many cooked provisions last night. But today the prisoners were well guarded, as they arrived en route for exchange. Soldiers kept sympathizing females aloof with bayonets & in one case charged on them. I heard of one who had her coat ripped down the back.

My sister Lucy was standing on her Aunt's step in Cathedral Street, hoping to do something. She was front, while Aunt Martha* with her provisions was endeavoring to operate in the rear—i.e. by the back gate. Lucy had a loaf of bread in her hand. A soldier seeing this said "If you will give me that Miss, I will hand it to the prisoners," Lucy said none, but not suspecting a trick handed it to Miss Gaillowdet, who gave it to the man. In a trice he arrested the pair and marched them off to the Provost Marshal's. Minnie Smith, in despair, offered the fellow ten dollars as a bribe. He arrested her too. After running about all day, we got them released at night fall. My brother John & Mr Bayard Smith went to see Genl Morris, now in command here, while I went in another quarter. [The following is crossed out: Morris was as rough as a brute, which is his general mood, though at times he can be goodnatured.] It was Lawrence, A.A. General, who was so tough.

The reports of the sailing of the Dane—French Iron Clad—the Sphinx, alias Alinde alias Stonewall seem now to be pretty well confirmed.** If she were to appear in the Chesapeake & blockade the James River for ten days, it would tell on Grant. I am curious

* Martha Sewall Glenn (1813–1881), widow of William Wilkins Glenn's uncle, William Carson Glenn, lived at 172 Cathedral Street.

** The ironclad ram *Stonewall* was purchased in Denmark in 1864 and was turned over to American authorities in Cuba in 1865.

to see what she will do, where she will come—and where is her mate. I would hope for more, had not the Confederacy been so terribly unlucky with its Navy.

Febry 24". Friends from New York report the exultant confidence there as universal. Nothing has been more astonishing during the past four years than the blind madness of these people. Until the interview held lately between the Southern Peace Commissioners and Lincoln & Seward,* it was utterly impossible to convince people in New York that the South would not be glad to return to the Union under certain guarantees. After the breaking up of that conference leading men for the first time opened their eyes to the fact that it was a question of subjugation or independence. In 1861 they were confident that McDowell would crush the heart of the rebellion in a week; in 1862 they were positive that McClellan would take Richmond and finish the war; in 1863 they declared the South was starved out and in 1864 they were more positive than ever that the forces under Grant were irresistible and could meet with no real opposition. This faith in brute force has made these people a terrible enemy.

Union people here are congratulating themselves upon the "improved" tone of society. They say that there is a much greater interchange of hospitality than there has been for the past three years. And they are right. On the 22d February, Tom Morris displayed from his window a large flag. So did the Meredith's. Now as both of these families use every endeavor to keep friends with Southerners, this is what I call offensive loyalty. There was no necessity of putting out a flag and very many Union people did not do it. Tonight Mrs. Tom Morris gives a small ball. Everybody is going. Two or three of us only will not go to Yankee parties. How soon people accomodate themselves to the force of circumstances!

Febry 25". Last night at Mrs. Morris', where the weak kneed Southerners flocked, Brigr. Genl. Graham & Col Lawrence appeared in uniform. Both made merry together, though the destruction of Charleston & the fall of Wilmington have barely been announced. Esau sold his birthright for a mess of potage. People now sell theirs for terrapins and champagne.

Genl. Morris issued stringent orders this morning forbidding the slightest intercourse with prisoners. Aunt Martha is prepared not-

* The Southern Peace Commissioners, who met at Hampton Roads aboard the *River Queen* on February 3, 1865 were Alexander H. Stephens, Robert M. T. Hunter, and Judge J. A. Campbell.

withstanding for a convoy to arrive tomorrow morning. She has a good woman to aid her and by being on the spot early in the morning when they arrive, before the police are about, is enabled to get a good deal to the prisoners. It appears the Yanks were very much surprised at the unbounded enthusiasm manifested towards the prisoners two days ago. The Military authorities were greatly incensed and when the prisoners arrived at the boat, all the extra blankets, clothing and provisions received by them were confiscated.

Poor Capt Beall who has just been executed as a spy was a man of noble character. He died like a hero. His letter to his brother a few days before his execution was simple manly and touching. He was taken in the Enemy's Country in Citizen's dress, but that does not prove he was a spy. There was abundant proof that he was not acting as a spy. This act will in all probability lead to retaliation.

March 3d. [*1865*] The members of the bar have been for the past few days discussing among themselves the course to be adopted in reference to the oath prescribed by Congress to be administered to those practising in the U.S. Courts. It goes into effect tomorrow. This oath is retrospective as well as prospective. You are required to swear "that you have not given aid, counsel comfort or encouragement to those in armed rebellion against the United States and that you will bear true allegiance &c." The oath will be very generally, I may say universally taken. At the majority of the members of the bar, I am not surprised. Many of them, though opposed to the war or really sympathizing with the South, have really been very prudent. They have stood firmly for four years so long as no sacrifices were required. After this display of heroism why should they be expected to quarrel with their bread and butter. Then there are others like Geo Brown, ex Mayor, who have shown nerve & pluck and are respected for it, but who after all are Yankees—and once Yankee always a Yankee. But there are two or three who really have surprised. Wallis for instance feels that he really can take this oath with a clean conscience; that he has only opposed this Government by the fair & legitimate exercise of his rights as a citizen of the country, and because, in the proper interpretation of the meaning of the oath, he has done nothing criminal *in law*. He probably however will not take it, because Judge Giles, in his entire subserviency to the Government, will not have the manliness to put the true legal interpretation on the oath and then, if indicted for perjury as he certainly will be, he would stand more than a fair chance of conviction, especially by Juries and in Courts constituted as they are at present. He does not consider sympathy, counsel or comfort extended to prisoners either privately in forts or more publicly while on parole, as coming within the meaning of the oath. They are not persons in armed rebellion. Thomas goes still farther. He was in arms after the 19" of April 1861. He drilled for some days. He was very violent. He had arms and munitions of war secreted for some time. He sees no difficulty in the oath however, as he does not consider either intentions or desires to come within the meaning of the oath. When men begin to discuss questions of ethics they generally manage to render a verdict to suit their own case.

The Legislature is concocting an oath for the State Courts. The opposition have managed to get rid of the retrospective part and think they have done a clever thing. The prospective part is stiff enough. It is recommended by Daniel Clarke and his friends. As Clarke eulogised Hicks lately in the Senate, I should not think he would mind oaths; and as for the men of the lower counties generally, those men, who swore openly at the polls at the late elections that "they had never desired the success of the South" will have no hesitation at swearing anything at all. O tempora! O mores! are either better than they were 2000 years ago. Where has virtue fled? Or was there ever any virtue to fly anyplace?

James W. Washington 12" Va. Cavalry, died a few days ago, at Fort McHenry. He was captured in the Shenandoah Valley. Most of the men taken there singly are treated as guerillas by Sheridan, sent to Fort McHenry & confined in cells. There are three cells there of the most horrid character. They cannot be 6 feet long or more than 2½ ft wide. I do not think they are high enough for one to stand up in, although I have not seen them for two years. They are side by side & have each an iron grated door which opens into a little gangway. At one end of this gangway is a door, with window lights in the top. This gives a dim light for a few hours a day to the cells. It is inhuman to confine a felon in such a place. Washington was stripped of his clothing when captured & clad in a summer suit. His treatment was so bad & his sufferings so great that he lost his reason and died.

The condition of many of the prisoners who go through here now daily for Exchange is heart rending. From Elmira down no provision is made for their meals. Some of them are very weak & require food. When the trains come straight through it is bad enough, but when there is delay, it is still worse. On several occasions five or six or more have died in the cars.

March 4. Abraham Lincoln is President of the Free States. Maryland is now a Yankee State. She voted for Lincoln and was represented in the Electoral College. Her citizens may be Rebels—but they are Yankee rebels.*

March 5. The poor fellow Washington alluded to above was the son of a cousin of Winter Davis who has recently married in second marriage, Davis' Bro in Law. Davis was very fond of her. During Washington's long & cruel confinement Davis has not troubled himself about him. Now that he is dead, Nancy Davis writes to her sister Lydia Howard "Mrs. Lyle (formerly Mrs. Washington) had lost another son. He was a wayward boy". How thoroughly does this war develop all that is wicked and selfish in the natures of people who pretend to be Christian.

Mr. Francis Hopkins has been here for a day or two from New York. He was very kind to the prisoners at Fort Lafayette and is now seeing about the distribution of money & clothes from the English fund raised at the Bazaar. He had no idea of the condition of things here and of the severity and brutality of the military authorities. So little is known of what passes here. No account is ever published in any paper. A paper which would make a fair statement would not be allowed a second issue. Yesterday he went to see the prisoners pass through. He was not allowed to approach them and was driven off several times with the bayonet, although he told the guard he was from New York & knew no one among the prisoners, but only wished to speak to them as a matter of curiosity. One of the men wrote on a small piece of paper, "For God's sake get us something to eat. We are starving" & gave it to a little boy, who gave it to Mr. H. Another message of the same kind was got from one of the ambulances. There were twenty five of them. They were closed in, so that it was impossible to see inside. Several of the prisoners, who were weak & unable to stand the fatigue of so long a journey & so long a fast, were already dead. No one was allowed to give a cup of cold water to the rest. Mrs. John S. Gittings went to see General Morris. He promised to send orders to the boat to have food supplied. If he did so or not, I cannot tell. He could not provide for those who were already dead.

Henry Sullivan has been fortunate enough to get a parole for his son who has been staying here for a few days, before returning

* Lincoln received 37,353 votes and McClellan 32,413 of the home ballot. Absentee soldier votes raised Lincoln's total to 40,171 as again 32,739 for McClellan.

to the Confederacy.* His description of prison life at Camp Douglas is heart rending. He says that 1200 men died there, not one of whom would have lost his life with decent ordinary care. He himself looks pretty well. He says he is sorry for it, but that in truth he cannot walk three miles & that it will take him some time to recruit before he can be fit for any duty. It is very evident that the aim of the administration is to land these men at the Exchange point, with the minimum amount of life of [*sic*] them & so broken down by starvation & discomfort that it will be a long time before they are fit to do duty.

March 6". Hon. Wm B. Read was here for a couple of days last week. He came with his wife to call upon Miss Mary McKim whose engagement to his son is announced.** Read has behaved so manly and so well from the beginning of this war that he has quite astonished many people who knew him well and gained the respect of people who formerly thought very little of him. He stood his ground in Philadelphia at a time when the Union Clamor was almost universal and when to stand alone required more independence than American politicians usually possess. He quite astonished me. I did not expect this of him, for I knew he was regarded in Philadelphia as a small politician—and I knew too from English officers that he was thought very little of in China when he was out there as Minister. The English had learned from experience that there was only one way to treat John Chinaman and that was as John Chinaman. If you acknowledged his superiority for one moment or even showed that you were dealing on equal terms, John was certain to entertain contempt for you. Read came out & thought that he knew more than the English. They only had experience. He had intuition. So when they were endeavoring to conclude a treaty the Emperor graciously offered to England & America to allow their ambassadors to come up the back way, to enter at the back door & to treat through a subaltern of the Govt. This the English refused to do. They declared they would go up as befitted their station, in their own boats, that they would be received in state and would only treat with the Emperor. They knew that any treaty made in any other way would not be respected by the Chinese and that they

* Henry Sullivan's son is probably Joseph Sullivan, whose arrest on April 27, 1865 for being in the Confederate army is reported in both the *Daily Gazette* and the *Baltimore American*.

** Congressman William B. Reade had two sons, neither is named in the *Dictionary of American Biography*.

would be sneered at for allowing themselves to be insulted. Read thought better, so he allowed himself to be carried up not in state, to be received by officials he knew nothing of & to be made a party to a treaty worth nothing. He had made a treaty however ahead of the English and he made the most of it in his despatches. He gained great credit at home, but very little in China. He was very clever with his pen and during the war wrote a great deal principally for the Philadelphia Age after it was started. When McClellan was nominated and wrote his famous letter, abrogating the platform, Read behaved very well, retired from the contest and wrote to the proprietor of the Age when they made up their minds to support McClellan, that he would not contribute to their paper any more. In a few days however, when he saw all his friends caving in & wheeling into McClellan ranks, he could not stand it. The old feaver came out. He was a politician and had to be in the ring. He had man [*sic*] enough to stand bravely up against large odds, with a very small party, but he was not man enough to stand up with no party at all. It was McClellan or nothing. So he took up the cudgal and battled bravely for him. I was disgusted but not altogether disappointed. I had been surprised to see him hold out so long. It was like Dr Johnson's dog—"The wonder was not that he danced so well, but that he danced at all". I do not think I ever knew a man who worked so hard for fame and for association with famous men as Read did. There was no end of correspondence that he would not write, no amount of trouble that he would stop at for this purpose.

Willy Smith, son of Mr Sam. Smith, who lately passed through here for exchange, says that his daily rations while in prison at Elmira if I recollect aright, were for some time four crackers & 3 oz. meat per day.

Mch 7". Andy Johnson still so beastly drunk that he is unable to preside in the Senate. The drunken exhibition he made on the 4" March in the Senate beggars description. (No report made of it in the newspapers gives any idea of the scene). (He could scarcely stand & could not talk coherently). In fact they tried as far as possible to gloss it over and hide from the nation the humiliation it had suffered.

March 8". Nothing is more curious than the changes in the opinions of people as they are affected by the progress of events. As an almost universal rule, men appear to have no opinions at all resulting from reflection and conviction. Their opinions are the result of mere chance. The successful campaign of a season will affect their views as decidedly as the decided victory will affect the Gold Market. Indeed their [*sic*] might well be a stockboard for public opinion. The turns would not be quite so rapid as at the Gold and Stock Boards, but quite as marked and indeed successful speculators in human nature could rival the Shoddy Princes and the Petroleum Nabobs. In Maryland Men were decided pro slavery men & Southern, then became Union Men and now are almost abolitionists. Men, two years ago, who were willing to sacrifice everything for the Southern cause, or rather to stake everything on its success, now swear in Court that they never gave aid counsel or comfort to the South and that they will protect the Union and forever resist its dismemberment. All this is very Contemptible but amusing.

When the revolution first broke out, almost every man in the Slave holding lower Counties of Maryland was pro Southern. They anticipated little war and were confident that Maryland would join the South. The prosperity of Maryland in their eyes was dependent upon the existence of slavery. In 1864 when a Convention was called, every effort was made to send proper men there to resist the abolishment of Slavery. It was a useless endeavor, for the Election was under Military control.* But it was at this time that the false swearing commenced which has since become so fashionable. No one was allowed to vote at the polls without first taking a strong Anti Southern oath. This was for the purpose of saving their slaves. This is the first time since the war commenced that there was a party in the State, putting itself under the name of the Democratic party, in alliance with the Democrats of the North and attempting to fight out the political struggle under a common banner. Defeated in the attempt to control the Convention, they again entered the arena to elect members for the Legislature in hopes of having a bill passed for Compensation for Slaves which had been freed by the Convention. Discovering that this was hopeless those of the planters who could afford it bought cattle and took to grazing while others endeavored

* Maryland's 1864 Constitution abolished slavery. The constitutional referendum occurred during the national election in 1864, yet, despite being tied to the reelection of Lincoln, it was rejected by the voters 29,536 to 27,541. Only when absentee soldier ballots were counted did the Constitution pass, by a margin of 375. A full, if somewhat biased, account of the circumstances of emancipation in Maryland can be found in Charles L. Wagandt, *The Mighty Revolution* (Baltimore, 1964). For an assessment of the 1864 Constitution, see Baker, *The Politics of Continuity*, pp. 104–10.

to obtain free labor. Owing to the high prices of cereals & beef, produced by the scarcity arising from diminished production, the profits in farming have recently been very large. Men have received double and treble the incomes they ever received before and delighted with this change, which they forget is but temporary, discover that slaves are an incubus after all and that they are well rid of them; that is as Slaves. Of course the blacks are largely still employed as farm laborers. Now comes another phase. The new draft has created a great demand for men. The conviction that the Northern Armies are soon to crush the rebellion induces men to believe that the present campaign will be short and attended with little danger. Negroes are easily induced to offer themselves as substitutes or for bounty money. Quite a trade is being driven in human flesh and smart negroes are actually selling their more stupid brethren & pocketing more than half the money received. The withdrawal of a large number of hands from the fields is producing a scarcity of labor. Men who formerly received $9 or $10 per month & board, now receive $16 and before long will demand $20. The price of board too which was $8 is now at least $12 per month. This has again set the landholders to thinking and they are not certain now if the violent unsettling of an established system of labor is after all a good thing. Slavery was most profitable in the planting districts where women & children could constantly be employed in light labor. It was not so profitable in the grain growing districts where women & children had but little out door work, but had to be fed & clothed. The advantages of the system in these districts however were that you could always control your labor and that you were not at any time liable to lose a crop or to sustain great loss from the impossibility of securing hands at the most important season of the year. This very state of things promises fair to occur this summer, when men will be converted again to the doctrines of slavery.

There are of course some men who reflect. The effect of thought and observation on their minds has been very different from that upon the minds of those who are solely influenced by self interest. When I proposed to buy the Exchange Wallis was afraid my opinions were so different from Frank Howard's and his own on the subject of slavery that we might not be able to agree. They were both decided emancipationists. Wallis and I had a long talk on the subject, he wishing to know what I did think. Today my opinions as to slavery in a Southern Republic are much strengthened, while theirs are completely changed, entirely upon political grounds. They are satisfied, as I am, that Republics as Monarchies, must be limited

—that there must be in every country distinction of classes—and that there must be families with large connections of powerful influence whose interest it is to resist the encroachments of the Executive power. They believe that this can be best effected in a Republican Country by the presence of slavery. The large land and slave owners will there represent the aristocracy. The whites will form the middle class and have their rights as such. The slaves form a lower Estate and fill the position for which they are best fitted. They have not the intelligence of the white and they are much better in a dependent condition than in an independent one.

March 10". That precious old psalm singing sinner, pothouse politician and Methodist, Thos. Holliday Hicks has been today lying in state in the Maryland Institute. His remains are on the way from Annapolis to Dorchester Co. No Governor ever received such a posthumous oration and no one was ever less deserving of it. The truth is Hicks was never employed before the Know Nothing days for any purpose except that of doing the dirty work of the Whig party. When the Know Nothing party was formed, most of the Whigs who were merely politicians and who looked only to self political preferment—in fact all the inferior men—joined the Know Nothing standard. This raised Hicks eventually to the Gubernatorial chair. He was made Governor by a party which could not boast of one decent intelligent high minded and high toned man in its ranks.* After Lincoln's election Hicks wrote on the 9" Novr. 1860 his famous to [*sic*] letter to E. H. Webster in reply to an application for arms.** He told Webster that as soon "as he had an additional supply, your people will be furnished. Will they be good men to send to kill Lincoln & his men; if not suppose the arms would better be sent South". On the 20" April 1861, he gave the orders to Mayor Brown and Marshall Kane to burn the bridges and then lied about a week afterwards and ever afterwards. Afterwards when the Federals had possession of the State Hicks became a Lincoln man. He got in on the winning side and staid there till his death. He was elevated at a time when Government controlled our elections to the U.S. Senatorship and having received that honor was to resign and accept in its place the position of Collector at the Port of Baltimore which

* An old but complete account of the Know Nothing Party can be found in Lawrence F. Schmeckebier, *History of the Know Nothing Party in Maryland* (Baltimore, 1899). Baker, in *The Politics of Continuity* discusses the evolution of the Know Nothing Party into the Union Party (pp. 31ff).

** The text of the letter from Governor Hicks is printed in Scharf, *History of Maryland,* 3:369

was much more lucrative and where the opportunities for stealing were infinitely greater. Death stepped in before Lincoln was ready to make the appointment under his new term.

Hick's inopportune death sadly disappoints Thomas Swann. Swann, who is another of those creatures who does not scorn the price of blood, expected to receive the appointment of Senator, for the balance of the term, after Hicks had resigned. This was part of the price to be paid him. But unfortunately Hicks died while the Legislature was in session and when the vacant senatorship created much more talk and discussion than it would otherwise have done. The Legislature finally decided to go back to the old plan, although it was not required by the late Constitution and to elect the New Senator, from the Eastern Shore, as the last one had been from the Western. This killed Swann's chances. Cresswell was appointed. He is no better, but still there is a sort of satisfaction to an outsider in contemplating Swann's discomfiture. In 1861 when Swann sent down to collect his coupons on his Virginia Banks, he took an oath which was virtually an oath of Allegiance to Virginia & pledging himself not to act against her. Bayne, who made the collections for him, knows this, but will not now disclose it. Some day we will get at it. I should like too to see published the list of all those hounds, such as Turnbull, Slade, Eaton, Cushing, Bailey, Hopkins & others who in the spring of 1861 subscribed $100 each to put arms in the hands of the police commissioners for the defence of the State against the forces called out by Lincoln.* All these will come to light some of these days—but when it is too late. Mankind is not very forgiving but it is forgetful. What damns you today is treated ten years later as a curious or an amusing piece of history.

* Among those Baltimore merchants solicited for contributions to put arms in the hands of the Police Commissioners were the following: Benner, Dennison & Co., bankers; Wyman, Byrd & Co., dry goods; John S. Berry, brick manufacturers; Austin, Dall & Co.; Hodges Bros., importers; Isaac Coale, Jr., & Bro., commission merchants; H. Tiffany & Co.; Eaton Bros. & Co., dry goods; Turnbull, Slade & Co., dry goods; Duvall, Keighler & Boyd; Rich, Chase & Co.; Henry Reiman & Son; Mills, Mayhew & Co.; Lanier Bros. & Co.; Miller, Cloud & Miller; Whiteley, Stone & Co., dry goods; Hambleton Bros. & Co.; Magruder, Taylor & Roberts; Wiesenfeld & Co., clothiers; Paynter, Davis & Co., attorneys; Thomas J. Carson, banker; Boyd Brothers & Co.; A. J. Albert, paperhangers; R. Walter & Bro., clothiers; Samuel Bevan & Co., dry goods; Meredith Spencer; Devries, Stephens & Thomas, dry goods; C. D. Slingluff & Son, grociers; Orendorf & Bean, grociers; McDowell, Robinson & Co., carpet importers; Cushing & Bailey booksellers; John Turnbull, Jr., carpet & oil importers; Orem, Hopkins & Co., cloth importers; Hurst & Co., dry goods; F. B. Loney & Co., hardware; F. Fickey & Sons. (John Thomas Scharf, *Chronicles of Baltimore* [Baltimore, 1874], p. 598. Baltimore City Directories are missing from 1861 to 1863; 1864 was used to identify firms listed.)

The past two days have been about the worst days for Gold & Stock speculators I ever knew. There has been a sudden heavy decline without any apparent cause other than the continued stringency of the money market, occasioned by a large temporary withdrawal of currency from the market, for the purchase of the 7.30 loan. This cannot last for the Government is so heavily in debt that it must pay out as fast as it can. It is now so heavily in arrears to contractors and these men are so hard pushed on account of the delays made by Government, that they are forced to pay $\frac{3}{4}$ to $1\frac{1}{2}$ perct per month for the use of money borrowed in these contracts till they can be paid. Washington Bankers make heavily at this business. The temporary stringency however cannot last. The Government must make money easy to float its own loans. An occasional stringency may help it, for it injures those who are speculating against the Government & buying for a rise based upon the continued depreciation of the currency. During the past year & especially since the removal of Joe Johnston & the commencement of the tide of success which set in then at that time, the Baltimore speculators have suffered heavily. Where $100,00 has been made $300,000 has been lost—and immense sums have been lost. Everybody speculates now and where men speculated once with $5000 they now speculate with $100,000. This is about the proportion.

Nothing really is more curious than the infatuation of the Northern people at this moment. Men who have been prudent and cautious for four years and who have carefully avoided Government Investments on account of the continued accumalation of the debt, now, that the debt has reached an untold amount and that $600,000,000 more is called for, suddenly abandon their convictions. Last year, after Grant's failure, or rather repeated failures, Boston Merchants who held Government securities prudently sold out one half of the amount. I heard of several very loyal men who did this. Now they are going in again. Never since the first day of the war have the subscriptions to the Government loan been so large or anything like so large as they are now. Even in Baltimore here men have caught the mania & the Johnstons, pretty shrewd Bankers, who three years ago sent all their money over to England & have since done no business, have now opened an agency for the loans. Joe said to Martin Lewis a few nights ago that they had for a long time forborne to do this on account of their Southern sympathies and their connections, but he simply thought he had been a great fool from the beginning & was determined to lose no further opportunity. Of such stuff are men made. Joe however is wise in this respect. He takes devilish good care not to buy Governments for his own account.

I was amused this morning at a very loyal man who is long in Gold and who is badly caught by the fall. No man in town, not even myself, would have been gladder to hear of Sherman's utter discomfiture than would he. Give the bulls a profit of 50 perct & the blessed Union may be forever dismembered & damned as far as they are concerned.

Mch 11. More prisoners. These poor fellows are not provided with food at all in the cars and they remain on their trip down, sometimes for two days without anything to eat. Mrs Ellen Gilmor saw one of them, as he passed down the street, stoop down, pick up some garbage and literally devour it. She had in her pocket a small vial of Mint Cordial. She stepped forward to the guard and asked him to give it to this poor fellow who seemed too weak to drag himself along. The guard struck her in the breast with his hand and told her to stand off. "Yes," said she, "that is all you are fit for, to make war on women".

Mch 12". I hear again today through Miss Williamson & her sister Mrs Mullen of the brutal treatment shown to prisoners. One man begged the guard for a morsel of bread. He was brutally refused and lay down & died in the street almost at once. Another one raised the car window. The guard said "faugh what a smell of small pox" Well may there be a smell," answered a prisoner "there are four dead bodies in here and we are stifling with the heat & the smell. The windows are all down—give us air or we shall suffocate". The guard closed the window by force. A man wounded in both legs was being supported by two Confederate surgeons who carried him toward an ambulance. The guard stuck him twice with the bayonet, telling him to move on, in spite of the remonstrances of the Surgeons aiding him. His conduct was so revolting that a Federal Surgeon finally came up and ordered him to desist, telling him he was a brute. This was however the only reprimand he received. These things were seen by Miss Williamson or her sister.

We have letters today from Savannah. The accounts are heart rending. The men have all gone off with the army. The women are left alone. Refined women born to affluence are sewing for bread or rather rice which is their principal food. The Yankees have cut down all the trees in the beautiful cemetery for firewood and have desecrated the graves.

March 14". People in the North are perfectly wild. They are now perfectly satisfied that sixty days more will end the "rebellion". Indeed they look upon it as already done and are preparing to return to specie payments. Gold which within the past nine months has been up to 285. has fallen rapidly. Today it has touched 176. Hundreds of people who have bought largely on margin are selling out at a heavy loss. It is a most depressing time, not that the news is so depressing but that the people are so depressed. I have still great confidence. I believe in Southern Gentlemen & Southern Generals, if Jeff Davis will only let them alone. I know perfectly well that the Generals who were imprisoned early in the war at Fort Warren were very anxious then to have the Sea Coast abandoned and to concentrate in the interior. I believe that the South is now much stronger for the change of policy. It strikes me too that it is much better for them to have Sherman near the seacoast than in the interior. He got to Savannah at a cost of $100,000,000 and with a loss of 50000 men, while he might have accomplished the same thing at a cost of $500,000 & with no loss of men at all. He abandoned the interior of a country where his communications had been cut off and changed his base. His march after all was a retreat and though this retreat ended in the Capture of Savannah, and enabled him to claim a victory, which he had not anticipated, this does not alter the fact that he abandoned the Country he had conquered. The English retreated from Spain. Sir John Moore fought a brilliant fight at Coruna & gained a victory; but his retreat had been a disastrous one.* Some days before Sherman reached Savannah Montgomery Blair assured Govr Pratt that Sherman was on his way to Beaufort where he intended to embark his forces and proceed to unite with Grant as soon as possible, for the purpose of capturing Richmond and thus crushing the rebellion in its last stronghold. As far as Blair knew the capture of Savannah was not contemplated then. Sherman finding that he was not opposed changed his plans as he advanced.

It appears to be now pretty clearly proven that Singleton's last mission to Richmond was for the purpose of making a trade & exchanging tobacco for bacon. A large quantity of tobacco was forwarded to Fredericksburgh for this purpose. By a singular coincidence a raid was made by vessels up the Rappahannock which reached Fredericksburgh soon after the tobacco arrived & captured it all. The South got no bacon. What Singleton made out of the transaction no one knows. It is an undoubted fact that a large trade has been at times carried on with the South by the connivance of

* General Sir John Moore was the British commander at the battle of Coruna on January 16, 1809, in the Peninsular War against the French.

officials high in Government employ. Butler made a fortune by selling passes and permits in New Orleans. He used to give clearances for small vessels in Lake Pontchartrain which he knew were destined for Mobile. I was cognizant of one transaction myself in England, where the party had a pass for two Cargoes from a member of the Cabinet. It was countersigned by Mr. Adams. He agreed to dispose of it to certain parties who employed me to draw the papers. It afterwards fell through because the terms were not satisfactory. On the Mississippi a very large trade of this character has been carried on in violation of the rights of neutrals.

March 15". The draft is to commence on this city in the 9" Ward.* Government commences with one ward & then stops. It shows the people what it will do if it must and then gives them to profit by this mild threat. It thus gets more volunteers, who are better than conscripts and avoids exciting the population by making a heavy draft. Frank Howard has joined an Insurance Club. He paid $30. The last draft he paid a little less. His argument is that he is a Marylander and Maryland has accepted her place in the Union; therefore he has no choice now that Lincoln is in for a new term. But I cannot understand how a man of his undoubted courage and determination can voluntarily contribute money to buy men to make war against his own brothers and the people he supports. I may do it—and very soon. But if I do, it will be because I am whipped—which I am not yet.

March 16. The N.Y. Tribune is rejoicing over the idea that the country is ruled by a President who was a farm laborer and a Vice President who was a journey man tailor. It would be quite as much to the purpose to say Knave and Sot. In the recent "honest efforts" made by Lincoln to obtain peace, his knavery and cunning were not to be surpassed. He allowed Blair to go to Richmond a second time with the most direct propositions to the South to treat on the basis of a junction of forces and war upon the French in Mexico provided the South would waive recognition for the time. The South did send commissioners. Lincoln meet [*sic*] them and declined to enter into any negotiations. The subject of war upon Mexico was discussed, as a continuation of the negotiation commenced in Richmond. Lincoln through Seward sends a despatch to France stating that this proposition made by Blair, came from the Southern Commissioners. R. McLane who has just returned from Paris, which he

* Baltimore's ninth ward was bounded by the harbor, Charles Street to the west, Franklin Street on the north, and the Jones Falls on the east.

left after the arrival of Duncan Kenner with the Southern despatches relative to Blair's mission says that Slidell and Mason both denounce Seward as a most unmitigated liar—in this attempt to falsify the truth and prejudice the Emperor against the South. But this is statesmanship. Lincoln told Govr. Pratt last week that he had completely fooled Blair, and had permitted him to go South with the impression that he was willing to enter into some such agreement on the part of the North—but that in truth he never had the slightest idea of doing any such thing and that he had succeeded through Blair in completely fooling the Southern people. This is quite possibly true. The opinion I formed was that Lincoln was very much exercised about the rumors of foreign recognition and that he did commence negotiations with an earnest desire to make peace; but that afterwards military successes and the demonstration of the weakness of the South caused him to change his mind and his plans.

Genl Singleton was also allowed to go South on a peace mission. Being unable to accomplish anything he was allowed to return on a tobacco speculation. He was to have tobacco for bacon. He entered into arrangements with a large New York House, took a large amount of greenbacks, went to Richmond, bought tobacco largely himself and induced others to enter into the trade. The tobacco was all sent to Fredericksburg, where it was to be shipped and the bacon was to be delivered. By a strange coincidence, several federal gunboats suddenly appeared, made a raid upon the town and seized all the tobacco. Singleton was very near being hanged in Richmond by the people who declared he had played them false.

So much for Mr. Lincoln's principles. Now for Mrs. Lincoln's. The story of the china is well known. A bill was rendered for $2100. I think this was the figure. Lincoln objected because it was not worth more than $900. "You forget Mr. President" said the tradesman "that I also gave a check to Mrs. Lincoln for $1200.

When the French Princes were entertained Mrs Lincoln gave the cook $50 extra to serve a dinner. After much irritable discussion she gave way to his demands. When the dinner was over she made a bill for $500—and took it to the Treasurer of the Dept of the Interior and demanded pay as these were Government and not private entertainments. She was new in the business then and it was some time before she understood clearly that she could only get pay for something actual required or used for permanent improvement. She returned in a day or two with a bill from the Gardner for plants, trees etc certified by herself for the amount. It was paid. This fact afterwards came out in the investigation of some accounts by the

Committee of Ways and Means in the Senate. Mr Boyer who was on the committee told me of it. Lincoln heard of it & went at once paid over the money and withdrew the check. The matter was hushed up for a time but soon leaked out. At another time Mrs. Lincoln wanted to have a cow paid for—and proposed that the cost should be charged to manure for public grounds. Some ladies in Washington declared that she appropriated the manure piles which had always been the perquisites of the gardener and devoted the proceeds to the payment of her ice cream bills. The complacent gardener who submitted to this and did all he was told afterwards received a commission. Mrs. Lincoln, it was said took his wife in the house as a companion and then drew in her name the salary allowed for a housekeeper, which Mrs. L. pocketed herself. But these were small things. The family grew rich by contracts. Contracts were sometimes given out with the understanding that Bob Lincoln was to have a joint interest and I did hear one man assert that he knew of one such agreement drawn up in Mr. Lincoln's own handwriting.

March 17". The facilities for crossing the Potomac were never greater than they are now. People pass to and fro with such ease that I inclined to think the thing is winked at by the Government and the route kept open for the purpose of letting their own Emissaries pass unmolested. There has been no little money spent during this war both in military and political circles. Many a blockade runner who has carried important advices to the Confederates has brought back private information to this Government. I suppose there is more of this now than ever. Almost anybody can go through who chooses.

Today I met Lawley in Broadway. He had just come through for a few days. He gives me the first news I have ever had that makes me at all despondent. Duvall came through about three weeks ago. He spoke very confidently and assured his friends that Johnston had 81,000 troops. As he is intelligent and as he had just come from Carolina, his statement was believed. Lawley on the contrary declares that Johnston has not more than 30000 men. If Johnston has but 30000 and Lee has but 60,000 the chances are indeed bad. Lawley still upholds Davis and declares history will do him justice and place him among the niches reserved for great men. His idea is that the blame of this failure rests with Joe Johnston who with a better and larger army than Lee's failed to give battle to a smaller army than Grant's. This may all be true; but certain it is that the removal of Johnston has brought nothing but discouragement. Mr. Randolph, late secretary of War, took a fair view of it in Paris. He said there was much discussion on the subject and that the Civilians in Richmond generally supported Davis. He thought Davis was right. The Army thought differently & so did General Lee. Bragg was the only man of any mark in the army who supported the President. Now is not this enough to condemn Davis. He commits an act at a critical period which he knows is disapproved of by the army. The subsequent demoralization has been frightful, and worst of all, for Davis, when Congress met, he found the sentiment of the Country was with the sentiment of the Army. The South had been sacrificed to his own bitter prejudices and the Richmond Clique which surrounds him. The worst feature about the whole business was the sending out Bragg as a spy to report on affairs at Atlanta. Bragg was the man who had been displaced to make room for Johnston. The wound to his personal vanity made it impossible for him to do justice to the handsome manner in which Johnston had treated him on that occasion.

March 18". I hear today of ladies in Charleston—Southerners—who have given parties to Federal officers. I am sometimes afraid that similarity of language is a powerful weapon in the hands of the conquerors. It gives them so many more opportunities to wheedle to cheat and to lie. The French invade Spain, the Austrians march into Italy, but the people do not come together. They cannot understand each other and the Conquerors and the Conquered are distinct and apart. But here, as everywhere, women will talk when they have a chance—and though no one has shown higher, nobler, more self sacrificing traits than the Southern women, still the courage of women is not ordinarly that independent courage which holds out bravely and firmly to the end, even after it is separated and cut off from its support. Those who were most courageous when with their husbands & brothers & sons may become despondent now that they are away from them, and if intercourse once spring up between them and their masters, its growth will be greatly facilitated by similarity of language—and thus a greater blow will be given to the South, by consequent demoralization, than by the defeat of an army.

March 19. Lawley is astonished to hear that Slidell has at last ceased to place faith in Louis Napoleon and that there are in reality no hopes of foreign recognition. The Richmond Cabinet does not yet understand this. Lawley says that when all the promises made by the Emperor are made public, his falsity will be shown in so contemptible a light, that were he a private citizen no common laborer, with honest instincts, would speak to him. But he is an Emperor. What then. The truth is both England and France always believed that the South could fight its own battles. England held back first to save her commerce and her trade. She commenced by fearing for those. She ends by fearing for herself. English Statesmen in conversation with French men have confessed that the great change in Maritime Warfare and the great superiority in the American Iron Clad Navy at the present moment render England no longer the first power at sea. But Enland has nothing to lose but Canada and she will gladly toss that bone to the big dog,—Uncle Sam, if he will be satisfied. France is different. Louis Napoleon has played a big game for Sonora. Will he abandon it. He must support the South or give it up. Maximillian is taking high ground on the frontier. His Generals salute the Confederate flag and the U.S. Consul is told he can leave Matamoros. This may be done as a sort of brag to attempt to force Lincoln to recognize Maximillian. Even if he do—and guarantee Sonora to Napoleon—is Napoleon fool enough to trust him? I have never yet understood the politics of England and France on this matter. They not only failed their only friend and natural ally on this continent but they have actually made the Southern people their most bitter enemies.

March 20". I hear today from Washington that Seward is anxious to have Lee and Grant agree to an armistice; but that Lincoln declares he will make peace himself and grant no other terms than those proposed at Fortress Monroe. Lawley mentioned today that while he was in South Carolina, after Blair's first visit to Richmond. Benjamin telegraphed him that there was a strong probability of peace coupled with an offensive alliance against France & England. This only shows how completely the Richmond Cabinet must have been deceived—or rather the faith they placed in Blair's assurances.

March 23d. News has come of the appointment of De Montholon as Minister to Washington. What does this mean? De Montholon was formerly consul to New York & an ardent Southerner. De Persigny told Robt McLane that when De Montholon went out in 1863, he endeavored to persuade the Emperor to recognize the South and that the Emperor was rather inclined to follow his advice; but that Dayton, U.S. Minister, had persuaded him that the war must last several years longer and that in the meantime the Emperor could establish his Empire in Mexico firmly without any opposition.

Mr. Bayard—a propos of McLane—told me a funny story of his father Louis McLane, who studied law with Mr Bayard's father, some sixty years ago. It shows the difference in tone between then and now. Louis McLane's father was quite a common man, who had been in the revolutionary war & was afterwards made collector. But he was without any social position. He was in love with Miss Milligan, who gave him some cause for pique and he soon after engaged himself to Miss Van Dyk. Mr Bayard thought very well of him as a promising young man and he had very agreeable manners. Soon afterwards Miss Milligan showing that she was not adverse to Mr. McLane, he jilted Miss Van Dyk and engaged himself to Miss Milligan. The affair made a great talk & Mr Bayard deeming Mc L's conduct as unbecoming a gentleman determined to cut him and break off all intercourse with him. Mrs Bayard knowing this would ruin McLane of whom she was fond, and force him to leave the State—and possibly for Miss Milligan's sake—actually went on her knees to her husband & entreated him to overlook the matter, which he finally did to a certain extent. Some time after when Mr B went to England he left his whole business in the hands of Mr McLane, who thus got his great start in life. Much was due to his abilities no doubt, but a wrong start might have had a very bad effect. Mr. McLane was at that time a young Federalist.

March 23d. The present financial panic is to my mind the most extraordinary event of this revolution. Six months there seemed to be every probability that the Northern finances would break down during the winter from depreciation of currency produced by inflation. To day the Government is on the eve of breaking from the appreciation of currency although the inflation is greater than ever. The uninterrupted successes of Sherman have given such credit to the government that for some time past the subscriptions to its loans have been unprecedented. The strong belief in a speedy peace, before the failure of the Peace Commission, gave great confidence abroad and large amounts of Govt. bonds went to Europe. The amount of Exchange drawn against these bonds became so large that it was a drug on the Market. Gold consequently began to fall. It has gone steadily down from about 214 to 151. As it has gone down speculators in gold, carrying it on margins, have been forced to sell and this facililated the decline. With the decline, provisions & merchandise that were shipped abroad at the high rates, cannot be exported. Speculators in provisions are forced to sell at ruinous prices—much less than the home value for domestic demand. All foreign goods paid for in gold find no market. Merchants who have invested their large profits in stocks are forced to sell their stocks to meet their payments. Stocks have fallen, some 30 to 40 per cent, and each day for the past ten days has only added to the panic, until it has got to such a height that nothing but a crushing Federal defeat can save the community from bankruptcy. A merchant of known prudence said confidentially this morning that three weeks ago he could have sold out his stock and assets at a profit of $1,100,000. To day he would close out at a loss of $300,000. It is not impossible that in a few days the National Bank circulation may be thrown out. Want of confidence in one is want of confidence in all, and they may be forced into liquidation. The green backs will furnish even then more than enough volume for all legitimate business. How Government is going to get on I cannot imagine, for the subscriptions to its loans must necessarily cease. It has all along ignored the fact that it was forced to keep money abundant in order to float its loans. It was in a dilemma either way. To make money abundant produced ruin from inflation & depreciation. Today it is on the verge of ruin from appreciation.

March 24". Genl Singleton has returned from Richmond. He took with him to Richmond a large amount of greenbacks which he invested in tobacco. All this he lost and those Virginians whom he induced to go in with him lost heavily too. They were very indignant at the seizure of all that tobacco at Fredericksburg by the Federals and were inclined to consider the whole thing a trick. Singleton was near being mobbed and hanged. How he got the permission from Lincoln is not known. But the whole thing goes far to confirm the story that was privately circulated last summer. It was reported then that Singleton was in league with Lincoln and that he was actually paid for going out West and making the strong peace efforts he did in opposition to the McClellan wing of the democratic party, this being desirable for the purpose of breaking up the democratic party and giving the Republicans an easier victory.

There was a curious story too afloat at that time about Ben Wood's paper the Daily News. Barlow told me then a gentleman, a friend of Wood's, had come to him, after McClellan had taken his stand in opposition to the Chicago platform, at the time when all the peace men and peace newspapers had wheeled into the ranks determined to support McClellan at all hazards rather than split the party, and asked him "what the party would contribute to the support of the Daily News, provided it would come out for McClellan"—suggesting that $15 or $20000 would answer the purpose. Barlow replied that he would consult his friends, but that he did not think they wanted the News as they considered its opposition would help them more than its support. A few days afterwards the same gentleman met him and told him that the matter had been arranged and that Wood had all the money he wanted. The conjecture was that Wood had received a large sum of money from the Republican Committee, for the purpose of inducing him to keep up his opposition to McClellan. I told the first part of the story afterward to Ben Wood. He appeared quite indignant and said that it was very hard that a man should stand up to a cause as he did at great personal sacrifice and still get no credit for it. I recollect however at the time, that for two or three days I was under the impression from the tone of his paper that he was about to give in and I learned at the same time from an employee of his office that he was making arrangements to sell out to his brother Fernando, who would then change the tone of the paper. I mentioned this to him. He denied it and about the same time came out as strongly for peace as ever. The Woods unfortunately have no character and no influence outside of their own circle. In his district in New York, Fernando is very powerful and Ben has a strong hold on the roughs. Beyond that they are hated and mistrusted and have no friends either among Democrats or Republicans. Their strength is in New York and they should confine themselves to the role of city politicians. As far as can be seen or known, Ben has been thoroughly bold and consistent from the beginning. Unfortunately he gets little credit for the apparent virtue he has manifested. He and Fernando I hear were both in this tobacco speculation of Singleton's and have both lost considerably.

Letters come from Fort Delaware imploring aid. The exchanges go on slowly and the rations have always been so small there. that it has been difficult for a prisoner to keep up his strength without receiving aid from outside friends, which was permitted in the shape of money.

News from the Shenandoah valley is sad. The distress there is extreme. An officer who took charge of a box sent there a few days ago for relief, reports on his return to Baltimore that he saw a woman up there, evidently a lady, standing on the ice watching the air holes. She was ragged and had an infant in her arms. She told him, when he questioned her, that she was standing there watching the air holes in hopes that a fish might come up and that she might catch something to give her children to eat. He told this to Mrs. Turnbull.

Mch 27". I learn from two or three sources that McCullough

Secry of the Treasury finds that he cannot restore the currency to a healthy state, as he calls it, as easily as he imagined. He did not care about ruining the Merchants and speculators, provided he could get the bone and sinew of the country to take his loans. But the honest laboring men are precisely the men who do not subscribe. It is the very speculators who make large profits who invest in Government loans. He ruins them and he finds to his surprise he stops his loans. Government has bought Gold largely in New York to keep up the price, it has bought up its own stocks to keep them from falling, it has induced several large operators to close out their short accounts in gold, for the purpose of staying a further decline. The trouble is that Government has succeeded so thoroughly in convincing the public that the South is speedily to be subjugated and that the public debt can easily be provided for, that the public has quite gone ahead of the desires of Government and has to a great extent anticipated a return to a specie basis. Scarcely anything but a Federal disaster can save the National Currency now, and it is disgusting to see how many a loyal citizen would gladly hail the news of a terrific defeat and of the slaughter of 20,000 men that would put $20,000 in his pocket by a rise in the price of Gold or merchandize.

Eggs have fallen to 30¢ a doz—Good sugar 18¢—Coffee 30¢ Oats are down to 70¢—a decline of from 30 to 50 per ct.

March 28. Govr. Pratt has been discussing the results of the subjugation of the South. He says if the South is subjugated the Northern people will confiscate the whole of their property to pay the debt—and ours in Maryland too. If he thinks so why has he labored so to effect the submission of the people of this state. He has done more than any ten men in the State to induce the people of this State to yield to "the force of circumstances" and to accept their present position as an integral part of Yankeedom.

No. 5

1865

March 29". News to day of death of young Arthur Gilmor. He passed through here a few days ago, for Exchange. He had then a chronic dysentery. He was very ill. His sister saw him and efforts were made to get him placed in the hospital here, but this was positively refused unless he took the oath of allegiance. This although he was known to be dying. The process of "exhaustion" as practiced by the administration has been terribly inhuman. The stoppage of the exchange of prisoners has cut like a two-edged sword, for in some of the Southern prisons the Northern constitution has given way and the men have died rapidly. I heard of 12000 men dying in one prison.

The accounts from the South are most conflicting. Communication now is frequent. This week, Mr. Brand has a letter from Burton H. telling him "to be of good cheer—that the people are more united & determined to gain the desired end"—and Jim Howard sends word that officers in the Commissariat Dept assure him that the question of supplies is now arranged and that Charley Marshall tells him that Genl Lee is more cheerful. Now these sources might be called undoubted; but Mrs. Murdock* brings word that Genl Lee rode down the line ten days ago, without receiving one cheer and that the men called out "General give us meat" to which he could only reply, with tears in his eyes "Boys, I have no meat for you".

I saw contracts for about 100 Bbls Whiskey awarded by the Govt. to its friend today at 3.70 to 3.90. The same whiskey—old Bourbon—was offered by others at 3.30. While the Md. Legislature was in session, when a Senator was to be elected in place of Hicks, decd, the Govt. awarded large contracts to members of the Md. Legislature. One member cleared $10000 on 400 Bbles Whiskey. The whole machinery of the War and Treasury depts was brought to bear. Consequently the Govt. candidate, Mr. Creswell, received the appointment.

March 30". Very busy at home. 86 permits came two days ago from Fort McHenry. The girls took 11 and have been hard at work procuring suits for 11 poor prisoners. Today a fresh batch has come and they are again at work.

* Mrs. Thomas Murdock may be Elizabeth C. Murdock of Winchester, Virginia, who married Dr. Thomas F. Murdock in 1854. Two Thomas Murdocks are listed as members of the Maryland Club, and no genealogical records have been discovered that shed light on the problem.

I am very anxious now to see Peace, on any terms short of subjugation. Two years ago when I declared myself willing to sacrifice Maryland, to stop slaughter and bloodshed, braver worded men than I, flourished imaginary swords and cried "Never, Never". Most of them are much meeker now—and, thinking that Maryland can no longer count upon a place in the Confederacy, are desirous of a reunion. Now when I say "Make peace, unite with the North, join forces and turn the French out of Sonora, kill any body else you choose" the few Southerners left say "Unite for the North, never!" "Yes, unite with the North! The South has won its fight. The Union is destroyed. Liberty has perished in the North. Reunite. Give the New England states a high tariff—navigation laws—everything her grasping spirit can desire. The more the better. Let her oppress the West as well as the South. When the West & the South make common cause New England fanaticism will cease to tyrannize.
When I said two days ago coffee was 22¢—I was wrong. This was in Gold. It is about 34 currency.

The draft is going on slowly, the Govt. drafting only in small districts and giving the people plenty of time to fill up their quotas by volunteers—who now never volunteer without being paid largely. In Baltimore the City Council allows every man who furnishes a substitute $200. The State allows $300 more. A man costs $900 to $1100 say $1000. Thus 300,000 men cost $300,000,000 dollars about half of which is paid for by State & City Governments and funded in debt bearing interest to be provided for by taxation. Was there ever so costly a war since the invention of currency.

March 31". Prisoners came up today taken in the recent fight on Grant's left. It was hardly a battle. Everything is relative and now a days war is made on so different a scale, that the engagement which terminated the revolutionary war for independence would scarcely be deemed more than a skirmish or at most a reconnaissance.

Among the prisoners are one or two first exchanged. After over twelve months weary imprisonment they are back again, without having had or taken time to go to their homes—if they had homes left to go to. It is to be hoped the Exchanges will go on as there is little if any balance against the South, notwithstanding the lying assertions of Stanton. It is rather a strange thing that the South should be indebted to Beast Butler for the exchange of its prisoners. In the quarrel between Butler & Stanton which was made public after Butler's failure at Fort Fisher, Butler made an expose of the whole negotiation concerning exchanges and showed evidently that the Administration deemed exhaustion the surest method of terminating this war, and that they were willing to exhaust the South no matter what the cost of life and suffering to their own men. It was the old story of Grant. When Grant advanced in 1864 with his immense army, confident of easy victory, he was little prepared for the terrific repulse he received. In a council of war held Meade advised a retreat. "No!" replied Grant "this is a battle of the Kilkenny cats and our cat has the longest tail". This is all in accordance too with the supposed policy of the Republicans. They wish to subjugate not to restore. If Southern States come back the democratic party regains the ascendancy and no one can fortell the consequences to the leading republicans after the effects of this war begin to be felt at the North. The southern States must be ruled as provinces. To return. When the story of the Exchanges came out it created so much indignation among the families and friends of those men who were still imprisoned in the South or who had already died there, that the Administration feared the consequences. Members of Congress finding that an attack upon the administration and a demand for the release of the prisoners would be very popular, determined to bring the subject before Congress. The administration feared the result of the Contest and gave in.

April 1". [1865] Grant moved two days ago. Lincoln, who has been at City Point for several days & intends, it is said, to await the result of this grand attack on Richmond, telegraphs today a slight check & a further advance. What this means no one can tell. Lying has been regularly systematized on so magnificent a scale, by the Republican Administration that it is often difficult to guess at the truth. The Newspapers lie in big letters. If even they tell the truth, they tell it in small. Most people read the large headings of the news telegrams. Few read subsequent details. Consequently the lies are generally credited. When Hooker suffered his very disastrous defeat and was driven across the tributaries of the Rappahannock, Stanton telegraphed North that Hooker had received a check & would assume the offensive in a few days.

The odds are certainly heavier against the South now than at any former period. Still within the past few days there have been received in town a letter from Burton Harrison, Secretary to Davis, a message from Charley Marshall, Secry to Gen Lee, a letter from Com Buchanan and one from Genl Trimble. All express hope and modest confidence. Trimble, when he passed through here for exchange after a long imprisonment with Northern Newspapers for his daily literature, was despondent. His tone is evidently much better now. Besides, I feel confident from what I know of Genl Lee that he is not the man to lead gallant men to useless and hopeless slaughter.

April 2d". Today we have the first positive news of very heavy fighting. News very meagre.

April 3d. A little before noon today news came of the evacuation of Petersburg & Richmond. The Mob soon took possession of Baltimore Street. Flags were run out everywhere, and many people were forced to hang them out. Hamilton Easter got a guard to protect his store. Several other stores were closed. At night many public places were illuminated. I heard of only one or two people who were mistreated & the mob was much quieter than usual.

Apl 4. Details come in very slowly and are meagre. Where are Genl. Lee and his army? Where are the officers of rank captured with the 18,000 prisoners they claim. Flags flying everywhere and great preparations being made for a general flag jubilee and illumination tomorrow.

Apl 5". News today of the capture of the Harriet Deford, at Fair Haven about 50 miles below Baltimore. A party of Confederates came into Maryland, a portion of them went on board in disguise, took possession of the boat & afterwards signalled for the rest of their band. A few days ago a Schooner was captured in the same way on the Potomack [*sic*].* Richmond has fallen. The war is at an end and still war is carried on in the now loyal state of Maryland.

Notwithstanding all the glorious news of the end of the Rebellion Gold still keeps at 150—and is steady. Everybody prophesied it would go to 125 when Richmond fell. Secretary McCulloch has just written a long letter in reference to a decision of the Courts of California in reference to legal tenders. The position of California has from the beginning a curious . She has acted as an independent and indeed a foreign state. When greenbacks were first issued, they were treated as an current money and dealt in at the broker's board. Several Government financial agents who endeavored to induce the Californians to be more loyal were very near being mobbed. Out there the laws were respected, civil law being paramount. The

* The *Harriet Deford,* owned by Isaac and Thomas Deford, in service between Baltimore and the Patuxent River, Capt. Albert H. League, was captured April 5, 1865. The schooner *St. Marys* with Capt. Howard was captured off the Patuxent River at Cedar Point on Friday, March 31, 1865. (Baltimore *Sun,* April 6, 1865.)

Government wisely refrained from interference. Then California was rather Southern. Now things were changed. The Californians have upon reflection decided that a grand railroad communication East is necessary. They think that unless the Union is preserved it may never be built. Therefore they are loyal. As this loyal party gets the upper hand it is not improbable that it may receive aid from the government to enable it to tyrannize, in return for which it will pass a state law or enforce the U States law relating to legal tender. Then California will have paper money—as a reward for becoming loyal. She asserted her rights and Govt. was afraid of her. She supports Govt.—from a venal motive—and now Govt. will trample upon her.

Apl 6". Today a proclamation of the Mayor appeared recommending a general illumination, at the suggestion of the City Council. Genl. Morris has also ordered 100 guns to be fired from Federal Hill and another hundred from Mt. Vernon Place. This is merely to annoy and insult the people around here, who are almost all rebellious. He hates this part of the town. When I was in Fort McHenry he had all his columbiads pointed at the Monument so that, if he should be at any time ordered to open upon the town, he would be able to explode his shells in the neighbourhood. The community generally are much perplexed to know what to do. If there is the slightest coercion practised every one will illuminate I should have gone to New York tomorrow, but I fear to leave my people. It will be a miracle exposed as our house is, if the mob do not smash our windows this evening. No lights shall be seen from them.

Apl 7. Last night the illumination was a total failure. About the Newspaper offices there was great display. Up town not one house in twenty was lighted up and not one in forty was really illuminated. I walked round ten squares and saw but five houses illuminated. To read the papers this morning one would think that the exhibition was brilliant. How contemptible newspapers are! And still from these history will one day be written. The town was quiet. The Mob made no demonstration and consequently the Southern men did not light up. I was much amused to see that about 25 window panes had been broken in Mt Vernon Place, by the firing of the guns. They were all however in the houses of loyal citizens—Gambrill, Eaton, Schumacher & Garrett—which stood together & nearest the canon.*

* John Work Garrett lived at 50 (now 16) East Mount Vernon Place, Charles A. Gambrill at 56 (corner of Charles St.,) George N. Eaton at 54, and A. Schumacher at 52.

This was all the harm Morris did by this foolish exhibition on his part. No body minded the noise.

I saw Wm. T. Walters yesterday. He was very extreme on the commencement of the war. In April 1861 when Fort Sumter was fired upon and taken by the Carolinians, Walters went around collecting money to fire a salute in honor of S. Carolina. He came to me for a subscription. I declined "You are afraid," said he "Yes" I replied "I am afraid to approve anything which my judgment does not tell me is right." A few months after when there really was danger in expressing your sentiments and just before the first arrests were made, Walters left with his family for Europe. He swore he would return by next steamer as soon as he found a place for his family. He did not come however and he has only just returned, after the destiny of Maryland is settled. He talks in a grand way about his astonishment at finding that the people of Maryland have made so little resistance to Military tyranny. The people have this advantage over him. They stood their ground. He ran away.

April 8". On my way to the New York train with Northey of the 60" Rifles and Glyn of the Rifle Brigade received a note from B. F. Ficklin, who is in Washington, just from Richmond and in dread of being caught. He little counted upon the evacuation of Richmond happening immediately after he left. F & I came up to Baltimore in the evening.

April 9". Ficklin disclosed his business to me. He wanted to get out Cotton. An order was issued some time ago regulating trade with the insurrectionary States. Permits were granted to parties allowing them to bring out cotton—paying 25% of the proceeds to the U.S. Govt and a small tax besides. The holders of the cotton were allowed to take back a portion of the proceeds sales—about one third of what they received—as mdze not contraband of war. This trade was soon stopped by Grant, who wished to prevent the sending of any supplies into the Confederacy. His object was to starve the Southern Soldiers out. Those persons having permits signed by the President and endorsed by the Secy of the Treasury found them worthless because Genl Grant refused to respect them. The tobacco recently seized and burned near Fredericksburg was tobacco carried up there under these permits. Before it got fairly out of the Confederate Lines the Military pounced upon it & destroyed it. President Lincoln's permit did not protect it. In old times there was said to be even "honor among thieves". The thieves now must be sadly demoralized with the rest of the world.

April 9". Went to New York and arranged our plans. Ficklin has 20,000 Bales Cotton in Alabama, paid for. If he gets this out he has no desire to take provisions back. All he wants is the money. He wants permits from the President, endorsed by the Secretary of War, so as to prevent the seizure of the Cotton by Military Authority. I am to get one third of the net profits. He gets one third of the proceeds for himself and Anderson of the Trediger Works. The other is to go to pay [the following names are crossed out: Sam Barlow Judge Pierpont and Stanton] the parties who enable him to procure cotton down South—Trenholm I suppose.

April 10". Stunned by news of the surrender of Genl Lee. Much as had feared the demoralization of the army resulting from bad food and retreats I was not prepared for this. In the evening had a long talk with Jerome and Travers. They talk of the war as over, and of the restitution of the Southern States to their rights, and of moderation just as if they believed that Puritans could be moderate or that the populace could be considerate. They say the South have fought like brave fellows and it is no dishonor to them to be over ran and broke down by numbers, and they pretend that this is the feeling of the Northern people. But was there ever a revolution where extreme counsels did not prevail. And this is a revolution—a social revolution consequent upon rapid growth of population, sudden increase of wealth, undue extension of territory and universal suffrage. Tariff did not break up the Union. Nor Internal Improvements, nor National Bank, nor Slavery. This latter fired the train but the mine that exploded was loaded with other combustibles.

We had a long talk about stocks. Stocks about 15 or 20 days ago were at a very low figure. The war was going on, the debt was increasing currency was multiplying and men who thought deemed it inevitable that everything having real value must appreciate. Suddenly stocks took a tumble. A large lot of stocks were forced upon the market by men who had lost fearfully by the fall in provisions and cotton, and who were compelled to sell; the desire to sell was encouraged by the shorts and a panic set in which would have destroyed any commercial community whose credit was not based in an irredeemable paper currency. The apparent cause of all this panic was anticipated peace. Many men who held a few stocks which they had purchased to make a small profit lost tremendously. Jerome got out of his stocks at a heavy loss. Seeing his judgment so mistaken he has held off for a little to watch the turn of the market. The market has rallied as suddenly as it declined and stocks are now higher than before they declined. He is still out. Today it was thought the almost positive news of Peace would put prices down. Instead of that they have rallied.

I take it for granted we shall have Peace. Genl. Lee is the only man around whom the whole South can rally. Davis must now be more execrated than ever.

April 11". Saw Thurlow Weed. Told him I wanted to get Stanton's endorsements to cotton permits and that *we* could make a handsome thing of it. He could no got to Washington but told me that Judge Pierpont was the next best man.

Stumbled across Lawley, on his way back to England. He left Richmond on Monday Morning at 6 o'c. At 8 he saw the Stars and Stripes from the distance. On Saturday evening the Cabinet had no idea of what was about to happen. Benjamin told L. that "Hunter & Campbell had given up, but that neither Davis nor Breckenridge nor he had. We shall be forced" he continued "to evacuate Richmond. Lee will fall back to Danville. The second stage of the War will commence and we shall come out victorious in our contest". Davis endorsed this opinion. Such people must lack common sense. They knew that Lee had not 30000 muskets south of the Appamatox. They knew that some of them had not had meat for over 10 days. They knew that Genl Lee had brought in a list of 1200 of his Veterans who had deserted, saying "how many others there are I know not; but these men have stood by me through every trial and they leave me now to get food". They knew that they had no cavalry and that the artillery horses were nearly starved on 3 H corn a day—and still they talked coolly of holding Richmond to the last and then retreating in safety. If this army had been well fed they could have counted upon it. The Yankees did not fight. If Lee's men had had the elan they have shown before, I have little doubt from what I hear that he would have gained a decided victory. But the men, after one or two brilliant & successful attempts gave up when ordered to retreat, straggled off, deserted and surrendered at discretion.

Mr Davis was in church on Sunday. A telegram was brought him from Genl Lee. He read it calmly. No one saw from his face that anything unusual had happened. He walked quietly from the church. By four o'c every one knew then Richmond was being evacuated. Horses, carts, wagons carriages everything was seized upon or brought into use. Confusion reigned everywhere. The heads of whiskey barrels were knocked out and whiskey rolled down the gutters. Men scooped it up in their hats and drank it—and drunken rioters soon made the Confusion more confused. Who got out and how they got out, no one knows. Mr Davis I suppose has gone to Danville. I wish it was some place where he can do no more harm. My friends who reproved me for saying long ago that if the South ever lost its independence, it would have no body to blame but Jeff Davis, have changed their minds now. Davis appears to have had no knowledge of men at all. He surrounded himself with inferior men. With the exception of Benjamin his first cabinet was a very poor one. Mallory Memminger Sedden have all helped to drag down the South. Even Trenholm the present Secy of the Treasury has turned out a great failure. But that was probably because his own interests were so large and his endeavors to secure himself influenced his actions in spite of his desire to act solely for the benefit of the Government.

There is hardly a chance now for the maintenance of the war this side of the Mississippi. Joe Johnston cannot have more than 25,000 men. They tell me that his ruling passion is jealousy of Genl Lee. They were in the same regiment in the old service. Lee was Col. Johnston was Lieut Col. But afterwards Johnston was appointed Quarter Master General and claimed to outrank Lee. He made this claim when he went South—but it was not decided upon. His popularity has been for some time on the increase and his power is growing. He would only be too glad to pluck fame from such an opportunity—and his more selfish and selfwilled character fits him better for such an emergency than the unseeking and modest character of Lee. If Lee had had the selfishness to assume a dictatorship, the result would have been different. There was much sense in the remark of Judge Campbell to Lawley "If you ever go into a revolution, don't go into one under a republican form of government". Johnston has probably nearly 30,000 men. Forrest has I suppose 12000. Forrest has genius popularity & power. If these two armies join and fall back, if forced, to Texas—they could get 30000 men, who would be determined men, across the Mississippi. An army of 50,000 men in Texas, with plenty of grass for horses and mountain ranges for defense could work miracles—if there was no dissension among leaders. What the South has wanted was one man. This war has taught me to believe in one man power. It is not the multitude which controls the destinies of the world. It is the influence of the one Man which sways them.

Lawley is still of the opinion that Johnston's Atalanta [*sic*] campaign was a great failure. He thinks Johnston really responsible for the utter break down of the South. He declares that Johnston took a splendid army of 72000 men, fell back with them against an army but little larger, abandoning three ridge positions which gave him great advantage & where he should have fought and finally left his army with 45000 men, thoroughly demoralized by retreat. He assures me that he has talked with many officers & he knows these facts. And he says that Johnston's removal was universally popular. This certainly is directly opposite to all I have learned. Lawley confesses however that he is not quite as great a believer in Davis as he was three months ago although he still believes history will do Davis justice and give him a high place among the men of the World. I am curious to see what will become of Johnston. Allan McLane, his brother in law, who will of course henceforth be strongly Union, although heretofore the family have been by way of being strongly Southern—in private—says that when the War broke out, Johnston was strongly opposed to the move of the South—and that it was only when Seward had ordered the revictualling of Fort Sumter, in a clandestine manner, which Johnston found out before hand through Allan McL, the Govt. having chartered two of his companys steamers, that Johnston determined to resign. This is rather in his favor. But no one can tell what men's motives are. As far as I can see soldiers have less principle than other people. They get their passions excited and fight for passion and for place. Most soldiers are Dugald Dolgettys.* McClellan certainly was one. He wanted to go with Johnston and Beauregard. He got a big appointment & fought against them. It is positively asserted that in addition to this he received a sum of money, as an equivalent for the value of the Presidency of a Western Rail Road, then held by him.

April 12". I learn that Stanton said two days ago at dinner "There is nothing left us but a foreign war. We have no commerce to damage. We may get the worst of it on land. But it is necessary to cement this shattered Union and the only way we can bring it together again". God Grant that it may be so. No body would see France and England involved in a war which would entail debt and suffering and involve them in similar ruin to that which stares this country in the face so gladly as a Southerner. England has been blind and love of money & commerce has made her cowardly. Napoleon has simply been too smart & has overshot his mark. Both thought the South could take care of itself against all odds & one sided neutrality. They will be terribly astonished yet. When I told

* Dugald Dalgetty was a character in Sir Walter Scott's *Legend of Montrose* (1819). He was a loquacious pedant and a brave but self-seeking soldier of fortune who would fight on either side of a cause.

the people in England that if the war was maintained long enough, it was clear that in the end three men and three guns and one gunboat must whip one man and one gun and no gunboat, and that if this happened the day might come when the American people would get tired of cutting each others throats and might possibly unite and cut somebody elses, they smiled at me. We shall see. If Stanton has these views he will carry them out, and in the excitement of the moment, while money is plenty and easily borrowed & taxation not fairly commenced, he can make war where he chooses. Stanton is the power now. Lincoln & Seward opened trade with the insurrectionary states. Stanton and Grant stopped. George Francis Train went not a great while ago with a cargo to Mobile. Grinnell and others furnished the money.* When he reached that port, his vessel was not allowed to enter. Lincoln's pass was of no avail. Train returned to Washington and appealed to the President. The President could not and would not interfere with Stanton although Train & his friends had risked the venture by the special permission of Lincoln.

I went to see Barlow to day to see if through him we could get at Judge Pierpont & get Stanton's endorsements, through him, to cotton permits. "You know" said Barlow "that Stanton will have to be paid" "Of course" was my reply "and we can afford to pay handsomely".

The course of the stock market is very curious. It is going up up up. But Travers, whose great principle was to be "a bear on a gold basis and a bull on a paper basis" got frightened last week, abandoned his convictions & though wiser than the herd does not profit by his wisdom. What I have predicted is being realized and yet I am a heavy loser although I stuck to my convictions until it seemed madness to hold to them longer. Crawford said to me last night "Theories may be very sensible, but any man who speculates on them will be ruined".

April 13. News today of the Wilmington Mob. They surrounded Mr. Bayard's house and threatened to smash all the furniture, if flags were not displayed. They went over to Dr. Kane's house & finding him at home, hurt him severely upon his refusing to obey mob law. They then went to Tom Bayard's and threatened his house.

* Glenn probably refers to one of the Grinnell brothers: Henry (1799–1874), a New York financier and mercantilist; Joseph (1788–1885), a former Whig Congressman and cotton manufacturer from New Bedford, Mass.; or Moses H. Grinnell (1803–1877), a former Whig Congressman from New York and a member of the Union Defense committee. Another possibility might be Iowa Republican Congressman Josiah B. Grinnell (1821–1891), who was a personal friend of Lincoln.

He hung out his flag as indeed was done at his father's house—in his father's absence. Mobs usually are antagonistic to the Military Authorities who finally subdue them. Mobs at present are encouraged and supported by the Military. The Provost Marshall stood by in Wilmington and enjoyed these scenes of violence hugely.

It would be horrible to believe that all this suffering and bloodshed had been in vain, as it will have been if the power in the hands of the people is not curbed. My great consolation has always been that this war would put restraint on the power orders. A Republic like a Monarchy, to be good must be limited. No government that is not limited can last. The curious question now is how is this form of Govt. to be limited? Will the people consent to give up the power in their hands? One would think not. The only way then is to take it away from them by a military dictatorship. As the people have more ideas of rights than in any other country this would soon be tempered down to a monarchy and that would possibly become more & more limited until the form of Government became, as far as possible & prudent, republican again. This revolution will take another phase yet. So far the war has been sectional. The Northern people have had nothing to revolutionize against. They have been gratified by the devastation and waste committed in the South. Some of these days when the Government tramples upon them they will take a different view of matters.

Dined with Lawley and L'Amy. L'Amy was very funny.* As he was an intimate friend of McClellan's, he could speak freely. Barlow dined with us. I asked what sort of a General McClellan was. "The very one" said L'Amy "I should like to fight against. I would know that he would take a book and a square and a compass and go to work and I would take two books and a square and a compass and beat him. When we were on the Chickahominy and McClellan commenced throwing up his first parallel seven miles from Richmond, Good God, said I, to Neville, at this rate when will we get to Richmond". L'Amy abused Hood a great deal for marching to Nashville and then sitting down quietly before the town and waiting until his adversary had time to get together enough troops to come out, attack and defeat him. L'Amy has a curious passion for war. He saw a good deal of fighting the first two years of the war. He was always with the Federal army, but is a great Southerner.

* *The Official Records of the Union and Confederate Armies,* Series I, vol. 6, indicates that a Captain or Mr. L'Amy carried dispatches from General Burnside to General McClellan during the Roanoke Island Expedition February 11, 1862.

April 14". Proclamation by order of President suspending further draft. This is a great relief to me. When I started from Baltimore on the 8", it was for the purpose of avoiding the draft. My ward was soon to be drawn and as the draft was very heavy, my chances were bad. I have never yet given aid or comfort in any form to the Govt. I have never even paid commutation money or subscribed to insurance funds for the purpose of procuring substitutes. Even when Richmond was surrendered, although by recent laws I would be disfranchised if I evaded the draft, I could not consent to furnish a man to war against my kindred. When Richmond fell I must confess I feared the time was coming when it would be foolish to resist in trivial matters, which could now entail no harm; and though I floated no flag and showed no lights on the day of the illumination, I doubted whether I should not soon be forced to acknowledge myself a subjugated subject. Still I was here, with my communications with Canada opened, in case of accident, determined to hold out until I knew what Johnston & Forrest intend to do. It is a relief to me to know that I am no longer in danger of being drafted.

There is a strange feeling of relief after all, although beaten, in the reflection that bloodshed is stopped. We blind ourselves to the fact that the condition of our people—as a subjugated people—may be ten times worse than our condition as a rebellious people. We merely accept the fact that ruin and rapine and slaughter are stopped for the moment and hope for a brighter future. For my part I think that although the Southern Armies are defeated the Southern people have won their fight. The Southern States may be held for one year or even five by military force, but the Union as it was is irrevocably destroyed and in our generation and the next the South & the North will live together as amicably as Poland and Russia. This state of things cannot last long under Republican rule. Now too that the war is over the North will be no longer a unit. The cry of the "Old Flag" and the "Union" was a terrible power. The faith of the North in the progress of the country and of free institutions was even still greater. I must confess I have often had my misgivings, when I reflected how the faith of the Jews in the Promise has kept them a nation to themselves, through hundreds of years, when other nations have arisen, passed away & left no trace. But now dissensions will arise and the demoralization and corruptions engendered by this war must produce their effect. The Northern faith is but a worldly faith and cannot last, like the heaven born faith of the Jews.

Lawley and I went last night to Barlows. Marble was introduced as Mr. Marble of the World. How vulgar! and how American. A man should lose his identity in a newspaper. Men should live and pass away and the public should not know they were gone. But Marble & Barlow & Hurlbert set quietly and tell you of the articles they have written for the next day. What can be expected of Newspapers in a country when they are merely used by men to exalt themselves and to subserve their own private interests.

Apl 16". News came late last night (Good Friday) of the assassination of Lincoln and Seward. It was only generally known this morning. The excitement soon became great. In Wall St it was intense, so much so that business was stopped & many houses entirely closed. One boy who declared that it served Lincoln right was beaten. An elderly gentleman who said that it was a shame to beat the boy barely escaped by the protection of the police, who got him in a house and kept off the mob. Later another man was mobbed for thinking Lincoln's death a good thing, his head was cut and as he was carried off by the police towards the Station house in Broad Street, where he was afterwards placed for safety, the excited mob rushed around & swayed to and fro looking very much as if it had "hay on its horns". At the corner of Wall & William St. orations were delivered from the high steps. Butler speaking and advocation [*sic*] death, destruction, & fire & sword for the South.

By noon the whole of Broadway was draped in mourning. The streets were filled. In the hotels the talk was extreme & blood & thunder men swore that Grant should be censured for paroling one single rebel in Virginia—that he should confine them in damp cells & feed them on saw dust till the heart was starved out of them. At the New York Hotel, policemen were placed in the rear of the Hall, in readiness, in case of a mob which was threatened.

At present there is but one feeling on the subject—and no one dares speak otherwise. After some thought I have come to a different conclusion. Seward is the man who for years has nursed and fostered and fed this irrepressible conflict, till it has grown to be the monster which is preying upon the country. Lincoln is the man who has aided abetted & encouraged the schemes of Seward, and by his unscrupulous cunning and shrewd duplicity has succeeded in dragging down the Nation far lower than Seward ever anticipated. Lincoln was elected President under the constitution. After four years of war during which crimes have been committed, by his permission & with his approval, which would have disgraced Nero, he steps into his
as dictator. This is the plain fact. The people of the North are only

fit for a Despotical form of government. They feel it; but so great has been the the influence of republican education on the minds of men that no man has been found sufficiently bold to throw off the ideas which control him grasp the sceptre and destroy free institutions. But the position which no bold man would strike for Lincoln has sneaked into—and there he was barricading & fortfying himself every day. I much doubt if Andy Johnson can start where Lincoln left off. As for Seward, he being the most conservative of the cabinet, there is much greater chance now of foreign war than there was while he was in power.

As far as the South is concerned, I cannot see that she is going to be really the loser, although extreme measures will prevail and much suffering will occur. But what future is for them when they cease to fight. Lincoln stopped recruiting in the Loyal States two days ago. But he is to continue it in the Slave States. His last speech shows too plainly his intentions. The South is to be kept in subjugation by armed negroes. They are to have equal rights with the Whites and the muskets of the armed force and the votes of their brethren are to crush the power of southern aristocracy. What could be worse than that? Talk of restoration of rights. The army is more liberal than the politicians. Passes were given last week to members of the Virginia legislature to come to Richmond and organize a state government. Lincoln countermanded the order & dismissed Genl Weitzel who issued it.

The history of this war has yet to be written. It is a great social revolution. This assassination is another great step.

Lawley got safely off for England on the Etna. We were very uneasy lest the ship should be searched—but it was plain that the restrictions on travel would be greater tomorrow than to day. The Etna was detained for despatches, but the delay this time was not dangerous. I went to the boat & saw everything looked straight before L. came aboard.

April 16". Breakfasted with L'Amy (Sylvester). He will not & does not write; but has in his head the best & most impartial history of the war of any man living. His criticisms are very shrewd, pointed and dryly humorous. He likes McClellan but laughs at the enthusiasm manifested for him as a Commander—and says the folly of his life was to come out as Presidential Candidate as a War Man on a Peace Platform. He cannot understand he says what became of the Southern army after the attack made by Stonewall Jackson on McClellan's flank in the beginning of the seven days battles. He says there should not have been a man or a gun left—that the confusion was hopeless and that a brigade of men, well in hand could have settled the whole affair. He regards Bragg as worse than a blunder. He was at Chattanooga when Rosecranz [*sic*] was removed. Bragg had there all the passes in his hands. Grant's army had not three days rations left. They had only Wagons & bad roads left for supplies and must have surrendered to Bragg, who would not have had to fire a gun. At this opportune moment Bragg withdrew 20000 men to attack Knoxville & Grant succeeded in opening railroad communications. When L'Amy heard Bragg was at Wilmington he immediately predicted its fall.

April 17. Excitement considerably subsided. People thinking again of stocks and mdze and the effect of the assassination upon them. Great outward demonstration however and almost every house in the principal streets of New York extensively draped. In Philadelphia, as I passed through on my way to Washington, the outward & visible signs were still more elaborate. There are certainly a great many people in the North who are prepared to make a demigod of Lincoln. They will be blind henceforth to all but the virtues with which they themselves invest him. The infatuation of these people is certainly extraordinary.

In Baltimore almost all the Southerners are frightened to death at the tragedy of last Friday night. They deplore pitifully the assassination of a man who has encouraged assassination for four years past and who has been the chief man to bring about the state of things which may render assassination frightfully common.

Last Saturday Mr W. J. Albert, one of the Vestry of Grace Church informed Mr Hobart, that if he did not remove all the flowers and floral decorations on Easter Sunday, that he would apply to the Military authorities and he forced Mr. H. to remove them. Such men as this compare Lincoln's entry into Richmond to Christ's entry into Jerusalem on Palm Sunday and his death to that of our Savior on Good Friday. Query—Were the two Sewards the two thieves?

April 18. In Washington to day, although I expected to find no one in their offices, the Treasury department was open and business going on quite as usual. This is a great country. In front of the Treasy. Dept was a dense file stretching all the way up and around the corner to the door of the White House, more than a quarter of a mile long. The people were waiting their turn to see the corpse which was lying in state.

In Baltimore today one branch of the City Council passed a resolution requesting the military authorities to banish Revd Mr. Bullock, Mr Hamner, & two others, as being too obnoxious to the loyal people of the State.* Thus teachers of the Christian religion are not to be allowed to teach unless they teach Yankee Republicanism. Two or three weeks ago the Unitarians had a meeting in New York and determined that for the future Jesus Christ was no longer to be styled our Lord, but Jesus Christ Esquire or Mr. J. C.

April 19". Today Lew Wallace takes command of this department again, which promises badly. He is a volunteer, vain & conceited and a blackguard. He is very extreme in his views & nothing has heretofore kept him under control but the power of the Government which has several times interfered, when his actions have been too outrageous. His animosity against the "Aristocracy" of Baltimore, none of whom know him or will receive him, is particularly keen. At the battle of Shiloh, this fellow got behind a tree. At another battle in Kentucky he called upon his brigade to march bravely forward to the attack and to uphold the honor of the flag that floated above them. He assured them that he would see them properly supported as he was going to the rear himself to order up the reserves. Several lampoons were written upon him and finally one was so annoying that Wallace determined to challenge the author, a Colonel, now resigned & in New York. The Col. accepted the challenge, stipulating only that he should have choice of trees. This so increased the laugh agst Wallace that he dropped the matter. These are the men taken from the field to tyrannize over women & children.

Wallace's first order issued this afternoon is to forbid the wearing of grey uniforms by a set of school boys—in town for Easter Holiday—because it is obnoxious to the loyal citizens of Baltimore. It is the same uniform as the regular West Point Uniform. There are also a good many returned paroled Confederates in town endeavoring to make their way home to their respective states. They have been ordered to change their grey suits within 24 hours. As they have neither clothes, money nor acquaintances many of them are now

* The following resolution was presented to the Baltimore City Council on the 18th of April 1865, and passed on the 26th: "Resolved by the City Council of Baltimore, that the military authorities in command of this department be requested to remove from our midst Rev. J. J. Bullock, Rev. J. E. Hamner and Rev. J. A. Lefevre, and all such dangerous persons as are inimical to our government." J. J. Bullock was minister of the Franklin Street Presbyterian Church, Franklin and Cathedral streets; J. A. Lefevre of the Fourth Presbyterian Church on Franklin Square; and J. E. Hamner appears in the 1864 City directory without a church.

shut up. So much for General Grants paroles. There is a mob law here higher than any other law. General Grant has certainly had some talk with the President and insisted as Commander in Chief that his paroles should be respected; but there has been a cabinet discussion about the matter and the determination seems to be to modify Grant's paroles considerably. Of course this can be done. Lee's army is gone and these paroled men have no one to protect them—unless Grant makes an issue with Andy Johnson & changes the form of government. This is our only chance now. Hancock refused to accept Moseby's surrender on the terms granted to Genl. Lee. Grant hearing it ordered him to accept the surrender at once, for said he to Mr. Garrett "What policy can be worse than that which drives so noted a guerilla chief to desperation".

Town quiet today. Every house draped though many of them with the scantiest possible amount of mourning. Bells tolled & churches open according to military orders. Some flags hung out where I little expected to see them.

April 20". Travers went to Washington today to finish arrangements for cotton permits and to try and find Ficklin, whom we have not heard of for several days. He is of course keeping very quiet until the assassin of Lincoln is discovered & having no pass is uneasy. Travers found business going on as usual in the departments. The event of the day was a dinner given to Grant by Col Lowe & the loyal League association, I think.* It was quite a large dinner. Lincoln, lying in State, was quite forgotten. This is truly a great people—utterly witless and as profoundly hypocritical as thoughtless people can be.

Meetings in different Wards in Baltimore declare that returned rebels & traitors shall not remain in the State. Two girls arrested for tearing up and burning a small Union flag. Jenny Cary arrested & taken to Guard house because she will not tell where Mrs Cary & Mrs. Pegram are gone to in Washington. They are at Genl Barnard's under a pass obtained by him. Such things go on and Northern people quietly assure us that peace is restored and that the country will be more quiet, more united & greater than ever. Wallace has just issued the following order in response to the resolution passed two days ago by a branch of the Council calling upon the military

* The Military Order of the Loyal Legion was founded in 1865. Its membership was made up of loyal officers of the United States Army, Navy, and Marine Corps, and its aims and line of descent were similar to those of the Society of the Cincinnati. Among the members were Col. John W. Lowe of New York, and Col. William W. Lowe of the 5th Iowa Cavalry.

to expel several hightoned clergymen. [The following newspaper clipping is attached to the manuscript:

LOCAL NEWS

To Clergymen. The following circular has been or will be sent, by order of Major General Wallace, to all clergymen in the city:

Headquarters Middle Department,
Eighth Army Corps,
Baltimore, Md., April 19, 1865

Circular—The conduct of certain clergymen in this city has, in some instances, been so positively offensive to loyal people, and, in others, of such doubtful propriety, to say nothing about taste, as to have become a cause of bad feeling with many well-disposed citizens.

As you must be aware, the recent tragedy, so awful in circumstance, and nationally so calamitous, has, as it well might, inflamed the sensibilities of men and women who esteem their loyalty only a little less sacred than their religion.

In this state of affairs you will undoubtedly perceive the wisdom of avoiding, on your own part, everything in the least calculated to offend the sensibilities mentioned. You will also perceive the propriety of requiring members of your congregation, male and female, who may be so unfortunate as to have been sympathizers with the rebellion, not to bring their politics into the church.

So profound is my reverence for your truly sacred profession, that, in the sincere hope of avoiding any necessity for interfering with the exercise of your office, I choose this method of respectfully warning you of the existing state of public feeling, and calling upon you, in the name of our common Saviour, to lend me your influence and energetic assistance, to be exerted in every lawful way, to soothe irritations and calm excitements. You know that what I thus request I have the power to enforce. You ought also to know that, to save the community from the dishonor and consequences of a public outbreak, it would be my duty to exercise all the power I possess, without regard to persons or congregations.

If you feel that you cannot yourself comply with this fraternal solicitation, or that you are unable to control evil disposed members of your flock, I suggest that it is better, far better, in every respect, that you should close the doors of your church for a season at least.

I have no fear that the kindliness of my purpose in thus communicating with you will be mistaken; and that you may not understand yourself as accused, or specially selected from the mass of your professional brethren, you are informed that a copy of this note has been or will be addressed to every clergyman in the city.

Very respectfully, your friend,
Lew Wallace,
Major General Commanding.

Official: D. P. Thurston, Capt., A.D.C.

[The Glenn narrative then continues.]

In the evening asked three or four men to sup at Bob's.* Charley Marshall came in as we were sitting down & supped with us. He gave me very satisfactory answers to my questions & only confirmed me in my opinion that there never was a cause so hopelessly botched in the world. He said that for 18 mos Genl Lee had been endeavoring to have negro recruits; that he had seen how the servants of officers fought and that he believed it was a mere question of discipline—and that if Gen Lee could have got them last September, he then had plenty of arms & could have organized them in time. He said that for the past six months Genl Lee had been urging upon Davis the absolute necessity of the evacuation of Richmond and the formation of a new base at Danville, but that Davis insisted on remaining till the last. He said he would not yield to Lee in this matter, although Lee had been appointed Commander in Chief, and that he was jealous of his prerogative to a fault. Will there ever be found a man hereafter to sympathize with Davis The pigheaded. Marshall said that one of their causes of failure was the Elective system, in the army, which was never abolished until too late. This gave them an undisciplined rabble instead of a well drilled army. He insisted that 10000 good men would have defeated Grants army. As it was the lines were very thin, the men about six feet apart and when the Yankees broke the lines and Lee commenced his retreat, the Virginians behaving like poltroons abandoned every thing, & gave themselves up rather than leave their State. They had no ideas beyond Virginia. Lee at last starved out having remained 72 hours without sleep and with little to eat surrendered 7842 muskets. While he was surrendering a great many stragglers came in & were paroled thus swelling the number to over 20,000. The last act of these gallant fellows, just as the flags of truce were about passing, was to charge the enemy & capture 4 guns, some colors & 1200 prisoners. They had no chance. Grant had cut them off from supplies, was moving on the shorter line and had by this time 15 or 20 men to Lee's one. Marshall said that Genl. Lee did not believe that Joe Johnston was jealous of him—other people think so however.

One of our party was Saunderson. He had sold out of the 11 Hussars made his way across, fitted himself out as well as possible in Virja. with horses and volunteered on Fitz Lee's staff. He lived five days on raw corn & was about the same time a Confederate officer. He lost all his money in the fire at Richmond.

* This may be the Rennert Hotel at Saratoga and Liberty streets in Baltimore which was owned by Robert Rennert. There is no restaurant or inn known as "Bobs." It is also possible that Glenn is referring to a personal friend.

Another was Dudley North of the 47". He was the last amateur to run the underground passage through Maryland, before Richmond fell. He got to Petersburgh [*sic*] in time to take a turn in the trenches and to see the evacuation.

April 21". Lincoln's corpse passed through Balto. Procession passed up Eutaw St & down Baltimore. All business suspended. Streets densely lined with spectators. The Negro Masons joined in the procession. The negroes in town were all wild. It was utterly impossible to keep servants in the house or to get any work out of them. Draped flags were displayed from almost all the windows in the Main streets. Our people are like whipped hounds and now that such a display can only make them contemptible are eagerly manifesting their loyalty. On the 19", I draped one window sill, from 10 to 3 o'c—during the time prescribed by Military orders for mourning. All the family were much opposed to this, but I thought they were wrong. Today we are almost the only house without some symbol of mourning.

Mrs. Cary & Mrs. Pegram who returned last evening from Washington were seized in the night & carried to the Provost Marshals although Wallace knows they are here with passes from General Grant.

Wallace has issued an order prohibiting all paroled Confederate soldiers from returning to Maryland unless they take the oath of allegiance. A large number who came here two days ago en route for Kentucky & Louisiana were taken to the Soldiers rest and placed under guard because they had on grey clothes, which color is obnoxious to loyal eyes. The larger portion succeeded in obtaining other clothes through Southerners here & were suffered to go at large.

April 22d. Mrs Cary & Mrs Pegram still in prison. I am curious to see where the conflict between Grant & the extremists will end. Grant sent up a long telegram to Wallace about Mrs. Cary. Wallace will not heed it. Grants paroles are set aside. If it only go far enough, I think the country will sustain Grant. The only chance now for the Border & Southern States is a Military Government—and for the whole country. Unless universal suffrage is abolished all the ruin & bloodshed has been for nothing. Grant has established his headquarters at Washington & sent Halleck to Richmond. What does this mean. Col Marshall said that Grant's staff officers told him to go where he pleased & that he should be protected by the parole given to U.S. officers.

Five men have been lynched & hanged in Indianapolis for

expressing satisfaction at the death of Lincoln.* see below *A*

I heard last week that Genl Lee had exposed himself in every possible way previous to his surrender and that Mrs Lee had written up here "Happy is he who found a soldier's grave". Marshall told me that it was true that Genl Lee had exposed himself very much, in getting his troops together but not from despair. It was rather to encourage the troops by his presence.

A—In the beginning of the War the West was the friend of the South. Men looked to the West for countenance and aid. The high prices of provisions & cereals have made the west first supporters of the War & finally supporters of Republicanism. Corn that was used five years ago for feed has been selling at very high rates. Small farmers have paid off mortgage debts or purchased farms from the profits of two or three years. What virtue could stand that?

April 23d. Sherman's proposition for Peace with Joe Johnston disapproved by Cabinet. Grant has sided with the cabinet & has gone out to North Carolina to take command. Sherman is virtually set aside. I am very sorry to see this. I had heard that there was great jealousy between Sherman & Grant, but I was in hopes that they would act together, especially now that the Washington Cabinet seems determined to ignore the paroles given by Grant. Mr. Charles Howards sons** and other Marylanders are at Fortress Monroe. They are not allowed to return to Maryland, unless they take the oath. If they decline this, they are to be sent to Halifax. I fear Grant has quite backed down & intends to submit to have his plighted faith treated with scorn. It is so wonderful that the Virginians could not understand this. It is so extraordinary that they could for one moment trust a government which has never had the decency to grant one single belligerent right but what has been wrung from it by force and which in the case of the Florida behaved with a baseness almost below contempt. What can these paroled men expect when they have no army left to protect them.

I scarcely know what to expect of Sherman. He is self reliant, very conceited and imperious. He may not submit cheerfully. He

* The Baltimore *Sun* of April 22, 1865, reports: "*Lynch Law.* Five Confederate deserters, who had taken the oath of allegiance, were Lynched and hung at Indianapolis on the 15th., for expressing pleasure at the assassination of Mr. Lincoln."

** Charles Howard's sons were: Francis Key Howard, John Eager Howard, Charles Howard, James Howard, Edward L. Howard, and McHenry Howard. All but Francis Key Howard saw service in the Confederate army.

was the principal of a military school in Louisiana. When he left there in 1860, he told Beauregard that he never would draw his sword against the Southern States and that he was going to Ohio where he intended to educate the people to a proper understanding of the doctrine of State rights. He certainly has changed his mind to some extent since then, but the general order issued by him, after agreeing on terms with Johnston, shows that his desire is to reunite the States as States with their rights as States as little impaired as possible. How I would like to see him & Johnston unite and take possession of the country. I should so like to see Stanton, who has for some time been the ruling spirit, foisted from his place. Knaves & cowards are bad rulers. Montgomery Blair said of him "Cameron was a knave, but Stanton is a coward and a liar to boot".

President Johnson made on T—day last a speech to some Yankee Delegation. He took a most extreme ground and declared that treason was a crime greater than burglary and murder for it was one which threatened the life not of one man but of a nation. He said that it was to be punished by death and confiscation. On top of this, Stanton issues an order declaring that the citizens of the lower counties of Maryland which have harbored Booth the Assassin and which have given such aid & comfort to the enemy, shall be brought by the Military Commander of the Dept. "to a sense of their criminal conduct". Everything tends to extreme measures. Now that the Southern Army is gone, there is no one to protect the Southerner from his false hearted and treacherous foe. Wo to the people whose rulers are the lowest of the land. Lincoln was a rail splitter. Johnson a tailor. Seward a school master. Stanton, Cameron & the rest of the same class. Thurlow Weed, a power in the party, was son of a ragman & Horace Greely, if I recollect, did not know if he had an honest father. The Virginians made a sad mistake when they laid down their arms thinking that after fighting like soldiers and surrendering to soldiers they would be treated as soldiers. This is not merely a sectional war. It is a great social revolution. Now that the War is virtually finished the common end which united the North is lost. The revolution is but begun. There is however one great difference between the French Revolution & ours. The French revolution went through all its criminal excesses before the army became a power. Here the Northern army has become a power before the ultra faction has had full sway. The army is dictatorial & conservative. This makes me hope that if we have a revolution of Government, it may come without the violent scenes of the French Revolution.

April 24". Prisoners still coming here, as if they had a right to under Grant's parole. Government seems determined to ignore it. They are not allowed to walk about in grey clothes. Mrs Cary & Mrs Pegram are released with orders to report from day. Mrs Pegram says "I gave my parole to General Grant. If he insists on my taking the oath I will do so". Wallace knows she is here by Grant's permission & still ignores it. How can Grant as a soldier permit himself to be thus set aside by an inferior. The Virginia soldiers have scarcely an appreciation of the falsity of the Puritannical Yankee or they would not have abandoned their colors so. Col. Marshall said that when they left Richmond, Fitz Lee had but one regiment left of his division when they crossed the first bridge. The rest had ridden off to their homes, refusing to leave Virginia. He also said that the commissariat was in so wretched a way that although Lee had ordered supplies to be collected for the whole army at Amelia C.H. ten days before the evacuation of Richmond, yet when the army reached there not a ration was on hand.

Marshall repeated the old idea that the difficulty between Davis & Johnston was a personal one, originating early in the war. Mr. Ed. Randolph told Robt. McLane in Paris that it was occassioned in a great measure by the jealousy of the wives of the two men. I suspect however it arose from a totally different conception of the plans of campaigns. Davis has shown himself as stubborn as he was ignorant in military affairs. I heard from pretty good authority that certainly on two occasions Genl Lee had said to Mr Davis "Mr President our ideas are so totally at variance, that I feel I could not do you justice in attempting to carry out your views & must resign" upon which Davis gave in. Mr. Randolph also said that in the first campaign Davis insisted on having an army at Harpers Ferry & another at Manassas, to make a show of holding the whole line & producing foreign effect, while Johnston told him that so far from having two armies he had in fact no army at all. This was one of the first differences they had.

April 25. The Atty General* who heretofore has declared [for] the military suddenly discovers that Grant has exceeded his powers and decides that no paroled rebel can enter Maryland, he having forfeited all rights of citizenship when he took up arms against his country. The pledges of a Government whether made by parole through an officer or by treaty through ministers are only kept while they can be enforced.

* The reference here is to U.S. Attorney General James Speed.

Newspaper editor shot yesterday at Westminster.* Small mobs in New York.

Rev. Dr Bullock, when attacked by City Council must needs appeal to Wallace. Wallace forces him to take the oath. Serves him right. Why did he not wait quietly till he was sent for. Nothing is gained by yielding.

Roads all guarded. Booth said to be in town. Boston Harbor was blockaded a day or two ago to prevent him from escaping. Nobody was allowed to leave Baltimore for a day or two after the assassination without a pass.

Lincoln was killed on the anniversary of the first call for 75,000 troops. He was buried on the 19" April.

The number of persons secretly arrested and confined is not known. Newspapers are forbidden to mention any names until Booth is caught. Ford, the leasee of the Holliday St Theater has been in prison for some days in Washington. Today he is arrested again. He is as innocent as Bob Lincoln. For several days many letters were opened in the Post Office & afterwards not delivered.

Genl Barnard—Topogr. Corps—said to Mrs Cary in Washington in reference to the late battles "The first two days we were uneasy. The third day we were driven". This accounts for the telegrams from Lincoln & Grant on which I based my hopes.

Apr 26. The arrests in Washington continue. A panic prevails among Southern people. Mr & Mrs. Green have been arrested on the charge of harboring Booth. Absurd. Green is on a gunboat handcuffed. Mrs. G. is in the old Capitol treated with indignity. Their house has been ransacked and every thing torn to pieces. Her sister Jenny Lomax went down from Baltimore to see her. Not one of her many friends would receive her in the house, & advised her to return to Baltimore without delay. They pretend to say how they have discovered a wide spread plot for the abduction of Lincoln. On this pretence they are striking terror into the hearts of obnoxious innocent people.

The treatment of Mrs. Pegram & her sister Jenny Cary at the Provost Marshals in Balto. was outrageous. Wiegel's familiarities were worse than disgusting. This has been reported to Washington.

* According to the Baltimore *Sun* of April 26, 1865, Mr. Joseph Shaw, age c. 35, editor of the Westminster (Carroll County, Maryland) *Democrat* was killed in Zachariah's Hotel while defending himself from a mob led by Henry Bele, which broke into his hotel room. Bele was wounded. Citizens of the town had wanted the paper suspended, and the press was destroyed by mob action on April 22, 1865.

What use? What redress have people now? What fools people were not to fight at first and fight it out. I have a right to say so now.

Apl 27. Booth caught in a barn in Virginia. He refused to surrender & died like a man, shot by the soldiers. He must have suffered a great deal, travelling with his leg so recently broken in Charles County.

The Radicals in Baltimore are pushing matters to extremes. They have formed a vigilance committee for the purpose of rooting out traitors. The Military authorities are informed of it. Some men are trying to excite the negroes to violence. At a meeting last night a minister told them that each man who brought a report of treasonable talk at his master's table should have $5.

I see the States Atty in Penna. has indicted Genl. McCausland & others for treason & burglary. They were at Chambersburgh & helped to burn it.* Yesterday the Attorney General declared these men belligerents & not entitled to asylum in a loyal state. Today a States Attorney declares they are citizens and files a bill against them as such.

I heard a funny story today about Capt. Geo Howard. When he was taken prisoner last, he was marched by a negro company. Suddenly he heard some one say "De Lar. deyve done caught Massa George at last". One of his own negroes was among them.

April 28. Mr. Edwd. Ingersoll & his brother Charles have been mobbed in Philadelphia.** Mr. E. Ingersoll though a strong states rights man and almost a rebel in his talk, has always insisted on the preservation of the Union as being necessary for the preservation of peace on this continent. But Philadelphia always was the most prim & narrow minded hole in America. The Quaker seems to be worse than the Puritan when his nature is developed.

The body [of] a Mr. Thomas, a lumber man, who committed suicide two days ago has been exhumed and sent to Washington, after being embalmed. There is some idea that he was in some way connected with some plot. All the inmates of a boarding house in Fayette Street where he lived have been arrested. Could anything be worse than all this?

* The raid on Chambersburg, Pennsylvania, on July 30, 1864, was part of Early's raid into Maryland. Confederate soldiers under the command of Generals McCausland and Bradley T. Johnson burned the town when ransom demands were not met.

** For an account of the Philadelphia riot see Nicholas Wainwright, ed., *A Philadelphia Perspective, the Diary of Sidney George Fisher* (Philadelphia, 1967), pp. 494–96.

A few days ago two gentlemen, Mr. Williams & Mr. Roderwald, were attacked on Baltimore St. by some Union shriekers. Williams took refuge in Webb's jewelry store.* A crowd soon collected in front and cried out "have him out—damn the secession sympathizers" &c &c. Webb sent at once to the Provost Marshall's for troops, there being no police force on hand. Woolley returned for answer that he could not send troops until he received word from the Mayor that he was unable to preserve the peace. Meanwhile Webb was in danger of being mobbed & having his store gutted and his jewelry carried off. The Mob fortunately made no warlike demonstration, although ample opportunity was afforded them by the civil & military forces.

The feeling, I learn, in the North is quite as bitter as it is here. Mr. Phelps writes John Carroll that people are only quiet because they have the assurance of the Government that the property of rebels and their sympathizers shall be confiscated and then says he "no man's property will be safe". Everything tends now to an attack by the Mob on the rich. We have no nobility here as was in France but we have rich people. They do as well and furnish quite a good plunder. There is but one chance & that is foreign war. I so want to see a war with England. The Yankees will get licked like blazes & the South will be relieved from tyranny, while English commerce will be destroyed, and English debt and taxation will be increased and the English people will suffer ten times as much as they would if they had behaved like honest & brave men instead of Pursuing the contemptible course they have. Wolseley however writes me word "I have no fear of a war with the U.S. Johnson has work enough *cut out* for every tailor in the country were they all in succession to be raised to the Presidential chair". The Fennian Brotherhood are making great efforts to stir up a war.** Immense placards have recently been posted up in this city calling upon "friends of Irish Independence" to come and list to one Walsh.

* No reference to the mob action before the jewelry store of George W. Webb at 185 West Baltimore Street is made in the press. Those involved may have been Henry A. Rodewald of "Star Mount" on Belair Road, and George Hawkins Williams (1812–1889), who was an attorney, active Democrat, and married to Eleanor A. Gittings.

** The Fenians were an Irish-American revolutionary society founded in the United States c. 1858. After the Civil War they were linked with the radical Republicans, particularly with Benjamin Butler. Although a constant topic of newspaper comment, no "Walsh" could specifically be identified in Baltimore. Patrick Walsh was listed among those Fenian Prisoners released from Ireland in 1870 and given a royal welcome in New York City. For further information see William D'Arcy, *The Fenian Movement in the United States: 1858–1886* (Washington, 1947).

Apl 29. Joe Johnston has surrendered to Sherman on terms granted by Grant to Lee. I wonder if Sherman & Johnston have any understanding beyond the terms of surrender. Certainly Grants paroles are not respected here. Grant & Sherman appear from this to be united in their policy. I trust they may. Our only hope is a Military despotism & it would be a great thing to arrive at it without anarchy. That & foreign war to be kept up till the North is thoroughly beaten and exhausted. Notwithstanding Grants instructions terms of surrender have been refused to Moseby. He is declared an outlaw.

Lincoln's corpse is still being paraded around in New York. The Republicans are using it for political effect. There should be two or three of the members of the Cabinet along and then they would have quite a Menagerie. Booth's heart and head have been cut off and embalmed. No one knows what was done with his body. Newspapers are forbidden to mention, as well as to speak of the exhumation of Thomas' body and of any arrests made. Talk of the Censorship of the press. The newspapers of the day carry not the slightest idea of the revolutionary excitement which pervades the country.

The financial excitement still continues. Stocks and goods which decline on the prospect of peace and the return to a specie basis are still going up. Stocks are up 20 to 40 per ct. Cotton goods have risen in the same proportion. People move like sheep in flocks & never reason. If money is plenty for the moment they buy everything. If it be scarce they sell. The great questions of political economy do not seem to bother them.

I learn that several hundred men have applied personally to General Wallace to induce him to adopt most stringent measures against Rebels and their sympathizers. The editorials in the American have been extreme and truculent.

Montgomery Blair, who is not an extreme writes from Washington that the assassination of the President is certainly a deep laid scheme concocted in the South. He cannot believe it. Probably Johnson may desire to nurse the wrath of the people of the North. He is a vulgar democrat who hates what he calls aristocracy. If he encourage this feeling it will get beyond his control.

In Philadelphia at the Continental the negro waiters wear huge rosettes, red white & blue, with Lincoln's portrait in the middle. On their left shoulders are knots of crape from which long streamers descend.

The old cook of Mrs John Hanson Thomas has shaken her face in her mistress' face saying "You are the slayer of my deliverer".

April 30". The murder of Shaw, the newspaper editor in Westminster was of the most atrocious character. He had been notified to leave but had returned to be with his family. He was dragged from his room, his arm was broken to make him loose his hold from the bannister, his 'brains' were beaten out & he was cut with a knife. There were five men. They are not under arrest.

The case of the Ingersolls was as bad. Mr Edward Ingersoll had no trouble until his pistol was taken from him by the Police. Then he was beaten. Mr Charles Ingersoll was beaten, it is believed, by the Police men themselves. Two of them got into his carriage. His face was so bruised that it cannot be recognized. After being dragged out he was stamped upon. It is feared that his internal injuries are serious.

May 1". [*1865*] The Ram Webb has met the fate of all Confederate Iron Clads. She ran out Red River, passed through the blockading fleet, steamed past New Orleans & was well on her way to sea when her machinery became deranged & she was blown up.

May 2d. H. G. Worthington, member from Nevada came up from Washington today. He had been to the Provost Marshal's to see Ben Ficklin but was denied access to him & not allowed permission to give him money. F. is detained on suspicion of being connected with the assassination. The only grounds are that they have no grounds.

Jennie Lomax returned today. She was seized four days ago & thrown into the old Capitol while in Washington endeavoring to get access to her sister Mrs Green. She was prohibited from writing or communicating with anybody. Her whereabouts was only discovered yesterday. Her released [*sic*] was procured by some friends here. None of her Washington friends did anything. They were too frightened.

Sister Mary got a pass today to go & see Percival Elliott. Four days ago we recd. a letter from him at the Lincoln Genl. Hospital, Washington, saying he had lost a leg in the late campaign in Virginia & was suffering from hospital gangrene. I telegraphed at once I would be down next day. But I found alas, I was not only debarred from getting to him but that I should in all probability be arrested and thrown into prison if I went to Washington. For the first time during the war my sisters opposed my going to the relief of a Southern man. I had often done it before, when others called it dangerous. Fortunately a pass is now obtained. Percy is better & I hope will pull through.

Ben Harris has been arrested in St. Mary's for advising returned soldiers not to take the oath. Civil law being now restored he is to be tried by court martial. Wallace has issued an order prohibiting sale of Booth's portraits or those of Rebel Generals in this department. We are getting back to the days when little children are sent to guard house for wearing red ribbons in white caps. In Richmond orders have been issued forbidding marriage to those who do not take the oath. In Charleston orders promise to be still more extreme.

May 2d. The arrest of Miss Jennie Lomax was fearful. She called to see Mr. Hunter on behalf of her sister. He cross questioned her closely, charged her with being the authoress of a letter which he had in his hand, which she never saw & finally gave a card to a detective & told her he would assist her. When she was going down the street, she found to her surprise she was a prisoner. She was hurried off & put in solitary confinement, without being permitted even to get a piece of clothing. After four days imprisonment she became so weak & delirious that they thought it advisable to take her to her sisters room.

The atrocity with which they are proceeding is dreadful. Men and women are confined on gunboats. No one is allowed access to them, nor are they permitted to defend themselves from any charges against them.

Worthington, member for Nevada, went today to see F. & learned that he was incarcerated on acct of suspicious circumstances. W. was allowed no communication with him. He was simply in Washington on cotton business, under his own name.

Judge Pierpont had arranged to get Stanton's endorsement on the permits I had obtained to get out cotton. The permits signed by Lincoln were for 250,000 Bales. Ficklin had gone on to Washington a day ahead of me and Judge P. He was arrested on suspicion & was kept over two months in close confinement without any charge against. For three weeks I could not even learn where he was. By the time he was released there was no object to be gained in carrying out our plan. The war was over. If it had continued a short time longer & we had perfected our schemes, Stanton & Trenholm would have been copartners in the operation. Each of them would have received a share of the profits.

No. 6

1865

May 5. I find in New York many Southern officers and soldiers—from Louisiana, Maryland & Tennessee principally. Some of these men have been at Fortress Monroe for three weeks, Genl Ord refusing to ratify Grant's paroles or to allow them either to leave or go back unless they took the oath of allegiance. Some of the officers begged their fellow prisoners to stand firm, telling them that as General Grant's word was not regarded they had no pledge whatever that Genl Ord's would be. But with that want of moral courage which appears to be a trait of American character, they soon gave in. To those that did take the Oath Genl Ord gave passes to go home, endorsing on the face of them "Rebel Deserters"—which was both an insult and a lie. So these men gained nothing by their conduct but contempt. The few who held out finally obtained passes to go to South America which was all nonsense, for now they are here, they can go where they choose. Marylanders however are not allowed to return to their state. They have lost all rights by being in rebellion—according to the dictum of the authorities.

Major Howard (Surgeon) who surrendered with Lee has given me some interesting facts, all of which go to show the grossest mismanagement in the Confederacy. I suspect the truth was that the people got tired out. From the battle of Bull Run to the last battle on the Chickahominy, no victory was ever pursued and the consequence was eventually that the North got fresh recruits and the South found itself after a victory weaker than it was before. This is the only fault I ever hear attributed to Genl Lee—a want of dash—of elan. His idea seemed to be to spare his men, to nurse them and he failed to overwork them on one or two occasions when a little overwork might have accomplished wonders. Ned Howard says that when men had broken rank and were making for the rear he has seen Genl Lee ride up and encourage them and expostulate with them. Then they would cheer him, but they would not reform. Presently Hill would come along. He would strike a dozen of them across the back with his sabre, order them up, call out a file of men to shoot them if they did not re-form and would soon have them to the front again. Ned's idea of Joe Johnston was that he was a better General than Lee. I think highly too of Johnston and have always thought that the South could afford to lose territory but could not afford to lose men. The trouble was that in losing territory

Johnston lost men. Men would not go far from their homes. Johnston knew this and after weighing the testimony well, it must be acknowledged that Johnston made a very great mistake in not giving battle in the Northern part of Georgia. A mistake which proved fatal, for the advance of Sherman changed the whole feeling of the North and the despair of Jeff Davis led to the removal of Johnston, which was virtually the end of the war & of all Davis ill advised acts the most ill advised. This unwillingness of men to abandon their homes led the Virginians to desert Lee at the last. The Southern army unfortunately was composed of men of too much intelligence and too much property.

To my surprise Ned told me that the scarcity of provisions was much less than was believed. There was abundance of provisions between Amelia C.H. and Danville but they were not made available for three reasons. The Commissariat was in such wretched condition that no forage or provisions were obtained except what was immediately in the vicinity of Rail Roads. He told me he saw himself abundance of everything twelve or fifteen miles off, which the owners would have been glad to give up. But no means were ever offerd for transportation. Then there were many who refused to sell for Confederate Money. And finally the Government had become so inefficient that it had not the power to seize what was necessary for its existence. Ned said that though the Army had been for some time on short rations, they had not really suffered but that on the contrary the health in his brigade and in those he knew most of was astonishingly good. His men got $\frac{1}{3}$ # bacon per day.

He said the men were tired of the war & even those who would have stood by Genl Lee to the death expressed their joy that the War was at an end.

Their idea was that they had fought for states rights and had been beaten and that they had lost slavery. They expected to come back into the Union and be as they were before the war. It is wonderful how little they understand the Yankee character. After all that has happened they trust it still. They will find before long that it would have been better to have died as freemen rather than to live as slaves.

May 6. Lincoln is buried at last after being paraded through the whole country, in order to excite the public mind. If Davis & Benjamin are caught they will certainly be hanged—for the purpose of "cementing the Union". The Republicans want an excuse to hold the South in subjugation.

Genl Barry, who was with Sherman at Johnston's surrender, says that the So. Carolinians are hounds. Everywhere through the State people came in & swore that they were always opposed to secession & were glad to get back again under the old flag. In Georgia & No. Carolina, he said men behaved like men. They said "You are our conquerors but we do not love you". How Maryland men now stand out after all the abuse they have received from Virginia! Over 20000 men left their homes in Maryland to fight for a cause. They risked everything for a principle. They are now exiles from their own land. No one state has produced as many men or anything like it, who were willing to leave it when it was in possession of the enemy.

May 16". New York has been & is filled with Southerners, some on their way home, others not knowing what to do or where to go. Barring the fact that there is no chance of getting employment for a Southerner or Rebel in New York, there is little else left to show that a war has existed for four years. It is already a thing of the past and these people, whose impressions last but a day, have already forgotten it. No one talks of it except newspaper scribblers and pot house politicians. It is really wonderful to see that in a whole country there is no one to think. The moneyed men are rushing madly to subscribe greedily for the U.S. 7.30 loan, as if it were better than gold. No one doubts for a moment the government's capacity and few understand that the loan at present authorized—of which 200 millions is yet unsubscribed for—will not suffice by a very large amount, to settle up all the debts of the Administration.

I hear that in Richmond people are shy of greenbacks. They insist on leasing ground for gold—rents payable in advance. They have seen the result of an over confederate issue & they fear a similar catastrophe. A burnt child dreads the fire. Now if a dozen states are restored to the Union, none of whom are interested in the payment of the debt, are willing to be taxed or believe in greenbacks, what is to be the result?

May 17. Tom Conolly—M.P.—known in England as "Mad Tom" sailed today. He paired off for six months & took to blocake running. He got out two Cargoes of Cotton and then lost his vessel and Cargo. He was afterwards with General Lee "en amateur". He was at Fort Steadman—where the men men [*sic*] went in, without charges in their guns and clubbed the Yankees. He said the surprise was perfect. Grant's army was cut in two and in twenty minutes they would have been thrown back in confusion & disaster to City Point. C. said to Genl Lee "For Gods sake General go in—now is your chance—you can ruin Grant with what you have here". But Lee would not do it. He said he could not afford such a risk. He had not troops enough near at hand. And still Genl Lee then knew that he could not hold Richmond and that when he evacuated it he must lose half his army. He felt that nothing but a miracle could save the cause and still he would not go in for a miracle.* Misfortune must have taken the heart out of him. It does out of everybody. It did out of Napoleon. It is very easy to be great when the tide is in your favor. It is hard for many people not be contemptible in adversity—& very very hard for one to be great when luck is running against him. Conolly sent out to Genl Lee & staff, an elegant set of equipments, comprising seventy saddles in all—a most handsome present. They reached Havana & are now in Galveston. He begged Genl Lee to go to England with him and offered him an establishment—house servants &c for three years. Conolly says the Southern women are the noblest creatures in the world; but he is coming back to marry Livia Peters a Philadelphian—and I take it the Philadelphians are the worst Yankees "in creation".

Byrne who was with Joe Johnston & Llewellyn Saunderson who was with Fitz Lee also sail for England this week. There were lots of young Englishmen with the Southern army.

May 20". There has been very little excitement over the capture of Jeff Davis. That he is to be hanged appears to be a foregone conclusion—and so he will be made a martyr of as Lincoln has been. Let him alone & he will go down to his grave unmissed & unhonored though not unsung. Everything tends to show that the South fought this war against Jeff Davis, who was their worst enemy. A letter published in the N.Y. Times today—dated Richmond May 15. written by a private secretary of a member of the cabinet gives a most sensible and clear statement of Davis' position—& after giving him due credit says he was a man "whose faults of temper & intellect would have ruined a far stronger cause than that of the South".** Davis appears to have had no knowledge of men. He surrounded himself with men of mean capacity & entrenched himself behind incompetency. The breaking down of the currency was one of the greatest & most fatal blows to the South. And still the South

* Douglas Southall Freeman, *Lee's Lieutenants* (New York, 1950) contradicts this view of the battle of Fort Stedman (March 25, 1865). Confederate losses were quite heavy.

** The unsigned letter to the editors of *The New York Times* from the private secretary of an unnamed member of the Confederate Cabinet can be found in the issue of May 19, 1865, p. 4, col. 6, and p. 5, col. 1.

started with a basis of credit the North never had—and the Southern men gave up their fortunes as no man in the North ever pretended to do. In the North people have only subscribed when they thought they could profit by it. What I always looked to to prove fatal to the north was what did prove fatal to the South—and all through the most shameful and hopeless incompetency and ignorance. But currency was not the only cause. Men had lost all confidence in the Administration. They had no security that munitions of war would be forth coming when needed and they were always afraid that the commissariat would fail. In fact so wretchedly was everything administered that the soldiers & people had no longer any confidence. I believe more and more in one man power. One man at the helm in the South was all that was needed to have carried through the cause not only triumphantly but easily.

I am going back to Baltimore. The members of the City Council and extremists of Maryland, who are all very common and very weak men, have been driving every Southerner out of Maryland. Consequently much Southern trade is lost to the City. Men have gone on North as of old. The Merchants & property holders finding this out have taken the matter in hand. The City Council has become quiet and the Military, which has been driven on to many extreme measures by the Loyal Leaguers, now follows their lead and keeps quiet too. Self interest is producing its effect. One can live home now without much molestation.

The treatment of the conspirators at Washington is atrocious. Hands, feets, & neck are manacled. Over the head a thick padded hood is drawn ostensibly for the purpose of preventing them from beating out their brains. Tried by a Military commission, for an offense punishable by the civil law, there seems to be no hope. The position of Dr. Mudd is very hard. He set the leg of a man he did not know & because he did not give him up, is to be executed for it after weeks of infamous torture.

May 21. It is well known now that the President Andy Johnson has quietly backed down from the policy inaugurated on his accession to the dictatorial chair. Prisoners who were not permitted to return to Maryland, even though they took the amnesty oath, now return to their homes unmolested. The opinion promulgated by the Attorney General that Rebels in arms, from states which had not seceeded, had lost their rights of Citizenship, appears to be considered by the cabinet after a little reflection as a dead letter.

Rumor says that Charles O'Conor has been called to a place in the cabinet. This can hardly be. He is an ultra secessionist. He is a man of very decided ability, & well balanced mind, but like all other politicians, he wants nerve. When McClellan received his nomination, many of the Democrats in New York were very indignant at the course it was understood he would pursue. Mr. O'C at the New York Hotel told Col Charley May that it would be ruinous to the peace party to permit McClellan to alter the platform one iota and that if he attempted to do so the Democratic convention ought to be called together without delay. He further said that he had held his tongue long enough, that now was the time to speak and that if McClellan did take ground against his party, he would come out in a letter and take a stand. Afterwards when McClellan showed himself a more decided war man even than was anticipated, I went to Ben Wood and asked him where was Mr. O'Conor's letter. He sent for it and received answer "that Mr O'C had no letter and had never authorized anyone to say he intended to publish one". All the peace men had backed down, prefering to support the Democratic nominee rather than make an honest effort to stop the war—and Mr. O'Conor went with them. Some time afterwards I was dining at Dr Carnochan's. Mr O'C & I had a long talk. He was looking forward anxiously to the establishment of the Republic of Ontario—to be composed of New York, Penna. N. Jersey & Delaware. He thought the country too large to be held together and the Republican form of Govt. a failure. He declared it was high time to form a peace party and said that the day after the Election whether Lincoln was reelected or not he intended to come out with a letter which he intended to be a nucleus around which peace men could rally. I asked him if he was in communication with organizations in the Western States which would support a peace movement. He said it had friends enough to give it strength. He did come out with such a letter, after the election. It was addressed to Mayor Gunther, but it had no force, was very ambiguous & no body suspected what was its intention. So much for a man whom everyone respects and who is regarded as one of the very best men in the North.

May 23d. The quarrel between Stanton and his enemies is getting to be a very pretty one. Sherman says he is a scoundrel and refuses to speak to him. Blair says he is a rascal and a liar and that he will forgive the Administration all their neglect of him if the President will only turn Stanton out and give him the Secretaryship for twenty four hours. Blair told Barlow that he had told Stanton that he was in league with Baker—and that Baker imprisoned men & extorted money from them for their release of which Stanton got half. Sam Berret said that in the commencement of the revolution Stanton was always at the Southern meetings in Washington & took a prominent part, declaring that the attempt to coerce the South was outrageous. When Berret was arrested Stanton wished to apply for a writ of habeas corpus for him; but Berret declined—wisely as it turns out. Stanton was at one time under great obligation to Senator Bright, early in his career. Bright had a claim against the Govt. for occupation of his property in Washington & was advised by some of the clerks to see Stanton. He declined at first but afterwards had an interview. Stanton, quite unmindful of any former intimacy, told him that the claims of such men as himself would not be paid until the rebellion was over & was very rude. Bright left & sent him word that when the rebellion was over he would horsewhip him wherever he caught him.

May 24. I cannot make out what the Administration is after. My own impression is that they are much surprised to find that Southern soldiers refuse to fight the battles of the North and to enlist for Mexico. After Blair's mission to Richmond it was considered quite certain that the Confederates would at any time join forces and make war agst Mexico and Canada if necessary. And so they would, if they could have gained nominal independence by it. But now that the cause is lost and they have nothing to gain, they do not intend to fight for their oppressors. The Rebs have had many offers made them and Genl. Lee himself I am assured has been approached. Even the prisoners in the different forts have determined not to fight for the North. No matter how fierce Andy Johnson may feel agst Napoleon, he cannot invade Mexico, with a large & hostile population at home. Some paroled men arrived here yesterday. They got as far as Augusta on their way to Louisiana. Whence they were shipped to Savannah & from thence to Baltimore. Here they are refused transportation & told they are to get home the best way they can. On asking what they were to do they were told in the Provost Marshal's office that they could get $500 bounty if they would enlist for Mexico. What is to be done with the Southerners if they refuse to be killed off in Mexico. Genl Lee will in all probability be indicted for treason. What do these men care about violating pledges. What law is left. The conspirators are being tried for a civil offense by a court martial. Ben Harris has been tried by a military tribunal for purely civil offenses—if they can be called offenses. And Bessie Perine who has been for months home by permission from General Dix and who was guilty of nothing but girlish folly, has also been tried by a court martial in Washington.

May 26". Quantities of soldiers here who live far away South & have no means of getting home. They solicit aid from door to door. One neighbor gave $200 away last week. The prisoners are still kept in the Forts. We receive here daily applications for clothing. Mother & the girls devote their whole time & means towards filling them. They come so often now that I am satisfied the prisoners at Ft. Delaware imagine that Mother is the head of a society. They can hardly think one woman would do so much.

May 29". I had a long talk yesterday with Dr S. and Govr P. about the calling of the Legislature together by Govr. Hicks and other matters. Hicks had professed to be entirely Southern, but at the same time had an old political party hatred of everything democratic, and he was very slow to act as the Southerners desired. They were considered too extreme by men like Hicks, who saw in the revolution that was about bursting over the country only a party quarrel among the Democrats. Dr Steuart had gone to Annapolis immediately after the outbreak in Baltimore on the 19" April determined if necessary to force Hicks to call the Legislature together with a view to calling a convention. Travel was entirely interrupted and Dr S. had driven down from the Annapolis Junction in Kilbourn's carriage. Dr S. used every argument he could to induce the Govr. to convene the Legislature immediately, but Hicks was not willing to accede altogether to his wishes. While they were discussing the subject Hagner came in crying out "Orders have been received from the President directing Butler to embark his troops and leave the harbor." This decided Hicks. Dr S. had brought the news that assurances had been given to Brune, Dobbin & Wallis, Commissioners from Baltimore, that the troops should be withdrawn from Cockeysville and that Belger had come up with orders from Genl. Scott to that effect. Hicks was satisfied that the Admn. were going to back down. He was quite safe. He immediately wrote the necessary proclamation, handed it to Dr. S. and asked him if it would suit. Dr. S. replied in the affirmative and was told that it would be ready with the official seal in half an hour. Dr. S. left to go and see the Commodore in charge. He met Govr Pratt at the door who said "Dont you go. Don't leave Hicks alone for half an hour or he'll change his mind. You can't trust him that long." Dr S. however did slip off for a few minutes, saw the Commodore, found that Hagner, although he was President of the Telegraph Co. had made a most singular mistake and returned at once. He got the proclamation. Fortunately a steamer came just then into the harbor. Dr S. went aboard, saw the Capt, who knew him well, told him to put him in Baltimore in two hours and a half and to name his own price, and in a very short time, Dr S. & the proclamation were beyond Hicks reach. Hicks soon found out his mistake for Butler had recd. no such orders & commenced telegraphing to Washington. But it was too late.

Dr. S. afterwards chartered a steamer to carry himself and his family to West River. As they were starting a man came aboard begging a passage stating that there was an urgent necessity for him to get to Annapolis. It turned out to be Govr Hicks brother* who had come over from the Eastern Shore, with the news that the people there had all changed their tone, that the feeling was entirely Southern & that it was absolutely necessary for the Govr. to espouse the Southern cause. Dr. S. wrote a letter by this man to Hicks urging Hicks to authorize him to go at once to Virginia and make some arrangement with Govr Letcher for the joint action of Maryand and Virginia. Next morning he recd. by special messenger from Hicks a letter, which I saw, assuring him that he concurred in the sentiments expressed but giving his reasons why such a step was inadvisible. [This sentence originally read ". . . . assuring him that the sentiments expressed coincided with his own. . . ." Glenn subsequently changed the wording to read as above. He also added in brackets: "I forget the exact words".] This letter no doubt saved Dr S. from indictment for treason. Hicks could not afford to have his answer produced.

Crump came to Annapolis somewhere about this time on a secret mission from Govr Letcher. He arrived in the morning. Hicks was at breakfast. He asked Crump to take some Whiskey. C. replied that he was not in the habit of drinking Whiskey at that hour and that besides he had had no breakfast. After stating his errand, Hicks left him. C. thought he had gone out to order him some breakfast, but after some time Hicks returned and gave him merely an unsatisfactory answer. C. then went round to see Govr Pratt, who asked him if he knew what Hicks had left him for. I am sure, continued he, Hicks went out to see Col. Lefferts, commanding the 7" N.Y. Regiment now here, to tell him your mission & to consult about arresting you". Crump was furious at the idea. He had entertained Lefferts in Richmond and he and Govr Pratt went round to see him

* Governor Hicks was one of the thirteen children of Henry S. and Mary Sewall Hicks. Only one brother was living at the time of Governor Hicks's death, Hooper Columbus Hicks (1819–post-1898), twelveth child and youngest son.

and find out what they could, but they learned nothing. Lefferts either knew nothing or was prudent.

May 30. The amnesty proclamation is out. No King of Dahomey* could be more absolute. Andy Johnson may as well sign himself, for the future JAH. He giveth and he taketh away. Sensible men have been wildly hoping and blindly believing to the last, that he intended to pursue a liberal policy. They are satisfied now. For my part I think it all right. God forbid these people should ever be united again. I want the South to be bound together by trial & suffering, that when the grand break up does come, they may be together. The most significant clause in the proclamation is the $20,000 clause. No man with that much property is to be pardoned. Is it to be war against the rich?

June 5". [1865] Lawley writes me most amusing letters from England in regard to the Times. Delane is worried to death at the very great mistake he has made in having a correspondent with Southern views in New York. He is very indignant that Mackay should have so misled the public and although Delane did his best to keep the Times right by publishing leaders in one sense while Mackay wrote in another, he is now much annoyed that M. should have written as he did. So Mackay is snubbed and to be recalled. On him is the wrath to fall. The truth is that Billy Russell was recalled because he would not write sufficient South. Mackay was sent in his place to write to order. Delane has himself to thank & no one else, and it is purely contemptible that he cannot be man enough to stand by opinions that he pretended to advocate. He is terribly afraid now of a war with this country. He will not publish North letters at all, for the present. There can be little doubt I think that in many instances the Times acts under instruction from the Cabinet. Lord Palmerston keeps Delane straight and Delane does his bidding, flattered with the attention shown him.

June 10". Baltimore is filled with prisoners paroled en route for home and young men returned. A great many privates are here who are not furnished with transportation by Government & who have to go hundreds of miles home as best they can. They solicit aid from door to door & receive clothing & money. Since it was found that the ostracising of returned men from the Southern Army had an injurious effect on the trade, the Loyal leaguers here have been

* The King of Dahomey was the monarch of an African kingdom known for the absolute rule of its sovereign, particularly in matters of human sacrifice.

remarkably quiet. Our boys walk about the street without molestation and several picnics and parties have been given to them. It is really very curious to see how quiet everything is. A stranger would scarcely recognize any signs of the bitter feeling which existed a short time ago.

June 11". No news from Washington. No one has an idea what the policy of the Govt is to be in regard to "Traitors and Foreign powers". The people have so entirely surrendered their liberties that they blindly acquiesce in the dictates of half a dozen men and support any proclamation issued by Andy Johnson.

I learn from returned men that in the 1" Maryland Cavalry and in the Maryland Infantry—the two bodies of Marylanders which had preserved their state organization—there were towards the end of the War more gentlemen & men of education than in any other regiments. Most of the rich men and men of any position had contrived to get their sons out of the army entirely, replacing them by conscripts, or had managed to get them soft places in some of the departments, so that towards the end the composition of many of the Southern regiments was very different from what it was at the commencement of the war. The Marylanders having gone to fight staid to fight and continued their organization to the last. Just before Lee's surrender at Appamatox they made a charge at High Bridge and were recalled, though they were driving the enemy. Genl Munford commanding complimented them, saying that Maryland had been the first to shed blood on the 19" April and the last to shed it in Virginia. The Maryland Cavalry & Infantry were both frequently complimented during the war. If any one man of ability could have rallied the whole Maryland force into a Maryland line it would have made a gallant record.

June 15". New York is filled with Confederate released prisoners. Most of them are destitute. They are furnished with transportation but not with food and while they remain in New York, waiting for steamers to sail, are forced to depend upon public charity. A gentleman came to night to the New York Hotel and appealed for lodging for himself & two friends. He said they would be content with one meal a day until they could get transportation. The kind treatment he received brought the tears to his eyes. I wonder if the government thinks this a good way of healing the bitter differencs and reuniting the broken parts.

June 16. Have just heard of Mr Henry A. Middleton's fate in South Carolina. Finding his position hopeless & his state abandoned he went to the Commander of the Fleet and asked him what he proposed to do. He said he proposed to preserve order and told Mr Middleton to put his negroes to work and if he had any difficulty with them to let him know. He accordingly returned to his plantation and made arrangements to cultivate it. Next day a squadron of cavalry came up, turned him out unceremoniously and without any further explanation whatever than that he was too persistent a rebel to be allowed to remain unpunished, began gutting his house and emptying it as soon as possible by the aid of the negroes, to whom they gave to understand that all the effects really belonged. Finally they fired the house & the outbuildings. He had time to pick up a small travelling bag, in which he placed two shirts. With this he marched off leaving his buildings in flames behind him. He was 60 miles from Charleston, which place he had to reach. He was 72 years of age. Mr. M. is now in New York. He has applied for pardon, in hopes of getting his property back. All the plantations in that neighborhood are in possession of the Govt. forces and the owners prefer to apply at once for pardon, in hopes of saving themselves from starvation. The worn out condition of the regions where the Federal armies have gotten foothold is fearful.

June 18". I hear that Rooney Lee has applied for pardon. Can it be so? If so it is the same old story we have seen in Maryland. Nothing could have been accomplished against us had we stood united. Everything was accomplished against a divided people and our liberties were lost. If the people of the South would stand firm, confiscation would be an impossibility. If they come in piece meal, they surrender virtually the last vestige of their liberties. Rooney Lee must have taken this step by the advice of his father. If Genl. Lee follows this step himself, acknowledges himself a rebel and humbly sues for pardon for an offence committed, he will damage his character. I cannot understand this servility. The Yankees are bad. But the Southerners appear to be no better. It may be that they are simply dispirited & exhausted. But in any event it is inexplicable to me.

The Yankees have not this excuse. They are fat and prospering and still their servility is abject. Andy Johnson issues proclamation after proclamation, forms provisional governments, lays down plans for ruling a subjugated people and delegates absolute powers to individuals as if these were all constitutional rights. No one objects. So many innovations have been made during the war, that now peace has come innovations no longer astound. People buy and sell and submit to dictatorship. In the North this war is totally forgotten already. It is curious.

June 20. Heard today from Sam Sterett just out of Fort Warren after two years confinement the story of the failure of the Iron Clad attack last winter. When Read, after his capture at Portland, effected his exchange he was put on duty near Richmond. He immediately said "What are these Iron Clads doing here. They are made to be lost. It is impossible that the Yankees can have so obstructed the channel that these boats cannot get down, for they hope one day to come up themselves". With that he explored the channel himself the first dark night. Genl Lee was informed of the fact that the Navigation was open past the Confederate obstructions. The plan was laid. But one Iron Clad was at City Point. The fleet was to go down, to seize or destroy this one Iron Clad, to destroy the pontoon bridge, thus breaking up all communication between Grant's wings & to seize the fleet of transports at City Point, taking them down the river and sink them many miles below, near Newport News, thus totally obstructing navigation for a time to come. The stores &c at City Point & wooden structures were all to be committed to the flames and Lee who had his army massed at Richmond was to attack Grants right wing. Afterwards, cut off from all supplies & the Confederates having command of the streams by small boats Grants surrender was almost inevitable. The fleet was committed to the charge of Capt Mitchell. As he neared the difficult point he became uneasy and sent Read down to explore a new channel. Read returned reporting 18 ft of water. Still Mitchell refused to go without exploring himself. The officers begged him not. The fleet had come up & when they recd. orders to anchor, they declared that if they anchored they would get aground. Mitchell insisted, made the reconnaisance, found water plenty and returned to find the Iron Clads aground and the scheme an abortion. The largest one got through alone easily. What is this. Is this luck or not? It certainly was hard luck to have a man so over cautious at such a time. It was bad luck to have Jackson killed. It was hard luck to have Longstreet wounded & his important movement defeated. It was carelessness in Hill to throw down Lee's orders near Antietam, but it was hard luck to have them found so soon by McClellan. So at Gettysburg there were faults but bad luck too. I am getting to be a firm believer in luck.

June 21. Genl. Lee I hear has applied for pardon.* Well! it only

* Elmer Oris Parker has written an interesting article on Lee's amnesty oath in *Prologue* (published by the National Archives), winter 1970. The text of the Oath reads as follows:

wanted this. People excuse him and say he does it for the good of the people. He sacrifices himself to show what is best for them to do. But has any man a right to set a fellow man an ignoble example? If Lee takes this step he lowers himself to the position of leader of the slave holders rebellion. The South itself accepts the situation the North has always allotted to it. To take an oath of allegiance when you are in chains & there is no hope of succor is one thing. To acknowledge you have been criminal is another. I trust the story is not true.

June 22. Baltimore is filled with prisoners returning to their homes. A Virginian today remarked to me that the drain on Baltimore must have been very large, for all the men he saw received new suits of clothes from Baltimoreans. So they do. The Southerners from Baltimore & Maryland who were in the South have fought nobly. Those who staid at home have behaved more than liberally.

June 23. Freedom of the Press is restored; but the Gazette is still afraid to attempt editorials and the Richmond Times of yesterday announces to its subscribers that it has been notified it will be stopped if it attempts to criticise political events as it has been doing.

June 25. At Church at Hanging Rock Harford Co.* Several Confederates there. The girls as usual pet them a great deal. One said "see here, you didn't kiss me when you came home. Now, I intend to find out if you kissed any of the other girls and if you did I shall never forgive you". The Papas were very funny. They were proud of their boys & spoke of them as brave fellows, quite forgetting how sulky they had been when they went and how often they had abused them for going.

OFFICE OF NOTARY PUBLIC
Rockbridge County, Va. October 2nd 1865
AMNESTY OATH

I *Robert E. Lee* of *Lexington Virginia* do solemnly swear, in the presence of Almighty God, that I will henceforth faithfully support, protect and defend the Constitution of the United States, and the Union of the States thereunder, and that I will, in like manner, abide by and faithfully support all laws and proclamations which have been made during the existing rebellion with reference to the emancipation of slaves, so help me God.

R E Lee

Sworn to and subscribed before me
this *2nd* day of *October* 1865

Chas. A. Davidson Notary Public

* "Hanging Rock" in Harford County cannot be located. There were five Episcopal parishes in Harford County: St. John's at Havre de Grace, Christ Church at Belair, St. George's at Perrymansville, St. Mary's at Emmorton, and St. James' Deer Creek near Dublin. This latter is near the Falling Branch of Deer Creek.

In New York last week I saw one pretty girl who would stick by Col Gordon. He had been repeatedly faithless to his wife, he had run away with his Major's wife and been forced to sell out in England (of the Coldstreams I think) he had left his wife & six children to take care of themselves, he had committed forgery in Vancouver's Island, been tried & convicted and lastly he had received in Baltimore $700 for Col Ransom to be handed him in Richmond and appropriated it himself. It was no use. He had fought & bled for the South. The lovely Sally would forgive him. As for the fact of his having condescended to obtain a commission in the Northern Army, in the beginning of the war, *that* she simply did not believe.

June 26". Baltimore is filled with Rebels. Many on parole, many on their way home from prisons, others having certified to their loyalty by taking the oath. Of course it is very interesting to converse with the more intelligent portion of them, especially those who have been in command and occupied positions which gave them an opportunity of informing themselves thoroughly on public matters. I hear but one opinion as to Davis & his Cabinet—and their influence upon the Southern cause. To think of such a chance so woefully botched by obstinancy & inefficiency. People talk about general causes, but my experience teaches me that there is no such cause as a good or a bad head. I believe in one-man power and the more I live, the more I see the influence that one man who leads exercises in his family, in his business circle, in a corporation, in his state or among a people.

The prisoners going home, reach Baltimore from Pennsylvania in a wretched half starved state. They are shipped with insufficient rations, kept two days or more cooped up in cars & arrive here worn out. Many of them are so weak as to be unable to get to the boat, which is more than a mile from where they stop. No provision at all is made for them. Nannie Howard, Mary Frick, Mrs. Winn, Mrs. Charles Howard, sisters and Aunt Martha are working all the time preparing sandwiches. Yesterday 200 poor fellows got a good meal served. Many other people are engaged in this work. Some gentlemen have organized a sort of Ambulance Corps to carry those who cannot walk, from weakness. Some of them who are very ill have been taken over to the Church Home Hospital.

June 27. Wm B. Paca & his sons have been acquitted at Easton.*

* The Paca homicide trial was reported in the Baltimore *Sun* of June 27, 1865. The case was heard before Judge H. H. Goldsborough in Queen Annes County of Maryland's Eastern Shore, with P. T. Kennard as State's Attorney.

He and his three sons armed themselves and rode over to the house occupied by his nephews. Paca was their Trustee. He had forbidden them to erect a fence around the garden. Finding them at work he & his sons deliberately shot one of the young men & his Uncle Jones with guns carried for the purpose and killed them stone dead in sight of their house and in the hearing of their mother. Paca gave up his idiot son as the assassin—but his little nephew—who has yet to be murdered before Paca's own children inherit the property—saw him kill his brother and gave his testimony before the grand jury. At the trial which followed the indictment all the respectable men were challenged until finally a jury was obtained of low illiterate and Anti Southern men. They were freely bribed and rendered a verdict of "not guilty". Judge H. H. Goldsborough during the trial descended from the bench & gave his testimony as a witness. The whole proceeding was most extraordinary. A Govt. man had shot two Southern men. The case was atrocious but the devil protects his own. Henceforth any man may kill a Southerner as he chooses. He will be protected. The men that assassinated Shaw, in Westminster a few weeks ago, on his return from the South have been also acquitted.

I find that Wm. B. Paca had before this obtained the confiscation of the property of another of his nephews, then in the Southern army,* and bought it in himself for $2 or $3000 although it was worth nearer $60,000. In summoning a Jury the Sheriff carefully avoided all gentlemen & took no talesmen except from among the commoner people. Five of the Jury had been connected with the provost Marshal's Office. It was simply a Federal outrage of the grossest character.

June 29. 11700 paroled Maryland Prisoners have already reported at the Provost Marshal's office here. John T. B. Dorsey** tells me that there were 22,000 enrolled in Richmond. Of course the actual number must have been larger. Military Commission, considered testimony & pondered verdict in the Washington trials. Verdict not yet made public.

State vs. William P. Paca, Tilghman C. Paca and James P. Paca, concerned the murder of Alfred Jones and John P. Paca of Edward at Wye Neck, Queen Annes County on March 8, 1865. The defendants were found not guilty in the Jones case, and the case against them for the murder of John P. Paca of Edward was moved to Caroline County for trial, where the defendants were likewise acquitted.

* The nephew in the Southern army was E. Tilghman Paca (1843–1922?).

** J. T. B. Dorsey was a captain and assistant quartermaster in the Confederate army.

June 30". My doctrine of luck is sometimes very considerably shaken when I reflect upon the inefficiency of men in the South to whom important commands were entrusted. Thus after the fall of Fort St Philip, occasioned by the passage of the fleet up the river, which could not have happened had not the chain obstructions been removed, Farragut to his great surprise sailed up to New Orleans. Guard had been kept at Fort St Philip in the most negligent manner. The inefficiency of an officer who permitted the enemy to come within gun shot and cut away a most important iron defense can not be excused. At New Orleans Lovell actually abandoned the city, saved his family & some valuables in a steamboat and made no attempt to man the forts or avail himself of the assistance freely tendered by the citizens. At Richmond the most important strategical feat of the war was rendered negatory by the incapacity of Capt Mitchell. He was afterwards removed; but not till the opportunity was lost. I learn now from Naval Officers who were at Mobile that Admiral Buchanan went into action at Mobile with the Tennessee, knowing that her steering gear was not sufficiently protected, that the smoke stack needed additional supports and that there was some defect in the ceiling. The Tennessee was the best ram built in the South. Buchanan was naturally very anxious to get her afloat and hurried her off the stocks. His career in the Virginia or Merrimac had perhaps made him over confident in the power of rams, but when he was notified by Officers, as he was repeatedly, of defects which required remedy and which could be remedied without going on the ways again, it was certainly very reprehensible in him not to attend to the matter. Officers say that had the steering gear alone been properly protected, the Tennessee would have defeated the fleet. With all Buchanan's gallantry and pluck, those, who are not his personal friends, say that he is very dogmatic and conceited and very unwilling to listen to any advice, especially from officers of lower rank.

The most fatal fault of Jeff Davis' character appears to have been his total want of knowledge of character. He had no power of discrimination at all and not knowing good from bad—he appears to have been the slave of his fancies and his prejudices. He clung to West Point officers with a too fatal adhesion, he ignored rising talent in the Provisional army, and it is generally acknowledged that he preferred Mrs. Davis' friends. This woman certainly had a very evil influence on the fortunes of the South. Her quarrel with Joe Johnston's wife (McLane that was) did much to augment that sad feud between Johnston & Davis. Mrs Johnston who did not think Mrs. Davis very refined—and she is Western to the back bone—christened her "The Squaw". Mrs. Davis never forgave it.

July 1. [1865] The Gazette is at last fairly launched into editorial existence. One leader today & two more for Monday. How far it will be allowed to go remains to be seen.

July 3d. I learn that a very large number of returned Baltimoreans —1000 I am told—have been presented by the Grand Jury of the Criminal Court for treasonable offences, such as horse stealing etc. How the C. Ct. of Baltimore City can take cognizance of offences committed in Frederick Co. is beyond my comprehension.

July 4". Left for Cape May to avoid the celebration of the "ever glorious Fourth". Very good fun for the stork—but poor for the Frogs.

July 5". I see that several officers who have been "pardoned" by the President, have been rearrested, charged with horse stealing—during the Maryland invasion.

July 6". The finding of the Court Martial has been made public today and an order has been immediately issued by the President condemning Payne Herold, Atzerodt & Mrs Surratt to be hanged *tomorrow*. Payne was certainly guilty. Herold aided booth in his flight—& is to be hanged for it. Atzerodt had a letter of Booths & one of his hdkfs. He had arms in his possession & it was supposed he intended to murder Andy Johnson. He is to be Hanged for it. Mrs. Suratt was a friend of Booth & evidently had communication with him. She is to be hanged for it.* If this thing goes on, women will be hanged for having Booth's photograph in their possession.

Dr Mudd is sentenced to hard labor for life. He dressed Booth's leg, when Booth went to him for medical assistance. Arnold has the same sentence & Spangler, the carpenter, gets six years of labor.

It is useless to comment on this trial. The prisoners were tried by Court Martial, in time of peace for a civil offence. Witnesses of infamous character were allowed to give testimony. Hearsay evidence was admitted and even opinions were admitted & permitted it seems

* Lewis (Louis) Thornton Paine (Payne) boarded in Baltimore with Mrs. Joseph Branson at Fayette and Eutaw streets the March previous to the assassination. Mrs. Branson and her daughters Mary and Maggie were known Confederate sympathizers, and were arrested but released after the assassins were discovered. Further information can be found in William E. Doster, *Lincoln and Episodes of the Civil War* (New York, 1915). Assassins George Atzerodt, Davy Herold, Mrs. Mary Surratt, and Paine were executed. Samuel Arnold, Michael O'Laughlin, and Edward Spangler were sentenced to life in prison, and John Surratt escaped.

to weigh as facts. The treatment and torture of the prisoners—the manacles upon their limbs and the hoods over their heads, thickly padded & drawn over their eyes, nose & mouth—were brutal.

July 7". The condemned were all hanged this morning. After the issuing of the Presidential order yesterday, a writ of Habeas Corpus was issued from the Supreme Court of the District, directed to General Hancock, in Mrs Surratts case. He refused to obey it & afterwards came into court with Atty General Speed, fortified by instructions from the President directing him to suspend the action of the Writ in this case.

President Johnson has been too ill for more than a week to receive anyone. This gives rise to surmises. Some say he has succumbed to his old weakness and been in a state of intoxication. Perhaps the condemnation of the Prisoners has had an effect upon him. He certainly had communications with Booth as was testified by the fact of the finding of a letter from Booth in his room—on the very day of the assassination. The President though confined has been able to attend to most important business.

July 8". How strange it is that men from the South should have so persistently misinformed their best friends in the North & in Maryland—in the strictest confidence too. I learn today that Duncan F. Kenner, when he passed through N. York, assured two of his friends that he had papers in his possession which would ensure recognition by France and that his positive confidential assertions were the cause of the failure & ruin of Henry J. Lyons and many others. This is of a piece with John Duvall's doings—only Kenner was a man in much higher position.

July 9. Genet of N. York tells me that he knows that Howell Cobb used the control that he had in Buchanan's administration indirectly to secure Lincoln's election, in order to force a separation. That he did this by producing dissension among the Democrats & breaking up the party. Genet says that he was one of a Committee who went on to Washington to remonstrate with him.

How far the secession of the Southern States was a long laid plan and who were implicated in it, remains to be seen. Certainly Maryland men had nothing to do with it. As early as 1850 there was a very decided Southern party in Washington, who established a paper called "the South" I think, the object of which was to show the North, that its ultra measures would only tend to force the South to withdraw. Mr Mason, Mr Slidell and others saw this paper supported. This first brought De Leon into notice. The paper was wretchedly managed and De Leon was recommended to Mr Mason as an efficient young man, then engaged in conducting some little village paper in Carolina. The paper fell through for want of support or perhaps it was only a campaign paper. De Leon in reward for his services was given a consulship to Alexandria, Egypt, by Buchanan. When the little Jew got away from his home associations he became a gentleman & married an Irish girl with money.

Henry Rodenwald of N.O. assures me that Benjamin is cursed in New Orleans. Letters from prominent men were written him repeatedly soon after the secession of Louisiana begging him to have New Orleans properly defended by batteries down the river & offering every assistance. Benjamin only laughed at their fears, answered them that the defences were perfect and moreover that they were not needed for he knew positively that in a short time, articles of peace, between the North & South would be signed. This is of a piece with what I have heard frequently before. Davis & Benjamin allowed Seward to hoodwink them to the last and with a blindness that seemed then extraordinary, refused to make any extensive preparations for defence, although the subject was strongly pressed upon their consideration by sensible men. Rodenwald says that Benjamin is too much detested at N.O. for him ever to find it pleasant there again.

July 11. Negro men now are all "gentlemen". The woman are "ladies". The Yankees never did know how to treat negroes. They first elevate them to an apparent equality with the whites and then punish them for taking liberties. I was much amused at Mrs Izard's Story. She went to S. Carolina to look after her property. The Negroes had put in a crop of rice & were working it. She was under the protection of Federal officers and officials and it was determined that she should have her property back, on condition that the negroes were to be allowed one half of the crop this year for their labor, after it was ready for shipment. All damage to animals from cruelty or injury to personal property was to be paid for by them out of their share. To this the Negroes objected. They had been taught to regard the property as their own & refused to give up one half of the crop. Capt. Gates, U.S.N. was unable to do anything with them. He treated them as equals. They were largely in the majority. In despair he sent for Mrs. I. She soon put the matter at rest. "Boys", said she "If you are free, recollect I am free too. This is my property and I intend to keep it." She retired. Gates again commenced "Gentlemen," said he, "you hear what Mrs. Izard says." It is too absurd to see these Yankees calling negroes Gentlemen and treating them like brutes. A Southerner treats them as children, enforces obedience from them as children & protects them as children. This is the relation which the negro in fact most enjoys. When freed they have always clung to the Slave States.

July 12". Col Browning is private secretary to President. I learn from a direct source that when he was lately in Baltimore, he said that Andy Johnson had been drunk for some time and that if he had been sober, he would certainly have respited Mrs. Surratt. Genl. Hartuff (I think this is the name) [John F. Hartranft] in command of the Military prison, wrote a note to the President the morning of the execution assuring him that he felt satisfied of Mrs. S's innocence. It had no effect. Browning himself was quite drunk in Baltimore. He had been to Cape May and they had feted him a great deal and he had evidently been drinking badly.

July 14". Lieut Jno. P. Black, with eleven men, entered Cedar Park West River, some weeks ago & commenced shooting the deer. They shot for over an hour, giving the Mercer's no reply to their remonstrances other than impertinence. They at last yielded they said to the appeals of the ladies. They frightened the sheep badly and drove the deer out of the Park. Out of 300 the Mercers only have got back about 75. They were English deer, the first of which were imported by old Col Mercer. Major Ed. Donaldson was in the neighborhood & determined to have Black brought to justice. He collected all the proof and had Black courtmartialed. The charges have been dismissed. [A short newspaper clipping of this affair is inserted here.]

> There being no evidence whatever to give testimony in any manner, or sustain the charges of committing waste, or being guilty of conduct unbecoming an officer and a gentleman, these were abandoned by the Judge Advocate. The specification in reference to the deer hunt was not denied, but the defense adduced evidence to show that no wrong was intended in entering the park above named; that no deer was either killed or wounded; that the accused did not know at the time he was intruding upon private property, and as soon as informed of it by the proprietor he immediately desisted, left the grounds himself, and ordered his men to do so, which they did.

July 19. A long speech of Govr Perry's of S. Ca. has just been published, in which he says that he opposed secession, that he always said slavery & the South had no chance except in the Union where they were supported by the Democratic party, and that the South never as really in earnest, that the heart of the masses never were in the war. This sort of talk has been very common since the failure of the cause. It is as unmanly as it is absurd. Never did a nation rise so unanimously and so gallantly, at the first note of war. Secession was I believe unpopular as a measure, but the call for 75000 men to invade the South aroused and united the people. The trouble was that there was no preparation for arming them. Davis and his cabinet refused from the beginning to make the necessary preparations for defense. They were afraid to incur the expense. They believed to the last there would [be] no war and when war came they were totally unprepared. I have heard several times of offers made to the Cabinet to import arms on private account, provided the Govt. would take them if needed, flatly refused. Now I learn in the most direct manner from one of the Southern Generals, that Davis & his Cabinet were implored before war commenced or rather at its comencement to import 1,000,000 muskets with the necessary side arms & small arms & ammunition. He was told there would be such an uprising of a people as was never seen and that there was no means of arming them. It was months before the blockade was virtually effective, but this was never done. After the war commenced Davis & Benjamin clung madly to foreign intervention. The truth is that with any other man than Davis—no matter scarcely who he was—the South would have been successful.

July 20". *Miss* Harris has been acquitted.* She shot Burroughs deliberately in the Treasury Department where I suppose she had friends who were employed. This place is a disgrace to the nation. One portion of it is filled with strumpets, brought there to be kept at Govt. expense. Men employed at Washington brought their women along and leading men obtained employment for them, so as to have them near at hand. Miss H. claimed that B. had trifled with her affections. Letters were admitted as evidence, which were evidently forged. The jury acquitted her, the crowd applauded her and Bradley, the advocate, an elderly married man, raised her veil & tenderly kissed her. Disgusting. Killing has ceased to be murder.

* The Harris case was reported in The *New York Times* of January 31, February 2, July 9, July 20, and July 24, 1865. Andrew J. Burroughs, a clerk in the office of the Comptroller of Currency, was shot by Mary Harris, who had arrived recently from Chicago. She was the daughter of William Harris of Burlington, Iowa, nineteen years old, and claimed that she had gone to Chicago and then to Washington after having been jilted by Burroughs and disowned by her parents.

July 21. Major Genl Heth has been spending the day with me. He sets my mind at rest on one question. He says the battle of Gettysburg ought to have been won, that the move was planned by Genl. Lee, as all his moves were, and that if Stuart—who was a gallant officer and could get more fighting out of men than any one else, but whose fault was a too great fondness for notoriety—had come up as he was ordered, instead of delaying to make his raid within three miles of Washington, the campaign would have been a success. But Genl. Lee could not tell whether Meade was massing on his right or left flank. He had no cavalry. Heth who was on the left sent Pettigrew to Gettysburg to bring off 2500 ps. of shoes. P. returned & reported cavalry & infantry too strong for his brigade. Heth did not believe it, rather reprimanded him and said he would go next morning with his division & get the shoes. He did go, stumbled upon a Corps of the enemy & lost 2600 men. This opened the battle of Gettysburg. When Genl Lee found out at last where the enemy was, it took him too long a time to bring his troops up. If he had struck a blow then, the whole North would have laid down its arms. Never were people so tired & so disgusted with war. Heth pays the very highest tribute to the gallantry of the Maryland men in his division. He says the reason was because they were gentlemen.

Talking about Genl. Joe Johnson [*sic*] he says his fault was that he never would fight and that among the officers of Lee's army it was considered not altogether satisfactory that battle had not been delivered before he reached Atlanta. They thought he should have fought farther North. He says there is no comparison between Lee's Virginia Campaign & Johnston's, as the latter claims. Lee, he says, attacked Grant whenever he got a chance, made at him wherever there was an opening, caught him by the throat with the grip of a bull dog, & only let him get off at all, because his force was so large and because he, Grant, entrenched himself front flank & rear where-ever he halted in his marches, moving in fact in entrenched parallel-ograms. Johnston on the contrary never made at Sherman

Heth says the misfortune of war is that it makes one callous to loss of life & suffering. One night after a hard days fighting, he & his staff flung themselves down to sleep, making a pillow of a pile of blankets they found. Next morning they found their heads had been resting on corpses. The discovery did not shock them.

July 22. Jim McLane has been to Virga. to see his bro. in law, Joe Johnston. He says that Johnston told him there never was any adequate provision made for the men who were willing to bear arms and eager to fight—that the Cabinet could not be convinced of the necessity of preparing for war and that consequently during the whole war the men never were properly armed. He said that to the last the Cavalry never were properly equipped, they never had sabres enough and that while the people were talking about arming the negroes, he could not obtain muskets for 2000 troops he wished to put in the field, most of whom had seen service. He said further that most of the machinery, which he had had packed at Harpers Ferry and had removed, reporting to President Davis, that there was none better in the world, was recently taken possession of by the Federals & brought north, in the original boxes which never had been opened. It had never been used. This fact was published a few weeks ago.

He said that there never was such an uprising among a people but that at last want of confidence in the administration paralyzed them and the conscription & imprisonment acts, administered as they were, made them hostile to the Government. When the conscription became general, rich men managed to get their sons employments where the danger was slight—in soft places & bombproofs as they were termed, and the rank & file were left to fight for the benefit of the wealthy. Under the impressment act the power of a foraging officer was arbitrary. He was not bound to assess pro rata. If a man refused to take the prices allowed by the sumptuary laws his property could be seized. And seized it was frequently. Men of means who staid at home, took the officers to their houses, entertained them & saved their property. Poorer people were victimized. Men who had sent fifty or one hundred miles for corn for their animals would have the wagon & team seized on its return, within half a mile of home. Women who had sons & husbands in the army, saw their horses & cattle taken away. They had no means of resistance and they naturally enough endeavored to persuade their men to leave the army & return to their homes to protect their families. These were of course individual cases, but there were enough of them to create very great dissatisfaction. In some parts of the country people concealed their stock in the woods and for the past 18 mos of the war there was a growing hostility to the Administration.

Genl. J. said that Swinton (of the Tribune) came to see him lately & told him he had an interview with Seward in June 1864 and that Seward had told him that the resistance of the South was too determined and that the Cabinet was deliberating what terms of peace to offer. Seward said that Sherman could not get any farther, that the conscription was very unpopular in the North, that there was great trouble in procuring money and that if the Govt. proceeded to take strong measures to provide men and means, they would certainly defeat Lincoln's reelection. He told Swinton to come & see him later at Auburn & he would talk more fully with him. This corresponds precisely with my observations at the time in New York & the Eastern States. In New York street rail road conductors & others told me that if the Admn. attempted to enforce the conscription, it would produce a riot. And that if there was not a conscription riot, there would be a bread riot before winter was half over. Food & articles of necessity were rising rapidly in price & much faster in proportion than labor. In Vermont I heard men say that the Southerners had fought like gallant fellows and they ought to be let alone. In the country people were staggered at the prices of oats, corn flour & everything else. Currency promised to depricate rapidly, distrust prevailed and it seemed evident that the North could not possibly sustain itself six months longer. Swinton after sometime went to Auburn. Seward told him that things had changed. Hood was in command. Sherman had defeated him & would soon march where he choosed—and so he did.

July 23d. Some of Genl Sherman's correspondence is just published. He writes to Grant Apl 25" from Raleigh [Short newspaper clipping inserted here]

> As to punishment for past crimes, that is for the judiciary, and can in no manner or way be disturbed by our acts; and, so far as I can, I will use my influence that the rebels shall suffer all the personal punishment prescribed by law, as also the civil liabilities arising from their past acts.

How false! This was just after he had proposed terms to Johnston guaranteeing the Southern people their civil rights. Stanton disapproved of it & Johnston subscribed to the same terms as Lee. If it had been agreed, Sherman here acknowledges he had no intention of fulfilling it.

July 25". Mrs —— has been here staying with S. S. Lee. She gives a frightful account of the barbar[i]ties of Sherman's troops in North Carolina. She & her sister, wife of Genl W barricaded their doors & betook themselves to the third story. They fortunately were not molested, but from the windows they saw houses sacked & women ravished.

At Fortress Monroe she endeavored to get a bouquet of flowers to Mr. Davis. She was stopped by a chaplain, who advised her not to attempt any such expression of sympathy, as it would be very dangerous.

At Washington she saw Prest. Johnson and thanked him for the pass he had sent her to return North. She then said she wished to put in a plea for Mr Davis & Genl Lee. Madam, said he, sternly, "the interests of the South require the blood of Mr Davis".

July 26". Harry Brogden said today, at dinner table, that last year he copied a despatch in cypher from Genl Lee to Mr Davis, urging the removal of Northrop, from the post of Q.M. General, saying that if the present management were continued he could not keep the army of Virginia together. All testimony goes to show the utter inefficiency of Genl Northrop. He was perfectly honest & that was all.

There were two other Confed. officers present—both of whom were on duty that time in Richmond. One of them said that after the battle of Cold Harbor Genl Lee urged the evacuation of Richmond, saying that he had then delivered such a blow to Grant, that he could not follow for some time and that he could get his army off safely and that it was a military necessity.

I am assured from half a dozen sources that Genl Lee assured Mr. Davis before the Peace Conference that the cause was hopeless and many people blame him for not making terms then, when he could. His infatuation was so blind that he would see nothing. He still looked forward to making a stand with Joe Johnston and even after he left him talked of a republic across the Mississippi which could not be overthrown. He knew at the time well, that the trans Mississippi troops had refused to cross to aid Hood last autumn. For my part, I am glad he did not have his eyes opened. I prefer this revolution to work out is [*sic*] end now. Reunion would have only stopped it temporarily.

July 30". News of the sufferings and privations of the Southern surpasses belief. The bare recital of some of their sufferings is incredible. The object of the Northern armies was not merely to conquer but by terror, rapine, devastation, rape and outrage to strike a blow that would leave a lasting impression. I hear now of high born & once wealthy friends wearing shirts made out of guano bags—material from which the odor can hardly be eradicated. Sisters gave [?] Elliott some old clothes to give away. They have been taken by Mrs. Joe Hager for her children. What a change for them! I have seen some of the Southern girls with their hair cropped short "a la victime". It was probably commenced by those who had the typhoid, which was once quite prevalent in parts of the South where the weather was oppressive and the people were poorly fed. Afterwards it was done to raise money—for there were always Jews and Jewesses to purchase silver and jewels and hair too.

Augt. 7t. [1865] New York is filled with Confederates. They appear to have but one idea which is that the South is ruined and no longer habitable. They rush to New York as the center of wealth and they expect to obtain profitable employment at the hands of the very poeple who have persistently oppressed them. To me this manifestation of indecent haste is painful. I cannot understand it. Genl Dick Taylor is on here staying at Barlows. Can he know that Barlow was the supporter of McClellan whose platform was "no peace but in submission".

Aug 12". There are some Southerners at Saratoga. It is race week. Col Rhett is here, of Fort Sumter fame and Genl Cheatham are here. What are they after? Why do they rush to Northern Springs as soon as paroled? Are the women after all the only staunch Southerners in the South? There is one gentleman here from Florida, on his way to the Brazil to see what arrangements he can make for colonizing two hundred Florida families there. They do not reflect that upon reaching there they will find the very difficulty to contend with they seek to avoid—the want of labor.The place for the Southerner is the South. He must not forsake his ruined home but strive to rebuild and restore.

Aug 15". The Ketchum forgeries have taken New York by surprise.* Ned Ketchum was the envy and admiration of all young men. Almost from the moment he arrived at age he was trusted to any extent by his father, who at last became so infatuated with his talents that he stood quietly by & allowed his son to engage daily in transactions of such magnificient proportions that he could himself hardly understand them. Young Ketchum spoke little. He looked wise and people thought he must know a heap. Shrewd men acknowledged his merit and pointed him out as the boldest operator of the day. But no one knew what he was after. Travers & MacVickar used to drive down with him in the morning and sometimes up in the afternoon. Occasionally I have been of the party. I did not think

* Edward B. Ketchum, 25, of New York City, was accused of forging nearly $2,500,000 in gold certificates. A member of the firm of Morris, Ketchum, Son & Co., he absconded with his ill-gotten gains and the company failed. For details see the Baltimore *Sun,* August 16 and 17, 1865.

that either of the others were at all in Ketchum's confidence. He was short & rather fat. There was nothing striking in his appearance. There has been nothing like his forgeries in the history of money. They amount to nearly $2,000,000 in gold checks, equal to $2,800,000 currency. Besides this he had abstracted securities to an incredible amount from the vaults of the house. His father is ruined. This is but one of the effects of over inflation. Excess of money is a wonderful demoralizer.

Only a week ago the World was astounded to hear of the defalcation of Jenkins of the Phenix Bank, N.Y.* Jenkins was a moral man, a church man, a family man. No man was more respected. Still he had picked up a girl in the dancing saloons of Broadway, the lowest holes of vice, and was lavishing wealth on her that he was stealing from the bank of which he was teller. Give me your Church going Christian to do the thing handsomely.

The most charming of these cases was the Strong divorce case.** Mrs. Strong was devoted to good works. So was Mr. Strong's younger brother. So the two, Mrs. S. and her brother in law, went to church together, taught Sunday School together gave charity together. They were the salt of the earth. One day Mrs. S. lost a son. She was frantic. She regarded it as a punishment for her sin and in her wild grief confessed to her husband that she had been untrue. She promised to sin no more and he for the sake of the children, agreed to keep the matter secret. In a few months Mrs S. began to sigh again for the pomps and vanities and flatly denied what she had before confessed. At this her husband declared he would sue for a divorce. She thought he would have no proof; but the hypocritical brother, who had ruined her, with his sanctified face confessed his sin. He declared that he knew he was wrong and that his only hope for salvation lay in acknowledging his error. So he sacrificed the woman who had trusted him. None but a Christian could have been such a scoundrel.

* Henry B. Jenkins, age 50, teller of the Phoenix Bank in New York, along with James H. Earle of Newark, New Jersey, age 31, and Genevieve Bower of New York, age 33, were accused of swindling over $300,000 of the bank's funds. Earle committed suicide when the swindle was discovered. For details see the Baltimore *Sun*, August 14 and 15, 1865.

** In the Strong divorce case, reported in The *New York Times* of March 10 and 17, 1865, Peter R. Strong, wealthy and socially prominent New Yorker, accused his wife of adultery with his brother, Edward Strong. In the case, heard before Judge McCunn of the Superior Court, Mrs. Mary E. Strong, daughter of John Austin Stevens, was defended first by William Curtis Noyes and, after his death, by a Mr. McKeon. Also involved in the case was the charge of homicide by abortion brought against Peter R. Strong, Mrs. Electra M. Potter, and Dr. John B. Dennis.

Aug 20". I learn from men connected with the Balto. & Ohio R. Road who usually have excellent means of information, that in his last debauch Andy Johnson was for four days in his room, walking up and down in his shirt, with whiskey bottle on the table, continually thrusting out his hands with a shudder and crying "take her away, take her away from me"—alluding to Mrs Surratt. Govr Pratt had an interview with him on Monday last, when he was certainly quite sober.

Aug 26". Mr. Gatchell tells me that when Genl. Dick Taylor was here he asked him "Why was it that you allowed yourself to be drawn into the Southern movement. You always used to see that you would go with the Southern leaders very far, but that when it came to secession, you would oppose them as you did not wish to break up the Union?" "The reason" answered Taylor "was a simple one. Men called the Southern movement a movement of the Southern leaders. It was on the contrary a movement of the Southern people and they were so unanimous in their determination that it became a question as to whether we should let him go in by themselves or whether men of capacity and experience should take the reins. This decided me. The people inaugurated the war and the people stopped it. They got tired and they abandoned the cause." This is all true. But why did they abandon it? Mr. Davis had everything his own way for two years. The Congress did as he wished, the people did as Congress decreed. There was nothing but inefficiency and want of system and the strength of the people failed merely because it was miserably and recklessly squandered away by Davis and his Cabinet. Benjamin, to my surprise is evidently held in as low estimation as any of the rest of the Cabinet. He certainly was very quick & had great capacity for work.

Aug. 27. Genl. Joe Johnston is here. I was talking with him this morning about the battle of Bull Run. He says that it would have been folly to attempt to enter Washington, on account of the strength of the fortifications and the number of troops under Patterson which could have been brought into action within a day or two. He says besides that the Southerners considered the war over and did as they pleased, many of them going off & the whole army being in a hopelessly demoralized condition. This puts at rest the story about the quarrel between Davis and Johnston & Beauregard on this point. What is one to believe? I had this story in the most direct manner. Genl. J. condemns Benjamin very strongly. He says Randolph was the best Secretary of War, but that when he found that he was to be a mere tool in the hands of the President, he resigned.

Aug 29". Govr Pratt says that when he was in Richmond in 1861, early in the spring—at a meeting with Gov Letcher & Genl Lee and others, they utterly discountenanced the secession of Maryland. Gen Lee especially said that it was the worst thing that could happen for the South; that they would be called upon in honor to defend the State without having the power.

Aug 28. Revd. Mr. Stryker who passed with Payne some of the last hours of his life, was much interested in him. Last year he noticed a man plainly dressed who was a stranger & who attended St. Barnabas, quite regularly morning and evening. After some weeks he spoke to him one day after Church and asked him if he had not been in the Confederate army. Payne told him he had. Afterwards they became more intimate and Payne came frequently to see him. Mr. Stryker found him gentlemanly, intelligent and earnest. When he saw in the papers that Payne had asked to have Mr. Stryker come to see him, he though it was the same man & went to Washington, where after long effort he obtained a pass. I am glad to hear all this of Payne. It is quite evident that no promise of gain influenced him. He was induced to join with Booth in the assassination of men whom he considered most wicked with the conviction that he was benefitting his cause and doing a deed for which his country would hereafter thank him. Now that the fight is over people are beginning to see that Lincoln's assassination was a very good thing. He was a weak & cunning creature in the hands of wicked and vindictive villains. No man can be worse than Stanton unless it is Holt. Seward was always superficial, unworthy of trust and tricky. Men went into fearful agonies of despair at the time of the assassination, merely because they were frightened to death and because they were afraid of military punishment, short and speedy, if not of Mob Law. It certainly was dangerous at the time to defend Booth and Payne. That was no reason why men should lie.

Aug 30". Montgomery Blair has made a speech. He opposes the registration law.* While he was in power Blair permitted the Radicals

* The Registry Oath became the major issue in the "redemption" of Maryland after the war. The oath, part of an act to register Maryland voters passed in March 1864, required a prospective voter to swear that he never gave direct aid to the Confederacy or to individual Confederates, and that he had never expressed sympathy for or hoped for the success of the Confederacy. The full text of the oath and 25 questions asked prospective voters can be found in Scharf, *History of Maryland,* 3:699–70. Scharf claims that this disfranchised two-thirds of the state's voters. Most historians have agreed that this oath was an attempt to disfranchise loyal as well as disloyal Democrats. The role of Blair in leading the anti-Registry forces has been variously portrayed. An analytical ac-

to go their own way in Maryland. They did their work so thoroughly that scarcely any honest man in the State, except those of extreme radical views who are rarely honest can be permitted to register. Consequently Mr Blair, now that he finds it his interest to be a little conservative, finds he has no constituency. Without constituency he has no power & is of no use at Washington. So Mr B. now thinks this law a shameful and abominable violation of a freeman's rights and opposes it tooth and nail. The President is in the same way. He is from the South and common as he is and false and vulgar as he has shown himself to be, he has this in common with Southern people—a hatred of Yankees. He must look to the Southern States for his constituency. He must secure votes for reelection among Southern people. But it is a long way to look ahead now, three years.

Sep 1" [1865]. It is cheerful to hear of some manhood still left. When Genl Wise reported to Genl. Terry under his parole recently, Terry asked him if he had applied for pardon. "Pardon" said he "Pardon! I'd rather take arsenic. Do you ask me if I have applied for pardon, you who have been a lawyer, you who should the Constitution of your country, if I have anything to ask pardon for?" Wise never was a man I admired. It is a pity however there are not more of the same spirit.

September 15". New York is crowded with Southerners and so is Washington. Everybody is asking for pardon and has some scheme for making a fortune as soon as he gets the necessary humilating document. Johnson is pardoning pretty freely. He does not know the names of a small fraction of the men to whom he extends "executive clemency". The patronage is confided exclusively to deserving men in Washington. Genl. Jos. R Anderson of Richmond, of the Tredegar Works, who of all men had done most to supply munitions of war, has three men now in pay. He will get through soon. When all that can pay have paid then there will be a general amnesty—not before.

September 30". The Democrats of the North have bowed down before Andy Johnson. They flatter and fawn and accept whatever he does. They implore him to be their leader and what is more the Southern people seem inclined to sustain them and to kiss the hand that smote them. They speak of Lincoln as that "joking old Nero" and they talk of Johnson as their salvation. Meanwhile John-

count is in Baker, *The Politics of Continuity;* but A. Leo Knott in *A Biographical Sketch of A. Leo Knott* (Baltimore, 1898) gives a lively and firsthand account of the return to power of the Democratic Party, led by former Governor Thomas Pratt, and its fusion with the Conservative Unionists under Blair.

son says nothing. He belongs to the conservative—heaven save the mark—wing of the Republican party. If that is strongest he will stick to it. If the Democrats come into power he will be willing to lead them. He is like the bone between two dogs. The dogs fight but the bone is not hurt. So he keeps quiet, willing to be the prize of the victor. When he finds which party is the stronger he will adopt any platform and issue any manifesto desired. Being neither Democrat nor Republican, I do not care much which side he goes; but in no event could I sustain a man who keeps my state uselessly under military law, does not permit its citizens the right of habeas corpus and undertakes to violate the rules of courts in regard to Negro evidence. The war is over and forgotten. Impressions never last here. The American people are the fastest in the world. They have buried the hatchet and military rule is absurd. You could not make the South fight now if you wanted.

Oct 10" [1865] Genl. Joe Anderson has obtained his pardon. Withers told me that he had procured his within four hours after he had an interview with his man in Washington; that it was a little expensive and cost more than it was worth, but that he could put any man through who desired to be "pardoned".

Oct 12. The excitement incident to the life of some large operators in New York is wonderful. In 1862 Leonard Jerome failed. Travers wound up his business & left him owing $300,000. On the 6th day of August 1862, he had $300 in bank & came to Travers to borrow $1000 to keep in bank for the purpose of making a show. Travers invited him home to dinner. After the usual amt of Champagne, Claret & Madiera, they went to the Billiard Room and had a chat. Travers told him that stocks were very low & promised to buy for him next day 2000 shares & carry them for 60 days. And said he do you go to your brother in law, who does not like to be outdone by me, tell him what I have done and he will do as much. He was right. As soon as he heard Travers had bought 2000 shares, he purchased 2500—so then Jerome who owed $300,000 & had $300 to pay it with suddenly found himself the apparent owner of 4500 Shares Stock worth $350,000. He caught the stocks on the turn. There was a great rise. He doubled his Stocks, played boldly & made a great hit. On the 6th day of August 1863, he had paid off his old indebtedness & was offered 1,250,000 dollars for his fortune. Since then he told me on one occasion he had come down to his office five days running and that if he had known any one morning what he would have to go through before the day was over to raise the money he required he would have staid home and let his name go to protest. A short time ago he was a very large holder of Pacific Mail. There was a promise of a difficulty between this company & the Atlantic Mail. If it had resulted in a quarrel the latter would have put in an opposition to the former which would have caused a great difference in the value of the Stock. The stock was on a stand still for a short time. Jerome pledged everything he could raise money to sustain himself. He had played his last card. If stocks had declined five per cent it might have nearly ruined him. He had property to the amount of $600,000 which he tried to sell at a sacrifice, but he could not sell any portion of it. He had nothing left except to remain quiet and submit to fate. He told me that he could not sleep. He had cold sweats in the night. In the morning he could take nothing for breakfast but a yolk of egg in a glass of Sherry. After days of suspense, the Pacific Mail bought out the Atlantic. The stock rose immensely, a large dividend was declared and Jerome's fortunes which had trembled in the balance, was not only made secure but immensely increased.

Oct 15. Mary Ficklin writes me from Charlottesville "I have lost heavily during our great struggle but I have enough left and better than that an undying hate to the Yankee that will last me as long as life. I saw much of the Cavalry and Artillery from Maryland. While I recollect them, I must & will hate the Yankee. No such glorious body of men, since war was known, ever left their own state or country to defend another. Never did any country turn out so much real worth in proportion to the number of men under arms. Such respectable material to fight the scum of Yankeedom". Genl. Lee spoke to Mr. Sam Smith of the Marylanders in the same way. Genl Joe Johnston said the same thing to Frank Howard & myself. Genl Heth talked to me of them in the same way.

Oct 26. I was talking some time ago with Genl. Joe Johnston about the first battle of Bull Run. Govr Pratt was present & remarked that the great error committed was in not following up the victory. "Five hundred men, said he, could have gone into Washington". "That is all very well," replied Genl. J., "but you must take into consideration, that besides the force sent forward under McDowell, there were still enough men left in the fortifications around Washington, to defeat our little army. Besides Patterson had nearly 30,000 men near Harpers Ferry who could be brought into action before we could march to Washington. But we could not follow even if we had wished. Our army was completely demoralized. Our men had gained a victory and they thought the war was over. Some went to look after the dead; others went to care for wounded friends. In some cases, a dozen men would go off with one wounded man. If we had determined to follow, we had no army to follow. The condition of the Yankee army was helpless enough. We did not know it. We could not have pursued if we had." I have always doubted this. The matter was simply there was no cavalry, & the Generals had no idea of the extent of the route & made no effort to inform themselves of it. In talking over the matter a few days ago with Genl. Dick Taylor while he said it would not have been practicable for Genl Johnston to pursue, he acknowledged that he held his regiment in readiness expecting an order to advance which never came.

Nov 20". [1865] Baltimore has burst out in Major Generals. I never before quite understood what Mrs Davis meant when she used to say "Mr. Davis has two faults. He is too fond of his first wife's relations and of West Point officers". The latter point I understand now too well. It is wonderful to find such men as Elsey, Lomax, Imboden & others exalted to high commands, which they got merely because they were West Point Men. Fitz Lee is a very good fellow—better than many of his compeers, but hardly a man for a division. Heth is decidedly the best of the lot, but I very much doubt if he has any remarkable ability. Kirby Smith has more dash apparently than any of them, but I have not seen much of him. Dick Taylor is superior to any of them & more brains than all put together. If Davis was too fond of his first wife's relations, tis a pity there were not more like Taylor. The best officer by all odds developed on the South was Forrest. He was no West Pointer but had the genius. As Fitz Lee said "He had the battle field glance". All the Generals speak of him in the same way. There must have been more such men, only they could not struggle up with Davis on top of them. He had no knowledge of men at all. Consequently we have had the officers we had and we have failed. I am sorry I ever saw them. I am sorry to know I have been worshipping strange Gods. I don't know what Joe Johnston means. He talks in a very curious way about the Southern people and spoke of his cause, at a Union dinner table which he attended lately, in a way I should not have spoken to my enemies. And Longstreet said two days ago "Well I am not sure it it not best as it is. We should have split up again if we had succeeded and fallen to pieces". If leaders are lukewarm what is to be expected of people.

Novr. 29". New York is still filled with Rebels, all having grand schemes and all asking for money—which is very hard to get although there is plenty of it, when a good scheme for large profit offers. Gustavus Smith who certainly has a very high reputation for intelligent capacity has been unable to get the funds to rebuild his works in Tennessee. I have been quite curious to know him. I had heard him spoken of so well. He is a very coarse looking man, with a great thick bull neck, a protuberant lip and a projecting chin. He may be a very good overseer, and he may know very well how to control a large force of men in a rolling mill and he may be a good practical engineer; but it is simply impossible that such a man, with such a countenance could be a man of any large views or have in him the capacity for a great general. His wife was with him. She is pretty well known as a loose fish. Lovell was also there. He looks more like a gentleman & is probably bright and quick but must want stability. I recollect perfectly well when these two men left New York, no doubt having procured high commissions before they threw up their positions in the North. When Farragut ran by the Forts and advanced upon New Orleans, Lovell instead of organizing resistance, let the city take care of itself and turned his whole attention to procuring money and a steam boat for himself and family to go up the river. After Smith reached Kentucky, he remained for several months drawing pay from the Federal Government before he crossed the lines.

It is only necessary to know the men of to day who will figure largely in history and whose descendants will repeat their names with fond pride, to feel the folly of Hero Worship. How humiliating it is, as we step behind the curtain, to find our Worthies all made of pasteboard and to be forced to acknowledge that the Gods to who we have bowed are all false and made of commonest clay.

Novr. 30". I saw Mr. O. today on business for which I came. How cautious these men are. They fear their own shadow. He has money provided for the defense of President Davis and Southern officers tried for treason. He left poor Wirz to the mercies of the two ignorant men, Schade and Baker, who volunteered to defend him,* simply because he feared to compromise himself. He has now given me *carte blanche* to employ what counsel I choose to defend Winder and to draw on him on condition that his name is mentioned to nobody. I shall do what I can as I have no fear of implicating myself by endeavoring to procure for a persecuted man a fair trial.

* Wirz was defended by General James W. Denver, Judge James Hughes, Charles F. Peck, and Louis Schade. No mention is made of Baker in the newspaper accounts of the trial consulted.

Besides which I sent Wirz's counsel money by mails & that is already known, no doubt, to the Government.

Dec. 1". [*1865*] It is a constant remark of old officers of the U.S. Army—West Pointers—that the line of demarcation between Southerner and Yankee is no where so strongly drawn as in Maryland. It is so however in Missouri and in that part of Louisiana which has been for some time under Federal rule. People in the South suffered every possible privation except loss of liberty. They were beggars but they were free. Where we were brought in constant contact with the Yankees as our Masters, the yoke was very galling and as resistance became more hopeless the bitterness which we were forced to conceal became more extreme. And this I take it will be the result of the intercourse that is now brought about by the subjugation of the South. The oppression of the Northern people will gradually make the Southerner more and more inimical to him. I laughed very much last week in New York. Mary Pringle had been staying with the Fishes, who having nothing to forget and forgive were very magnanimous and ready to forget and forgive everything. They were one day commenting on the State of the Negro and expressing a hope that the conservative party might succeed and that the planters might be supported. When they turned to Miss Mary to receive at least her approval of these views she quietly said "I take as much interest in your politics as I do in those of England and France". "Oh! Mary", cried one of the girls. "Yes continued she "you need not think for a moment I would care if a French fleet would come in and bombard New York. I would rather like it, I think, if they were to lay it in ruins". The company was horrified. And still this is true genuine Southern feeling. Still fools write about the perfect consummation of a blessed reunion.

Reunion is perfect among West Point officers and Navy men. As a general rule every soldier, bred to the profession, is a Dugald Dolgetty. It matters little to him which side he espouses. I have been amazed to see how they fraternize. Heth when he went to St. Louis calld at once on W. T. Sherman who ought to be infamous to every Southern man for his march through South Carolina. While I was in Richmond, Joe Johnston, Genl. Heth & Genl Elsey were dining with Brig Genl. Mulford, who by the way invited me to come along which I declined to do. And in New York I see this thing every day. They tell one "My dear fellow you civilians don't understand this *esprit de corps*." It would be a curious thing to learn exactly what influenced each old West Pointer to take the side he did, to learn why McClellan fought for the Yanks and why Joe Johnston went South. Joe Johnston & Heth are both intimate now with Sherman and have accepted favors from him. Heth showed me letters a few days ago which Sherman had given him and which had been of the greatest service to the new Express Company of which Johnston is President.

Decr. 12. I insert the following for the purpose of showing of what history is made. Genl. Morris was known in the army as Black Bill. Randolph Ridgely, Bob McLane, Kit Tompkins and all the army men of that date knew that he had more than once swindled at cards and had once been courtmartialled for some very dirty trick. Early in his career he had been courtmartialled for conduct unbecoming an officer and a gentleman and got off on the plea set up by his Counsel, Jas. A. Bayard, that though unbecoming a gentleman it was not unbecoming an officer there being nothing unmilitary in the offence. This was about the woman he married, being forced by his fellow officers to make her his wife. He was placed on police duty early in the war because he was not considered fit for field duty and he remained on duty principally as a jailor till his death. This is the man who dies "honored by the whole nation". [A newspaper clipping is inserted here with the following notation by Glenn: Part of this extract has been mislaid, especially that which says he was "honored by the whole nation". It will be found in the *N.Y. Herald.*]

Captain Morris was promoted major November 4, 1853, and attached to the Fourth Artillery, and placed on duty as commandant of Fort Kearny, Nebraska Territory. He was relieved of this command by Colonel D. S. Miles in 1860, and ordered to the command of Fort Ridgely, Minn. where he was on duty until shortly before the commencement of the rebellion, when he was ordered to Fort McHenry, Baltimore. He was in command at this point on the memorable 19th of April, when the riots occurred in the streets of that city, and he caused much surprise and no little indignation among the secessionists by his promptness in training his guns on the riotous city. Here General Morris remained during the entire war, his career marked by no startling events, but his conduct always distinguished by firmness, fortitude and faithfulness.

It was shortly after assuming command at Fort McHenry that Colonel Morris (he had been promoted Lieutenant Colonel, May 14, 1861) took the important step of refusing to answer a writ of habeas corpus granted by a Maryland judge, in order to obtain possession of a soldier of the garrison of Fort McHenry. Against the advice and arguments of all his friends, legal advisers and fellow officers, Colonel Morris deliberately concluded to refuse the surrender of the culprit;

and though the habeas corpus had not been formally suspended he decided that the commencement of hostilities necessarily suspended it. He as the first officer who resisted the execution of the writ of habeas corpus after the war began, though hasty historians have given the credit of this action to General B. F. Butler.

This action, calm and deliberate, was a fair illustration of the character of General Morris. He always acted with a firmness only intensified by its deliberation and coolness. He possessed great perseverance, and was of iron will, though mild mannered and affectionate to an unusual degree. He was a man of fine personal appearance and dignified and courtly manner.

Decr. 15" 1865. It certainly is right and proper that men who manifest decided capacity and who develop great ability should be reward [*sic*] by position and the consideration of the people whom they serve, and that they should be allowed a place in the Councils of the Nation. But smartness is by no means Capacity and adroit Charlatanism is not ability. What is to become of a nation when all the clever mounte banks and humbugging quacks are exalted to the high places. Such men have really no weight of character. Their elevation turns their heads & they are too weak to be virtuous. In the present day wherever you turn, you find power and control in the hands of the weak, the uneducated & the unscrupulous—men who are willing to sacrifice anything and anybody to gratify a false ambition. John Woolley I see is made a General. He was a bootblack & afterwards a messenger. Though very civil to me, everyone else tells me he is a thorough blackguard. Genl Lew Wallace was on here a few years back peddling Agricultural impliments. He borrowed money from Jas T. Earle then President of the Agricultural Society and forgot to pay him. Earle applied for it when he came back as a Major General and mirabile dictu got it. Sam Barlow who is a good enough fellow in his way and as near a gentleman as a man without advantages in youth can be, was a messenger boy. He managed to get together a great deal of money and has been the leader of the McClellan part of the Democratic party for a year past—and a nice botch he has made of it. Belmont, an imported Jew & a supposed natural son of Rothschild is another leader and chairman of the Democratic Central Committee. He is a good enough fellow too. But what is to become of a country when such people have the control. This drunken tailor, Andy Johnson, seems when he is sober to have more sense and more adaptation to high bred society than almost any of the crew. Raymond, of the New York Times, who has just gone over to the support of Johnson, started life as a Printers Devil and is a thorough & unscrupulous blackguard. As far as I can learn the principal cause for this exhibition of virtue on his part arises from the fact that he was not honored by the House of Representatives with the position of chairman of any of the leading committees.

January 1" 1866. Henry Winter Davis is dead. He died after a very short illness. He was a very good popular debater and an excellent stump speaker. He was very false, very unscrupulous and the worst man in political life I ever knew in the State. He never was bound by what he had sworn to yesterday, he never regarded the position he might take tomorrow. He was untrue to every pledge he made, he had been deliberately cut even years before the war commenced by every gentleman friend in the State and his malignity had become so extreme that he was notoriously and openly opposed to every action which met the support of the high toned and the honorable. He courted the mob because he knew he could only be sustained by the blackguards and the rabble. When I went to the Gazette [?] I found to my surprise the following [?] [Newspaper clipping inserted here.]

The Honorable Henry Winter Davis, for some years a Representative in Congress from this city, and one of the most prominent among the leaders of the Republican party, departed this life, on Saturday last, at his residence on St. Paul street, after a brief but painful illness. He was a native of this State, having been born at Annapolis, and, as we learn, was about forty-seven years of age.

The readers of the GAZETTE do not require to be informed, that between Mr. Davis and the conductors of this journal there were vital and irreconcilable differences of both opinion and principle. The condemnatory judgements which we have from time to time passed upon his public conduct, were as deliberate and conscientous as they were decided, and they must stand unchanged, as they were recorded. But we should do injustice to ourselves, not less than to the memory of an opponent whose career is closed forever, if we were to deny to Mr. Davis the possession of high intellectual faculties and many estimable and attractive personal qualities. Those who have observed the origin and course of the political organizations with which he was connected here, since the decline of the Whig party, cannot have failed to perceive to what a remarkable extent, they were the creatures of his individual ability and energy, and how largely they depended, for their vitality, upon his single mind. As a thinker, he was bold and original, with powers of reasoning which were at the same time comprehensive and singularly acute. His oratorical talents were conspicuous, and would have been so at any period; for with but little imagination or illustrative power, he was able, by his vigorous and earnest tone, the ingenuity, spirit and independence with which his views were presented, and his remarkable fertility and force of language, to produce effects upon his audiences, whether popular or cultivated, which few of his contemporaries have surpassed. In professional discussions he was equally able and successful, whenever he sufficiently withdrew himself from political occupations to do justice to his capacity. To the day of his death, he was a laborious student of those branches of science and literature to which he was addicted, and the fulness of mind, which he derived from such occupation, was one of the chief secrets of his superiority to the herd of commonplace politicians among whom his lines were cast.

Of the personal qualities of Mr. Davis, in strictly private life, those who knew him well spoke always very warmly. It cannot be doubted, we believe, that he was generous, genial and full of hospitality, or that he attached closely to him those to whom he was attached. The animosities by which he narrowed the scope of these kindlier gifts ought not to prevent them from being mentioned in his honor, now that all mere animosities should be buried with him.

I was utterly astonished and refused to let it go to press. On enquiry I found it had been contributed by Wallis. I was astonished at this, because only two days before Wallis had furnished me with Davis last public letter in which he took open ground in favor of negro suffrage and declared in the most revolutionary manner that it was absolutely indispensable for the country to give to the negro "the ballot and the bayonet". This while he knew that the over populous negro districts were threatened with insurrection during the recent [?].* I went to Wallis and told him my view. It was useless to argue with him. He thought a man was dead and his strong feelings for the Morris family evidently influenced him. I did not discuss the matter long knowing his weakness. If his bitterest enemy were to come to him tomorrow, he would overlook his faults and lend him his aid. So I went to Frank Howard & told him I could not let the piece go in. But Frank was evidently greatly softened by the death of a man who had married his wife's sister, and whom he had abused so often and so roundly in print as a scoundrel. He thought it was magnanimous and as he had not written or suggested it himself—he

* The farmers of the 1864 Constitution favored emancipation but not equal rights. Representation and voting were confined to the white population only. With the end of the war and the Democratic election victory in 1866, the Union Party began to look upon the Negro as a potential voter, with Davis leading the radical minority faction who supported Negro enfranchisement and the 14th Amendment. John A. Creswell became the leader of the radicals after Davis's death. With the 1867 elections the radicals had become Republicans and, as a minority party, their only hope lay in the enfranchisement of Maryland Negroes. This occurred with the ratification of the 15th Amendment and the passage of the Federal Enforcement Acts in 1870. For additional information see Wagandt, *The Mighty Revolution,* and Margaret Law Callcott, *The Negro in Maryland Politics, 1870–1912* (Baltimore, 1969).

was very anxious for it to go in. I told him it was wrong to let family matters influence a newspaper and that it was false and fair [*sic*] to eulogize a man whom we regarded as infamous. Better to say nothing of him. But Frank was in a forgiving mood for the moment, he flattered himself that it would be a good "coup" and that the paper could afford to be most liberal and he was anxious for the piece to appear. As it was a matter more of taste than of principles, I determined not to insist upon my rights and to waive the question. So it appeared. For the future we may as well eulogize Schenck and Fish and Stanton and the whole lot. I don't think there is one single one of them who has not more virtue than Winter Davis. Lots of people today have complimented Frank on the piece. When I have seen them, they have whipped right round and said "they saw evidently it was written by a relation and that under the circumstances it was the best thing to be done". No decent man I have yet seen, who felt he was not hurting my feelings, has yet approved the piece. How American all this is! Where is virtue, if vice is not to be held up in ignominy. Men lie and cheat and fail taking care first to make their moves comfortable and in a short time they are again in business. Women go astray and society receives them. Men who are notorious libertines entertain handsomely and are courted. That Frank Howard should so break down astonishes me. I wondered at him last year when he consented to subscribe to buy a substitute to take the field against the South where five of his own brothers were fighting, but I wonder more at this. It is the old cry O! tempora! O! mores!

No. 7

1866

Jany 24. State convention met today to discuss the proper means of doing away with the Registration Law.* The history of the whole affair is queer. On the 4" Jany Jno Thomson Mason wrote me from Annapolis asking if the Gazette would not advocate the calling of a convention of disfranchised tax payers. I answered him that it was useless to attempt such a movement unless it was started by leading men and that no one man nor indeed any set of men from any one district could expect the whole state to send delegates at their call & I asked him to let me know who were his supporters. Meanwhile I talked the matter over with Frank Howard and on Saturday Jany 6", asked eight or ten prominent lawyers to meet at my house & consult. After much talking we determined to have a convention. A committee had already been appointed to memorialize the Legislature. As there were a large number of men who did not choose to sue humbly for a restoration of rights, we concluded a convention would afford field for discussion and at least start an agitation which we would keep alive until the obnoxious laws were in some way repealed. I then got together about as many leading merchants who met in my house on Monday 8" and who endorsed the movement. Determined now to push it, I prepared the annexed circular, to which I signed the names of Govr. Pratt, Chas Webb—a well known Mason & myself. I had 150 copies printed which I circulated through the state & then day after day kept the matter alive in the columns of the Gazette.
[Newspaper clipping inserted here.]

Baltimore, January 10th, 1866

Sir—A number of influential gentlemen in the counties and in the city of Baltimore, earnestly desire that a Convention of delegates, representing those citizens who are opposed to the present Registration Law, may be immediately called. They wish to give expression to

* Popular opposition to the Registry Law, and mass meetings at which such Union leaders as Montgomery Blair denounced the law, led to an Anti-Registry Law Convention in Baltimore in January 1866. The convention, meeting at the Temperance Temple on January 10th, had the support of the legislature as well as the conservative leaders of both parties. Blair was the presiding officer. Convention resolutions, demanding an immediate repeal of the Registry Law, were presented to the General Assembly, but that body refused to act. This left the entire issue of the Registry Law up to the voters in the fall of 1866, hence the importance of having Swann appoint conservatives to register voters. For the text of the resolutions see Scharf, *History of Maryland,* 3:677–78.

> their views concerning the continued disfranchisement of a large proportion of the people of Maryland, and to take into consideration appropriate measures for their relief. In response to letters from prominent men in the counties, private meetings have been held here, and after consultation with a number of leading citizens, who cordially approve of the movement, a call has been made for a Convention to meet in Baltimore on the 24th of January instant.
>
> It is proposed, as you will see by certain resolutions which appear in the Baltimore papers, that primary meetings be held throughout the State on or about the —— day of January, and that delegates from each county and the city of Baltimore, equal in number to their respective representation in the Legislature, be appointed to meet in Convention in Baltimore on the day designated.
>
> It will be apparent to you, that in order to render this movement effective and beneficial, the aid of the ablest and best men in the State is required. We therefore solicit your active co-operation, if you approve of the plan, and beg that you will confer without delay with those who agree with you in your county, and see that it is represented in the Convention by its best men.

There we would say "We are requested to say so & so. We are informed thus and thus" which meant in reality that I requested Frank Howard or that he informed me. The call was responded to heartily by the newspapers. It was taken up throughout the state and excellent delegates were nominated in each county. Frank Howard & I arranged all preliminaries & he was to see to an address. On the 23d. I said "Frank have you the address ready" No replied he, I have been unable to get any one to prepare it". "What said I, here are all these people coming here, not one of whom knows what is to be done and everyone supposing that there is a central committee to look after things. Let me think" So without more ado, I went off and found Judge Merrick. After some talk he promised to prepare one that evening. After tea I went to Barnum's and after much trouble, I got together about twenty delegates and had a caucus. I had John Wethered called to the chair & gave him a list of names of men to appoint on a committee of resolutions. Finally after much polemic, a motion was made to appoint such a committee, he read out the names and the meeting adjourned. I staid with the committee, who made a rough draft. I promised to have an address ready & we adjourned to meet next morning. Next morning we met at ten and had so much discussion that no one had time to look at the address which I had barely had time to read over with Judge Merrick & which I cordially approved. So we adjourned to meet at Convention no one else having seen the address. In convention Montgomery Blair was called to the chair, chiefly because there was no one else who would have it. Govr Pratt & prominent Southern Men did not wish to have the movement appear too Southern & declined—and while many delegates were quite willing to use Blair, but not to honor him, they found themselves forced to accept him, because there was no other available name proposed. The resolutions were finally presented and adopted with little alteration and the address was adopted almost without being seen. When the Committee reported, Archer the chairman requested that Judge Merrick might be permitted to read the address, simply because he was the only man at all familiar with it. So the convention adjourned. For the work done, all the delegates might have staid at home & left the whole business in the hands of Govr Pratt, Judge Merrick Frank Howard & myself. We had however the satisfaction of seeing one of the most respectable conventions the State ever saw, assembled at response to an irresponsible call & of finding great feeling and much determination manifested on the subject of our violated rights. Besides, the real object attained was the appointment of an important executive committee which can act with authority when the proper time arrives.

Jan 26. Montgomery Blair said in his room last night that in the autumn of 1861, six months after the fall of Fort Sumter, the Cabinet at Washington was utterly despondent and that Lincoln and all the Cabinet members, except himself, were in favor of abandoning the war and recognizing the South. He alone opposed it. Soon after, successes gave them heart and they changed their tune. How much of this curious history ever will be known? Here was a war waged by a people who felt they had no right to wage it and encouraged by leaders who knew they were wrong—in a mere party political spirit. How they blundered on in the fatal maze they entered into will never be told, how often they sat down weary and despairing and ready to give up can not even be guessed. How they were allowed finally to blunder out by the absurd folly of Davis and his underlings, every one knows. Finis coronat opus. To be successful is to be virtuous. Political leaders now, who have been false to every principle of civil liberty they have sustained and advocated since their boyhood, endeavor to persuade the public that they have been loyal and true men and devoted to a consolidated union and opposed to State soverignity from the day that S. Carolina seceded.

Febry 1". [1866] The two Woolley's from Kentucky have returend to Tom Chiffelle's school (near Catonsville).* Last year complaint

*Thomas Philoteos Chiffelle (d. 1891), South Carolina civil engineer who

was made that these boys were "the grey". They did wear a grey uniform the same as is worn at West Point. After some talk the matter was taken in hand by the Provost Marshal, who ordered that all the boys should take the oath of allegiance. Some of them were eight or nine years old. These two boys manfully refused. They were sent to Fort Delaware. Some time after, notwithstanding all this, an order was issued forbidding the wearing of the obnoxious grey & the boys who had taken the oath, by the advice of parents to save expense of a new suit, had humiliated themselves for nothing.*

Feb 7". Met Montgomery Blair at Opera in Washington. He had had a semi official interview with the President, had announced to him the passage of certain resolutions by the Maryland Convention endorsing his reconstruction policy and had endeavored to obtain from him some expression as to his intentions regarding the disfranchised citizens of Maryland. But never a word did he get.

Feb 8". I went with Govr Pratt today into the Audience Chamber. Mrs. Waddell was along. The object of the interview was to have her parole revoked so that she could go abroad and join her husband. Govr P. said to him after this business was arranged satisfactorily, Mr President About two thirds of us in Maryland are disfranchised. Every unregistered man is ready to support you. And almost every registered man is opposed to you. Now if you will only assure us that you are opposed to the continuation of the present registration law, we will sweep the State & elect your friends". Mr. Johnson smiled. Not a word would he say. Still when Burton Harrison was recently released, Mr. Johnson charmed him. He left satisfied that he was doing the best he could for the South. And when the Va. Clergy delegation had an audience he said rather solemnly—no doubt suiting himself to his company—"Gentlemen, this country is in more danger than you think and I intend to save it". He tells Raymond he intends to stand by his party. And so on all round. It is impossible to tell what he means—and I sometimes think he is drifting along from day to day, waiting like Wilkins Micawber "for something to turn up".** And still this is the man whom half the Southern politicians are ready

designed canals and water works in the Baltimore area, became principal of the Maryland Military Institute in St. Denis (nine miles south of Baltimore, near the Patapsco River, and c. four miles south of Catonsville) in 1862 and served to 1891.

* The order of April 19, 1865 concerning the gray uniforms worn at the Catonsville Military Institute is given in Scharf, *History of Baltimore City and County* (Philadelphia, 1881, p. 151).

** Wilkins Micawber is a character in Charles Dickens's *David Copperfield* (London, 1849).

to bow down to and worship, before they even know what his views are.

March 1". [1866] The President did, after all, veto the Freedman's Bureau Bill.* It gave him immense additional power, if he had chosen to use the patronage but it would have ensured the hostility of the entire South to him and of a large party in the North and West. It would have been a gain of temporary power and a loss of popularity. There was great danger too of its throwing the power really into the hands of the radicals. They have gained strength by the long delay of Johnson, who has shown himself very unwilling to meet the issue forced upon him. I do not understand him except upon the general principle that you cannot understand a politician. For weeks before his veto he had not a friend among the radicals. His friends now say that he was anxious to wait till the 4" March, when the portfolios of the Cabinet expire, as he did not intend to continue Harlan and Stanton in their places. We shall see what truth there is in this.

March 5". Charles Kean & his wife—Ellen Tree as was—are again here, after a long trip through the South. They complained bitterly of fare and accommodation and have been half starved. But they are more Southern than a Southerner. They tell most extraordinary stories of the insolence of negroes and of the support they get in the South & West from the officers of the Freedman's Bureau. Their account of the pluck of the women is delightful. Mrs. Kean told me of an occurrence which took place in New Orleans. A lady wished to obtain some favor of Genl Canby and took with her to visit him a young friend. "Mind" said she "you say nothing to offend him or he may refuse our request". She kept quiet during the audience till Genl C. turning round remarked "Why is it that you Southerners will not visit our Northern ladies". "Your what?" said she "Our Northern ladies". "Women! Sir. Ladies do not follow an invading army." On another occasion she said a boat load of ragged prisoners, just exchanged stopped at New Orleans. The women crowded to the wharf with shirts. Two were allowed to go on board at a time with what they could carry. Finally the boat was ready to start and they were ordered off. They made a rush to say their good byes and could

* The Freedman's Bureau Bill, passed by Congress in February 1866, extended the life of the agency that had been set up to help former slaves obtain homes, jobs, and land. The most controversial aspect of the new bill removed cases involving freedmen from local courts to Bureau courts, were persons accused of interfering with the rights of freedmen would be tried without jury and without appeal.

not be gotten rid of. Officers charged them, but they made away for the files of soldiers & closed in behind them. Then the artillery was dashed through them at brisk trot and brought back again. All was of no avail. Finally the Col. in command drew up his guns and announced his intention to fire upon them if they did not disperse. At this the women spontaneously waved their hdkfs and cried out with one voice "Fire". This is called "la bataille des Marcheurs".

Kean & his wife told me that in Mobile they were so sick when they played that they had to have a physician behind the scenes, to tinker them up between the acts. He says he has often been so ill from the gout that he had to be almost carried to the theatre, but that after he had hobbled on the stage the excitement relieved him and he actually played himself well.

March 7". Kean is very hoarse today. "Ah! me" he says "anything but hoarseness. An actor can contend against anything but that. Gout! fever and even small pox I have played off but never hoarseness." He is getting old.

March 8". The Southern Fair is assuming large proportions.* The women have had a great time. They have three cliques among them—the charitable ones, the South Carolina ones and the lower house as they call it. Among many of them a universal sort of grab game has been going on and several of them have actually been spending money they received as donations on fancy articles for their tables which they will be unable to get rid of probably, except at a sacrifice. Some people write from the North "Don't make a political affair of this." As if anyone was giving to relief distribution in the South except those who had Southern sympathies or who wanted to make Capital out of their charity to the South. I have had a good many circulars distributed recently by prominent men. The returns are made to me as chairman of the Finance Com. T. J. Carson recd a letter today for answer to an appeal made to

* The Managers of the Southern Relief Fair, in Baltimore, from April 2 to 13, 1866, at the Maryland Institute Hall were: Mrs. B. C. Howard, President; Mr. J. Hanson Thomas, Mrs. Charles Howard, Mrs. J. S. Gittings, Mrs. W. Prescott Smith, and Mrs. J. J. Bankhard, Vice Presidents; Mrs. Peyton Harrison and Mrs. Doris Hoffman, Treasurers; Miss Frick, Secretary, and the following members of the Executive Committee: Mrs. J. Harman Brown, Mrs. Samuel Hoffman, Miss Louisa Hoffman, Mrs. Charles J. Baker, Mrs. P. Preston Parr, Mrs. Samuel W. Smith, Mrs. T. Parkin Scott, Mrs. Thomas Murdoch, Mrs. Gustavus Lurman, Mrs. Robert H. Carr, Mrs. J. H. B. Latrobe, Mrs. Joshua Vansant, Mrs. A. DuBois Egerton, Mrs. John F. Hunter, Mrs. Allan Dorsey, Mrs. Richard Norris, Mrs. James F. Purvis, Mrs. Louisa Carmon, Mrs. James M. Anderson, Mrs. F. W. Elder, Mrs. James Hodges, and Miss Emily Harper.

Fisk & Hatch New York Bankers. They say "We note your remarks in regard to the Circular enclosed by you. Please state if you can *assure* us of the *entire loyalty* of the *parties* who have *control* of the *movement* and of their *thorough sympathy* with *Northern sentiments* and feelings. And that the influence of the Society will not be used to foster any spirit of opposition or ill will towards the loyal people of the North.

Apl 14". [*1866*] The Southern Relief Fair is over. Its success was simply unparallelled and it reflects great credit on the women of Maryland. As soon as it began to assume large proportions men managers were called in to help and as many of these were not men of high social position or refinement I was called in specially by some of the ladies and made Chairman of the Finance Committee. I was invited to meet the Executive Committee and one evening faced alone twenty two women. It appears there were three parties. First the conservatives, second the South Carolina party headed by Louisa Hoffman and thirdly the Third Estate—composed of the outsiders who did not belong to the haute volée. Afterwards a fourth party was developed. The President Mrs Ben Howard struck off on an independent tack, would not account to the Treasurer and held on to her funds to the end of the Fair in violation of all law and order. These parties were all working against each other. Each one was ready to cheat in a quiet way to get the biggest share for her party or to make the best show at her table. Never before did I see so much envy hatred malice and all uncharitableness as was developed by this Charitable undertaking. On the night referred to, to my surprise, I succeeded in harmonising all the discordant elements. Each party assured me that I had given them the advice they had wanted and before I went they voted me an unanimous vote of thanks. Alas! for the vanity of human conceit. I learned afterwards that before I left the house the South Carolina party and the Third Estate were up in arms, each declaring that I had been brought in by the Aristocratic Conservatives to bully them. But what was funnier was that the very resolutions which had been passed to meet certain difficulties and which had been signed by the Treasurer, the Secretary being absent, as follows [Newspaper clipping inserted here]

AT A MEETING OF THE OFFICERS AND EXECUTIVE COMMITTEE OF THE ASSOCIATION FOR THE RELIEF OF SOUTHERN SUFFERERS, held on the 26th day of February inst. it was

Resolved, That this Association cordially approves of the appointment by the Assistant Managers of a Finance Committee, composed of Wm. W. Glenn, Joshua Vansant, and John L. Weeks.

That the duty of the Finance Committee shall be to receive and take charge of the funds contributed for the relief of Southern sufferers, and to hold the same subject to the future order of the Executive Committee.

That the Finance Committee be instructed to give to each person a proper receipt or certificate for all sums paid in or contributed, in order that each person shall thus have full credit for all amounts contributed or collected by them.

That the Managers are requested to pay over to the Treasurer of this Association, or to the Chairman of the Finance Committee, all sums collected by them, with the exception of such small amounts as may be reserved for the purpose of purchasing material for their respective tables, said amount so reserved, in no case to exceed the sum of one hundred dollars for any one table.

That all persons requiring additional funds for the purchase of such material, are requested to make written application for the same to the Executive Committee, who will provide therefor, by draft, on the Finance Committee.

That the Auxiliary Managers be and they are hereby requested to act as collecting agents for this Association, and to solicit contributions therefor.

By order,

MRS. PEYTON HARRISON
Secretary

were next morning deliberately violated by the Secretary herself, one of the Women who had called me in, who declared that she would not part with one cent of the money. As I came in to help the ladies and not to oppose them, I of course yielded and gave her her own way.

As chairman of the Finance Committee I authorized Miss Molly W. Kemble, who was very earnest in New York, to organize a sub-committee there. I had always mistrusted even Southern women who had resided much in New York and breathed the air there. But here was one who lived among friends who had very strong Southern feelings and whose mother was a South Carolinan. I was a little less cautious than usual and giving her pretty free rein was astonished to hear from her one bright morning that she had appointed Jessie Fremont as chairman of her sub committee. This was bad enough. I knew Genl Fremont and his wife were both incorrigible negro shriekers. I recollected when he was out for the Presidency, head of a very small niggir party, which flaunted in our faces, blazoned on banners, the words "Freedom Free Soil and Fremont"—and I knew Jessie would be a very hard pill to stomach. But Miss Molly declared she was enterprising and indefatigable and that her name and influence would be worth $100,000. So I wrote "let her be charitable if she chooses but dont let her attempt to be sociable. If she comes on to Baltimore she will not be received." But the New Yorkers were not content to stop here. They wanted more influential names and so they asked permission to add those of Genl Grant and Admiral Farragut. Here was a go. This was a firebrand. I telegraphed promptly "Impossible" and the New York committee subsided and in fact ceased to exist. These people cannot understand Southern feeling. We are disfranchised, denied political privileges, prevented from performing certain occupations unless we subscribe to oaths that require us to perjure ourselves and we have but one weapon of defence. That is the social weapon. This we use freely. We do not know these people socially and they shall not visit at our houses. In New York they declared us narrow minded and illiberal and vowed we would lose a great deal. We shall make $150,000 which is a pretty penny. The Crowd from beginning to end was enormous. The crush at night was indescribable and I suppose 10000 visitors came in daily on an average. The number of raffles was incalculable. The rage for gambling among the women was intense. Many things went off at very high prices. In the drawings unfortunately there was strong suspicion in more than one instance that there was considerable cheating and one old lady who had a very valuable doll house which had been superbly fitted up by certain artesans and given her for the fair, raffled it off at an indefinite amount, returned a certain sum as the profit, first detaining $300 as the cost to which she herself was entitled. It was exclusively a ladies Fair and some of the female developments, to those behind the scenes, were curious and interesting.

April 20. The Idiosynecrasies of self made men are very curious and there is certainly more force of character developed by them, than in the men of society. Refinement and education and training have their advantages, but they develop elegance rather than force. Some months ago Ben Ficklin & I determined to get up ourselves a Southern Express, worked & officered by Southern men. While we were arranging for the capital, Genl Heth and Genl Hanson with Mike Harman and some others took up the charter and went with great flourish of trumpets to establish a grand national affair employing the soldiers of each army in the different states of the Union. Genl Joe Johnston accepted the Presidency and Heth soon got assurances of patronage from his old enemies Grant & Sherman. Books were opened over the country. 50,000 shares were offered to the public at $100 a share making a capital of $5000000. $1 was paid in and subscribers were told confidentially that about $3 more was all that would be required. I saw Genl Johnston & told him the difficulties & told him I was sorry I could not work with him or serve under him. I told Heth that such a concern could only be successful by starting as a Southern concern and making an issue with Adams Express which was exclusively Northern. I told him that he would ruin it if he made it a military Alms House and that confidently as they counted upon Ben Ficklin accepting the Superintendence he would never touch it. Heth laughed. People scrambled for the stock. Offices were established all over the country. Soldiers were employed. Wagons & harness were bought and everything was done but open routes. Here was the hitch. Adams & Co. with their Capital had purchased exclusive privileges everywhere. Ficklin came home & would not touch the concern. $4 more was called in and then $5. The stock which rose in the beginning to a high premium declined more rapidly. Heth abandoned the ship. Others followed suit and early in March it was nearly wound up. At this juncture Ben F. was called in and offered absolute control and his own terms. The temptation was great & he took the risk. It has been an awful risk & we have worked like Turks. I have raised for him over $40,000 and through another friend raised $20,000 more. Last night there was a meeting of Directors to discuss matters and to see how far they were still willing to stand by. After the meeting Mike Harman, a man raised to wealth by his own efforts from the humblest beginning, came to see me. He & I and Ben were talking. And we all knew that Genl Joe Johnston was no more fit for the place he occupied than was a link boy—notwithstanding his long service as Quarter Master General and as General in the South, he seemed to have no business idea of organization and an utter indifference to and contempt for detail. Much as I thought of him from reputation I am I must confess considerably staggered and more than ever convinced of my old plan, never to pass conclusive judgment on any man till you see him. Nevertheless his name just now is great & we are determined to retain him. "Great Lord" said Mike "it is curious what a big man our President is among men who don't know him as well as we do. I'll tell you what gentlemen. We'll just have to keep him as an ornamental head piece. He'll look d—d well and be of service to us that way." It was very funny & very clever.

April 22d. A most extraordinary attempt at defamation has occurred here which has caused great feeling and excitement. For two years past the town has been flooded with anonymous letters. Most of them were left on Tuesday mornings, the day after the meeting of the German Cotillon Club. Suspicion was directed to one John Henry Keene, a young lawyer, son of a small Methodist Minister, who by push and perseverance had succeeded in effecting a lodgment in society. He was forbidden several houses, finally the "German" was reorganized and he was left out or virtually turned out, for he had gotten in there without authority or invitation. Soon after this he attempted to get into the Maryland Club and was black-balled. This made him furious and shortly afterwards he wrote to Frederic Bernal British Consul telling him that he had conclusive proofs against his wife and that she was undoubtedly the author of all the letters.

Bernal was stunned. He went to Robt. Gilmor Jr. for advice. Bob declined to give it or to aid him because he said he belonged to the Church. So he went to Robt. Gilmor, *père,* who of course, as he has done all his life, did exactly what he ought not to have done and then talked loudly about it at every street corner. Bernal had several difficulties to contend with. In the first place he actually permitted himself to discuss in his own mind his wife's innocence. Secondly he allowed old Bob Gilmor, who had no sense of nicety, to insult his wife by asking her if she was guilty or not; and finally Bernal has but one arm and was afraid of Keene.

The affair dragged on in a most disgraceful way. Several men had the bad taste to support Keene on his own *ex parte* statement and were sufficiently infamous to lend their aid to the slander against an innocent woman. Prominent among these was John Edgar, Mr. Dick Moale, and Mr Horace L. Brooke. Mr. Thomas Morris & family declined to give opinions, but cut Mrs Bernal and asked Keene to tea. Those who belonged to the Maryland Club or the German generally supported Mrs Bernal. Those who were not in either or both of these exclusive organizations discussed the matter pro & con freely. It was a great subject for evening talk at the Baltimore Union Club—a recent Yankee organization. Bernal was led by Bob Gilmor Sr. into an awkward correspondence and Keene finally finding that Bernal did nothing, assumed, I presume, naturally that he was afraid and one morning published the whole correspondence in the American with comments in the local. Keene certainly had the best of the correspondence. The story went from Baltimore to New York and there was a growing feeling that Bernal for some reasons preferred not to meet the issue squarely. Finally Keene endeavord to have Mrs Bernal presented by the Grand Jury. This would have affixed a stigma to her name which would have lasted her through life. No matter if a woman is afterwards acquitted, the fact that such a suspicion could have rested against her is enough to taint her character. Bernal was finally roused partially from his indifference and torpor. The advice of proper parties were taken and in a few days the whole devilish plot was unravelled. Keene had employed detectives Peirson and West* to aid him in the discovery of the writer of the letters and in trying to light upon the party who should bear the odium that now attached to him. He gave them so much trouble that they very soon began to suspect him and, once on this track, found unmistakable proofs as to the real authorship of the letters. One of the plans hit upon by Keene to catch Mrs Bernal was to write her anonymous letters about himself of a most filthy character, telling her what he Keene had been doing. These letters were given to the detectives to copy and deliver. Next morning Keene would deliver them in answer an anoymous letter charging him with the dirty practices mentioned in his own letter. The proof was conclusive. As no one but Keene, the writer, knew what was in these letters except the party who received them, of course the answer came from one of the two. Unfortunately for Keene, the detectives did not deliver his letters. They retained them. The answers however came all the same, of course written by Keene himself. On one occasion Peirson said to Keene "this answer is hardly plain enough". Oh! replied Keene, you'll have a plainer one tomorrow" and tomorrow a plainer one came. This was but one of the proofs. It was shown before the Grand Jury most conclusively that Keene was the author of the letters and that many of them had been gotten up and concocted with Mrs. Solomon Hillen at her house. Keene was on very intimate relations with her and she had always been suspected. Before going before the Grand Jury, when he was summoned, Bernal made a collection of different anonymous letters from several ladies who had received them—one of them of too filthy a character to be made public—and compared them. Three of them were written on an out of date foreign letter sheet, rather uncommon & exotic, of the same character as that in which Keene had conducted his Bernal correspondence. Besides this experts pronounced the handwriting unmistakable. He not only used remarkable paper in several instances but did not conceal his B's & K's which were of an outré character. The whole affair looks like insanity. I cannot imagine a man being so vile and so base. Nor so utterly & ridiculously foolish as to imagine

* The detectives mentioned in connection with the Bernal case were Joseph T. Peirson and D. Pinkney West.

he could fool detectives with his childish tricks. His spite against Mrs Bernal was that he had been turned out of the house by her and Mrs Hillen's ill feeling had evidently been excited in a similar way, for Mrs Bernal is plain spoken & had given her a piece of her mind.

April 27. The Grand Jury finally dismissed the Bernal Case today. Bernal did not ask them to indict Keene, as he should have done & so the Gr Jury did not take it upon themselves to take such action. Bernal has acted in a most wretched manner and has been badly advised. This fellow Keene has been making attack after attack of the most infamous character and Bernal has been contented to remain passively on the defensive. His wife's reputation has been assailed, an infamous charge has been made against her, and still Bernal takes no aggressive step in the matter. In the eyes of some he suffers more than his wife does.

I have just heard of conversations held by Tom Morris with two former friends. He complains bitterly of his ostracism. He says "you are the conquered and yet you behave as the conquerors. I am made to feel this war in social life—though I have been victorious. My wife is made to feel it. My children are made to feel it. Men frown upon me in the street"—and said to Buck de Courcey [?] "even negroes have scowled at me". Now this is delightful. Here these men ban together and ostracize us. We are not allowed to vote nor to practice professions unless we take repulsive oaths. In our turn we punish them socially and I am glad to see they feel it so deeply. I trust it may rankle for a long time to come.

April 28". The chances of life are wonderful. In the private letters of George Washington recently published he says to this effect "pack up my valuables & remove them. The contest is hopeless—not that I fear Howe's Army, but that the New Yorkers & Pennsylvanians are so demoralized that they are not to be relied upon". Still he was eventually victorious. I have already spoken of some of the wonderful turns of Jerome's fortunes. My experience has been curious latterly. I went on to New York ten days ago and wanted $50,000 for the Express. I made offers absurdly advantageous if the project proved a success. I offered private security to wealthy men and in spite of all my efforts could get nothing. In Baltimore, I half determined with Ficklin to throw up the whole concern. Today in Richmond after much talk with the Board, I finally came to the conclusion that they were not willing to back Ficklin up as I wished him backed up and that it was no use to trifle. So I had a talk with Ben and he resolved to get out while he could do so at a small loss. I had made several offers through the day to the Board through Mike Harman, all of which had been refused. About four o'clock, I went to see him. I asked for the return of $15,000 of my paper which he held. "What for" asked he. "Because, said I it is no use. The Board will not stand by us and Ben and I will just toss up while we can save ourselves. That's our conclusion". I went upstairs, tired out and disappointed. I hated to give up so big a chance. But there was no help for it. In an hour I was to leave for home. In less than fifteen minutes to my surprise Harman came after me & in a few minutes the Board not only accepted the proposition I had made most favorable to Ben and myself, but actually added to it what I particularly wanted, but was afraid to ask for lest they should not consent to it. If we are successful Ben will make a big reputation & he will add largely to his means. We will both be successful in spite of ourselves. [The lengthy newspaper clipping here is omitted, as not particularly pertinent to the above.]

May 8". Nobody seems to know what is doing at Washington or what is to be the eventual result of the President's inactive policy. The Radicals, since they carried the Civil Rights Bill by a two thirds vote over the President's veto, seem to be a little quieter feeling satisfied that they have now the power in their own hands. There was much apprehension that Johnson would use his partonage after Congress had adjourned and put his own men in the offices through the country, so as to use their influence to control the elections. To prevent this Mr Trumbull, a few days since introduced into the Senate the following amendment to the Post Office Bill, which was carried. This effectually curbed the President and took all power from his hands.

[Brief newspaper clipping on the above inserted here.]

The question was taken on the reconsideration of the vote by which the following amendment was adopted:

No person exercising or performing the duties of any office which by law is required to be filled by the advice and consent of the Senate shall before his confirmation by the Senate, receive any salary or compensation for his services, unless he be commissioned by the President to fill a vacancy occurring by reason of death, resignation or expiration of term of office during the recess of the Senate, and since its last adjournment, or removed for acts done in violation of the duties of his office; the case and cause of removal to be reported to the Senate at its next session.

It was decided in the affirmative as follows:

YEAS—Messrs. Cowan, Davis, Doolittle, Edmunds, Fessenden, Foster, Guthrie, Lane (Kansas), McDougal, Morgan, Nesmith,

Norton, Poland, Riddle, Saulsbury, Sherman, Stewart, Van Winkle, Willey, Williams and Wilson—21.

NAYS—Messrs. Anthony, Chandler, Clark, Conness, Creswell, Harris, Henderson, Howard, Howe, Lane (Ind.), Morrell, Nye, Pomeroy, Ramsey, Sprague, Sumner, Trumbull and Wade—18.

ABSENT or NOT VOTING—Messrs. Brown, Buckalew, Cragin, Dixon, Grimes, Hendricks, Johnson, Kirkwood, Wright and Yates—10.

To my great surprise they reconsidered it two days ago, the reconsideration being carried by a vote of 21 to 18, ten Senators being absent.*

May 9". Genl. Johnston was this evening in my room, signing some papers, when my little son, Johnny came in with his slate on which was a half worked sum. I laughed and said he was not yet up to long multiplication. "Never mind" said Genl J to him "if it be any consolitation, I will tell you, that I did not learn to read till I was ten years old". At tea George McHenry was here to whom I told the story. Ah" said he "that is perhaps the reason why he never advanced." The more I see of Genl. J. the more I am satisfied that he must have given great dissatisfaction in the position he occupied in the South. He is a very jealous man. He throws difficulties in the way of those who operate with him and when he is off and they take responsibility which is absolutely necessary for them to take, he is dissatisfied next morning. He evidently hates detail. Men now tell me that that was one reason why his Army was not at times in more efficient order.

I hear some strange stories now. Charlton Morgan tells me that some time before his brother, John Morgan was killed he told him that the "Yanks are too strong for us. They outnumber us too largely, for us to succeed". And Jim Howard (Col) says that he knew for months before Lee's surrender that "the thing was up." He said that he got daily the most urgent letters from women and their children urging him to grant furloughs to particular men that they might get bread to put in their mouths. The men themselves received direst appeals from their families. The consequence was that there were daily desertions. This no army and no cause could stand long. Burton Harrison, is still an ardent admirer of Mr. Davis and devoted to Mrs Davis and the family. He is still young and has lived exclusively with them for a long time—of course he is somewhat prejudiced. Burton privately abuses Joe Johnston and declares he had no right

* Maryland's Senators in the 39th Congress were Reverdy Johnson, who served from 1863 to 1868, and John A. J. Creswell, who filled Senator Hicks's unexpired term in 1865.

to surrender and that if he had not disobeyed orders & surrendered, Mr Davis never would have been captured. Quite probable. But does this make Genl. J. wrong. Certainly Morgan by his disobedience of orders helped to bring about the very result he wished to avoid while he deemed it inevitable.

Living as we do in the midst of great events, knowing many of the leading actors intimately and having every access to information, it is still almost impossible to form an impartial judgment on what is to become history. When we see how rivalry and party jealousies, have interfered with the best plans, how heedlessness has brought on battles prematurely and decided the fate of campaigns, how blind chance has overcome impossibilities how bold front and brag has pulled men through tight places and how leaders like skilful jugglers, taking skilful advantage of some unforseen occurrence, have changed their whole pre arranged programme, we can well understand how difficult it is ever to get at the truth. Still some bold and ignorant men will write books from hearsay and newspapers and call it history. And a hundred years hence some clever fellow in his closet, will say "now that the smoke of prejudice has passed away and time has allowed us to criticise impartially, we will give to the world a philosophical account of the events of the last century". What folly! I laugh to think how many great knaves and weak fools will then be historical, and how many men will have credit for great actions who never had brains enough for an original thought or independence enough for manly action. At the battle of Cowpens Col John Eager Howard was retreating as fast as he could according to positive orders. Closely pursued he was forced to fight. He turned & won the little skirmish, heralded in history as a battle. Its results were good. If he had failed he would have been shot. As it was history makes him a hero. We know that he was a plain countryman, his brother Cornelius Howard, a plain surveyor. They knew nothing of their ancestry and never could trace it. Their father or grand father had come over her and they had got much land when it was worth a song. Land became valuable. The Howards became rich. They boast of the plain & rough but bold old Colonel, mount the arms & crests of the Arundel Howards and impose on a great many people who know no better. What a terrible thing an Almanach de Gotha or a Peerage would be in this country. How it would unveil many a grand lineage.

July 13". [1866] Mr O'Conor and Govr Pratt had today a final interview with President Johnson relative to Mr Davis. They have got from Mr Johnson the "kindest assurances" but Davis is still a prisoner.* They hope for relief as soon as Congress adjourns. So every body has been hoping for eight months past. But put not your trust in Presidents. On the 26 May Mr O'Conor telegraphed me to meet him at the cars. I found him and Shea on their way to Fortress Monroe to have an interview with Mr Davis and Mr Brady, with Burton Harrison, on their way to Washington. Mr O'Conor begged me to urge Govr Pratt to go along. Having no confidence in Mr Brady, knowing that he felt not the slightest interest in Mr. Davis and that he was only acting for notoriety and pay, I did urge Govr Pratt to go along and he went down next morning. It was well he did, for he soon found that Brady had not the manliness to talk out. The President declined to see them on Sunday. This was to get time. Monday they went according to appointment at twelve o'clock, but were kept waiting till two o'clock, when the President was called off to a Cabinet Meeting. This was evidently what he had been delaying for. When it was over he had a free talk and said frankly that the Government was not ready to go to trial with Mr Davis and that if his counsel insisted on trial he must either be bailed or paroled—and that one of these things should be done. Burton Harrison was in great spirits & Brady assured him that Stanton was favorable to Davis' conditional release. Next day however, Govr Pratt, at the request of Mr Davis, had an interview with Stanton & requested additional privileges at Fortress Monroe to be granted Mr Davis. Stanton's manner was so short and rough that it was evident he was in no friendly mood. Wednesday the 30" May, after seeing Govr Pratt, I wrote to Mr O Conor & Burton Harrison, telling them both to be on hand & ready for trial on Monday in Richmond and not to place too much reliance on seeing friends. Mr. O'Conor wrote me back word to get Mr. G. Wm. Brown & Govr Pratt to join them, *en route* for Richmond on Saturday. Mr Wm. B. Reed came along & he Mr Brady & Mr Brown went to Richmond while Mr. O'Conor & Govr Pratt went to Washington. Judge Underwood at Richmond was prepared to do nothing. The counsel waited for instructions from Washington. Mr Brady made a joke of the matter and Mr Reed got angry because Mr O'Conor had neither given him latitude nor furnished him with instructions. So between them allowed the Court to adjourn.

* Counsel for Jefferson Davis included Thomas G. Pratt, James T. Brady, William B. Reed, William George Brown, Edwin A. Vansicle, Thomas H. Edsall, Burton N. Harrison, Charles O'Conor, and George Shea. The case was tried before Judge John C. Underwood.

Meanwhile the President had given most positive assurances to Govr Pratt & Mr O'Conor that Mr Davis should be released. The Atty General, Speed, agreed to it. (Chief Justice Chase suddenly became virtuous, declined to sit on the Case because Virginia was still under military rule and he did not choose to attempt the exercise of legal jurisdiction under such circumstances.) (And Mr Speed agreed to go to Richmond to have Mr Davis bailed. Just as the three were starting they heard however that the Court had adjourned—so they determined to apply to Chase.) The trouble then was to find Underwood. Wednesday, the President was still decided and Mr O'Conor telegraphed to me to send him some Maryland decisions that would help the case & strengthen the President. That night I went to New York and next day Com. Vanderbilt was telegraphed to to know if he would go on the bail bond. Friday night I came back. Horace Clark Augustus Schell and Horace Greely, who had also volunteered were also on the train, the former going in place of Vanderbilt who was sick and all going on as bondsmen. Horace Greely as Davis' Bondsman. Heaven help the mark. Saturday morning Mr O'Conor telegraphed me to find Judge Underwood who was in Baltimore. He had been in Baltimore and had left for Alexandria. I telegraphed back "Send to Alexandria". It was no use. Judge Underwood did not intend to be found and was not found. His game I think was to force Davis Counsel to sue out a writ of habeas corpus. This would have placed him under the jurisdiction of the Court and he would have been lodged in Richmond jail where he would have died. He is much more comfortable where he is. Another Cabinet Meeting had taken place. The President no longer talked confidently and it was evident that the hopes of Mr Davis' release were groundless. Seward was violent and talked of Mr Davis' implication with the assassination of Lincoln. "Look at me" said he—and he is a humble object to look at. He evidently wishes to have Mr Davis tried by a military commission.

Monday June 11. Govr Pratt went back to Washington. Mr O'Conor staid there. All the others went home. It was evident that the President as usual had made up his mind to yield & so the matter stands, Mr Johnson having gone back from the most positive promises. He appears determined not to break with his cabinet. Six months ago when Govr Pratt assured him that if he meant what he said, he must discharge Stanton & Seward, he answered "It shall be done Governor". A few days ago, Govr Pratt said after some conversation, "I am delighted to hear you talk so, Mr President, but why in God's name, don't you do something? And why do you keep around you a Cabinet who are not only opposed to you, but who are false to you—who not only thwart you, but who actually tell all that happens at the Cabinet Meetings, to your political opponents within half an hour after the meetings are over." All that Mr Johnston does is to declare that he is firm in his policy. But what is the use of being firm and staying quiet and getting beaten and losing State after State merely from inactivity & want of boldness. Mr Johnson told some radicals in Govr Pratt's presence "The South has done more in fourteen months than I expected to see accomplished in several years. Slavery is abolished. The Confederate Debt is repudiated. The people are submissive. What more do you want? Why do you go on demanding exaction after exaction. You are actually trying to cut off the heads of the Southern and thus leave the legs to manage political affairs. I must oppose such policy. If the people choose to sustain it, the blame be upon them. It shall not rest upon me". But having talked thus Mr Johnson stops. He takes no steps, to prevent the success of a policy which he says will ruin the country and which if carried out will destroy it—for said he "the country is this day in greater danger of disruption than it was at any time during the war". How hard it is to make a large minded statesman out of a petty pot house politician.

July. Burton Harrison tells me Mr. Davis told him a few days since at Fortress Monroe, that Col Myers, his brutal jailer said to him recently "I always thought they wanted you to die here till now. And now I believe they want you to live". This only confirms our opinion. For some time President Johnson considered Davis' death as an excellent solution of a troublesome question. Now, he considers it would cast a stain upon his name, in the eyes of the world.

Talking of Mr Davis how Joe Johnston hates him. I was arguing with him not long ago that the proof that Mr. Davis had no money in England lay in the fact that Mrs Davis had actually subsisted on charitable contributions. "That proves nothing, said he, she would take a quarter from any body".

August 7". Registration commences today.

How curious are the changes of fortune. Ben Ficklin & I had built up the National Express. A month ago I would not have taken $1,000,000 for our share and as much more for the position we should have attained in it. A personal difficulty arose between Ficklin & the directors which gave birth to an intrigue against Ficklin. This has now gone so far that Ficklin has very foolishly tossed up. I stand by my friend, although I know there is no one but him & myself who will carry this thing to a success. I have told Allnutt that now I am out the concern must either smash or become Yankee. The former will happen I suspect, as there is not a man in the concern capable of controlling men & choosing proper agents.

Sep 4". [*1866*] Mr Bayard tells me that Mr Davis says that there is not one word of truth of what Craven says in his book about Hunter.* He never uttered such words. The Book he says was prepared for Craven by Miles O Reilly who had been on Hunter's staff. O'Reilly put all this in himself.The Book was reviewed in the war office & expurgated before going to Press.

Sep 10". Charley Marshall told me that Mr Davis, when Johnston was before Atlanta wrote to Genl Lee telling him that Genl J. had made a failure and asking him who he should appoint in his place. Genl Lee answered the President that he did not see that Genl Johnston had made a failure and that in any case it was a very dangerous moment to make any change. Soon after without noticing this letter Mr Davis wrote back to know what Genl Lee thought of Hood. As Marshall read the letter he remarked "Genl Lee, I am afraid Mr Davis is being activated by personal feelings towards Genl Johnston". Genl Lee reproved him and told him he should not utter such sentiments. He wrote back to Mr Davis that Hood was a good Brigadier General, but that his career as Commander of a division had not been successful, that he did not know if he had improved sufficiently to command a large force, but that something could be learned from the history of his connection with a corps". Hood was appointed. Long after, after the surrender, Genl Lee said to Marshall, referring to this conversation "Colonel, I fear you were right".

Sep 24. The National Express has come to an untimely end. There was not a single man in it after I left who had the pluck to back it heavily.

Oct 18". [*1866*] Col Peyton, Lee's Adjutant, told me while dining with me yesterday, that he had never despaired until April 6" 1865 and that three days before Genl Lee was confident of holding together his army and making good his retreat. But he had a long line & it was important there should be no gaps. Pickett got very drunk & left a very wide gap. In this Sheridan entered unopposed, while Pickett was reposing in a fence corner. After the battle of Five Forks the game was evidently up—Lee's plans having been defeated by failure to carry out his orders. This agrees with the telegrams of

* John Joseph Craven's *The Prison Life of Jefferson Davis* was published in 1866.

Grant at that time. I recollect perfectly well that the impression produced upon me was that he anticipated failure.

When Genl Mulford, Commissioner for Exchange, was talking over these matters after the close of the war, he said "I know as much about these matters as most men and I tell you that the South lost from its own mismanagement". Mulford is a plain man but a good fellow & sincere. I knew him at Fort McHenry, where he was as Captain with his company during my first imprisonment.

Novr 3. [1866] Another sad fiasco, resulting from hopeless imbecility. Govr Swann, a Virginian by inheritance, false to his education and his early associations, clung to the Union party and was elected Governor. Now that the war is over and he was in the Gubernatorial chair, he thought the conservative game was the best to play. He disgusted the radicals and soon found himself in a minority in his own party. As he was very desirous of going to the United States Senate his only chance was to turn to the disfranchised voters of the State. Accordingly he made a sort of bargain with two or three of the party leaders of the Southern Element here that he would appoint registers who would permit men to register without too close a scrutiny by which means we should be enabled to get control of the Legislature, call a new convention and remodel the present "bayonet" constitution. In the electoral districts the candidates were to be divided. We were to have one half who were to vote for Swann as U.S. Senator. The Swann men were to have one half who were to vote for a convention.

After the registration, prior to the State election, there was to be held a city election, the first week in October. The registers could not be got ready for this election. But they were not needed. In passing the registration laws, they were only made to apply to state elections. This was the only municipal election in the State of any importance and it was overlooked. Swann should have had sense enough to avoid all questions by appointing his registers sooner. He did not, and when the election was held he should have taken some steps to see that his party men were allowed to exercise their privileges. As he had delayed in the first instance so now he trifled. He said first one thing than another and finally determined to let the election go on, declaring that if it was not fairly conducted he would remove the Police Commissioners, appoint good men,* secure the Legislative

* The Baltimore City Police Department has been under state control since 1858 and it is the governor, not the mayor, who appoints the police commissioners. The irony of the situation in 1866 was that election violence during the mayoralty of Thomas Swann prompted the state take-over of the police!

election and then take away the franchise from the city so as to get rid of the scoundrels now in power. The Election was held. None but radical judges were appointed. There were few boxes for rejected votes, in fact only in a very few precincts. Men who had served in the Federal army were refused permission to vote, and the election was a farce.

Instead of turning out the Police Commissioners Swann again began to temporize. The law was explicit. During the war the radicals had made it to suit themselves so as to give them absolute control over this force. It was a clear case for following Judge Taney's advice to my father, when he first went on the bench.* "Glenn," said he, "whenever you are in any doubt, find out the common sense and the merits of the case. Decide upon them. You will find that you can always make the law to fit." But Mr Swann would not do. He trifled for several days and said he wanted support. He sent to the Gazette to get that paper to back him up. Then he wanted countenance from the gentlemen, very few of whom would give it to him directly because they regarded him as a leader of the Street mob, as a man who had been head of the most disgraceful ruffianism during the worst days of the history of this city and because they trusted neither his words nor his intentions. Finally he determined to take testimony to prove charges which were portent. Counsel was employed, money was raised for fees and the affair dragged wearily along, although the November election was approaching. Meantime the radicals raised a great storm. Baltimore was as quiet almost as a churchyard and they declared that it was in a state of revolution. Finney came on here and wrote the most incendiary letters which were circulated through the North, about the rebel element and its threatening aspect, in which was not one word of truth. The Northern Press raised a storm and troops were promised from Pennsylvania to protect Mayor Chapman & his supporters.

Finally Swann saw that the law was clear and having received assurances from President Johnson that the peace of the city should be preserved if necessary by U.S. Troops he decided to remove the commissioners. This he did on Wednesday Octr 31".

Novr 1". [1866] Mr Swann, strange to say, made no appointments yesterday. The elections are for the 6". Time is precious. This afternoon it is understood that the new commissioners are General Horn and John T. Ford, the theater man. Genl Grant came up today. He

* Roger Brooke Taney was a close friend of Judge John Glenn of the United States Fourth District Court, and had administered the oath of office to him.

had a conference with Judge Bond of the Criminal Court, Mayor Chapman, the Police Commissioners and other radical rascals. Finally he sent for Horn and Ford and enquired if they had received their commissions. They told him no but signified that they expected them. Grant then said to their very great surprise, that Govr Swann was all wrong in this matter and he was sorry he had taken this step. "Genl" said Horn, "I went into the ranks as a private. I have risen to the rank of Major General. These men refused my vote." "Such occurences, replied Grant, "are certainly unfortunate, but they will happen and this does not alter my mind. If there is any trouble here and the Military is called in it will raise a row in the North and create an excitement which will be injurious to the country". Ford was perfectly taken aback. He saw Frank Howard late in the evening and said "Mr Howard, I knew Genl Grant only by reputation, and had heard of him as a conservative man; but I assure you the man rambled on incoherently and talked as much like a fool as any man I ever listened to. The conclusion I came to was that, although it is evidently the interests of the country and of President Johnson that this odious tyranny and extremism should be removed from Baltimore, yet if President Johnson and Govr Swann insist on carrying out the determination of Govr Swann, it will create a breach between Genl Grant and the President. Genl. Grant has elected evidently to stand by the radicals in this instance.

Novr. 2. Swann has appointed James Young and W. T. Valiant as Commissioners. The present commissioners had their offices guarded so that no one could approach them. They locked up all their doubtful men, for it was very evident that as Govr Swann had law so clearly on his side, more than one half of the present police force would at once enlist under the new commissioners if they had a chance. The day passed without anything being accomplished, the new men being unable to make the demand.

Novr. 3. Young and Valiant succeeded today in making a demand for the books &c which was refused. They drove about in a hack followed by a large crowd cheering them. They stopped in front of an office which they had taken for the occasion. There they staid trifling, until about noon, when they were accosted by a bench warrant from the Criminal Court for an attempt to break the peace. The sheriff who had been swearing in special policemen, was also arrested. No bail was permitted except upon a pledge not to exercise the functions of their office &c &c. So now all three are locked up in Jail. Govr Swann called upon Genl Canby, in command. A large number of troops have been sent here. Genl Canby of course could not interfere except in case of a riot. The election is on Tuesday the 6". Judge Bartol of the Court of Appeals came to the city in the afternoon. A writ of Habeas Corpus was applied for and granted. It was not however served from carelessness or neglect.

Nov 5. Writ served this morning. James, the Warden of the Jail, decided that he had three days to make the return it [*sic*]. The counsel for the Prisoners showed clearly that three days was granted by law in order to give time to bring in the person of prisoners who might be away at some distance but that the whole intention and meaning of the writ of habeas corpus was the immediate delivery of persons from custody. Judge Bartol allowed the three days. So the old commissioners hold on, and the election is held tomorrow under the auspices of the city clique and all its subordinate villains. Swann has been beaten out of his boots and altogether there has been a display of trifling imbecility and want of manliness in Swann, Schley & Latrobe the Counsel and the Judge which are shameful. Swann made up his mind what to do one month ago and never did it.

Nov 6". The radicals were so uncertain about their chances of conducting the election today, that they failed to have sufficient cooperative preparation for their rascalities. Therefore although in many precincts they rejected an immense number of votes they actually to the surprise of everyone lost the election by a small majority. Their defeat was partly owing to their own trickery. They had tickets printed with the National flag in color on their paper, so that it showed through. This was found out & the conservatives in some wards prepared similar tickets. Voters bringing these tickets were allowed to vote without challenge.

Nov 7. The object of detaining the prisoners is now passed away. Still Judge Bartol insists on having the case argued. What in the devil does he want argued.

Nov 10. After long winded speeches Judge Bartol has delivered a long winded decision, discussing questions which were hardly involved, declaring the New Commissioners properly in office and still holding them to bail to answer for conspiracy & an attempt to break the peace. Thus a policeman is right to arrest a thief & knock him down but may be indicted for assault. Law has long since ceased to be a protection for right. It is become a sharp game where the honest and the innocents have no very good chance.

Novr. Matters have settled down quietly. The new police commissioners have taken possession and so ends the fearful row about which the Yankee papers made such a noise.

Thanksgiving Day. Genl Dick Taylor has been for some time in Washington riding his jaded political hobby horse—Expediency. He has proposed to accept universal suffrage for the South for all who can read & write and to receive at the same time an universal amnesty and to have the disabilities removed under which Southerners now labor. The President was pretty well pledged to issue a general amnesty today. It would have been a graceful act. But no pardon has come. What is to be expected of a low born cur no matter what his cleverness. He never can have the appreciations of a gentleman. Andy Johnson was the son of a prostitute in New Berne N.C. He had a reputed father. His mother could not support him and he was taken by the city as a pauper boy and apprenticed to a tailor. I first heard this from Dr Hanks who lived years ago in North Carolina. Since then I have heard it from others.

Dec 21. [1866] The Supreme Court have just made a most important decision. They have decided that no man can be deprived of his right to a trial before civil courts where they are in the exercise of their functions. What a farce! There will be no more military commissions—until they are deemed necessary. Then, the Supreme Court will be respected as is and was its Constitution. Notwithstanding this Mr. Davis is still kept in prison.

1867 January. At the meeting of the Legislature, Govr. Swann began immediately to press his claims for the Senatorship, asserting roundly that he had made a bargain to give us registers who would allow every man to register who would take "the oath" so that we could control the Legislature, on condition that he should have the Senatorship. Absurd! Govr Swann did make such a bargain for Baltimore City with Montgomery Blair & Govr Pratt. But what has Montgr Blair to do with Southern men or Maryland politics. Govr Pratt sent for Mr. Gatchell Mr Wallis and myself to ratify the bargain. We all laughed. I said "Govr Swann's main object is to defeat Cresswell and prevent him from again going to the U.S. Senate. He hates him so bitterly he will make any sacrifices to accomplish this end, and the only hope he has of defeating Cresswell is to fling himself into our arms. When he really does anything I for one will be willing to reward him." The others agreed with me. Govr Pratt after our conversation still tried to engineer the matter, but Swann trifled so, lied so & cheated and deceived him so at every turn that finally even he became disgusted. When the Legislature met, I took very good care to put leading men from the Eastern Shore right on the subject but Swann took equally good care to make terms with the Members, promising offices to friends of different parties and the use of his Executive power & influence. As a two thirds vote was necessary to accomplish our reforms the Legislature was at last forced to elect him Senator. In fact many of the members had regularly sold themselves to this creature. In return we were to have an enfranchising law, which was got before he was elected, a police bill, a Convention call and a Bill calling for a new election in Baltimore City and getting rid of this Scoundrel Chapman who is now Mayor elected in fact fraudulently. We shall probably get a Police Bill but I expect, now that Swann has the Senatorship, we shall be cheated out of the two last and be forced in City and State to remain for two years more under Republican rule.

Feb 23d. [*1867*] There is a pretty row in the Camp. It is has been for some time past doubtful whether Govr Swann would be allowed by the radicals to take his seat in the Senate, so bitter are they against him for throwing open the registration to so large a portion of the voters of this State. Today he went to Washington & had an interview with Montgomery Blair. Blair assured him that he had no chance whatever. Lieut Govr. Cox it appears is entirely in the hands of the radicals. During the war he was medical inspector. He gave Shrynek a large contract for beds & mattresses, in return for which Shrynek presented him with his fine house & furniture. He refused to purchase drugs in Baltro. because Canby would not allow him a handsome percentage for himself. Last term a suit was docketed agst Leary brother of the City Counsellor, damages $20,000. It was instituted by one of the ring who had not got his fair share of the spoils. Cox's complicity was very evident and they paid the whole claim rather than have the exposure. Wallis was atty for platff. Cox now owes, says Blair, at least $50,000 which he has not settled with Govt. The game was that as soon as Swann presented his credentials his election was to be referred to the Judiciary Com., where he was to be tied up until our Legislature adjourned. Then Cox, who would be Govr, was to appoint Cresswell and finally Cox was to petition Congress to place such a form of Government in Maryland as would be best calculated to preserve order, the reins of power being at present in the hands of parties not well affected to the Union. For this he is to have a quittance from Govt. It was a rascally scheme. Swann wd. not have cared if he could have made anything by it, but the idea of being defeated by Cresswell was too bitter a pill for him and he declared at once he would decline to accept the nomination.

Feb 25. There has been great talk today behind the scenes about Swanns probable course. Maddox (senator) assures me I know nothing about it and that Swann will resign and Cox will be Govr.

Feb 26. This morning I went to Annapolis. Cox's family were down to see his inauguration, the crowning glory of his political career. His friends were confident. I began to think I was wrong so I went after Govr Thomas and Jones of Somerset. They told me that Swann had acted until eight o'clock last night as if he were really going to resign the Governorship when he had sent for them, Judge Carmichael, Miller (speaker) and one or two others. His object was to induce them to take the initiative. He had said in Washington "The Legislature has placed me in a very false position. I will throw the responsibility on them". Swann is always very funny about the responsibility. He has always some little game to shift it somewhere. But this time it would not do. "Really" said Govr Thomas, "now that the Legislature have elected you Senator, it does seem to me it would rather stultify itself by asking you not to accept the position". And so Swann, who had made up his mind anyhow to cling to the Governorship if he could not get the Senatorship, was obliged to act on his own responsibility. Cox never knew his determination until this morning. Swann deceived him to the last moment. Never was man more mortified than this vain conceited jackanapes Cox and never were men more disappointed than his friends, who all were promised the privilege of a finger in the pies. [A lengthy newspaper clipping follows.]

Special Correspondent of the Baltimore Gazette.

THE INAUGURATION THAT DID NOT COME OFF—THE WHY AND THE WHEREFORE.

Annapolis, Feb. 26, 1867.

If the uses of adversity are really sweet, then Lieutenant Governor Cox has nearly a surfeit from the very big pill he had to swallow to-day. The sweetness, too, must have all been inside for the pill was very certainly not sugar-coated.

On Saturday afternoon it was confidentially rumored behind the scenes that Gov. Swann had been to Washington and had been very positively informed by influential friends that there was no chance of his being allowed to take his seat in the Senate. Relying upon this assurance it was stated that he had said positively he would not send in his resignation as Governor, but that feeling keenly the unfortunate position in which he had been placed by the Legislature of Maryland who had elected him a member of a body which refused to receive him, he would send a message to them informing them of the facts and placing upon them the responsibility of action. This, of course, created great consternation among the Coxites, who had large baskets full of loaves and fishes ready to distribute. Whether or not they remonstrated is not known, but on Sunday afternoon Gov. Swann appeared to have reconsidered his determination and gave orders to have engrossed all the bills which had passed, in order that he might sign them on Monday prior to his resignation. On Monday afternoon an application was made to him for a pardon which he referred over to Cox, Governor in embryo.

These facts were a renewed assurance to the Cox men that Governor Swann was determined, at all hazards, to resign, and they continued to make their little plans and arrangements with every confidence. Late in the evening, however, it appears that Governor Swann determined, before taking too rashly a step which might in its consequences be so important to the interests of the State of Maryland or to his own, to have a long consultation with gentlemen of known sagacity, with whom he had not yet consulted. It was well understood by them that the nomination of Governor Swann would be so tied up in the Judiciary Committee of the Senate, if ever it got there, as to virtually exclude him from a seat in that body, and it was also very positively asserted and quite generally believed that Mr. Cox was in some way deeply committed to some of the Radical leaders. It was their opinion, as it was the opinion of many leading Conservative men, that under the circumstances it would be best for Governor Swann not to resign.

This morning all was still in doubt. The Cox party was in good spirits and the Cox family had arrived in force to see the expected inauguration. But by the time the House met it was well-known that Governor Swann had determined to remain Governor for the present and, by the time the Senate met, Lieutenant Governor Cox had prepared a written answer to make to the communication of the Governor. He was determined this grave responsibility should rest on the shoulders to which it of right belonged. No doubt what occurred in the Senate appears in your reports. Shortly after these communications were read Mr. Cox left his seat and walked out as crestfallen as a chicken with a clipped wing. He was heard to declare outside that never again could he speak to Governor Swann except on official business. Over the rest of this sad story it is but proper to draw a veil. There are family and other griefs which should be sacred.

Feb 27". The smash in New York has been awful. Twelve men lost eight millions of dollars. Jerome who had made $3,000,000 on Pacific Mail within the past two years undertook to double his fortune and is ruined. No more sleigh rides, with eight horses and outriders & torches and camel's hair shawls for wrapping. When he got in difficulty like most men the desire to save himself was stronger than his principle. He sold stock freely while he was pretending to sustain the market. Some of his friends talk very hardly about him.

1867

Mch 5. The radical Congress met today. The whole power of the Government is in their hands. Johnson is really an insignificant cypher and even his best friends pity a man who has almost made himself contemptible by losing such opportunities and letting such vast power pass from his hands. Two weeks ago Greely urged him to reorganize his cabinet and turn out Seward and Stanton. He said "For universal amnesty the South will give universal suffrage. For universal suffrage let us give universal amnesty. I will go in your cabinet and we will so split the Republican party by this move that the conservative element will triumph". Conservative! ! Heaven bless the mark; but it was a suggestion. Johnson thought about it and after nearly making up his mind abandoned the project. His character if he has any is pitifully passive. Judge Black said to him You are like Fort Sumter before the rupture. I told Mr Buchanan one day "Mr Prest. either abandon Fort Sumter or fortify it. If you leave nothing to take there can be no fight if you make it impregnable it will not be attacked. I tell you Mr Prest., either fortify your Executive power or resign and go to Tennessee. It is your duty to pursue one course or the other." Johnson calmly submits. He is making the appointments now to suit the radicals. Judge Black wrote the veto message for him on the military reconstruction bill. It was an able document.

Mch 20. Home today from Norfolk, where I went to take Miss Mildred Lee on a visit to Dr Wm. Selden. The negroes are well organized there and their Republican leaders expect to carry the State. Genl Lee, I hear, as well as other leading Southern men are for using all their influence to control the conventions under the Military Bill. They say if they do not, the Yankees will. My own impression is that these Southern gentlemen make a great mistake. The more resistance they make the more oppression they will certainly induce.

Mch 23d. The Legislature adjourned today. There were among its members many men of capacity and position, more than one generally found in such a body. But on the whole it was as corrupt a Legislature as ever met at Annapolis. They were very loose too in their way of doing business. They juggled and swapped off measures, defeating the Municipal Bill which they should have passed so as to enable us to depose Mayor Chapman and the most disgraceful ring which ever swindled citizens and passing a Bill for a Convention, which is so imprudent and impolitic in view of the Military Reconstruction Bill that nothing is left now but to defeat it by the vote of the people. If we were to secure a convention now, we should either have it controlled or set aside by the Radicals. In either case we should be territorialized.

Mch 24". Have just left Mrs Davis, for whom I have been trying to make some arrangements about the release of Mr Davis through Mr John Garrett. Wilson has lately "got religion" and has introduced a resolution into the Senate, calling for the release of Mr Davis or his trial. Thad Stevens has also signified to Mrs Davis' friends that if she wishes and will come to him, he will help her. Now Thaddeus is not a bad hearted man. He will curse you or ruin you or pick your pocket or confiscate your property, if he can make anything by it, but he will not cut your throat needlessly. So Mrs Davis has hope of him. She counts upon Wilson because Wilson actually signed a memorial for her to the President asking for Mr Davis' release, on condition that it was not to be used unless Wendell Phillips signed it too. Phillips however would not sign. Still Mrs Davis thinks it is time to act and as it is very evident now that Stanton is the power behind the throne, the effort is to get at him. Garrett thinks if he can get Stanton and Grant to make application it must be listened to. All have given up any hopes of President Johnson. Those who were most deceived in him and had most confidence in him, now confess there is no reliance whatever to be placed upon him. He is not partial to Mrs. Davis. She sent to old Blair some time ago a letter in blank signed by herself to be filled in by him and intended as an application to Johnson. She wrote & sent with it a private one in which she spoke about the Yankees and the President and said she supposed this treatment was meant as retaliation on a helpless man for an insult given when he was free and she did not know what Mr Johnson wanted to keep Mr Davis there unless it was for him to learn to sew. When Blair went to see the President he gave the *quondam* tailor the wrong letter by mistake. When Mrs Davis saw my smile she said "Mr. Glenn, I don't believe Mr Blair did this intentionally." I did.

Mrs Davis looked so like a squaw today. I never see her but that I think of this epithet given her by Mrs Lydia (Joe) Johnston. She talked as usual—steam always up ready for a go—and the larger the company the greater the speed. Today Govr Pratt & I were alone with her. She was berating him for not going to Fortress Monroe according to promise. "You promised, but you did not come. We expected you, but in vain. We looked for you, but you never appeared. We waited and waited but n-a-a-r-y Pratt." Western this!

Mrs Davis told a very characteristic anecdote about Mr. D. I suggested that Mr D. might be released if he would be willing to leave the country. Of himself, she said, he would never consent to it. When he makes up his mind you can't bend him. It is just the same spirit which made him dispute with Breckinridge about the time of the death of his father and still refuse to be convinced even after old Mrs Breckinridge herself said she recollected all about it perfectly.*

I could not but laugh at what Cameron said to a gentleman two days ago in Washington. How is Mr D. said Cameron. "Oh replied P. he is very feeble". That's singular said Cameron for Mrs Davis, is now in Baltimore, at Mrs Gittings, where she has gone to be confined. There is no truth whatever in the report.

There is one thing I cannot understand and that is about the money affairs of Mr. Davis. When I undertook to procure counsel for McCue** or any other Southerner who was about to be tried by Military Court, I was told by —— to draw on him for whatever I wanted. Now I never did draw for no money ever was needed. The massacre of Wirz's closed this atrocious business. I undertook to procure counsel at a time when men were afraid to have their names known in connection with suspected Southerners. I afterwards learned that —— was authorized to draw on England for £20,000 for any such trials, Mr Davis' included. Now this was not all the money that was abroad. A considerable sum was divided. Mr Mason got a slice, Benjamin got a portion, Slidell got some—and some I feel sure was set aside for Mr. Davis. This was Secret Service money which could not be used after the collapse. The money to provide for Mr Davis' trial, as I understand is a separate fund. A large amount of money too has been subscribed in the South and I am informed that there is in hand for Mr Davis at least $250,000. Now Mrs Davis is always talking about his poverty and the necessity for

* The Breckinridge referred to may be Joseph Cabell Breckinridge of Kentucky, whose wife was Mary Clay Smith. He died young, leaving among his children John Cabell Breckinridge who became a Confederate general.

** John W. McCue of Scott County, Virginia, an 18-year-old Confederate soldier who had served under Moseby and whose father was a Confederate officer imprisoned at Fort Delaware, was arrested for the murder of Richard N. Ryan of Croom, the assault of Francis Coffron, also of Croom, and the plundering of John W. Coffron's store at Croom. Croom is in Prince Georges County, Maryland, south of Upper Marlboro. An account of the incident appears in the April 28, 1865, issue of the Baltimore *Daily Gazette*.

his working for a living. She declares positively she does not know of any fund except one of $8000 on which she is drawing. I can only account for it in two ways. The Trustees of this fund must want to keep it for Mr Davis' family. Mrs. Davis herself is extravagant and besides she has a family who prey upon her, as far as they can. Mrs Davis can hardly be telling me a deliberate story. And still it is so hard to know when to believe women.

Mrs Davis talking of some one said "Ah! he did not know how Mr. Davis doted on West Point." Unfortunately we have found it out. The South fell a victim to this spirit and to Mr Davis' unchangeable obstinancy.

May 11". This morning I got a letter from Genl Rooney Lee, saying that "Unless Mr Davis' counsel were very confident, they were making a very great mistake in bringing him up to Richmond for the May term of Court, where he would be transferred from Military to Civil Custody". This made me a little uneasy. Since the opening of negotiations I have known very little what was going on. When Garrett told me that he had obtained from Stanton the assurance that when Mr Davis was brought up to Richmond for trial, he should not be more uncomfortable there than he was now at Fortress Monroe, both he and I felt that this was a very great step. As Garrett had got so much more than any one else, I told Mrs Davis by all means to let him control matters entirely and to keep Govr Pratt her Baltimore Counsel, quiet for the present. This was the advice she wanted, but she hesitated about telling Govr Pratt to drop his efforts. So I did it for her, much to her relief. After which I kept out of the way. I could do nothing and it was no use for me to interfere.

Soon after I got this letter from Rooney Lee, I received a telegraph saying the [*sic*] Mr Davis would be carried up to Richmond under charge of Genl Burton and would have apartments at the Spotswood House. This as least was carrying out Stanton's pledges in good faith and promised well. I drove up to Garretts to ask if there was any cause for uneasiness. "I trust not said he. You have heard from time to time that I felt very confident of success and I have every reason now to hope for the best. Still nothing is positive. Mr O'Conor, you know, has been to Washington on different occasions, and latterly he and Stanberry got on stilts; but I smoothed matters over and now matters appear to be all right." He advised me to go to Richmond by all means and so I started in the afternoon.

At Washington took the boat for Acquia Creek. Saw a man who

looked so like Greeley that I was astonished. He was so much cleaner than Horace that it never occurred to me that this was the man. However when we got in the cars, I heard the creature say with a strong northern accent "These cars are very comfortable & would do if we could only have a little more fresh air at something less than a dollar a pint". Ah! thought I, wrong after all. There is the inevitable Yankee. Since Greeley commenced to interest himself in Mr. Davis' release, he has certainly been consistent. I dont exactly know his motives. I think he felt flattered by Mrs Davis' personal application. When she wrote to Mr Frank Blair to apply to the President, she also appealed by letter to Greeley. Greeley immediately interested himself and has been doing what he could since.

May 12. [*1867*] Sunday. Breakfasted this morning with Geo Shea, who also came over last night. Shea has been very useful to Mr O'Conor, who has kept him running to and from Washington. Mr O'Conor thinks very well of his capacity and prudence. He is rather a vulgar little fellow very conceited, who boasts a good deal of what he has accomplished and is sometimes very mysterious. I am satisfied he told me one or two lies about matters, when there was not the slightest possible sense in it. He said there was only one little snag in the way now and that he hoped would be removed before the day was over. It was a mere way of talking. Shea had all his work cut out for him and fetch and carried just as Mr O'Conor directed him.

At noon I went to the Spotswood and found Mr & Mrs Davis alone with Genl Joe Davis & Burton Harrison. Mr. Davis looked very much older and more careworn than I had any idea of. He was very cheerful and the fact that Garrett still had great confidence in his release on bail was comforting to him. We talked on general subjects till Church was out and people began to come in. In the afternoon I went to see Mr O'Conor who was staying with Mr Wm. B. Read at Ould's. He was out however having gone to Mr James Lyon's to complete the list of names for the bond.

In the afternoon we heard that some alterations were being made in the Libby and were very uneasy. Mr. J. Randolph Tucker sent down to see & found the report unfounded.

J. Minor Botts requested to have his name put on the bond, having got wind of what was going. He said he did not wish to offer it if was to be refused. It was declined.

May 13. I had got a ticket to go into Court with the Counsel. Dr Minnigerode, Genl Joe Davis, Shea & myself went in together. None of us knew what was going to take place. Even Mr Wm. B.

Read, who was the only one of the Counsel with whom Mr O'Conor had consulted much, did not know if Mr O'Conor was to speak or not. Stanberry had said to Mr O'Conor "If many of your colleagues are there I trust they will have discretion enough not to do too much talking" and Mr O'Conor had taken this as a hint to him. However Mr O'Conor did speak and to my surprise said things that were at least undignified. To be sure he knew that Underwood might play false at the last moment and that the presence of Evarts, the tool and âme damnée of Seward, boded apparently no good. But that was no reason why he should praise Underwood and applaud the Government. Fortunately he spoke so low that but few heard him. Near as I was, I did not know what he said until I read it in print next day.

It was very evident that all the little speeches had been prepared beforehand. The performance proceeded slowly and with great gravity. It was intensely exciting. Even when it was announced that bail would be taken, those most interested felt that some of these creatures, whose low natures were not to be trusted, might play us a trick yet. When the bond was nearly completed, the Judge asked Chandler Dist. Atty what he proposed. Chandler replied "Adjourn the Court till four o'clock". A tremor ran through our veins. We all felt that some delay might be fatal. Mr. O'Conor was greatly excited & manifested it. He spoke to Chandler & the Judge, said why he wished the bond kept open and offered any personal pledge. His proposition was accepted. Mr James Lyon leaned forward & told Mr O'Conor "We can furnish as much security as you want. Let us complete the bond". "For heaven's sake, replied Mr O'Conor quickly "tell me something I do not know". There was some feeling about this piece of rudeness in Richmond. It must be recollected it was a moment of intense excitement. Mr O'Conor had been working out the details of this business for five weeks & he had promised to keep the bond open for Gerrit Smith & Com. Vanderbilt.

Only when Underwood said "The Marshal will discharge the prisoner" did I feel a sense of security and relief. Mr Davis was the only perfectly impassive spectator. He sat at the table as if he had been a spectator of something to which he was totally indifferent. When the indictment was read I felt very uneasy lest Mr Davis should be arraigned. I expected to see him stand up and to hear a voice say "prisoner hold up your hand". But Underwood knows about as much law as any other Mountebank. The bond given was not even a joint and several one. It was only a general bond. Each man is responsible only for $5000. However this may have been arranged to suit the Northern bondsmen. Botts name was on the bond. It was thought this morning better perhaps to accept his offer. It seemed to be agreed that twelve names should be from Virginia. The rest were to be taken from the North. Chambers leaned across the table & said "Mr. O'Conor did you say twelve?" "With Mr Botts, replied Mr O'C. "thirteen". I could but laugh. It showed too plainly how little he counted for.

An hour after Court had adjourned I went with Miss Norvill [*sic*] Caskie to congratulate Mrs Davis. Mrs Davis showed a warmth of heart and a true feeling which quite overcame me. Mr Davis was pleasant but impassive. No one would have suspected that he had just gone through a scene which must have been one of intense excitement to him.

Miss Norville was in a wretched state. Mr Davis had requested Mr Caskie to dine Genl Burton & Dr Cooper. They were to dine there today at five. Miss Norville has to sit at the head of the table and play hostess to these Yankees. No matter how kind & how considerate a man may be, he is still a Yankee & it is very hard to have [to] break bread with him sociably. No one else was asked but Burton Harrison. He was a prisoner at Fort Delaware while Burton was there.

In Baltimore where Genl Van Vliet has recently been ordered as senior in command, an invitation has been sent him to the Maryland Club. This is the first break down. I suppose it is all right. The war is now over two years. As we all go to New York & go to clubs there, we cannot close our doors to them here.

Mr Davis is going to step off quietly to night to the steamer Niagara which sails tomorrow for Canada. His children are there. He will be too glad to get his daughter again. I much doubt if he likes her being in the hands of Mrs. Howell. I know he cannot bear her and that is a point on which he and Mrs Davis are not of perfect accord. Mrs Davis of course has some feeling for her mother.*

May 22d. Mr Davis has been for some days in New York. Burton Harrison writes me that he is completely worn out by visitors and that he is so broken down that he had at last to take him, almost bodily, and put him in a carriage, to drive him out to Mr O'Conor's where he could be more quiet. Still his organization is one of those which require the stimulus of excitement. That is the cohesive power

* Mrs. Davis's mother was Margaret Louisa Howell (Mrs. William Burr Howell). The Davises had two daughters: Margaret Howell (Maggie), born in 1855, and Varina Anne Jefferson (Winnie), born in 1864. Winnie was with her mother while Jefferson Davis was imprisoned at Fortress Monroe.

which keeps his animal nature together. He looks as if he would tumble to pieces the moment he was deprived of the active principle of his life. Rest to him will probably be ruin.

What a lucky man Mr. Davis has been. With all his faults of temperament and lack of perception of character and with all the ruin many feel he has entailed upon the South, he comes out of prison a hero. Two years of persecution have softened the hearts of those who at one time felt most bitterly against him, and his cruel mistakes if not forgiven are forgotten.

May 25. Maj Gen Van Vliet was last evening elected a member of the Maryland Club at the request of Mr Geo. S. Brown and Mr John Lee Carroll. It may have been very well to give this gentleman the courtesies of the Club. If men accept his hospitality, they must return it. But it is another thing to make this man a present of the Club and to give him the privilege of asking for an invitation for any Yankee scrub he may wish to talk to. The Government made this Club a political Club. It denounced the members, took possession of the building and did everything to put us in opposition to its representatives. We are as much anti Yankee as the Carlton in London is anti radical and we should preserve our type. One half the members thought so. But the Governors elect and as usual when the responsibility is thrown upon a few men who are known they very rarely have the courage to act independently.

June 10". I sometimes get disgusted with Newspaper business. Popular as is the Gazette—among educated men—and large as is its State influence, it is after all only a provincial paper. It has no effect upon the affairs of the Nation and the pursuit as occupation, to me, never rises to the dignity of a profession. Often I laugh at the nonsense I write and think how aggrieved the public would feel did they know often the contempt with which they are treated. To day as I was cooking up a money article, filling the place of a man that was absent, I was reminded of Lafayette's story of Tallyrand. Mr Morris said that Lafayette told him that once, when Tallyrand was Bishop of Autun, and they were swearing all sorts of oaths over flames and altars to various Goddesses, he Lafayette approached an altar where Tallyrand was officiating. As he came up, Tallyrand leaned over and said "Don't laugh".

Mr Morris also said on Lafayettes authority that Tallyrand considered Alexander Hamilton one of the greatest men of his day and that when Aaron Burr called on Tallyrand, he declined to receive him. "You can tell him, if you choose" said he to the friend asking for an audience pointing to a likeness of Hamilton over his mantel "what you saw there".

June 14. How foolish and silly conceit makes us. Wm. Geo. Brown who certainly is a man of very respectable capacities has been talking away at the Convention about the liberation of the negroes and stated he would undertake to say that there was not a man in the State who would have the institution revised if he could.* How silly. Brown always had his head filled with a parcel of Yankee ideas about the progress of civilization and such like sentiment and he believes that everybody must believe as he does. But Mr Brown arrives at his convictions merely because his mind is not strong enough to soar higher. His reach of thought is not sufficiently extensive. The really able men I know think that slavery is an essential part of democratic institutions. They think that the men of the South were high toned, liberal, thoughtful, statesmenlike because they were aristocratic and that this aristocracy arose from Slavery. Any form of government which becomes absolute becomes tyrannical and nourishes the seeds of its own destruction. Democracy is only good where the people are not democratic, and in the South where slavery made the institution of caste and separated the common laborer from the landed proprietor, democracy worked very well. There was always a great deal of talk about the inhumanity of a forced separation of families. But after all this was very little done. Certainly to nothing like as great an extent as the voluntary separation of families in the Northern States.

Sept 1". [*1867*] Home yesterday from a months trip to the Virginia springs. Never in my life did I see so many young women travelling around loose. There were a number of married ladies, all young, moving around most independently and not a few single ones who had gotten there, I scarcely knew how and expected to get home as best they could. Still I saw but one symptom of fast life. Society seemed so good that one woman, whom I knew to be a devil, passed for a model of marital devotion and virtue.

It was a great relief to me to find that Custis Lee had not applied for pardon. While we were walking one day he said to me

* The Constitutional Convention assembled in Annapolis on May 8, 1867. Former mayor George William Brown was a delegate from Baltimore's Second Legislative District. The new constitution accepted many of the provisions of its predecessor, including a prohibition against compensation to former slave owners. While not making a strong statement for equal rights, the constitution based representation on total population, abolished poll taxes, and allowed Negroes to testify in the courts. It was adopted by the voters 47,152 to 23,036.

that he had tried hard to dissuade the General from making an application for himself and that he had told him that he would gain nothing by taking such a step for that he could put no reliance whatever on the words and pledges of the men who were persuading him to make the application, as they said, for the public good. Genl Meade, Custis said, was among those who were most earnest in their entreaties. Genl Lee finally yielded to their persuasions, after much deliberation. He very probably has more than regretted it since.

I don't exactly make out Genl Lee. Intimate as I was with the family, and often as I saw him, several times a day in his own cottage, at the White Sulphur, besides elsewhere on the grounds, he scarcely ever spoke a word to me more than what he would have spoken to a stranger. Once I asked him about his old sorrel mare, which he brought back from the Mexican War and once I spoke of Traveller. Both times his eye lighted up for a moment and when he spoke of his "gallant grey" he referred to the battles of the Wilderness and how well the horse had carried him.

To men he seems perfectly inanimate and still he observes keenly and enjoys quietly a pipe although at the time he makes no sign. Once he told Sister Mary how amusing it was to have Yankee Generals presented to him and to hear them say to him as they often did, how glad they were to meet him and how time and again they had given their pickets orders not to fire at him as they would see him riding in front of his lines. You know, said he, Miss Mary, when I did go in front of them I always went very quietly and on foot.

General Lee seems happiest when he can get hold of a nice little girl, young fresh, or two at a time and forget himself for a moment. With ladies he will talk rather soberly but somewhat freely. With men not at all. It was painful to be with him. He reminded me of a man who feels that life had closed over them and that there was nothing left for him but death. His condition seemed to be morbid. He never seemed to read and his only amusement appeared to be letter writing. I could not reconcile such a condition of mind with so fine a character as General Lee's. He has had his glory, enough to satisfy the most ambitious, and he has still years of usefulness before him in impressing that character on the youth of his country.

Going up the road one day, I met a boy on his way to Lexington. Where are you going said I? To the Military Institute? "I don't know, said he. I'm going where Genl Lee is." And this is a common feeling in Virginia and the South. The devotion of some of the women, and indeed men too to Genl Lee is simply marvellous.

I was much amused one day at the talk of a Louisianian who like others from that section considered Beauregard the great central orb around which the world revolved. "And what, asked a bystander, do you think of Genl Lee down there?" "Oh!" said he shaking his head with a grave kind of earnestness, "Beauregard thinks very well of Lee".

Mrs Lee said that the Genl. had dreaded coming to the Springs very much, that he disliked meeting so many new people, but that he had gotten along better than she expected. He was seized ten days ago with a severe cramp colic from which he recovered very slowly. At one time, at the Sweet, I feared from the low fever he had that he was going to have typhoid and I was satisfied that his depressed condition of mind had a good deal to do with his physical condition. He recoved very slowly and said that he had never been so ill and had never taken so much medicine before in all his life.

Septr 22d 1867. In the Gazette of the 19th appeared the following extract from the N.Y. Express.

> Gen. Beauregard Resolves to Support the Government. A few evenings ago a party of Southern gentlemen gave a dinner to General Beauregard at the New York Hotel. In the course of his remarks on the occasion, the General stated that he had received tempting offers from English capitalists to take up his residence in England as superintendent of extensive engineering works in that country, but he had concluded, upon calmly surveying the different Governments of the world, their status and their inherent strength, that this country possessed the most stable Government of any existing on the face of the earth, and that, for his part, he was determined to spend his life under the flag of the Government that was the most stable and least liable to disorganization. It was nothing short of sheer nonsense to talk of another rebellion. If they wanted to raise one they could not. It was utterly impossible and will be impossible for them to do so for the next generation. Before the war he was in favor of State sovereignty, but he had had that dogma essentially whipped out of him, and thought that all should now bend their energies towards again building up our Union to that magnificent status among the nations of the world to which its destiny evidently points. In conclusion, he would urge them to give the Government their united support in every manner, making it their pride to add lustre to the common glory of a united people.—N.Y. Evening Express, Sept. 17.

[The text of Glenn's narrative now continues.]

On the same day Genl Beauregard sent a letter to the office denying it. Late at night he sent down and stopped its insertion. Next day he came & brought a letter slightly altered, then stopped that and finally brought a third one for publication. The three letters I keep.* It is very evident that Bory said somethings he ought not to have said, to suit the Northern palate, never thinking they would have been repeated South of New York. He had a long talk in the Gazette office and was in evident trouble to know exactly what to say.

Sep 24". The Judicial nominations under the new Constitution were made to day.** There was no opposition and only Southern men stood any chance. The public expected everything and had a right to expect to get good men. The primary elections were remarkably well attended and the voting for delegates was very spirited. In some wards there were several tickets. The surprise is great at the result. Three good men got in. Of the others, Robt Gilmor is a child in learning & experience. Pinkney alias Whyte alias White, his true name, has not been a citizen for six years & probably never tried a case and Garey is a pettifogger who has neither ability nor integrity.

Sep 25. I never saw more universal disgust at the result of the labors of the Convention. Part of the ticket was carried by Pinkney Whyte, who is an adroit party manager. He did it up in the regular old style of democratic jobbing. Bob Gilmor secured his nomination by money. He had a paid set of *claqueurs* in the gallery to applaud his name whenever it came up. What a farce! this system of elections. What an idea that people are capable of self government when the State Convention, recently in session, which had an opportunity to make its Judiciary independent of the populace and to make the Judgeships permanent offices, preferred to make them temporary and elective.

Sep 28". I never saw more universal indignation at the result of a convention then exists now. There never was a time when the unanimity was so perfect. There is no opposition and all that was to do was to select good men. Campbell Pinkney, alias Whyte alias

* For the text of General Beauregard's letters see Appendix E.

** Judges were elected for 10 years under th Constitution of 1850, and for 15 under that of 1864. The Court of Appeals consisted of Judges Brice Goldsborough, James L. Bartol, S. Morris Cochran, and Daniel Weisel, the latter elected in 1864. The Constitution of 1867 reduced the number of judicial districts, and necessitated new judicial elections.

Baltimore City judges elected in 1867 were: Orphans Court, Josiah Balderson, Thomas Bond, and Bolivar D. Daniels; Supreme Bench, T. Parkin Scott, Chief Judge; Henry F. Garey, George W. Dobbin, Campbell Pinkney (Whyte), and Robert Gilmor. Judge Garey was assigned to the court of Common Pleas, Judge Dobbin to the Superior Court, Judge Pinkney to the Circuit Court, and Judge Gilmor to the Criminal Court.

White his true name is a young man comparatively without practice without experience and totally unknown. He went to New York before the war to live. From there he went South. The war over he went back there. Now he is brought here and by very adroit party engineering among the low democracy of the outside wards he is foisted upon the community. It is a direct insult. To day it kills Pinkney Whyte, his brother. Next month it will be forgotten.

Robert Gilmor totally unknown has also secured a nomination. He went to day to ask Teackle Wallis if he was included in the general indignation. Wallis told him plainly that as it was too evident that no one would have put his name before the Convention, he must have put it there himself, and that not only his youth and inexperience were against him but other things. For instance the fact that he was going about to ward meetings with Milton Taylor, a trading politician, was very bad. The fact that he used money at the legislature to have a large amount of taxes improperly refunded on the Gilmor Hotel was against him; and the fact that he was cognizant of and probably party to the transaction made by his brother, a few months ago, when the Gunpowder water power was sold to the City by the aid of Chapman,* the thieving Mayor whom everybody has denounced, was still more against him. Especially as it was known that Mace, Chapman's henchman, had been paid by the Gilmor's very handsomely, for himself and Chapman of course. It is really inconceivable, considering the strong line of demarcation between the Gilmor's friends and those men and the strong sectional feeling that exists, they being Union Men, that the Gilmors should have any transactions with them whatever. However when a man has failed as often as Willy G. has and ignored every debt as long as his father has, it is not to be wondered at that they should have lost all tone.

Of Garey the third objectionable Candidate, I say nothing. He is too low. He has the support of the Masons & odd fellows, who actually say now they must be represented on the bench.

What folly to have the judiciary nominated by the people and voted for by them. To think that we should have a state convention

* According to Scharf, *History of Baltimore City and County,* p. 220; "As early as January, 1866 Mayor Chapman recommended to the City Council the purchase of the water rights of the Great Gunpowder River for the purpose of securing an additional supply of water to meet the future wants of the city. The City Council adopted the suggestion and authorized the issue of the necessary water stock, and the purchase was accordingly made. It included the water rights of the whole stream from tide-water to Meredith's Bridge, a distance of twenty-one miles. . . ." Also included were 16,000 acres of land and two factories, for which was paid $265,000.

which had only to act and was assured before hand of support, and still, with all our experiences, had not the manliness to give us a good Judiciary. They even put the salary so low that no decent man will take the office, scarcely. For two days every effort has been made to get up an independent ticket. I have been applied to and I have seen or had seen every lawyer who would at all suit the place. Wm. Geo. Brown would take it he said, if it were $5000. per an.; but he cannot live on $3500 and so on. The two or three good men we could have gotten have already had their names before the Convention and cannot, in etiquette, consent to run against the Candidate chosen.

Octr 1" 1867. Every effort has been made and every good man has been spoken to. We cannot find three men who are willing to run, if nominated against the regular ticket. The truth is few good men will consent to accept the pitiful salary.

The nominations are still going on. Primary meetings are held and men are nominated for conventions where again members of the Legislature, among other Candidates, are to be nominated. The Legislature elects the United States Senator. Primary meetings are already being manipulated by Pinkney Whyte who wishes to go to the Senate, for which place he has no particular fitness further than that he is sharp shrewd moneymaking and unscrupulous. But the object of our Constitution is to remove the election of Senator as far as possible from the people, that the Senator may be selected by good men and that he may not go into office by the popular vote of the mob whom he flatters and whose good will he gains by low familiarity. But this has gotten to be, under our system, only a theory. Here is Pinkney Whyte actually packing the primary meetings who refuse to nominate any man for the Legislature who will not agree to vote for him as Senator, when the time comes. After his sale of the Gunpowder water power to the city, through Mayor Chapman, whom of course he bribed, this man has cheek enough to do anything.

Octr 4". Mrs Lincoln is in New York, as Mrs Clarke, trying to sell her old shawls and laces for immoderate prices and threatening disclosures against certain parties if they are not disposed of speedily. A long and disgraceful correspondence on the subject has gotten into the Newspapers. Lincoln during his term invested $50,000 in 5.20 Bonds and after his death Congress gave his family $25,000 of which 22,000 were invested. Besides Lincoln made his son Bob partner in several fat Government contracts. Bob ought to be rich.

When Mrs Lincoln left the White House, she took plenty of time and stole a great deal of Government silver, spoons forks etc and a large quantity of linen and stuffs. She once bought a lot of China for $1500 in New York & made the seller give her $1500 in cash & send in a bill for $3000. When Lincoln refused to put his signature to the Bill prior to sending it to the Department to be paid, on the ground that it was exorbitant "You forget, sir, said the man that I gave Mrs Lincoln $1500.

She took from her gardner the perquisite of the manure heap from the stables and appropriated it herself. On one occasion when she entertained Prince Napoleon she went to the Secry of the Interior to have the bill paid for by the Government, on the ground that it was a government dinner. When he refused & said he could pay for nothing which was not an addition of some sort and properly certified, she made her gardner make out a bill for plants, pots etc of the required amount, certified it herself and drew the money. Lincoln afterwards refunded the amount. These matters came before committees in Congress and were hushed up at the time. It appears that there is nothing too low, too contemptible, too disgraceful for these degraded creatures to do.

1867

Dec 20. Mr & Mrs Davis, who recently left by Steamer for New Orleans have enjoyed themselves a great deal in Baltimore. He has had every manifestation of sympathy a man could desire and I am not surprised that he talks of settling here and would like to go into business here. He will do well yet. He is born to luck. His imprisonment at Fortress Monroe and persecution by the Yankees have helped him immensely. If he had been allowed to go free, he would have had so few friends, that he would have been almost forgotten in a few years. The feeling against him was so strong that he would found [*sic*] no sympathy from anyone. Long imprisonment has changed all this. Now he is a sort of a martyr.

A day or two before he left I drove him up to Brand's in Harford Co. He talked a great deal about Mexico and about Albert Sydney Johnston, who had been a great friend of his. He ranked him as the first General the South had. So did old Scott, or rather as one of the first. Old "Fuss & Feathers"—who was well named, certainly thought most of those men who thought most of him. Mr Davis has his prejudices too, though in this instance he may have been right. The other two men, who Mr Davis said he & Scott both thought highly of were Genl Lee & Prescott Smith. I may possibly be wrong about the last named. I asked about Genl Lee & said "Can you account for his conduct. He is certainly the most whipped man, I ever saw. He doesnt seem to rally. He broods over his defeat and does not strive to interest himself in the daily affairs of life and endeavor to fight the battle which is now going on. He keeps aloof from people and won't even talk, if he can help it". "The misfortune, replied Mr. Davis, was that Genl. Lee was whipped long before he surrendered. The truth is, said he, he never understood the importance of the struggle and how necessary resistance was to the death, if we hoped to maintain any liberty whatever." I knew very well that there were many things which Mr Davis did not understand and one thing was the situation. Tom Hall said not long ago, at Wallis' table, that a few days before the evacuation of Richmond, when it was evident that the existence of the Confederacy was a matter of a few days, and after he had applied to one of the departments to try and obtain some original documents, which he had prepared and which he desired to secure before the final crash, Mr Davis sent for him and actually proposed to him to start a newspaper, in the interests of the Government, so much hampered was he by the constant attacks of the Press. This is only a piece with other things which I know. Mr Davis is a man who wont see what he does want. He reminds one of Sam Weller,* who, when the Judge told him to look into the gallery and see if his father was there, looked straight up into the ceiling and said he did not see him.

Mr Davis strong point is cultivation. He will talk to you about everything from science down to the shape of a dog's tail, and have something to say about everything, showing that he has read or talked about it before. During a long ride to Harford & back, he was as pleasant as he could be and if I had not seen such men before, I would have thought that I had wronged him in my estimate of him. But, as a rule, men of high cultivation are not men of original opinions. They take so much from other people that borrowing becomes second nature to them. Mr Davis' opinion of men certainly cannot be worth a great deal. He must have selected them more from personal feeling than from any other motive. Benjamin must have been a very bad counsellar for the South and a very mischief making man. From what we now know, he must have been very corrupt and he must have used his great capacity for work to encourage disorganization. Genl Joe Johnston has twice assured me that when

* Samuel Weller appears in Charles Dickens's *Pickwick Papers.*

Benjamin was Sec. of War, it was his constant habit, to answer, in person, letters from soldiers applying for a furlough, when these men referred to any one who had political influence.

The day before Mr Davis left, I mentioned to him a talk I had had with Burton Harrison about his going into business, and a conversation I had also had with Mr Garrett. Mr. Davis was going into business with Frazier Trenholm & Co, L'pool, but their failure has knocked this. He likes the idea of a connection here and if ever he is released by the Govt. we shall probably see the Ex President of the C.S.A. getting commissions on cotton in Baltimore. Mr Davis has had a great deal of money sent him, but it seems to slip like quicksilver through his own fingers and Mrs Davis' besides.

1868

Jany. We have had *La Grande Duchesse* here. Tostée tried the *cancan* and, finding it took, she kept it up.* I declined to take a lady to see it. How other men, who knew what this lascivious dance meant, could go with young girls, I do not understand. It was as bad as bad could be, and any woman who was married, or ought to have been, must have known very well what it all meant. The only most outré to my mind, was that Tostée didn't take her clothes off at once. The dance only lasted two minutes and in no ways belonged to the play. It was almost impossible to conceive why or how it became introduced. I was very much amused at the virtue (?) of Mrs Lizzie Read. When she saw my *critique* on this play, written from New York, she could not let her daughters read it. But when the play was here she let them go to see that. This performance is a very significant sign of the times. Women tell me that young girls now know of and discuss things about which young girls twenty years ago knew nothing. I am sure it is so.

March 5". [1868] It has long been evident to me that Andrew Johnson was a mere maker of phrases. He writes and talks, but he never acts. One by one every friend, who believed in him or hoped for any thing from him, gave him up and recently even Judge Black has abandoned him. When the Stanton–Thomas row** occur[r]ed

* Lucille Tostée appeared in the title role of Offenbach's *La Grande Duchesse de Gerolstein,* which opened in New York on September 24, 1867, and came to Baltimore on February 3, 1868. It played at the Hollyday Street Theatre until February 13.

** When Secretary of War Stanton was finally dismissed by President Johnson on February 21, 1868, he refused to vacate his office, ordered the arrest of Adjutant General Lorenzo Thomas, the Secretary *ad interim,* and posted a guard and a despatch went over the wire late at night saying that the National Dem. Executive Committee, which was in Washington, intended to remain in permanent session and not only to counsel, but to aid the President, it did look to me at last as if issue was joined. I went to Washington next morning & found that all the excitement was in the telegraph wires. The letter dated 23d Febry., is a picture of what I mean. I have since been several times to Washington. I have not seen Mr Johnson for I do not want to. He is helplessly imbecile, I think, sometimes. I have seen several men who have seen him intimately. All give me the same account. He is as undisturbed as he would be by the announcement that he was threatened by a Magistrate's Warrant. He talked about impeachment as if it were a little matter which concerned him individually and speaks about want of proof and legal . . . [A portion of the Glenn manuscript is missing at this point. The available documents continue as follows.] . . . little dinner we had to day Genl B.* told me an amusing thing of the last commission he issued. It was in Florida & given to a man who took great trouble to assist him to escape and raised a yawl for him to get off in, which had been sunk some time before in the river. Just before starting, Genl B. said to his Aide "Colonel," make out a commission as Lieut Col. for Capt I am going to raise him two steps." At first the man who was a good fellow and rather a plain countryman, did not quite see the use of it as there really was no longer any Confederacy, but after a moment he turned round and said "General, I think if you dont object, I'd like to be a full colonel. There's a man close by here who calls himself Lieut Colonel, and he is rather a sorry kind of a creature, and it would worry me to have him rank me." "Good!" said Genl B. "Make out a Colonel's commission" & it was made out.

Feb 14". [*1869*] I called to see Mr Thornton, the British Minister yesterday. In course of conversation, he said "In the Alabama matter we have given up everything—and indeed said he, if we don't the very first war we have Alabamas will steam quickly out of every American port & prey upon our commerce. Americans will not stop to consider the difference between the cases. Mr Johnson wrote a few days ago to Wallis "I suppose they will ratify the treaty.** It

over his records. He remained entrenched in the War Department building until the impeachment of Johnson had failed on May 26, 1868.

* General Beauregard was in charge of the Confederate Military department of Florida and Georgia from 1862 to the end of the war.

** Reverdy Johnson was Minister to England from 1868 to 1869 while the *Alabama* Claims were being negotiated.

has been settled upon the basis originally laid down by our Government". England has got to eat some leek and eventually will get into a fight when she is kicked into it.

Nothing shows the degraded condition of socity more than a party I witnessed yesterday. F. Secretary of Legation, begged me to stay in Washington to dinner. So I staid. We dined at 7. & at half past 9. I said "Upon my word, if you have ladies at the theatre, your guests you ought to be there". "Oh!" replied he "make my excuses. I shant go. I will be here to receive them at supper at 11 o c". When we got to the theatre, the ladies said "pray where is F? It is too bad of him, not to come". At 11 o'c we all left & went round to Welcker's* where the supper was to be. No F.—so we ordered supper without the host. He came at 12 o'c. The supper was a beautiful one. We got through about 1 o'c, after which the rooms were cleared & we began to waltz to piano music. Soon after a quadrille was formed and Count T. with another Frenchman** & an Italian & an English attache danced the can-can with four ladies. The men had cigars in their mouths & two of them put their hats on. They imitated as closely as they could the Jew dancers of the Casino and one figure was made by one man mounting upon the shoulders of another and then performed a pas seul. One of the young ladies was Miss G. a sweet & lady like looking girl, step daughter of Admiral Dahlgren.***

1869 August 26. A few days ago at the White Sulphur Springs Com Maury told me that he had been invited while in England by Napoleon to come to France and build what ships he wanted. And that while building them Napoleon sent his officers to see what armament was needed, which Com. Maury was assured should be provided. He, Com. M. said he formed the idea that Napoleon was going to use this fleet to send with Confederate officers & French ones to the Pacific to take S Francisco & then offering California his protection & its own form of government to make it virtually independent. Com M. thought this programme was changed by the agreement of Seward to recognize the Mexican Empire. Seward it will be recollected did send in such a treaty to the Senate, but the word Empire was stricken out & Republic inserted. When the news

* John Welcker had a restaurant at 424 15th Street West in Washington, D.C.

** Cards from Count L'Corti and Count Turenne (Turessey?) of the French Legation can be found in the Glenn Papers, MS 1017, Maryland Historical Society.

*** Romaine Madeleine Goddard was the daughter of Madelene Vinton and Daniel C. Goddard. Her mother married Admiral John A. Dahlgren in 1865.

of this reached France other circumstances must have transpired to make Napoleon stand by his change of views. Certainly he never favored the Confederacy again.

Rev W. F. Brand came to day to ask my advice. For three months past a R. C. Priest, with the Jesuits at Loyola College, has been in correspondence & conversation with Bishop Whittingham. Three days ago he told Bishop W. he would come the day after & make open profession of his faith. "Do you think" said the Bishop if, you get in there now, you will get out again" "Oh! doubtless! was the answer. But he was no more heard of. I advised Brand to sue out a writ of Habeas Corpus. This afternoon they got letters from the poor fellow, saying that he had been ill and that physical suffering had chastened his spirit—that he was not a Priest (Bishop W. had his priestly certificates) that he wanted to get out to marry, that all he had said was false, that it must be regarded as unsaid & so on & so forth. He has evidently undergone some very severe dosing or rigorous treatment and is now laboring under extreme fear.

Septr 5". [1869] On my return to Baltimore I find my duel with Quentin Washington very much talked about & for once I am very popular. Washington who is dyspeptic and can't waltz, wrote an account of a fancy ball to the Richmond Despatch in which he spoke very disparingly of the Baltimore ladies & said that the Virginia girls kept their embraces for their fathers & husbands. This certainly was true of all the modest minded ones who could not waltz. I wrote a letter for the Gazette & put in one paragraph about this letter. It was so severe that it irritated Washington. All the Baltimore ladies cut him & when I got back to the White, after a week's absence, I found him livid with rage. His second Col Pickett deld. me a communication late that evening, Saturday. I answered it Sunday. Not hearing from him and having written to two ladies that I wd. come over & dine with them at the Sweet, I drove over in my carriage. There was an awful rain & the streams rose, so that I could not cross that night. But I got back next morning before nine o'clock. I recd a rigmarole about my absence, then some more correspondence & finally a challenge. When I got it I asked Mr L. L. Conrad to act for me. Until then Col Wade Hampton had deld. my letters. But I did not wish to ask him to go out with me as he was not from Maryland. Pickett, who had been Confederate agent in Mexico, when he deld the challenge, apologized to me and afterwards said to Ould (Judge Robt. O.) "I wish I could stop this. Glenn has behaved most handsomely. His letters have been models. But my principal is wild and as an old school mate I must stand by him" Col Sutherlin* proceeded to arrest us, but I begged Ould to stop this & not to humiliate me. I had not gotten into this affair & I would rather be shot than be arrested. And be made ridiculous. By this time the affair had become notorious. But as there was little law in Western Virginia we were not troubled. Govr Wise however with some gentlemen determined to stop it. He and Hon James Lyons, Ex Senator W. [*sic*] T. Caperton, Jas G. Berret of Washington Tazewell Taylor of Norfolk, Genl Lindsay Walker & Genl Pickett got together late Wednesday night & arranged matters according to their lights. They then wrote me a letter prescribing terms which I could accept honorably. This letter was given to me Thursday morning at 7 o'c. I at once rejected. Judge Conrad, of La., formerly Secry of War, finding I had gone out, came himself out on the ground & told Washington I was right not to accept these terms. It was no use. Pistols were loaded & ground measured. We won position & choice of weapons. They the word. Genl Walker then came up & begged me again to accept the terms offered which he said I could do. But I told him "No. I knew where I was & I stood on high ground. There could be no settlement, unless it was based upon a withdrawal of offensive terms by Washington". After ten minutes had elapsed, I sent Conrad to say I was tired of waiting & that the affair must be settled. Walker asked for five minutes more. Before they were out Pickett brought another proposal. Ould who was also on ground said "Glenn, you can accept this, but there is a point" "I will have no point," I replied and I took a piece of paper & wrote my terms. They were signed rather to my surprise & much to my satisfaction. Dr Ball came as surgeon & a negro carried his instruments. This was the company, across the creek, a little more than half a mile from the hotel. My second was delightful no nonsense, Perfectly cool & thoroughly refined. Ould was consoling. It will be settled said he after the first fire. Berret amused me. When he thought I wd. certainly accept the prepared compromise, he said "It's all right all [*sic*] boy. It is settled. You'll have all the eclat without any danger. I wish to the Lord I could get such a chance."

Octr 28" 1869. When I found my name on the Committee to invite the President & Cabinet to visit the State Agricultural Fair,**

* Colonel Sutherlin may be W. T. Sutherlin of Danville, Virginia. He had opened his home to President Davis during his flight from Richmond, and in 1869 was appointed a Commissioner to discuss the Virginia—West Virginia debt.

** The Maryland State Agricultural Society, founded c. 1847, resumed its annual fairs after the war. The first was held at the Pimlico Fair Grounds

I determined to let it stay, simply because I would attract more attention by declining to serve than by performing the duty. One of the Committee being unable to attend I put Heth—Major General—in his place. Monday, 23d, we went down. Prescott Smith was to take charge of everything in Washington & of transportation and I to attend to arrangements in Baltimore. In order not to be kept waiting, we wrote word to Genl Porter requesting him to inform the President what our mission was and begging him not to delay us—as we had the other members of the Cabinet to see. When we called at the White House, we were ushered in quite promptly & we expected to be received with great dignity. We were—at least supposed to be—a most respectable committee representing what was supposed to be the most important society in the State, delegated to invite a man supposed to be a gentleman & certainly Chief Magistrate of what is supposed to be the greatest nation on the Earth. Smith advanced to Grant, rather impressed with the importance of his mission. Grant rose from the table where he was sitting & held out one hand. Then just as Smith was about to commence his small oration, the President riding rough shod over ceremony, caught him by the coat & said "Smith I have just written you a note, telling you I want a car tomorrow at noon, for Philadelphia, for myself & family. You will please see to it & not forget it". Smith, evidently annoyed & mortified, took out his note book & made the memorandum in due rail road style. "Is that all" said he "Mr President" "Yes" he replied. "Then Mr. President" said Smith, taking Genl Grant by the arm, "I want now to introduce *you* to some of *my* friends". I smiled at the Presidents. . . .

[This concludes the available portions of the narrative of William Wilkins Glenn.]

(now Pimlico Race Track) from October 26 to 30, 1869. Among the members of the committee sent to invite President Grant (who apparently did not attend) were W. Prescott Smith, General Henry Heth, Samuel M. Shoemaker, Charles G. Kerr, and William Wilkins Glenn.

APPENDIX A

The following letters of William Wilkins Glenn, written during his incarceration in Fort McHenry, are illustrative of his political views at the time of his imprisonment. The text of the letter of October 3, 1861, is taken from *War of the Rebellion—Official Records of the Union and Confederate Armies,* Series II, Volume II, p. 781, The letter of Nov. 30, 1861, is in the Maryland Historical Society, Glenn Papers, MS 1017.

Fort McHenry, October 3, 1861.

Maj. Gen. John A. Dix.

Dear Sir: Mrs. Glenn has this morning showed me a note addressed her by you in reference to some communication had by yourself with the authorities at Washington in reference to the terms upon which I would be released from confinement. Having already more than once taken an oath to bear allegiance to my State and to support the Constitution of the United States and never having violated this oath in the slightest particular I know of no ground upon which any other could be demanded of me. In no case do I hope I will ever be so wanting in that self-respect which I owe to myself as an American citizen as to take any oath whatever under compulsion. Much less would I consent to take any oath the strict and honest observance of which would oblige me to be false to myself by ignoring the one I had already sworn to. I have always been a conservative citizen.

I have never until lately mingled in the slightest degree in politics. I advocated a policy upon the election of Mr. Lincoln which if pursued would I believe have preserved the Union. I purchased a large interest in The Exchange for the purpose of advocating that policy. Even now I look upon separation as an evil and that the benefits to be derived from it can in no event compensate for the loss of the manifold advantages enjoyed under the Union. I never have hesitated to say this. At the same time I look upon the preservation of our constitutional rights, the only safeguard of liberty, either civil or religious, as the duty of every good citizen, in the performance of which even greater evils than separation should be cheerfully submitted to. In any action that I have ever taken I have never forgotten that Maryland was a State in the Union. I have never had the slightest communication with any of the seceded States or committed any overt act in opposition to the Government. Under these circumstances I cannot see why any oath should be asked of me.

The Daily Exchange has been stopped by force. Though disputing the right to commit the act I still submit to the superior power of the Government. I shall not edit The Exchange nor republish it nor contribute to any paper so long as the censorship of the press is exercised in Baltimore. Denying the right of the Government to hold me under arrest without trial I still acknowledge the fact which is patent that I am a prisoner. As such I should be glad to accept my release under conditional parole, pledging myself also not to connect myself with any anti-Administration newspaper until I am in a position to express my views freely and unrestrictedly.

Your obedient servant,

W. W. GLENN

Fort McHenry
Novr 30" 1861

Major Genl
John A Dix
Sir

My brother informs me that you lately stated to him that my release from imprisonment depended upon my giving a pledge the precise nature of which is not specified. I infer however from conversations had with Col Morris that the pledge proposed is that I shall commit no act of hostility to the United States and that I shall not contribute editorially to the columns of any newspaper.

As I have never committed any act of hostility against the General Government, I am at a loss to comprehend upon what grounds any such pledge can be asked of me. I certainly have opposed and am opposed to the policy of the Republicans and regard the inauguration of peace measures as the only possible chance for the preservation or reconstruction of the Union, the permanent disruption of which would be a calamity too sad to be contemplated without grief. But this is no treason; nor have I been guilty of the slightest act which can be so denominated. I cannot therefor nor do I think I should be asked to consent to give a pledge which would in itself be a tacit acknowledgement that I had been inimical to the United States Government.

As to my editing a paper, the attempt now would be simply

foolish. I have no idea of doing so while the present censorship of the press continues. Even if I had, I have no desire to be incarcerated a second time.

If the Government still thinks I ought to be looked after, I am just as much at its disposal at my residence in Baltimore, as in any Fort; and I have no intention of absenting myself from my home & family. I have heretofore been very careful not to put myself in an attitude which could even be distorted into treason and I shall certainly not be less particular now when I am well aware that the Administration thinks proper to regard me as a suspicious character.

I cannot possibly see what more can be desired nor can I imagine what the Administration gains by pursuing a course which must finally result in making enemies of many who are still friends of the Union.

I remain with much consideration

Yours very respy
[s] W W Glenn

P.S. Since writing the above I have been shown a note written by you to Mrs Glenn in which you say "It is in Mr Glenn's power to remain here & to be released from arrest by complying with the conditions proposed by himself".

I accept these terms & have requested my brother to furnish you with a copy of my former letter to you in regard to this matter, in case you have mislaid the original.

W. W. G.

APPENDIX B

The following letter is from the War Department Collection of Confederate Records—Union Provost Marshal's File—Record Group No. 109—in the National Archives.

Head Quarters Baltimore,
2, Dec. 1861.

Col. W. W. Morris,
Comg. Fort McHenry,
Colonel,
Mr. W. W. Glenn is discharged from custody at Fort McHenry and will be put on parole here under my direction.

I am, very respectfully,
Yours,
[s] John A. Dix,
Maj. Genl.

APPENDIX C

The following letter from William Wilkins Glenn to an undesignated correspondent apparently was never sent. It provides some additional insight into the arrest of Judge Richard Carmichael and others, who were seized at Easton, Maryland, on May 27, 1862. Judge Carmichael was confined in Forts McHenry, Lafayette, and Delaware until December 4, 1862. This letter is part of the Glenn Papers, MS 1017, in the Maryland Historical Society, as is the "Statement of Judge Carmichael from himself" that follows it.

Baltimore May 31" 1862

My Dear Sir

I am at last enabled to write you some details about the Carmicheal [*sic*] affair. Immediately on receipt of the news of the Judge's arrest, with no other information than that gathered from the American, I determined to see the leading members of the bar and some of the Judges and see if they were or were not willing to express their sentiments in regard to the outrage. I wrote you about my visit to Mr. Meredith. That was on Wednesday. McLane would cooperate, he was inclined to do something. Judge Crain spoke in a manly way. Frick thought something should be done. Dobbin would cooperate and Mr. Fred Brune was ready to meet these Gentlemen; so was Steele. Besides these I found none of the older members of the bar who would think about it. They could only say that all remonstrance was useless and could have no good effect. Friday, after much running around, I saw all the parties myself and arranged a meeting at two. Before this I saw Mr. Meredith again, who was confirmed in his opinion that Judge C. had acted disloyally and that his arrest was quite as justifiable as any one else's. Judge Crain, who had at first consented to see Judge Martin with me, thought on reflection that he would rather some one else would do it. Two o'clock came. Mr. Dobbin had not understood the message properly and had gone to the country. Crain was missing. Steele had gone up the street. McLane insisted on my going up the street as there would be no meeting and declared he would not do anything anyhow until he saw Mr. Pearce, who was to come up that evening. Their [*sic*] was nothing left but to give it up & I accordingly went in and told Mr. Brune that my two days labor running after and dogging men was a hopeless, fruitless, thankless effort and that I should now leave people to look after themselves. While I was at dinner Frick came to the door & told me that he wanted me to call again at St. Paul St. at Six o'clock and meet Judge Chambers, Judge Bartol & Mr. Pearce. I saw at once that this was merely an attempt to procure Judge C's release but I determined not to lose the occasion. I went for Mr. McLane & we went. Judges C & B had been to the Fort & had an interview with Judge Carmicheal from whom they gathered the following facts: McPhail & his crew came to Easton on several days before the arrest & the Judge expecting it, instead of leaving Easton as usual, after Court hours, staid there saturday, came in town again Sunday & Staid again monday afternoon. Nothing however was done by McPhail. Tuesday, while the Judge was on the bench, engaged in the discussion of a Law point, the Jury in the box, McPhail appeared and walked to the side of the bench on the left hand of the Judge, stretched out his hand & said "Good morning Judge," His head was covered. The Judge thinking he was going to make some application, took his hand saying at the same time—"Take off your hat Sir". McPhail obeyed. "I arrest you Sir," said McPhail. "By whose order." "By order of the Marshal of Baltimore." (McPhail says he said Provost Marshall) "I recognize no such authority," at this moment Bishop the Know-Nothing-Swann rowdy walked up to the table struck upon it and said "the Court is adjourned; shall I assist you to arrest him" cried he to McPhail & immediately pushed for the opposite side of the Bench drawing out his pistol—the Judge called out to the Sheriff to preserve order—but the Sheriff had disappeared. Bishop jumped up & knocked the Judge twice on the back of the head with his pistol, the cock of it coming in contact with his skull & hurting him severely. Two men then rushed upon him one on each side & seized the Judge's Arms; Bishop then drew off to strike him in the face & while thus held fast, the Judge raised his feet to Bishop's breast to repel him. The next blow knocked him senseless & he was dragged along from the Court—on his first return to consciousness caused by the motion & air, shortly afterwards, he found himself in a helpless condition—his eyes suffused with blood from his head. At this moment he heard Cassell one of the police, say "don't strike him any more, their [*sic*] is no call for such treatment". And he thinks to this man he owes his life. Sam Hambleton & Martin had disappeared together with the Jurymen & the rest of the crowd. They dragged the Judge into the Registers Room & the only man who seemed to take any interest in his condition was an oysterman, who ran across the Street & returned with a bucket of water for him to wash the blood from his face. I think it was Nabb who heard the noise & ran across to the Court. He was arrested as he entered the Court House—having been heard to say two days before, that they should not arrest the Judge. Their were eight men with McPhail. The troops were three miles off & on landing captured every body so as to prevent the news of their arrival from reaching the town. If their had been any resistance to the arrest they promised themselves doubtless a gory time. To return, after relating this, Judge Chambers read a letter from Pearce who was ill on his back it was sensible & manly & more than I expected. But he is too sick to do anything & will hardly be able to be again in his seat in the Senate soon. Besides, I have no confidence in him, that he will do more than write private letters. They discussed about one hour about the prospects of a release before I got them to the point, assuring them that they could rest satisfied that Judge C. would be able to get no release on terms that he would subscribe. After this the discussion was short. Brune desires to act prudently. McLane who always talks all round a subject and who has really amused me lately while he annoyed and almost provoked me, preferred to rely upon the superior wisdom of Judge Chambers. Judge Bartol spoke properly but wished to take no action that was decidedly unwise. My proposition to call the facts of the outrage—the time place & manner of it without any discussion as to its legality at all—to the attention of the Governor giving him the opinions of the respectable portion of the bench & the bar was not listened to—a protest was dangerous—a remonstrance was unwise—the only thing was a proper memorial to be presented by Pearce—and finally it was actually considered *advisable* that this memorial should come from Judge Carmicheal himself. Not, mind you, from friends whose countenance and support would be a solace & comfort to him in his prison—but from himself, to be signed afterward by his friends, and the upshot of the whole matter, depend upon it is that Mr. Pearces hands are not even to be fortified with a memorial of respectable names, but he is to be left to do his best, if he happen to get well. As for me—as you know—I am nobody here. Nobody minds me or even listens to what I have to say. The community is going to the devil or rather gone there—and I am its slave—when I thought you were too hard upon them, I did not think they are what they now show themselves to be. Frick has manifested more interest than any one else—other gentlemen actually laugh & say it is all coming right & more than one do not hesitate to say they are glad of it—as if they had not had enough of it already to arouse any spark of manhood that still slumbered xxxxxxxxxxxxx etc.

Yrs Sincerely
[s] W. W. G.

P.S.
Hadcastle the foreman of the Grand Jury was arrested here but released upon an interview with Genl. Dix.
P.S. June 3d. The end of all this was that today Judge Chambers wrote up that after a consultation with Judge Carmichaels friends,

among whom was Pearce, it was deemed *advisable* to do nothing for the present.

Statement of Judge Carmichael from himself.

On the 27 May 1862, whilst sitting as Judge of the Circuit Court for Talbot Country, during the trial of a cause, the jury in the box, and a witness on the stand, a stranger approached the Judge & saluted him quietly saying "Good Morning Judge" & extending his hand. The Judge took his hand and looked at him, waiting for him to speak. "I arrest you" said he. "By what authority" asked the Judge. "I am Mr. McPhail, the Provost Marshal," replied he. "I do not recognize your authority" said the Judge, whereupon he called for the Sheriff. The Sheriff did not answer. McPhail then said "I have the force". "You shall see" replied the Judge, at the same time ordering the Crier of the Court to call the Sheriff. At this juncture the Judge discovered a stranger addressing some words to Mr. Powell, one of the Attornies engaged in trying the cause. This fellow proved to be Bishop a detective and notorious bully. The crier repeated that "the Sheriff did not answer". He was ordered to make another call upon the Sheriff. One of the Jury now rose & addressing McPhail, said "Is the Jury discharged." The Judge ordered him to sit down telling him that he could not speak to any one without the permission of the Court. McPhail then put on his hat. The Judge said "Take your hat off sir". McPhail obeyed instantly. Bishop then turning to McPhail said "Don't take off your hat," and added "Shall I take that man from off the bench. McPhail assented. At this moment the crier was making the second call for the Sheriff, when Bishop rushed across the room, seized the crier, forced him violently into a chair and addressed to him words which the Court did not hear. He then came up and seized the Judge by the throat. The latter instantly rose saying "Unhand me Sir". The demand not being heeded, he pushed Bishop from him. Simultaneously he received a blow upon the head from what proved to be the handle of a heavy pistol. The blow was rapidly repeated bringing blood which flowed in streams down his face. Force was now used to push him from the bench. Bishop was still before him. As the Judge was urged forward he pressed Bishop before him and forced him off the platform. He then attempted to make a stand by holding with one hand to the desk and placing the other against the wall. His head was borne down and forwards by these efforts of his own & by the force of those pushing and beating him from behind. At this moment the Judge perceived Bishop with his arm drawn back in the act of striking him with his fist in the face. The Judge spurned him from him with two sound kicks, thus breaking the force of the blow. As he dealt Bishop the last blow he was pushed from the platform of the bench. Bishop now joined the others in the rear. A great force and weight was borne upon the shoulders of the Judge, depressing his head and a blow was dealt him which laid him for a moment unconscious. He was then held by force and another severe blow dealt him on the head.

The Judge has a confused recollection of attempting to call for help at this period and of a blow which crushed the voice in his throat. When he became somewhat restored to consciousness, he heard a person rebuking an attempt at further violence. His name was Cassell. He was one of the participators in the outrage. The Judge is not certain that Cassell struck him. Bishop was the only one who seized him by the throat or dealt him blows, that he can say he saw. All the others were behind his back.

"Everything" says the Judge "I have related occurs to my memory with entire certainty, though my recollection was not quite clear until after I had slept upon my wounds. Many things may have occurred which I did not see nor hear". The Insolence and vanity of the Man Bishop after the troops were brought to sustain the outrages done on this occasion were offensive beyond expression.

APPENDIX D

The following documents written by William Wilkins Glenn form an interesting supplement to some of the tumultuous events mentioned in his narrative. Perhaps Glenn intended to include them in the final version of his work. Possibly they were prepared at the time for publication in sympathetic newspapers outside of Maryland. Dated June 29, July 28, and August 4, 1862, they touch on the arrests of Baltimore's Mayor, Police Commissioners, and other prominent civilians. The difficulties of the City Council over the "Bounty Bill" are also detailed. These documents may be found in the Maryland Historical Society, Glenn Papers, MS 1017.

June 29th 1862

Among the different means resorted to for the purpose of holding the people of Maryland in a wholesome state of subjection, perhaps the most common is the arrest and incarceration of citizens of all classes for the most trivial causes.

It has more than once happened that some of our most inoffensive citizens have suddenly found themselves carried off to Fort McHenry without being aware that they had ever committed any act which entitled them to the distinction of the notice of the military authorities or the police. Once in Fort McHenry they are kept in some out-houses prepared for the reception of State prisoners and retained there until the number became too large for the space allotted them. Those who are willing to take the oath of allegiance as prescribed by

Government are usually set at liberty after the space of a few days; while those against whom there is no charge whatever are not unfrequently released upon giving a pledge not to render any aid or comfort to the enemies of the Union. When the prison rooms or rather barracks become full the inmates are shipped in a lot to some distant Fort and the quarters prepared again for newcomers. The facts of the arrest of private citizens are frequently entirely unknown and it is by no means a common thing to find a statement of the prisoners in Fort McHenry in any of the newspapers. By some chance however a list of those under arrest and the nature of the charges against them was procured at the last transfer from Fort McHenry to Fort Lafayette, and published in the daily papers. The accompanying statement was clipped from the columns of the Maryland News Sheet. It is worth perusal. Not having made a special examination of all these cases, I will not pretend to say what was the amount of treason committed by each individual; of those few which I have enquired into I will give you the particulars which I have obtained. David Bendann is a young Jew one of two brothers who have a large photographic establishment in one of our main streets. They are well behaved and quiet young men who confine themselves almost exclusively to their business in which they have been most successful. While David Bendann was working some weeks past in his office a captain in the Federal army entered and in rather an abrupt manner requested him to take his portrait, saying at the same time that he was sorry to be forced to sit in Baltimore, as the photographic art was not nearly so well understood here as in Philadelphia. Mr. Bendann then advised him to wait till he got an opportunity to get a picture taken in Philadelphia. The officer said "No; that he was obliged to get one at once & that he would have it taken now." Mr. Bendann then remarked to him that he would ask him to pay beforehand as he had lost so much money by soldiers & officers ordering pictures and then never paying for them, that he had determined to work for no more except when paid in advance. The Captain became very indignant, swore and threatened—and finally pitching the money on the counter told Mr B to come at once & give him a sitting. Mr. B. who was by no means inclined to put up with such insolence pushed back the money saying that he declined to do any such thing, as he was accustomed to work only for gentlemen. The Captain on this became furious and drawing his sword advanced upon Mr. Bendann. The latter however far from being intimidated cooly drew a revolver from a drawer and told the Captain to advance at his peril. After a little swagger the latter withdrew.

Shortly afterwards Mr. Bendann was arrested. No other charge has been preferred against him. No investigation has been made in his case.

William H. Cowan was employed by a client indicted under a charge of using treasonable language. In the course of the defense he asserted that there was no law which made it treason to cry "Hurrah for Jeff. Davis." He was sent to Fort McHenry. The cause of Judge Carmichael's arrest has already been stated. Mr. Powell was arrested because in the discharge of his duty as State's Attorney he was prepared to prosecute parties who had been indicted for conspiracy by the Grand Jury. Mr. Nabb was arrested because he declared that Judge C. should not be arrested if he could prevent it and because he rushed to his assistance while he was being so cowardly and attrociously maltreated.

Perhaps the most extreme cases of all are those of Mr Porter & Mr Meyer. Mr Porter is a most quiet and orderly gentleman and highly respected as a good citizen. After the receipt of the news of the disastrous defeat of McClellan and when wounded Generals and officers were being brought in numbers to the city information was given Mr Porter, by a person in whose reliability he confided, that Genl. McClellan and his Staff had taken refuge in the Galena & that he had offered to capitulate, but that Genl. Lee had demanded an unconditional surrender. The party in question assured Mr Porter that he had seen Genl Harman [?], who was in the James River Steamer sick, & that he had this statement directly from him. Mr. Porter copied it almost verbatim as I have given it and showed it from time to time to his friends.

Mr Piggott obtained a copy of it for the same purpose. Mr. Meyer procured a similar statement from some other source; from a Federal officer he says for the news had spread like wildfire through the town—and handed it during the morning to a large number of customers principally females who came to purchase ribans [*sic*] & muslins at his counter. Such officiousness was objectionable to Genl. Wool. He declared that he would put a stop to the circulation of all rumors so injurious to the Federal army. These three men & one or two others I think were taken to the Fort without delay. It turned out to be perfectly true that Genl. McClellan had established himself on board the Galena, and the report of the demand for a surrender was reported in the Richmond papers. You will observe in the extract quoted above that Mr. Cowan and others were charged with de[c]lining to take the oath. It may not be amiss to remind you that there is a regular oath prescribed by the constitution for all persons holding office in the state, Members of the Legislature, Members of the Bar &c. This oath requires you to bear true allegiance to your state and to support the Constitution of the United States. The test oath at present administered by the Federal authorities requires you to bear paramount allegiance to the United States. The doctrine of State Sovereignty is utterly ignored and no one who has on any previous occasion taken the oath as administered since the formation of the Constitution, can possibly subscribe to the oath now prescribed without forswearing himself. In case of arrest the surest method of purging one's self of suspicion and proving one's self a "loyal" citizen is to commit a perjury.

[sgd] W.

July 28". 1862

The extreme measures resorted to by the Military authorities of the Federal Government in those portions of the Confederate States in which they have succeeded in gaining a foothold have become matters of history. The proclamation of Hunter, the orders of Fremont & Halleck in Missouri, of Butler in New Orleans, of Grant in Tennessee, of Boyle in Kentucky and latterly of Pope in Virginia are of public record and have been fully commented upon, at home and abroad.

The cause of despotic tyranny pursued towards the citizens of the State of Maryland is not so well known and it may perhaps not be uninteresting to many of your readers to be more intimately acquainted with the accts of intimidation practiced by the Government against the people of a state still in the Union and in which the supporters of the Government still claim that there is decided Majority in favor of the Union—or rather now that the secession of the Southern States may be considered as a fact—in favor of remaining with the North. Maryland it must be recollected has never declared in favor of secession. At the time of the Establishment of a provisional Government in the South, there was a very small portion of the people in the State in favor of such a course. There was a very decided majority comprising a large portion of the talent and ability of the State in favor of the Union, as it was. Many of the leading men were however opposed to any attempt at coercion and were satisfied that re-union could never be accomplished by force. The attempt to reduce the people of the South to subjection by arms to [*sic*] believed not only to be an unwise one, but they were also satisfied that the calling out of troops by the President, in one State for the purpose of quelling an insurrection in another was an unconstitutional measure. The people of Maryland were told this. They were assured that the marching of Northern Volunteers over Maryland soil for the purpose of making war against her sister Southern State could be lawfully and should be resisted. This led to the uprising of the citizens of Baltimore on the 19" April 1861 when the Massachusetts Volunteer troops were attacked with stones in the streets and the demonstration made was so formidable that it was deemed prudent by the Government to stop the passage of troops by this route, at least for a time.

The North was electrified. Deceived by the Misrepresentations of the Governor of the State, they had relied confidently on the cooperation of Maryland and impressed as they were with the belief that all Southern sympathy was confined to but a small number of the citizens they were ill prepared for so rude a blow to their delusive convictions. Since that day the animosity and hatred constantly manifested towards the state has known no bounds. As the astonishment and disappointment of the coersionists were extreme so have their animosity and malice been beyond measure. Shortly after that as is known abroad the commissioners of Police two of whom were gentlemen of the highest standing and the Marshal of Police were thrown into prison and this notwithstanding the acknowledged fact that the united exertions of these gentlemen and of the Mayor of the City, had alone prevented the massacre of a large portion of the Northern Volunteers—notwithstanding the fact that in spite of any southern proclivities they may have had they labored manfully & nobly to preserve order & peace in the city & to protect without destruction every person within its limits—the Mayor and Marshal of Police having themselves marched through the streets at the head of the Northern troops for the purpose of more fully protecting them.

The arrest of the Mayor of the City followed soon after—and although martial law was not actually declared the City was virtually placed under the control of the Military authorities. Columbiads and Mortars of heavy calibre were mounted at Fort McHenry; two other forts were built, one on the outskirts of the city and another in one of the suburbs and garrisoned; and the citizens were given to understand that in case of disturbance or in case of the entry of the Confederate troops into Maryland that the City could be laid in ashes at very short notice. On one occasion certainly after the defeat at Manassas the shot furnaces were heated to a red heat and every preparation made for a bombardment of the city.

The subsequent arrest of the members of the legislature is a matter of history. With the exception of the Members from Baltimore City, these gentlemen had all been elected some time previous and before the question of separation had even been mooted. It is but fair to suppose that they represented in a great measure the opinions of their constituents. They declared emphatically that coercion could not bring about re-union and recommended the recognition of the Southern Confederacy. At the same time they disavowed all intention of passing any act of secession. The people of the State they said were the only ones who had a right to decide the future destiny of the State and if such decision should be rendered necessary by the subsequent course of events, they would no doubt assert and use that right in their own good time. For this they were arrested in the month of September last, prior to the autumn elections and consigned to a Military prison. About the same time the Editors of two newspapers were arrested, one of which papers had neither advocated nor advised the secession of the State but had confined itself to discussing the constitutionality of the measures adopted by the Government and to comment freely upon the inevitable results consequent upon the course that was being pursued.

Soon after the arrest of these men, the elections were held. They were conducted under Military surveillance. The result was most satisfactory. A most "loyal" Governor was elected without opposition—and the Legislature which convened shortly afterwards was found to be composed of Members unanimous in their support of the Government. A Treason Bill was passed—a special tax voted to meet the War quota assessed by the National Government on the State and among other things a Bill passed, declaring the old police commissioners *functe officio* and organizing a new board & a new police. The Police Commissioners in Fort Warren and the Marshal were however not released. Their authority is gone but they are still held as dangerous citizens. Nor were all the members of the old Legislature released. Several months after their powers had virtually ceased by the election of other members and some time after the new Legislature had actually convened, such of them as were willing to pledge themselves that they would render no aid or comfort to the enemy were allowed to return to their homes.

Those who insisted that they had done no wrong, that their arrest was illegal and that they were entitled to & claimed an unconditional discharge remain there still. No charge has been preferred against them and all right of trial has been denied them. They are shut up in Fort Warren, with but a few occasional exceptions, their friends denied access to them, and to a great extent their very existence ignored. When Genl Dix, then Commander of the department was applied to by the friends of several members who were willing to give the pledge desired, to know why they were not released, he frankly confessed that they had not been arrested in his immediate district & he had forgotten all about them; and during the last week of the Session of Congress when Bingham's Bill providing for the release of all state prisoners, after incarceration for a certain period without trial, was under discussion there was actually no one in the Senate who could say whether or not any Members of the Maryd. Legislature were still in Confinement. The Senators from Maryland were of course not present.

The Mayor of the City is with them. He has declined to resign his office and from present appearances if Maryland is not meanwhile rescued from her thraldom, will be kept there until his term expires. We have then now in the State a most "loyal" Governor & a "loyal" legislature. In Baltimore we are kept in order by a "loyal" police, duly installed by a "loyal" legislature—and a large military force is also stationed in and around the city. We have in addition a city Council the popular branch of which was elected last autumn & is consequently most "loyal". Then judges were also elected who preside in our city Courts, all of whom are "loyal" men. The Justices of the Peace were nominated and elected as men of known "loyalty". The Constables are "loyal". The Sheriffs are "loyal" and in fact almost every man who occupies any office whatever is or professes to be a most "loyal" citizen. Surely there can be neither sense nor policy we would think in treating a State inhabited by so "loyal" a people as a subjugated province.

No. 4

August 4th 1862.

The accounts I have already given you of the despotic measures constantly resorted to for the purpose of intimidation in the State of Maryland are but single instances among a host of others which it is useless to relate. There is an occurrence however of very recent date which though little known, of our State, is in fact an outrage to public liberty and a violation of the rights of every freeman in the city of Baltimore, second only in character to the arrest of the Members of the Legislature. I allude to the forced resignation of the members of the Second Branch of the City Council.

Notwithstanding the efforts which are constantly found necessary to check more effectually exhibitions of sympathy with the South and notwithstanding that the authorities found themselves compelled to increase the stringency of their measures from week to week the Governor of the State is none the less anxious to convince the World at large of the perfect loyalty of the state of Maryland. Indeed the greater the obstacles which he finds in his way the greater seems his determination to convince himself & every body else that they are at best but of a temporary character. Accordingly when the President called upon the States to furnish 300,000 additional troops, Governor Bradford was one of the first to come to his aid and one of the first to assure the people at large that Marylanders needed no incentives to induce them to rally speedily to the support of so glorious cause. Facts told a different tale. Govr. Bradford was soon compelled to submit to the force of circumstances & follow in the lead of the Yankee States. There was another difficulty which presented itself so soon as he determined to offer bounty to recruits—the State Legislature. That to be sure was a most "loyal" body and had been elected last Autumn without opposition & protected by the bayonets of the military. But since that period many eyes had been opened to the character of the war and it became a very serious question with the Governor whether if he did call the Legislature together he could safely count upon their support of his extreme views. Rather than run such a risk he determined to relieve himself from all difficulty by applying to the wealthiest and most influential citizens who professed to be "loyal" and accordingly he convened a number in the city of Baltimore to meet him and consult upon the means of raising the necessary fund. But here again he was doomed to a sad disappointment. Had the Legislature been convened many of its members would undoubtedly have voted for the appropriation. They dispose of other people's money. Among these "loyal" citizens he found none to contribute. They were asked to dispose of their own.

Rested then the City Council as the Governor's last resort. A Bill for an appropriation of $300,000 had been introduced already & passed the First Branch; but the Council had adjourned without any final action being taken on the Bill. The President of the First Branch who during the confinement of Mayor Brown in Fort Warren is *Ex officio* Mayor, a very ordinary individual and at all times eager to outstrip even the Governor in his manifestations of loyalty, immediately called the Council together. It met. A Bill appropriating $300,000 for bounty was introduced and passed almost unanimously in the First Branch, which is the lower house of the Council. It is composed of men elected annually one from each ward and is supposed to represent the people more particularly than the other Branch the members of which are elected biennially, one from every two wards. The First Branch had been elected last Autumn under a military Rule. The members of the Second Branch had been elected a year previous, about the time of the Presidential elections, when a perfectly fair vote was had & when the citizens of Baltimore were fully aware of the necessity of their being represented by conservative men. It is but fair to suppose that they represented fully the views of a large number of the citizens.

When the Bounty Bill was sent up to the Second Branch on the 22nd July last the members with but one exception voted against it. They took the ground that this bounty was for soldiers to be furnished by the State to the Government, and that it was therefore a Government Measure and not even a State measure; but that if the State choose to furnish men and bounty too that was not their business but the State's. It was their business however to protect the citizens of Baltimore and they had no idea of imposing upon them so onerous a tax. The vote was received with decided marks of disapprobation by the gal[l]ery. Cries of "Traitor" "Hang him" &c were uttered as the speaker who expressed the sentiments of his fellow members took his seat. The first Branch then asked for a committee of conference which was of course granted and the Council adjourned to meet next afternoon at five o'clock. There was great dissatisfaction expressed at the result of the vote by the "Union Shriekers" and threats of violence were heard. Application for protection was made by some of the members to the Marshal of Police and assurance was given that no one should suffer any injury.

On Monday afternoon July 23rd the Council accordingly met. A number of people were assembled in front of the Council Hall having met in obedience to a call made by so called Union Men of the City. A number of placards had been posted during the morning through the City calling upon Union Men to rally in the afternoon in support of their rights, which should not be trampled upon by traitors. The Council having no other business a second vote was immediately taken. The fury of the spectators in the Gallery was more intense and more insulting than it had been the day before; and it was only through the efforts of the police that they were obliged to leave. They did not go far however but stopped with the crowd in the street to vent their indignation on the obnoxious members—one member an old man was knocked down & beaten, the President of the Second Branch was attacked and badly bruised and one other member was only protected from serious injuries by the police, who thought it was high time to put an end to the disturbance. This last gentleman was conducted home in safety and there the matter was supposed to rest, the Bounty Bill having been finally disposed of.

The usual parliamentary laws regulate the action of the Council. By them, when a question has once been finally disposed of by a deliberative assembly, the action taken is conclusive and the Bill cannot be brought up again in any form by the same assembly. I must remark here that not one of the ruffians who made this infamous assult was arrested. They never are. The invariable practice is to allow every outrage upon so called secessionists to proceed to a pitch, when there is danger of united resistance. When a stop is put to it. Those who commence the attack, are told to go about their business. Those who attempt to resist are usually sent to the Station House.

The disgust among the loyal Union men when they found their threats had been of no avail was great. A Town meeting was called for the following Monday and loud hints were circulated about mobbing and tar and feathers. The President of the Second Branch called upon Genl. Wool commanding in this department and laid the whole case before him. Genl. Wool assured him that he had acted from conscientious motives & that had he been similarly situated he would have pursued the same course. The members then hoped to hear no more of the matter. Next day however, Mr Miller the most prominent member, was requested to call on General Wool. He did so and had a private audience. General Wool stated to him frankly that there was a great pressure upon him, that the Government wanted means and men badly and had to have them; that Governor Bradford was sadly disappointed in the action of the friends he had convened and that his main hope and reliance was in the City Council. Genl. Wool then spoke of the indignation of the Union men in the City, of the town meeting that had been called and the probabilities of an outbreak. He said nothing however of three forts and six thousand armed men ready at his beck and call, and kept here for the special purpose of preventing disturbance. He finally urged upon Mr. Miller the propriety of resignation as the only means of reconciling the difference that existed. Mr. Miller and his friends had a consultation. They understood what Genl. Wool's advice meant—resignation or a Fort. Threatened by the mob, not fully protected by the police, and with the prospect of a residence in badly ventilated quarters and soldiers rations for an indefinite period, they concluded to resign. To their shame be it said they voluntarily laid down, on the 25th of July last, a sacred trust with which they had been invested by their fellow citizens, under intimidation. Most of the members were men of the middle class & several of them old. From one or two however better things were to be expected. Fortunately there are younger men and better men in the State whom no threats can induce to yield up their rights. Men who make no surrenders, who subscribe to no oaths. On such as these Maryland bases her hopes in this her hour of sore trial.

Since the resignation of these men, there is no barrier left between the citizen and the ruffian—matters are worse than ever—numerous arrests have been made, houses searched & floors torn under the pretense of looking for concealed weapons. On the walls of the city in conspicuous places, placards have been placed with the following inscriptions "Union First, Peace last—Traitors Read—Posterity will treat with scorn the traitors of to day—Every vestige of treason must be crushed out"—and many other such.

Another election has been held. A "loyal" Second Branch has been elected & has assembled. In violation of all law and precedent it has at once taken up the Bounty Bill which will be passed almost immediately.

APPENDIX E

The following three letters are mentioned in the Glenn narrative under date of September 22, 1867, and may be found in the Maryland Historical Society (Glenn Papers, MS 1558). The letters were written by General Pierre Gustave Toutant Beauregard, the flamboyant "Hero of Sumter" and the triumphant victor of First Bull Run, otherwise known as "Old Bory." His literary efforts early in the war were marked with a "singular infelicity" that he apparently carried over into civilian life.

LETTER No. 1

Baltimore Septem 19. 1867

To the Editor
of the Baltimore Gazette
Dear Sir—

I notice in your paper of this morning an article copied from the New York Express of the 17th inst., in which certain political opinions are stated to have been expressed by me, at a dinner given to me by some friends at the N.Y. Hotel. Not having been present at that dinner, I cannot have uttered the sentiments attributed to me on that occasion.

Being still an outlaw on my own native soil, I do not feel called upon to express any public views relative to our Govt.—But I am at liberty to state, that, unless the conservative element of the Country soon awakens to the dangers which threaten the liberties of the Country, I confidently believe, that our form of Govt. will ere long be changed to a Military Despotism, after a period of anarchy more or less prolonged.

Resply. Your Obt. Sevt.
[s] G. T. Beauregard

LETTER No. 2

Baltimore—Septe. 19. 1867

To the Editor of the
Baltimore Gazette—
Dear Sir—

I notice in your paper of this morning an article copied from the New York Express of the 17th inst. in which I am stated to have expressed certain political opinions at a dinner given by a friend at the New York Hotel. [Part of the next sentence has been crossed out and the following written in pencil above it: "No such opinions were expressed by me."] As the dinner was private, I am surprised at that publication which says either too much or too little.

Being still an "outlaw" in my own native country, I do not feel called upon to express any public views relative to its Govt., but I am free to state, that unless the conservative element of the country soon awakens to the dangers which threaten the liberties of the country, I confidently believe that its form of Govt. will, ere long, be changed to a Military despotism, after a period of anarchy more or less prolonged.

Resply. Your Obt. Svt.
[s] G. T. Beauregard

[On the back of Letter No. 2 is the following in pencil: "At the public dinner alluded to I was not present having respectfully declined the invitation. I [?] present and therefore could not have expressed any such sentiments. I [?]. No such opinions were expressed by me."]

LETTER No. 3

Baltimore—Septem. 20. 1867

To the Editors of the Baltimore Gazette
Dear Sirs—

I notice in your paper of yesterday an article copied from the New York Express of the 17th inst. in which certain political opinions are stated to have been expressed by me at a dinner given to me at the New York Hotel. The dinner was a private one, & the statement of the Express, being but a brief & incomplete abstract of the remarks which I made whilst conversing with the few friends present, conveys an erroneous impression of the views expressed by me on that occasion. Being still an "outlaw" in my own native country, I do not feel called upon to publicly uphold its Govt. especially at this time when the country is divided in opinion as to whether Congress or the Executive constitute *the Govt.*—but I am free to say, that unless the conservative element of the nation soon awakens to the dangers which threaten the liberties of the country, I confidently believe that its form of Govt. will, ere long, be changed to a military despotism, after a period of anarchy more or less prolonged.

Yours very truly
[s] G. T. Beauregard

GLOSSARY

The following is an alphabetical listing of persons and places mentioned in the narrative of William Wilkins Glenn. No attempt has been made to elaborate on those persons who have been the subject of biographies or who have been fully identified in generally available biographical directories. Likewise, no Civil War battles, nor generally known battles and personages of previous wars, have been identified. It is hoped that this glossary will add to the usefulness of the Glenn narrative and the enjoyment of the reader by clarifying some obscure relationships and placing some unfamiliar personalities in a relevant setting.

ACQUIA CREEK (Virginia)
: Creek emptying into the Potomac River south of Washington, D.C. Stafford, Virginia, was the town nearest the steamboat landing.

ADAMS, CHARLES FRANCIS (1807–1886)
: United States Minister to Great Britain from May 1861, to June 1868. Arbitrator of the *Alabama* claims, 1871–1872.

Alabama, C.S.S.
: Confederate naval steam sloop built by Laird in England in 1862. Commanded by Rear Admiral Raphael Semmes of Maryland, she sank fifty-eight Union ships valued at $6,500,000 before being sunk off France by the U.S.S. *Kearsarge* on June 19, 1864. Claims

against Great Britain for American shipping lost to the *Alabama* were the subject of postwar negotiations.

ALBERT, WILLIAM JULIAN (1816–1879)
Baltimore attorney and director of the Baltimore and Cuba Smelting and Mining Company, and the First National Bank. A strong Unionist, he was a manager of the Union Club, a Lincoln elector in 1864, and a Republican in the House of Representatives from 1866 to 1874.

ALEXANDER, GEORGE W. (1829–1895)
Colonel and assistant adjutant general in the Confederate army. Resident of Laurel, Maryland, in the postwar period.

ALLNUTT, JAMES W.
Baltimorean and president of the Bank of Commerce in Baltimore from 1855.

ANDERSON, H. PERCY
Major in the British army; attached to the British legation in Washington, D.C., in the early 1860s.

ANDERSON, JOSEPH REID (1813–1892)
U.S. Military Academy, 1836; owner of the Tredegar Iron Works in Richmond, Virginia, from 1858. Brigadier General, CSA, 1861. Resigned in 1862 and returned to Tredegar for the duration of the war. Resumed position as president of Tredegar when it began postwar operations in 1867.

ANDERSON, ROBERT (1805–1871)
From Kentucky. U.S. Military Academy, 1825. A major in the U.S. Army, he was breveted Major General April 13, 1861. Appointed to the command of the forts in the harbor of Charleston, South Carolina, he withdrew his forces from Fort Moultrie to Fort Sumter on December 26, 1860. Following bombardment by Confederate forces on April 12–13, 1861, he evacuated Fort Sumter on April 14th. He retired from active service October 27, 1863, because of ill health.

ANNAPOLIS JUNCTION (Maryland)
Junction of the Annapolis and Elkridge Railroad with the Washington branch of the Baltimore and Ohio Railroad 20 miles west of Annapolis and approximately 18 miles from Baltimore.

ARCHER, HENRY W. (1813–1887)
Harford County, Maryland, attorney and member of the House of Delegates, 1845. In 1866 he was Chairman of the state Anti-County.
Registry Law Convention in Baltimore, and in 1867 served as a delegate to the Constitutional Convention from Harford County.

ARMY AND NAVY CLUB (London)
Located at Pall Mall and George Street near St. James Square, it was established in 1837 with members among the commissioned officers of the Army and Navy. Its headquarters, built in 1847, were demolished in 1961 to make way for newer quarters.

ASHLEY, EVELYN (1836–1907)
Private secretary to Lord Palmerston from 1858 to 1865, and his biographer (1876). He became a Member of Parliament in 1876.

ATWOOD, MRS. G. C.
American actress, married to a Bostonian, made her debut on the Philadelphia stage in 1854; living in 1870.

BAKER, LAFAYETTE CURRY (1826–1868)
Counterspy and special agent for the State Department. Self-styled "Chief, National Detective Police," he was appointed special provost marshal for the War Department on September 12, 1862. Appointed Colonel of the 1st District of Columbia Cavalry, 1863, and Brigadier General of Volunteers, 1865, he organized the pursuit of John Wilkes Booth. Author of *History of the United States Secret Service* (1867).

BANKS, NATHANIEL PRENTISS (1816–1894)
Massachusetts Congressman, 1853-1857, and Governor, 1858–1861. Appointed Major General of Volunteers in 1861, he headed the Department of Annapolis and then the Department of the Shenandoah. After field commands he was briefly (September–October 1862) in charge of the Military District of Washington, then moved to the Department of the Gulf 1862–1864. After the war he returned to Congress.

BARLOW, SAMUEL LATHAM MITCHELL (1826–1889)
New York corporation lawyer and comptroller of the New York *World*. He had been involved in the Mexican Treaty claims in 1846 and 1847 along with Reverdy Johnson and William Wilkins Glenn's uncle, David M. Perine. A Democrat, he was a supporter of Buchanan in 1856 and McClellan in 1864.

BARNARD, JOHN GROSS (1815–1882)
U.S. Military Academy, 1833, and a member of the Corps of Engineers. Chief engineer in charge of the defenses of Washington from April to July 1861. Named Brigadier General of Volunteers in September 1861. Served in Corps of Engineers until his retirement in 1881.

BARNEY, ESTER ANN (b. 1814)
Baltimorean, sister of James H. Barney.

BARNEY, JAMES H. (1820–1882)
Baltimorean, lived on Cathedral Street, served as a volunteer in

in the Mexican War. A founder of the Maryland Club, he was its president from 1870 to 1875. Appointed Baltimore City Collector, 1868.

BARNEY, JOSEPH NICHOLAS

Entered the U.S. Navy as a midshipman, 1835; dismissed in 1861. Joined the Confederate naval service, commanding the *Jamestown* in 1862, the *Harriett Lane* briefly in 1863, and the *Florida* from 1863 to January 1864. Held the rank of lieutenant commander.

BARNUM'S CITY HOTEL (Baltimore)

Established in 1825 on the southwest corner of Fayette and Calvert streets, it was one of the principal hotels in Baltimore throughout the nineteenth century.

BARRON, SAMUEL (1809–1888)

Entered the U.S. Navy as a midshipman, 1812; resigned April 22, 1861. Joining the Confederate naval service, he held the rank of commodore. Chief of the Bureau of Orders and Detail, 1861, he was in charge of the coast defenses of Virginia and North Carolina. Sent to England in the summer of 1863 to bring over the Birkenhead Rams, he remained in Europe as "Flag Officer Commanding Confederate States Naval Forces in Europe."

BARRY, WILLIAM FARQUHAR (1818–1879)

U.S. Military Academy, 1838; served in the Artillery. Named Brigadier General of Volunteers, 1861, he became Chief of Artillery of the defenses of Washington from September 1862, to March 1864. After the war he headed the Artillery School at Fortress Monroe.

BARTOL, JAMES LAWRENCE (1813–1887)

Resident of Caroline County, Maryland, he was Associate Justice, Maryland Court of Appeals, 1857–1867; Chief Justice, 1867–1883.

BATH, MARCHIONESS of—see THYNNE, HARRIET BARING

BAYARD, JAMES ASHETON, Jr. (1799–1880)

Resident of Wilmington, Delaware, and U.S. Senator from Delaware, 1851–1864. Practiced law from 1864 to 1867. Appointed to the U.S. Senate, 1867, he served until 1869. Delegate to the Democratic National Convention, 1868. He was married to Ann Bassett.

BAYARD, THOMAS FRANCIS (1828–1898)

Son of Senator James A. Bayard, practiced law in Philadelphia to 1858, and in Wilmington, Delaware, to 1869. Elected to his father's Senate seat in 1869, he served until 1885. Secretary of State in the Cleveland administration, 1885–1889; Ambassador to Great Britain, 1893–1897.

BAYNE, LAWRENCE P. (1815–1885)

Baltimore banker and officer of the citizens' meeting to provide candidates for mayor and city council in the election of October 10, 1860.

BEALL, JOHN YATES (1835–1865)

"Captain" Beall, officially an Acting Master in the Confederate naval service, was arrested in December 1864, near the Suspension Bridge at Niagara Falls, after an unsuccessful attempt to release prisoners at Johnson's Island and blow up a train near Buffalo, New York. Charged with guerrilla activity and with being a spy, he was hanged on Governors Island in New York Harbor on February 24, 1865. Beall had several prominent Baltimore connections, including Andrew Ridgely, one of his attorneys; James A. L. McClure; Mr. & Mrs. John S. Gittings; the Reverend J. J. Bullock; and Mrs. Basil B. Gordon (Elizabeth Skipwith).

BEALL, WILLIAM N. R. (1825–1883)

U.S. Military Academy, 1848; resigned as captain in 1861. Commissioned captain in the Confederate army, he was appointed Brigadier General in 1862. Commanding Port Hudson when it surrendered in July 1863, he was released on parole in 1864 and acted as agent in the exchange of prisoners with offices in New York.

BEAUREGARD, PIERRE GUSTAVE TOUTANT (1818–1893)

U.S. Military Academy, 1838; resigned in 1861 and was appointed Brigadier General in the Confederate army. He commanded the attack on Fort Sumter; was at First Bull Run and Shiloh; commanded defenses in South Carolina and Georgia to 1864. In 1865 he was with Joseph E. Johnston in the Carolinas Campaign. After the war he was involved in railroading and Louisiana politics.

BELGER, JAMES (d. 1891)

New Yorker; a noncommissioned officer in the U.S. Army, he rose through the ranks to become quartermaster major in 1861; colonel in 1862. He was a quartermaster officer at Baltimore, 1861–1863. Dismissed November 3, 1863.

BELMONT, AUGUST (1816–1890)

Son of Simon Belmont of the Rhenish Palatinate, he came to the United States in 1837. Partner of the banking house of August Belmont & Co. Served as consul general for Austria in New York, 1844–1850; Minister to the Netherlands, 1853–1857. He traveled to London in 1861 and to Paris in 1863. An active Democrat, he was a member of the Democratic Central Committee.

BENDANN, DAVID (1841–1915)

Baltimore photographer, artist, and fine arts dealer in partnership with his brother Daniel at 282 Lexington Street. He later went exclusively into the art field, leaving the photography business to Daniel.

BENJAMIN, JUDAH PHILIP (1811–1884)

New Orleans attorney and politician, he served in the U.S. Senate first as a Whig and then as a Democrat from 1853 to 1861. Con--federate Attorney General, 1861; Acting Secretary of War (August–November 1861); Secretary of War, 1862; Secretary of State (February 1862–April 1865). Fled to England at the close of the war and practiced law until his death. Frank Lawley was a close friend and was writing a biography of Benjamin at the time of his death.

BENTLEY, RICHARD (1794–1871)

London publisher and "publisher in ordinary to the Queen."

BENTINCK, GEORGE WILLIAM (1803–1886)

Conservative Member of Parliament from Norfolk West, 1852–1865, and 1871–1884. Nickname "Big Ben" may have been coined to distinguish him from George Augustus Bentinck, Member from Taunton in 1860.

BERNAL, FREDERICK K.

Consul for Great Britain in Baltimore from c. 1861–1867. His wife's Christian name was Augusta. Neither was a Baltimorean.

BERRET, JAMES G. (1815–1901)

Democratic mayor of Washington, D.C. He was arrested on August 24, 1861 and confined in Fort Lafayette. He was released in September 1861, after taking the oath of allegiance and resigning as Mayor of Washington. He was affiliated with the Merchant's National Bank.

BISHOP, JOHN L.

Baltimore City policeman from 1859, he acted as deputy marshall to James L. McPhail in the Carmichael affair. He does not appear in the 1864 Baltimore City Directory.

BLACK, JEREMIAH SULLIVAN (1810–1883)

Pennsylvania attorney and state judge; Attorney General in the Buchanan administration, 1857–1860; Associate Justice of the United States Supreme Court, 1861–1883. He served as a Constitutional adviser to President Andrew Johnson.

BLACK, JOHN P.

Second lieutenant of the 1st Battalion, Delaware Cavalry. Appointed May 5, 1864, and mustered out August 3, 1865.

Blackwood's Edinburgh Magazine

Founded by William Blackwood in 1817 and still published. In the 1860s it was managed by John Blackwood, son of the founder. Fitzgerald Ross wrote several articles for *Blackwood's* during the Civil War.

BLAIR, FRANCIS PRESTON (1791–1876)
Kentucky editor and Republican party organizer, he was the father of Montgomery Blair. Moving to "Silver Spring" in Montgomery County, Maryland, he became active in the peace movement in 1864, and in 1865 went south for peace talks with Jefferson Davis.

BLAIR, MONTGOMERY (1813–1883)
Son of Francis P. Blair, he moved to Maryland in 1853, where he practiced law and became an active Free Soiler. Presided over the 1860 state Republican convention; appointed Postmaster General 1861–1865. He was considered too moderate for radical Republicans, and by 1868 had become a Democrat.

BLUNT, ATWOOD
Resident of Granite, Baltimore County, Maryland, where he moved from Montgomery County in 1853. He owned 300 acres of farmland, and in 1871 was owner of the quarries at Woodstock across the Patapsco River from Granite.

BOND, HUGH LENNOX (1826–1893)
Baltimore attorney and active American Party (Know Nothing) politician. Judge of the Baltimore Criminal Court from 1860–1868, he became U.S. Circuit Court Judge in Baltimore in 1870, and in 1871 investigated the Ku Klux Klan in Raleigh, North Carolina.

BOOTH, JOHN WILKES (1838–1865)
American actor, son of Junius Brutius Booth, born in Harford County, Maryland. Assassinated President Lincoln on April 14, 1865, and was himself killed on April 26 after an escape through southern Maryland. He is buried in Greenmount Cemetery in Baltimore.

BORTHWICK, SIR ALGERNON (1830–1908)
Editor of the London *Morning Post* from 1852, he became owner of the paper in 1872. A close friend of Lord Palmerston, he was in a position to know the inner workings of the British cabinet. In 1864 he joined Palmerston's secretary, Evelyn Ashley, in the "Owl."

BOTTS, JOHN MINOR (1802–1869)
Virginia attorney and Whig member of the House of Representatives, 1839–1843 and 1847–1849. He was a delegate to the Southern Loyalists Convention in 1866.

BOYER, BENJAMIN MARKLEY (1823–1887)
Pennsylvanian, elected to the House of Representatives as a Democrat in 1865 and served to 1869.

BOYLE, JEREMIAH T. (1818–1871)
Kentuckian, commissioned Brigadier General of Volunteers in 1861, he served as military governor of Kentucky from 1862 to 1864, when he resigned from the U.S. Army.

BRADFORD, AUGUSTUS WILLIAM (1806–1881)

Maryland attorney and politician, he was born in Harford County and moved to Baltimore County in 1838. He was an active Whig, and from 1845 to 1851 Clerk of the Baltimore County Court. He represented Maryland in the Peace Conference in January 1861, and that year was Union Party candidate for governor. Governor of Maryland from 1861–1865, he was unpopular with Southern sympathizers in the state. His country residence on Lake Avenue and Charles Street, Baltimore, was burned by Confederate raiders in 1864. After his term as governor he retired briefly from public life, but in 1867 was appointed by President Johnson as Surveyor of the Port of Baltimore.

BRADY, JAMES TOPHAM (1815–1869)

New York attorney and Breckinridge supporter in 1860. He was appointed in 1865 to a commission to study corrupt practices in the South. In 1866 he was one of Jefferson Davis's attorneys.

BRADY, SAMUEL (1789–1871)

Mayor of Baltimore, 1840–1842, and Baltimore County Commissioner, he lived with his son, also Samuel Brady (1834–1890), off the Dover Road at its intersection with Falls Road north of "Brooklandwood" in Baltimore County.

BRAGG, BRAXTON (1817–1876)

U.S. Military Academy, 1837; resigned in 1856. Commissioned Colonel, later Major General in the Louisiana Militia, 1861, then Brigadier General in the Confederate army. In charge of coast defenses on the Gulf, he later served under Albert Sydney Johnston in Kentucky. Became commander of the Army of the Tennessee, and in 1864 went to Richmond as Davis's military adviser.

BRAND, WILLIAM FRANCIS (1814–1907)

Episcopal clergyman and rector of St. Mary's Church in Emmorton, Harford County, Maryland. He conducted a school for boys and at various times taught Burton N. Harrison, two of Jefferson Davis's sons, and William L. Glenn (son of William W. Glenn). Historian of the church as well as a teacher, he published a life of Bishop Whittingham in 1883. He served as rector of St. Mary's until his death in 1907, and was succeeded by William Lindsay Glenn.

BRATTLEBORO (Vermont)

City on the Connecticut River in Windham County, Vermont, near the New Hampshire border.

BRECKINRIDGE, JOHN CABELL (1821–1875)

Presidential candidate as a Southern Democrat in 1860, he had served in Congress from Kentucky and from 1856–1861 was Buchanan's Vice President. Served as U.S. Senator from Kentucky in 1861, then resigned and became a Brigadier General in the

Confederate army. On February 4, 1865, he was appointed Secretary of War.

BRENT, ROBERT JAMES (1811–1872)
Baltimore attorney, member of the 1851 Constitutional Convention. Attorney General of Maryland from 1851 to 1852. He was married to Matilda Lawrence, who was descended from the Hagers of Hagerstown. Among his children were Mrs. William Keyser, Mrs. Dunbar Hunt, and three daughters who remained unmarried and were not mentioned in his obituary.

BRIGHT, JESSE DAVID (1812–1875)
Democratic U.S. Senator from Indiana, 1845–1862. He was expelled in February 1862, for having recognized Jefferson Davis as President of the Confederacy. He was unsuccessful in a bid for reelection in 1863; he moved to Kentucky, served in that state's House of Representatives in 1866, and moved to Baltimore in 1874.

BRIGHTON (England)
Popular seaside resort on the English Channel c. 50 miles south of London.

BROGDEN, HARRY HALE (1837–1905)
Resident of Prince Georges County, Maryland, and member of the Confederate signal corps.

BROOKE, HORACE L. (1832–1899)
Baltimorean and partner of Rogers & Brooke, general commission merchants and agents for the Avalon Nail Works, which was located on the Patapsco River between Relay and Catonsville.

"BROOKLANDWOOD" (Baltimore County)
Estate of Alexander D. Brown on Falls Road in Baltimore County, Maryland, c. nine miles from Baltimore City. The house was built in the 1790s for Mary Carroll Caton, daughter of Charles Carroll of Carrollton. It is now owned by St. Paul's School for boys.

BROWN, ALEXANDER DAVIDSON (1824–1892)
Son of George Brown of the banking house of Alexander Brown & Sons in Baltimore; his country home was "Brooklandwood" in Baltimore County. In the postwar period he served on the staff of Governor John Lee Carroll c. 1876–1880.

BROWN, GEORGE STEWART (1834–1890)
Partner of Alexander Brown & Sons; member of the Maryland Club; lived in Baltimore near Cathedral Street and Madison Avenue. In 1876 he was appointed a Trustee of the Peabody Institute, serving to 1890.

BROWN, GEORGE WILLIAM (1812–1890)
Baltimore attorney and partner of Frederick W. Brune, Jr., whose sister he married. Elected Mayor of Baltimore as an Independent in 1859; led movement to moderate feelings after the riot of

April 19, 1861; arrested by General Dix on September 12, 1861 and imprisoned until December 1862. In 1872 he was appointed to the Baltimore City Supreme Bench and served to 1875.

BROWN, SAMUEL

Resident of Woodstock in Howard County, Maryland, his home was near the intersection of Old Frederick and Old Court roads.

BROWNING, WILLIAM A. (d. 1865)

Colonel and private secretary to President Andrew Johnson. He was succeeded by Colonel William G. Moore.

BRUNE, FREDERICK W. (1813–1878)

Baltimore County attorney and member of the firm of Brown and Brune. He was married to Emily Barton.

BRUNE, JOHN CHRISTIAN (1814–1864)

Baltimore merchant, brother of Frederick W. Brune, elected to the House of Delegates from Baltimore City in April 1861.

BUCHANAN, FRANKLIN (1800–1874)

Marylander; entered the U.S. Navy as a midshipman in 1815; Superintendent of the Naval Academy, 1845–1847; accompanied Perry to China; commander of the Washington, D.C., navy yard when he resigned in 1861. Commissioned Captain in the Confederate Navy, he commanded the Chesapeake Bay squadron in 1862, the CSS *Virginia (Merrimac)*, 1862, and was appointed Admiral later that year. He was defeated by Admiral Farragut at Mobile Bay. He was married to Ann Catherine Lloyd, a daughter of Maryland governor Edward Lloyd (of "Wye" in Queen Annes County). After the war he became president of the Maryland State Agricultural College (afterwards the University of Maryland).

BUCHANAN, JAMES (1791–1868)

Democratic President of the United States, 1856–1861.

BUCHANAN, JAMES M. (1803–1876)

Baltimorean; Minister to Denmark, 1856–1861; friend of William W. Glenn's uncle, David M. Perine. He was married to Jane Ellen Carns of Arkansas.

BUCKLER, THOMAS HEPBURN (1812–1901)

Baltimore physician, born at "Evergreen" in Baltimore County. Among his patients were Roger B. Taney, Robert E. Lee and President Buchanan. A Southern sympathizer, he moved to Paris in 1866 and remained there to 1890.

BULLER, REGINALD J.

Regimental instructor in musketry for the Grenadier Guards, he was commissioned in December 1858.

BULLOCK, J. J. (1812–1892)
Presbyterian clergyman, he was pastor of the Franklin Street Presbyterian Church in Baltimore, and later Chaplain to the United States Senate. He was a native of Kentucky, and died there in 1892.

"BULSTRODE PARK" (England)
Country residence of the Dukes of Somerset near Gerrard's Cross in Buckinghamshire.

BURKE, MARTIN (d. 1882)
A Marylander, he entered the Army in 1820, and was promoted to lieutenant colonel in 1861, commanding the Narrows of New York Harbor, including Fort Lafayette. He retired in 1863.

BURTON, HENRY S. (c. 1818–1869)
U.S. Military Academy, 1839; served in the Artillery. Commanded Fort Delaware from June 1862 to September 1863. Promoted to colonel in August 1863. Later breveted Brigadier General.

BUTLER, BENJAMIN FRANKLIN (1818–1893)
Attorney and Democratic politician from Lowell, Massachusetts. Delegate to the Democratic Convention in Baltimore, 1860, he supported Breckinridge. Elected Brigadier General in the Massachusetts militia in April 1861. Commanded the District of Annapolis, 1861; occupied Baltimore on May 13, 1861. Commanded Fort Monroe, May–August 1861. After the capture of New Orleans he was military governor, May–December 1862. In 1863 he was in command of the Army of the James, and in 1864 he was sent to New York City in anticipation of election riots. He was a radical Republican representative to Congress from Massachusetts, 1866–1875, and managed the impeachment proceedings against President Andrew Johnson. Elected Governor of Massachusetts in 1882.

BUTTERFIELD, WILLIAM (1814–1900)
English architect known mainly for his public buildings and Gothic church architecture. Designed All Saints, Margaret Street, in 1859.

BYRNE, C. H.
Englishman; designated "Captain," he was described as a "volunteer aide-de-camp" on the staff of General Patrick R. Cleburne. He is reputed to have lost a leg at Manassas, but fought throughout the war.

CAMERON, SIMON (1799–1889)
Pennsylvania Republican and Secretary of War, 1861–1862. Censured by the House of Representatives for corruption in his department.

CAMP DOUGLAS (Illinois)
Training camp for Illinois volunteers; located south of Chicago.

After the fall of Fort Donelson 30,000 Confederates were imprisoned there. Dismantled in November 1865.

CAMPBELL, ALEXANDER WILLIAM (1828–1893)
Commissioned colonel in the 33rd Tennessee Infantry, CSA, 1861. Captured July 1863; exchanged February 1865; commissioned Brigadier General in March 1865.

CAMPBELL, JOHN ARCHIBALD (1811–1889)
Alabama attorney; Associate Justice of the U.S. Supreme Court, 1853–1861; Confederate Assistant Secretary of War, 1862–1865. Served as a Peace Commissioner in both 1861 and 1865.

CAMPBELL, JAMES MASON (1810–1869)
Baltimore attorney and member of the City Reform Convention in 1859. He was married to Roger Brooke Taney's daughter, Ann Arnold Taney.

CANBY, EDWARD RICHARD SPRIGG (1817–1873)
U.S. Military Academy, 1839; Commander of the Department of New Mexico. As Brigadier General of Volunteers, he commanded troops during the New York draft riots.

CAPE MAY (New Jersey)
Fashionable seaside resort on New Jersey's Atlantic coast, long popular with Baltimore society.

CAPERTON, ALLEN TAYLOR (1810–1876)
West Virginian attorney, Whig politician, member of the Confederate Senate from 1861 to 1865. In 1875 he entered the U.S. Senate as a Democrat.

CARLISLE, EARL of—see HOWARD, GEORGE WILLIAM FREDERICK

CARLTON CLUB (London)
Conservative political club, established in 1832 and still extant. Its quarters, on Pall Mall, were bombed in 1940.

CARMICHAEL, RICHARD BENNETT (1807–1884)
Queen Annes County, Maryland, attorney, Democrat politician, and Judge of the Queen Annes County Circuit Court, 1858–1864. In 1861 he was Presiding Judge. He died and is buried at "Wye."

CARNOCHAN, JOHN MURRAY (1817–1887)
New York physician and Professor of Surgery at the New York Medical College. He was married to artist Estelle Morris and lived at 45 Lafayette Place.

CARPENTER, WILLIAM H. (1814–1899)
Newspaper editor, born in London, proprietor of the *Western Continent* before coming to Baltimore. Commercial editor of the *Patriot,* 1856; part owner of the *Exchange,* 1859; editor of the *News Sheet,* 1861–1862; editor of the Baltimore *Sun,* 1879; editor of the *Baltimore Book.*

CARROLL, JAMES (1817–1887)
Baltimore County resident, son of James Carroll and Achash Ridgley. Owner of "Summerfield" an Old Manor Road near Glen Arm Road. "Summerfield" was once part of the Ridgley estate "Hampton."

CARROLL, JOHN LEE (1830–1911)
Howard County, Maryland, attorney, great-grandson of Charles Carroll of Carrollton. Practised law in New York from 1858 to 1861, returned to care for his father Charles Carroll and lived at "Doughoregan Manor." Elected governor of Maryland as a Democrat in 1876 and served to 1880.

CARSON, THOMAS J. (1813–1869)
Baltimore banker and partner of Carson and Co. His residence was 82 West Madison Avenue.

CARTER, EDWARD F. (1816–1897)
Baltimore newspaperman, business manager of the *Times* and *News Sheet,* part of the *Gazette* management, 1861–1865.

CARY, JANE MARGARET (1843–1895)
Daughter of Jane Margaret and Wilson Miles Cary of Charles Street, Baltimore. Familiarly known as "Jenny," she was a red-headed beauty, member of the pro-Southern "Monument Street Girls," who defied Federal orders, and along with her sister introduced James Ryder Randall's "Maryland, My Maryland" to Baltimore. She is responsible for setting the poem to music.

CARY, JANE MARGARET CARR, Mrs. Wilson Miles Cary (1809–1903)
Founder of the Southern Home School for Girls in Baltimore, and leader of social and charitable projects in the city.

CARY, WILSON MILES (1806–1877)
Baltimore politician and state senator, 1846–1852. Married to Jane Margaret Carr. His children were Wilson M. Cary, Jr. who served in the Confederate army, Sara Nicholas Cary (Mrs. James Howard McHenry), Hetty Cary (Mrs. John Pegram), and Jane Margaret Cary (Jenny).

CASKIE, MARTHA NORVEL (b. 1845)
Daughter of wealthy Richmond, Virginia, tobacconist James Kerr Caskie and his wife Martha Norvel.

CASSIDY, WILLIAM (1815–1873)
Albany, New York, journalist and Democratic politician. As editor of the Albany *Atlas (Atlas & Argus)* he supported Governor Seymour. In 1868 he was secretary of the New York State Democratic Committee.

CATONSVILLE (Maryland)
Town on the Frederick Turnpike seven miles west of Baltimore

City in Baltimore County, and the location of the Glenn's estate, "Hilton."

"CEDAR PARK" (Anne Arundel County, Maryland)
West River estate of Richard Sprigg Mercer, located north of Galesville.

CHAMBERS, EZEKIEL FORMAN (1788–1867)
Chesterton, Maryland, attorney and Whig U.S. Senator, 1826–1834. Chief Judge of the Second Judicial District of Maryland and Judge of the Maryland Court of Appeals, 1834–1851. Declined appointment as Secretary of the Navy, 1852. Delegate to the State Conference Convention, 1861, and the Constitutional Convention, 1864; ran unsuccessfully for governor, 1864.

CHANDLER, LUCIUS H. (d. 1876)
Norfolk, Virginia, attorney and politician. Born in Maine, moved to Norfolk in 1850. Ran successfully for Congress as a Unionist in 1865 but was not seated. Ran for Congress in 1868 as a radical and defeated. His death by suicide supposedly resulted from his political frustrations.

CHAPMAN, JOHN LEE (1811–1880)
Baltimorean and owner of the Maryland Glass Works. Mayor of Baltimore, 1862–1867. President of the Western Maryland Railroad, 1866–1868. Naval Officer of the Port of Baltimore, 1869–1873.

CHASE, SALMON PORTLAND (1808–1873)
Ohio Republican, Secretary of the Treasury, 1860–1864; Chief Justice of the United States Supreme Court, 1864–1873.

CHEATHAM, BENJAMIN FRANKLIN (1820–1886)
Major General in the Tennessee militia; promoted to Brigadier General in the Confederate army, 1861. Division commander under Polk and Hardee.

CHESTER (England)
Ancient city and railroad center south-southeast of Liverpool in the county of Chester.

CHURCH HOME AND HOSPITAL
Episcopal hospital opened in 1858 on Broadway in east Baltimore. Buildings formerly owned by the Washington Medical College. Still extant.

CITY POINT (Virginia)
Railroad terminus of the City Point and Petersburg Railroad, on the James River near the mouth of the Appomattox River.

CLARK, HORACE FRANCIS (1815–1873)
New York City attorney, Democratic Representative from New York, 1857–1861. Prominent in financial, political and railroad circles. Signed Jefferson Davis's bail bond.

CLARKE, DANIEL (1835–1876)
Attorney and state senator from Prince Georges County, Maryland, 1865. Married Governor Pratt's daughter.

CLAY, CLEMENT CLAIBORNE (1816–1882)
Alabama Democratic U.S. Senator, 1853–1861. Member of the Confederate Senate from 1861. Sent to Canada in 1864 to negotiate peace. Imprisoned in Fortress Monroe after Lincoln's assassination.

CLIFTON HOUSE (Canada)
Hotel near the Suspension Bridge at Niagara Falls, Ontario.

Clipper
Baltimore newspaper (1839–1865), owned and edited by William N. Tuttle (d. 1864).

COBB, HOWELL (1815–1868)
Georgia Democrat, member of Congress, 1844–1857; Secretary of the Treasury, 1857–1861; Chairman of the Confederate Convention, 1861. Brigadier General in the Confederate army, in charge of the Department of Georgia from 1863.

COCKEYSVILLE (Maryland)
Baltimore County town 15 miles north of Baltimore City on the York Road.

COLENSO, JOHN WILLIAM (1814–1883)
Anglican bishop and author. Bishop of Natal and Suffragan Bishop of Cape Town, 1853. A biblical scholar, he wrote the controversial *The Pentateuch and Book of Joshua Critically Examined* (5 vols., 1862–1865). Excommunicated, 1866.

COLFAX, SCHUYLER (1823–1885)
Indiana Republican member of the House of Representatives, 1855–1869. Served as Speaker of the House, 1863–1869. Vice President of the U.S., 1869–1873.

CONOLLY, THOMAS (1823–1876)
Member of Parliament from Donegal (Ireland), 1849–1876, and Sheriff of Donegal.

CONRAD, CHARLES MAGILL (1804–1878)
Virginia; Whig U.S. Senator, 1842–1843. Moved to Louisiana and served in the House of Representatives, 1849–1850. Secretary of War under President Millard Fillmore, 1851–1853. Served in the Confederate Congress, 1861–1864. Practiced law in New Orleans after the war.

CONRAD, LAWRENCE L. (1840–1884)
Maryland attorney.

CONSTABLE, A. G. A.
Captain in the U.S. Army, in charge of mortar boats at Cairo,

Illinois, in late 1861 under Flag Officer A. H. Foote. He had been a major in the service of the British East India Company. On November 20, 1862, he was appointed military Provost Marshall in Baltimore, and resided at 51 North Charles Street, at which time he is referred to as "Major."

COOPER, GEORGE E. (d. 1881)
Pennsylvanian; surgeon in the U.S. Army since 1847; promoted to major, May 21, 1861. After the war he settled in San Francisco.

CORBIN, FRANCIS C.
Virginian; resident of Paris at 59 Rue de Varennes.

CORCORAN, WILLIAM WILSON (1798–1888)
Washington, D.C., banker and philanthropist. His mother was Hannah Lemmon of Baltimore. Left the United States in 1862 and remained abroad until the end of the war, when he returned home with an extensive art collection to found the Corcoran Gallery.

COWAN, WILLIAM H. (b. 1822)
Baltimore attorney, born in Ireland. In 1860 he presided over a meeting of Southern sympathizers at the Liberty Fire Company Hall at Liberty and Fayette streets.

COX & COMPANY (London)
Army bankers at Craigs Court, London.

COX, CHRISTOPHER CHRISTIAN (1816–1882)
Associate editor of the Baltimore *Patriot* and Lieutenant Governor of Maryland in 1864. (He served only one term for the office was abolished, not to be revived until 1970.)

CRAIN, PETER WOOD (1806–1892)
Charles County attorney, member of the House of Delegates, 1841–1842; appointed Associate Judge of the Maryland Court of Appeals, 1846.

CRESWELL, JOHN ANDREW JACKSON (1828–1891)
Easton, Maryland, attorney. Began political life as a Whig, became a Democrat, and attended the 1856 National Convention. Member of the Maryland House of Delegates, 1861. Became a Republican and served as state adjutant general, 1862–1863. Member of Congress, 1863–1865, but failed reelection. Delegate to the Republican National Convention in Baltimore, 1864. Appointed to the U.S. Senate, March 9, 1865, served to 1867. Delegate to the 1866 Philadelphia Loyalists Convention; delegate to the Border State Convention in Baltimore in 1867; delegate to the Republican National Convention in Chicago in 1868. Postmaster General, 1869–1874; counsel on the *Alabama* Claims, 1874–1876.

CRICHTON, Honorable CHARLES F.
Ensign in the Grenadier Guards, commissioned April 1861.

CRITTENDEN, JOHN JORDAN (1787–1863)
U.S. Senator from Kentucky, 1817–1819, 1835–1841; Attorney General, 1841; U.S. Senator, 1842–1848; Attorney General, 1850–1853; U.S. Senator, 1855–1863, A lifelong Whig, he was a friend of William W. Glenn's father. The Kentucky whiskey mentioned in Glenn's journal for October 1861 appears on an inventory of Judge John Glenn's estate in 1853.

CRUMP, WILLIAM WOOD (1819–1897)
Virginia attonery; Assistant Secretary of the Treasury for the Confederacy, appointed May 20, 1864. A defense attorney for Jefferson Davis.

CURZON, ROBERT, Baron Zouche (1810–1873)
British diplomat and author, expert on ancient manuscripts. Married Emily Wilmot–Horton. His estates were "Parham" in Sussex and "Ravenhill" in Staffordshire.

Daily Exchange
Baltimore newspaper founded in 1858 by Charles G. Kerr and Thomas W. Hall. In 1859 it moved its offices to Baltimore and North Streets, and Henry M. Fitzhugh, Francis Key Howard and William H. Carpenter were added to the partnership. In 1861 Fitzhugh purchased the interests of Kerr and Hall, and W. W. Glenn in turn purchased Fitzhugh's interest. On September 19, 1861, the paper became the *Maryland Times,* and on September 24 the *News Sheet* both under the partnership of Edwards F. Carter and William H. Nielson. These were succeeded by the *Gazette* on October 6, 1862, which was run by Carter and Company until June 21, 1865, when ownership reverted to Glenn & Company (Glenn, Howard, and Carpenter). W. W. Glenn sold his interest in the paper in March 1872. It continued publication until 1882. The Maryland State Library in Annapolis has a complete set of the *Exchange* from 1858 until April 1861. The Maryland Historical Society owns a complete set of the paper for 1861, as well as a set of the *Maryland Times* and the *News Sheet.* The Enoch Pratt Free Library has the *Gazette* for 1864 and 1865. The rest of the paper is in scattered issues.

DALLAS, ALEXANDER GRANT (1816–1882)
Hudson's Bay agent in Victoria, Canada, from 1857, he became governor of Rupert's Land in 1862 and served until 1864.

DANVILLE (Virginia)
A major railroad center on the Dan River near the North Carolina line. This was Lee's objective when confronted by Grant near Appomattox.

DASHWOOD, MAITLAND (1813–c. 1880)
Member of the Grenadier Guards and magistrate for the county of Kent (England). His seat was "Hall Place" in Kent.

DAVIS, ALLEN BOWIE (1809–1889)
Montgomery County, Maryland, gentleman farmer, president of the Montgomery County Agricultural Society, and one of the founders of the Maryland State Agricultural College (later the University of Maryland). He was a delegate to the state Constitutional Convention in 1850, and in 1862 sat in the House of Delegates from Montgomery County. His home was "Greenwood" near Brookeville, but he spent his winters on Madison Avenue in Baltimore. He was married to Hester Anne Wilkins, an aunt of W. W. Glenn.

DAVIS, HENRY WINTER (1817–1865)
Baltimore politician and member of the House of Representatives from Maryland, 1855–1861. He lost his bid for reelection as a Republican, but was returned in 1863 as a member of the Unconditional Union Party and served until his death. In Maryland he had supported Governor Hicks, and had campaigned for Bell in the presidential election of 1860. He was outspoken in his opposition to Lincoln's suspension of the writ of *habeas corpus,* and equally outspoken for the cause of the Union. In opposition to Lincoln's plan for reconstruction, he sponsored the Wade–Davis Bill and then the Wade–Davis Manifesto (1864). He supported Lincoln in 1864 only after Montgomery Blair resigned as Postmaster General. His second wife was Nancy Morris of Baltimore, sister of Lydia Morris (Mrs. Francis Key) Howard.

DAVIS, JEFFERSON (1808–1889)
U.S. Military Academy, 1828; Secretary of War, 1853–1857; Mississippi Senator, 1856–1861. President of the Confederacy.

DAVIS, JOHN W. (1823–1888)
Member of the House of Delegates from Baltimore City, 1851–1853. Member of the first Board of Police Commissioners, 1860; arrested and imprisoned, 1861. Became Sheriff of Baltimore City, 1870; Maryland State Treasurer, 1872. He also served as assistant to Robert Garrett of the Baltimore and Ohio Railroad.

DAVIS, JOSEPH ROBERT (1825–1896)
Mississippi attorney, nephew of Jefferson Davis. Appointed a Brigadier General in the Confederate Army, he served in the Army of Northern Virginia.

DAVIS, VARINA HOWELL (1826–1906)
From Natchez, Mississippi, she was Jefferson Davis's second wife and author of a two-volume memoir of his life.

DAYTON, WILLIAM LEWIS (1807–1864)
New Jersey Senator, 1842–1851; vice presidential candidate, 1856; Minister to France, 1861–1864. Influential in denying French aid to the Confederacy.

DE HORSEY, W. H. B.
Lieutenant Colonel in the Grenadier Guards, commissioned 1857.

DELANE, JOHN THADDEUS (1817–1879)
Editor of the *London Times,* 1841–1877. Carried on a program of impartial and accurate reporting. Personal friend of Lord Palmerston.

DE LA RUE, THOMAS (1793–1866)
London printer and inventor, resident of Westbourne Terrace, Paddington.

DE LA RUE, WARREN (1815–1889)
Son of Thomas de la Rue, Doctor of Philosophy, inventor, member of the Royal Astronomical Society, and the Chemical Society.

DELAVAN HOUSE (Albany)
Albany, New York, first-class hotel near Capitol Park.

DELEON, EDWIN
Journalist and former consul to Egypt, he acted as Confederate commissioner in France until fired by Judah Benjamin. Reputed to be a personal friend of Jefferson Davis.

DE LHUYS, EDOUARD DROUYN (1805–1881)
French attorney and diplomat; French minister to London, 1849; Minister of Foreign Affairs, 1851–1855, 1862–1866.

DENISON, ROBERT M.
Baltimore County resident and member of the House of Delegates, 1860–1861. His city residence was 73 Courtland Street. He was a member of the Maryland Club.

De PERSIGNY, VICTOR FIALIN, Duc
French Minister of the Interior, friend and spokesman of Emperor Louis Napoleon, he followed his master into "poverty, prison and exile." As publisher of the newspaper *Constitutionel,* he was a leading Confederate champion.

DERRY (Ireland)
Londonderry, Northern Ireland. Seaport on Loch Foyle.

De WINTON, Sir FRANCIS WALTER (1835–1901)
British army officer and aide-de-camp to Sir Fenwick Williams when he was commanding the British forces in North America, 1861. He was also with Williams in Nova Scotia from 1864–1867. Retired from the British army with the rank of Major General.

DIMICK, JUSTIN (1800–1871)
U.S. Military Academy, 1819; Colonel, First U.S. Artillery, 1861. In command of the prisoner of war camp at Fort Warren in Massachusetts from October 1861 to January 1864.

DISRAELI, BENJAMIN (1804–1881)
Member of Parliament, conservative leader in the House of Commons, 1861; later Prime Minister and Earl of Beaconsfield.

DIX, JOHN ADAMS (1798–1879)
U.S. Senator from New York, 1845–1849; Secretary of the Treasury under President Buchanan, January–March 1861. Appointed Major General in the Volunteers in 1861, he commanded the Department of Annapolis in July, the Department of Pennsylvania to March 1862, the Middle Department to June 1862, the Department of Virginia to July 1863. From July 1863 until his resignation in November 1865 he commanded the Department of the East. He became Minister to France in 1866.

DOBBIN, GEORGE WASHINGTON (1809–1891)
Baltimore attorney; chairman of the Judiciary Committee of the state Constitutional Convention of 1867. Later judge of the Baltimore City Supreme Bench.

DONALDSON, JAMES LOWRY (1814–1885)
U.S. Military Academy, 1836; entered the artillery. Quartermaster and major, 1861, he was breveted colonel in 1864. In 1865 the Baltimore City Council "ordered that a sword be presented him for faithful and meritorious service during the war for the Union." (Baltimore *Sun*, June 9, 1865.)

DONELSON, ANDREW JACKSON (1799–1871)
Nephew of Rachael (Mrs. Andrew) Jackson and confidential secretary of President Jackson, he was appointed Minister to Prussia in 1846 and served to 1849. He was married to Elizabeth Martin Randolph.

"DOUGHOREGAN MANOR" (Howard County, Maryland)
Estate of Charles Carroll of Carrollton. The manor is still in the possession of the Carroll family. Located off Route 144 west of Ellicott City, it was the home of John Lee Carroll during the 1860s.

DUBLIN (Maryland)
Harford County town at the intersection of Routes 440 and 136, five miles south of the Susquehanna River crossing at Conowingo.

"DUNROBIN CASTLE" (Scotland)
On Dornoch Firth in Sutherland county on the northeast coast of Scotland.

EARLE, JAMES TILGHMAN (1814–1882)
Maryland state senator from Queen Annes County; postwar president of the Maryland State Agricultural Society. He was a leader in the 1866 Anti-Registry Law Convention.

EARLE, WILLIAM W. (1833–1885)
Brigade Major in the Grenadier Guards, stationed in Nova Scotia from 1862–1863. Became military secretary to General Sir C. H. Doyle in North America, 1865–1872. Promoted to Major General in 1880.

EASTER, HAMILTON (1810–1895)
Baltimorean; owner of Hamilton Easter & Co., importers and retailers of dry goods at 199 West Baltimore Street. His residence was on Liberty Road in Baltimore County.

EASTON (Maryland)
County seat of Talbot County on the Eastern Shore of Maryland. Located on the Tred Avon River.

EDGAR, JOHN M. (c. 1819–c. 1893)
Baltimore attorney.

EGREMONT, Lord—see WYNDHAM, GEORGE

ELDER, ROBERT N.
Baltimore County farmer; owned "Rockland," 11 miles north of Baltimore on the Reisterstown Road near Garrison Forest Road.

ELKTON (Maryland)
County seat of Cecil County, located six miles from Newark, Delaware and served by the main line of the Philadelphia, Wilmington and Baltimore Railroad (now Penn-Central).

ELLICOTT CITY (Maryland)
County seat of Howard County, west of Baltimore City on the Patapsco River, and the intersection of the Frederick Turnpike and the Baltimore and Ohio Railroad's main stem.

ELLIOTT, PERCIVAL
Private in the Confederate Signal Corps. Stationed at Fort Sumter in December 1863.

ELMIRA PRISON (New York)
Federal prison on the Chemung River in Elmira, New York. Began in May 1864 after prisoner exchanges were halted. Held 10,000 prisoners, mostly enlisted men. The death rate was 5 percent per month.

ELZEY, ARNOLD (1816–1871)
U.S. Military Academy, 1837; resigned, 1861. Lieutenant Colonel in the First Maryland Artillery (Confederate). Promoted to Major General, 1862, in command of the Department of Richmond. After

an outstanding military career, he took up farming near Jessup in Anne Arundel County, Maryland.

ERLANGER, EMILE

Son of Emile, Baron Erlanger, of the European banking house of Erlanger et Compagnie, Paris, Frankfort, and Amsterdam. Married Matilda Slidell.

"ESCRICK PARK" (England)

Country seat of Beilby Richard Lawley, Lord Wenlock, in York.

Etna, S.S.

Steamship owned by J. Florio of Palermo, Italy, in service between Glasgow and the Mediterranean.

EUSTIS, GEORGE (1828–1872)

Louisiana Representative to Congress, 1855–1859. Became secretary to the Confederate legation in Paris. He had sailed with James M. Mason and John Slidell on the *Trent* and with them was held at Fort Warren. After the war he settled in France.

EUTAW HOUSE (Baltimore)

Baltimore hotel on the northwest corner of Baltimore and Eutaw streets. It was purchased by Robert Garrett & Sons in 1845. During the war it was managed by R. B. Coleman.

EVARTS, WILLIAM MAXWELL (1818–1901)

Massachusetts Senator, 1861. In 1863 he was sent to England by the War Department to assist in the legal attack on Confederate shipbuilding in that country. A principal in the prosecution of Jefferson Davis, 1867. Attorney General, 1868–1869. Counsel for President Johnson in 1868. Counsel on the *Alabama* claims, 1872.

EXPRESS—see NATIONAL EXPRESS AND TRANSPORTATION COMPANY

FAIRHAVEN (Maryland)

Anne Arundel County resort and steamboat landing off Herring Bay approximately 20 miles south of Annapolis. The hotel was in operation until the 1930s.

FALLS, MOOR N. (1805–1876)

Baltimorean; member of the firm of Syackman, Falls & Co.; president of the Baltimore Steam Packet Company (Old Bay Line). His residence was 279 Madison Avenue.

FARRAGUT, DAVID GLASGOW (1801–1870)

Entered the U.S. Navy as midshipman in 1810. Was living in Norfolk in 1861. Commanded the New Orleans expedition, 1861. Rear Admiral, 1862; Mobile Bay, 1864; promoted to Vice Admiral, 1864; the Navy's first Admiral, 1866.

FICKLIN, BENJAMIN F. (d. 1871)

Son of Charlottesville, Virginia, clergyman Benjamin Ficklin.

Supervised the building of a road between Charlottesville and Scottsville. He was in England on official Confederate business from October 1861 to November 1862, when he returned with dispatches. Variously called major or colonel. He was in Glasgow, Scotland, in 1864 in connection with the blockade runner *Dare*. After the war he was briefly superintendent of the National Express and Transportation Company. His wife was Mary Ficklin of Charlottesville.

FIELDING, Sir PERCY R. B. (d. 1904)
Officer in the Coldstream Guards, he rose to the rank of General and was a Knight Commander of the Bath. He married Lady Louisa Isabella Harriet Thynne (d. 1919).

FINNEY, CHARLES GRANDISON (1792–1875)
Clergyman, abolitionist, and educator, he was president of Oberlin College in Ohio from 1851 to 1866.

FISH, HAMILTON (1808–1893)
New York Senator, 1851–1857. Commissioner for the relief of prisoners at the end of the war. Secretary of State, 1869–1877. Married to Julia Kean of New Jersey.

FISH, WILLIAM S.
Connecticut resident before the war. Appointed Provost Marshall at Baltimore on January 1, 1863; held rank of Major, later Lieutenant Colonel. In office to January 15, 1864, he was court-martialed and found guilty of fraud and corruption.

FISK & HATCH
New York City banking house. Bankrupted by the panic of 1873.

FITZHUGH, HENRY M.
Secretary to the "Independent Reformers" of 1860, who were responsible for the election of George William Brown as Mayor of Baltimore. He purchased a one-third interest in the *Exchange* newspaper in 1859.

Florida, C.S.S.
Screw steamer purchased for the Confederate navy in England in 1862. Commerce raider in the West Indies and the South Atlantic under the command of John N. Maffitt; also commanded by Joseph Nicholas Barney. Captured in October 1864.

FOOTE, HENRY STUART (1804–1880)
Mississippi Senator, 1847–1852; Governor of Mississippi, 1852–1854. Moved to Tennessee and served in the Confederate Congress from that state.

FORD, JOHN THOMPSON (1829–1894)
Baltimorean, partner in the Old Holliday Street Theater, 1856–1874, as well as several other area theaters and Ford's Theater in

Washington, D. C. Ford's Theater in Baltimore was built after the war and stood until the 1960s.

FORD, ROBERT (d. 1884)
Leonardtown, St. Marys County, Maryland attorney. Associate Judge of the 7th Judicial Circuit, 1867–1882.

FORREST, NATHAN BEDFORD (1821–1877)
Tennessee planter and businessman. Entered the Confederate army as a private. An outstanding cavalryman, he rose to Brigadier General by 1862; was a Lieutenant General by the end of the war. Returned to planting and became involved in railroading after the war.

FORT DELAWARE (Delaware)
Federal prison on Pea Patch Island in the Delaware River south of Wilmington near the present entrance of the Chesapeake and Delaware Canal.

FORT FISHER (North Carolina)
Confederate fort at the mouth of the Cape Fear River guarding Wilmington, North Carolina. Not captured until January 1865.

FORT JOHNSON (South Carolina)
Confederate fortification (there had been a fort there since 1776) off James Island in Charleston Harbor opposite Fort Sumter.

FORT LAFAYETTE (New York)
Federal prison in New York Harbor.

FORT ST. PHILIP (Louisiana)
A brick and stone sod-covered fortification of 52 guns on the north side of the Mississippi River below New Orleans. Together with Fort Jackson across the river, Fort St. Philip effectively controlled the river approach to New Orleans from the Gulf. During the night of April 23–24, 1862, Union naval forces under Admiral David G. Farragut fought their way past these forts and arrived off New Orleans on April 25th. The forts surrendered April 28, 1862, and the occupation of New Orleans under Major General Benjamin Butler was completed by May 1, 1862.

FORT WARREN (Massachusetts)
Federal prison in Boston Harbor.

FORTRESS MONROE (Virginia)
Fortification held in Union hands on Old Point Comfort, it commanded the entrance to Hampton Roads and controlled Chesapeake Bay shipping.

FOSTER, JOHN GRAY (1823–1874)
U.S. Military Academy, 1846; Corps of Engineers. Commanded troops in Annapolis, Maryland to December 1861. Brigadier

General, later Major General of Volunteers. Commander, Department of North Carolina, 1863, then the Department of Virginia and North Carolina to November 1863. He later commanded the Department of Ohio and the Department of the South.

FOX, AUGUST H. LANE
Captain in the Grenadier Guards, commissioned 1857.

FRANKLIN, JANE (1792–1875)
Widow of Sir John Franklin (d. 1847), the Arctic explorer, she fitted out five ships to search for her husband between 1850 and 1857.

FRANKLIN, WILLIAM BUEL (1823–1903)
U.S. Military Academy, 1843; Corps of Engineers. Promoted to Brigadier General in 1861, he held various commands in the Virginia and Maryland theater. He was captured in Maryland by Harry Gilmor on July 11, 1864, but escaped the next day. He retired from the army in 1866.

FRASER, TRENHOLM & COMPANY (Liverpool)
Liverpool shippers and brokers who acted as Confederate financial agents throughout the war. George A. Trenholm was the Charleston, South Carolina, partner (he was also a member of John Fraser & Co. of Charleston). Charles K. Prioleau was the resident partner in Liverpool.

FREDERICK (Maryland)
County seat of Frederick County and a principal western Maryland city. It is located approximately 40 miles west of Baltimore and 40 miles northwest of Washington, D.C.

FRÉMONT, JESSIE BENTON (1824–1902)
Daughter of Thomas Hart Benton and wife of John Charles Frémont.

FRÉMONT, JOHN CHARLES (1813–1880)
Joined the U.S. Army in 1838. Republican candidate for president in 1856. Appointed Major General of Volunteers in 1861; he commanded the Western Department. Transferred to the Mountain Department, he was relieved of command in June 1862.

FRICK, MARY SLOAN, Mrs. William Frick (d. 1865)
Widow of Baltimore Judge William Frick and mother of William Frederick Frick.

FRICK, WILLIAM FREDERICK (1817–1905)
Son of Judge William Frick of Baltimore. Attorney, Harvard graduate, he was a commercial and corporation lawyer. He married Ann Elizabeth Swann, resided on Lexington Street in Baltimore, and had an estate, "Hilltop," in Baltimore County near Irvington on the Frederick Turnpike.

FROUDE, JAMES ANTHONY (1818–1894)
English novelist and historian, editor of *Fraser's Magazine,* 1860–1874. He was married to Charlotte Maria Grenfell.

GALLENGA, ANTONIO CARLO NAPOLEONE (1810–1895)
Writer, lecturer, correspondent for the *London Times,* he had lived in North America in the late 1830s, and returned to report conditions in 1863. From there he went to Italy with the French army, and in 1865 to Denmark.

GAREY, HENRY FAITHFUL (1821–1892)
Baltimorean; delegate to the 1867 Constitutional Convention; elected to the Baltimore City Supreme Bench and served on the Court of Common Pleas from 1867 to 1877.

GARNET, HENRY HIGHLAND (1815–1882)
Born a slave in Kent County, Maryland, he escaped and became a Presbyterian clergyman and active antislavery spokesman in Washington, D.C. In the 1880s he was named Minister to Liberia.

GARRETT, JOHN WORK (1820–1884)
Baltimore banker and president of the Baltimore and Ohio Railroad, 1858–1884. During the war he supported the Union and saved the railroad from confiscation. In the postwar period he led the reestablishment of economic links with the South. His residence was on Mount Vernon Place, and his country home was "Montebello," at Harford and Hillen Roads.

GARRICK CLUB (London)
Club made up of literary men and actors, founded in 1831 and located at 13–15 Garrick Street, Covent Garden, London.

GATCHELL, WILLIAM H. (1799–1878)
Baltimore Police Commissioner, 1860–1861; arrested and imprisoned in Fort Warren, he later became a judge of the Appeal Tax Court.

GENET, HENRY W.
New York attorney, president of the New York City Board of Alderman in 1861; member of the Union Defence Committee of New York City.

GERMAN COTILLION CLUB (Baltimore)
Social club organized in 1856. Among the original members were William Wilkins Glenn, John Lee Carroll, C. Oliver O'Donnell, and other members of the city's social elite.

GILES, WILLIAM F. (1807–1879)
Maryland attorney and Judge of the Fourth U.S. District Court, 1853–1879. He succeeded John Glenn, the father of William Wilkins Glenn, in that position.

GILL, GEORGE M. (1803–1887)
Baltimore City attorney and politician. Member of the Reform Convention of 1859, the Anti-Registry Law Convention of 1866, and the Constitutional Convention of 1867. His residence was 227 North Charles Street.

GILMOR, ARTHUR (d. 1865)
Private in Company E, Second Maryland Cavalry. Harry Gilmor was the unit's Lieutenant Colonel.

GILMOR, ELLEN WARD, Mrs. Robert Gilmor (1811–1880)
Wife of shipping magnate Robert Gilmor III. Resident of "Glen Ellen," in the Loch Raven area of Baltimore County. Her sons Meredith and Harry Gilmor served in the Confederate army.

GILMOR, HARRY (1838–1883)
Son of Baltimore Countians Robert and Ellen Ward Gilmor, born at "Glen Ellen." Joined the Confederate army in 1861 and was given command of Company F, 12th Virginia Cavalry, then command of the 2nd Maryland Cavalry. Captured September 1862; exchanged February 1863. In July 1864 under the command of General Jubal Early he raided into Maryland and burned the railroad bridge over the Gunpowder River at Magnolia in Harford County. He was captured in February 1865, and released at the end of the war.

GILMOR, ROBERT (1808–1875)
Baltimorean and head of the import house of Robert Gilmor and Son, he was the grandson of the company's founder and had been attaché to the American mission in Paris. He was married to Ellen Ward Gilmor, was the father of Harry and Robert Gilmor, and resided at "Glen Ellen" in Baltimore County.

GILMOR, ROBERT (1833–1906)
Baltimore attorney, son of Robert and Ellen Ward Gilmor, he became a judge of the Baltimore City Circuit Court in the postwar period.

GILMOR, WILLIAM (1843–1896)
Nephew of Robert and cousin of Harry Gilmor, he served as a private in Company C, 2nd Maryland Cavalry, and settled in Baltimore after the war.

GILMOR HOUSE (Baltimore)
Hotel on Monument Square and Court House Lane, this 150-room building was later known as the St. Clair and then Guy's Hotel. It was closed during the war and used as a prison by the Provost Marshall.

GILMORE, JAMES ROBERTS (1822–1903)
Boston author and cotton merchant, he visited Jefferson Davis in

July 1864 with Colonel James F. Jaquess in an attempt to reconcile the warring states.

GITTINGS, CHARLOTTE CARTER RITCHIE, Mrs. John Sterett Gittings (1822–1895)

Wife of John S. Gittings (1794–1879), founder of the Baltimore banking house of John S. Gittings & Co. Her home was on Mount Vernon Place. She was from Richmond, Virginia, and one of her sisters married into the Harrison family of Lower Brandon, Virginia.

"GLEN ELLEN" (Baltimore County, Maryland)
Gothic revival house built in 1833 for Robert Gilmor of Baltimore. Located on the Gunpowder River, it adjoined "Hampton," on property that is now part of the Loch Raven Reservoir.

GLENN, ANNE (1823–1893)
Wife of Baltimore attorney John Glenn, sister of Ellen Smith (Mrs. William Wilkins) Glenn, she was from Philadelphia. In March 1863 she was delivered of her first child, John Glenn, Jr. (1863–1938).

GLENN, ANNE ((1823–1893)
Daughter of Baltimore Judge John Glenn and his wife, Henrietta Wilkins Glenn, and eldest sister of William Wilkins Glenn.

GLENN, ELIAS (1840–1868)
Baltimorean, second son of William Carson Glenn and first cousin of William Wilkins Glenn; during the war he served as a private in Company C, 1st Maryland Cavalry.

GLENN, HENRIETTA—see HARWOOD, HENRIETTA GLENN

GLENN, HENRIETTA WILKINS (1804–1891)
Baltimorean, widow of Judge John Glenn, and mother of William Wilkins Glenn, Anne Glenn, John Glenn, Henrietta Glenn Harwood, Mary Glenn, and Lucy Glenn. As a beneficiary of the Judge's estate she owned the house at Charles and Madison Streets in Baltimore and "Hilton" in Catonsville.

GLENN, JAMES SEWALL (c. 1836–c. 1916)
Eldest son of William Carson Glenn and Martha Sewall Glenn and first cousin of William Wilkins Glenn. During the war he was a private in Company E, 1st Maryland Cavalry.

GLENN, JOHN (1829–1896)
Baltimore attorney and realtor, son of Judge John Glenn and Henrietta Wilkins Glenn, and brother of William Wilkins Glenn. His law practice was limited because of progressive blindness. In 1859 he married Anna Smith of Philadelphia and moved to "Hilton" in Catonsville.

GLENN, JOHN MARK (1858–1950)
Son of William Wilkins Glenn and Ellen Smith Glenn. He became

an attorney in 1882 and was known for his participation in municipal reform in Baltimore City. From 1907 to 1947 he was Director and a trustee of the Russell Sage Foundation.

GLENN, LUCY (1842–1919)
Youngest child of Judge John Glenn and Henrietta Wilkins Glenn, and sister of William Wilkins Glenn. In 1879 she became the second wife of Colonel Ambrose R. H. Ranson.

GLENN, MARY (1828–1882)
Daughter of Judge John Glenn and Henrietta Wilkins Glenn and sister of William Wilkins Glenn. She was active in the Episcopal church and died unmarried.

GLENN, WILLIAM LINDSAY (1863–1930)
Second son and youngest child of William Wilkins Glenn and Ellen Smith Glenn. His mother died within a month of his birth and he was raised by his aunt, Anne Glenn. Educated in Harford County, Maryland, by the Rev. William Brand, he was ordained an Episcopal clergyman in 1902 and became the rector of St. Mary's Church in Emmorton, Harford County, Maryland.

GLYN, Sir JOHN PLUMPTRE CARR (1837–1912)
Rose to the rank of Lieutenant General and Colonel commanding the Rifle Brigade, and was Knight Commander of the Bath.

GOLDSBOROUGH, HENRY HOLLYDAY (1817–1899)
Easton, Talbot County, Maryland attorney, member of the House of Delegates in 1858, and president of the state senate in 1860. Maryland State Comptroller, 1863, elected on an antislavery ticket. A member of the 1864 Maryland Constitutional Convention, Lincoln elector, 1864; judge of the 11th Judicial Circuit, 1864–1867.

GORDON, GEORGE T.
Former member of the Coldstream Guards; entered the Confederate army and became a lieutenant colonel on J. E. B. Stuart's staff and later on that of Ambrose Powell Hill. As a member of the 4th Brigade, 34th North Carolina Infantry, he was wounded at Gettysburg.

GORDON-IVES, GORDON MAYNARD (1837–1907)
From Bentwood Hall and Gaston Grange in Hampshire, England; a captain in the Coldstream Guards, he later became Deputy-Lieutenant of Essex.

GRAHAM, LAWRENCE PIKE (1815–1905)
Entered the U.S. army in 1837; cavalry. Brigadier General of Volunteers, 1861; in 1862 he was in charge of cavalry instruction near Annapolis. He continued in the army after the war.

GREELEY, HORACE (1811–1872)

Founder and editor of the *New York Tribune*. Lincoln supporter, he advocated immediate emancipation. In 1866 he signed the bail bond of Jefferson Davis. In 1868 he ran for president against Grant.

GREEN, CHARLES

British subject, resident of Virginia, he was a business partner of Andrew Low in England. He was arrested and imprisoned in Fort Warren because of the activities of his brother-in-law, John Low. A wealthy merchant, he had subscribed to the cotton loan.

GREEN, THOMAS

Washington, D.C. resident, originally from Virginia, he owned the Van Ness Mansion in Washington and reputedly was involved in Confederate underground activities, including a plot to kidnap President Lincoln. His wife, Anne Corbin Lomax, was a sister of General Lindsay Lunsford Lomax and Virginia (Jenny) Lindsay Lomax.

GREENHOW, ROSE O'NEAL (1818–1864)

Washington, D.C. widow, confidante of presidents and senators, she became a leading Confederate agent. Arrested and imprisoned in Old Capitol Prison in Washington in 1862, she was banished South on her release. She went to England, running the blockade from Wilmington, North Carolina, lived abroad for a period, and was drowned while attempting to return through the blockade off Wilmington on October 1, 1864.

GRENFELL, GEORGE ST. LEGER (c. 1807–1868)

British soldier of fortune, he entered the Confederate army and served as adjutant general to John Hunt Morgan. A member of the landed Grenfell family, he had been in a French lancer regiment, then went to Tangier. He entered the service of Abu-el-kader and served for four years, then went into Turkish service in the Crimea. Captured while attempting to free prisoners at Camp Douglas, he was imprisoned in Fort Jefferson in the Dry Tortugas and died attempting to escape.

GREGORY, WILLIAM HENRY (b. 1817)

Member of Parliament from Dublin City, 1842–1847. Losing a reelection bid, he ran as a Conservative from Galway County, Ireland, in 1857 and served to 1872. In 1871 he was a member of the Privy Council, and later was appointed governor of Ceylon.

GUNTHER, CHARLES GODFREY (1822–1885)

New York City merchant and head of C. G. Gunther, furriers, he ran as a Democrat for mayor in 1861. Winning the position in 1863, he served as Mayor of New York to 1867 and was noted for his opposition to Boss Tweed.

GUTHRIE, JAMES (1792–1869)
Louisville, Kentucky, railroad promoter and president of the Louisville and Nashville Railroad. He served as Secretary of the Treasury under Pearce, 1853–1857. A member of the 1861 Peace Convention, he also attended the Virginia Peace Convention and the Kentucky Border Conference. A Democrat and McClellan supporter, he was elected to the U.S. Senate in 1865 and served to 1868.

GUY'S HOTEL (Baltimore)
Hotel on the northeast corner of Monument Square and Fayette Street, it was torn down in 1881 to make way for the U.S. Post Office.

GWIN, WILLIAM MCKENDREE (1805–1885)
Tennessee attorney and physician, his father had been a close friend of President Andrew Jackson. He practiced medicine in Mississippi until 1833, then served in Congress from 1840 to 1842. Moving to California in 1849, he entered politics in the San Francisco area, and in 1850 was elected to the U.S. Senate. Arrested in November 1861, he was sent to Fort Lafayette, but was released in December. Going south, he made his way through the blockade and was in Paris from 1863 to June 1864, where he promoted the settlement of Southerners in Sonora, Mexico. He returned to the United States in 1865 but did not resume his political career. He was married to Mary Bell and had four children.

GWINN, CHARLES JOHN MORRIS (1822–1894)
Baltimore attorney and politician, he represented Baltimore in the House of Delegates in 1849. He was a delegate to the 1850 Constitutional Convention. In 1876 he became Attorney General of Maryland under Governor John Lee Carroll and served to 1880. He was married to Matilda Elizabeth Bowie Johnson, daughter of Reverdy Johnson.

HAGERSTOWN (Maryland)
County seat of Washington County in western Maryland, located in the Hagerstown Valley between South Mountain and the Alleghenies, c. 25 miles west of Frederick, Maryland.

HAGNER, ALEXANDER BURTON (1826–post-1905)
Annapolis, Maryland, attorney and president of the Telegraph Company. He represented Annapolis in the House of Delegates in 1854, supported the election of Bell and Everet in 1860. Moving to Washington, D.C., he became Judge of the Supreme Bench and served from 1879 to 1903. He was married to Louisa Harrison of Elk Hill, Virginia.

HALL, THOMAS WHITE (fl. 1830–1880s)
Baltimore publisher and organizer of the Baltimore Board of Trade in 1836. He was an owner of the *Exchange* from 1858–1861, then published the *South* from April to September 1861. Arrested, he was imprisoned at Fort Warren. From 1867 to 1869 he edited *Southern Society* and in 1876 in conjunction with Severn Teackle Wallis, published the Baltimore *Clipper*. In 1881 he became City Solicitor.

HALLECK, HENRY WAGER (1815–1872)
U.S. Military Academy, 1839; he was appointed Major General in the army and served as Lincoln's military adviser and General in Chief. He was a better administrator than field general and was not at all popular in Washington.

HALPINE, CHARLES GRAHAM (1829–1868)
Irish author and former Washington correspondent for the *New York Times,* he served on General David Hunter's staff at Hilton Head, South Carolina, and wrote war articles under the name of "Miles O'Reilly."

HAMBLETON, SAMUEL (1812–1886)
Easton, Maryland, attorney; he represented Talbot County in the state senate, 1844–1850; House of Delegates, 1853. President of the Chesapeake and Ohio Canal, 1853–1854; member of Congress, 1869–1873.

HAMNER, JAMES GARLAND (1798–1887)
Baltimore Presbyterian clergyman, his residence was 135 St. Paul Street. He had been pastor of the Fifth Presbyterian Church in Charlottesville, Virginia, but apparently was not formally attached to a Baltimore congregation.

"HAMPTON" (Baltimore County)
Home of the Ridgely family, located north of Towson, Maryland, off the Dulaney Valley Road, about eight miles from the center of Baltimore City. The house, built in the 1790s for Charles Ridgely, is now a National Historic Site.

HAMPTON, WADE (1818–1902)
South Carolina planter, became Brigadier General in the Confederate cavalry; promoted to Major General in 1863 and Lieutenant General in 1864, he commanded the cavalry of the Army of Northern Virginia. In 1876 he became governor of South Carolina, and from 1879 to 1891 served in the U.S. Senate.

HANCOCK, WINFIELD SCOTT (1824–1886)
U.S. Military Academy, 1840; serving in the infantry in 1861, he was appointed Brigadier General in the Volunteers. From 1861 to 1864 he served in most of the major campaigns in the east.

In 1864 he became a Brigadier General in the U.S. Army and ran for president as a Democrat in 1880.

HANK, JOHN WILLIAM FLETCHER (1826–1881)
Baltimore physician, he received his degree from the University of Pennsylvania. From 1856 to 1862 he served as Vaccine Physician for the city.

HANNEGAN, EDWARD ALLEN (1807–1859)
Indiana attorney; U.S. Senator, 1843–1849. Appointed Minister to Prussia, he served 1849–1850. On returning to the U.S. he moved to St. Louis, Missouri, and resumed his law practice.

HARDCASTLE, JOHN
Baltimore commercial agent c. 1860–1864.

HARDEE, WILLIAM JOSEPH (1815–1873)
U.S. Military Academy, 1838; resigned 1861 and was commissioned a Brigadier General in the Confederate army. He was appointed Lieutenant General in 1862 and in 1864 commanded the Department of South Carolina, Georgia, and Florida.

HARDY, JOHN W.
Baltimorean; law clerk of William Wilkins Glenn.

HARLAN, JAMES (1820–1899)
Secretary of the Interior under Andrew Johnson, 1865 to July, 1866.

HARMAN, MICHAEL G.
Resident of Staunton, Virginia; called "Colonel"; vice-president of the National Express and Transportation Company.

HARPER, EMILY LOUISA (1812–1892)
Youngest daughter of Robert Goodloe Harper and Catharine Carroll, daughter of Charles Carroll of Carrollton; therefore a first cousin of John Lee Carroll.

HARPERS FERRY (Virginia)
Railroad center at the junction of the Shenandoah and Potomac Rivers. The Baltimore and Ohio Railroad crossed the river here, one branch continuing up the river and the other heading for Winchester, Virginia. The Chesapeake and Ohio Canal went along the north bank of the Potomac River. The town was also the site of a key Federal arsenal.

HARRIS, BENJAMIN GWINN (1805–1895)
St. Marys County, Maryland, attorney and Democratic politician. Member of the House of Delegates, 1833, 1836. Served in Congress, 1863–1867. He was tried by a court-martial in Washington, D.C. in May 1865, for having sheltered two Confederate soldiers and was sentenced to prison. President Johnson commuted the sentence.

HARRIS, JAMES EDWARD, 3rd Earl of Malmesbury (1807–1889)
Member of Parliament from Wilton, elected 1841. Secretary of State for Foreign Affairs, 1852, 1858–1859; Lord Privy Seal, 1866–1868, 1874–1876.

HARRISON, BURTON NORVELLE (1838–1904)
Attorney, he received his early education from the Rev. William Brand in Harford County, Maryland. Graduating from Yale as a Phi Beta Kappa, he taught mathematics at the University of Mississippi. Came to Richmond as personal secretary to Jefferson Davis. Met and married novelist Constance Cary (1846–1920), niece of Wilson Miles Cary, who visited Richmond with her cousins Hetty and Jennie Cary. After the war he practiced law in New York City.

HARRISON, MRS. DABNEY CARR
Widow of Captain Dabney Carr Harrison, son of the Rev. Peyton Harrison, a member of the 56th Virginia Volunteers, who entered the Confederate service on September 23, 1861, and was killed leading a charge at Fort Donelson on February 16, 1862.

HARRISON, HUGH T. (1809–1872)
Episcopal clergyman; rector of St. John's in Ellicott City, Maryland, and later of the Elkridge Episcopal Church. Married Eliza Thompson of Alexandria, Virginia.

HARRISON, PEYTON (1801–1886)
Baltimore Presbyterian clergyman, he resided at 90 Read Street. During the war he was without a congregation. His wife was Jane Carey Carr (1808–1859). Three sons died in the Confederate service : Lieutenant Randolph Harrison of the 15th Virginia Infantry, Lieutenant Peyton Randolph Harrison of the 2nd Virginia Infantry, and Captain Dabney Carr Harrison.

HARRISON, WILLIAM GILPIN (1802–1883)
Baltimore businessman and politician. President of the Baltimore and Ohio Railroad, 1853–1856. Ran for Congress unsuccessfully against Henry Winter Davis; member of the House of Delegates from Baltimore City, 1861. Became a director of the Canton Company and the Franklin Bank, and president of the Union Railroad Company. Married Anne E. Ross of Frederick, Maryland.

HARTINGTON, Lord
Spencer Compton Cavendish (1833–1908), Marquis of Hartington and 8th Duke of Devonshire, compiled an enviable political, governmental and social career. A liberal supporter of Lord Palmerston, he was elected a member of Parliament for North Lancashire in 1857. During the Civil War, following his visit to America, he served as a junior lord of the admiralty and an under-secretary at the war office.

HARTRANFT, JOHN FREDERICK (1830–1889)
Colonel in the 4th Pennsylvania, 1861, he became a Brigadier General of Volunteers in 1864. Medal of Honor winner for bravery at 1st Bull Run, he was Mrs. Suratt's jailer at Washington, D.C. Republican governor of Pennsylvania, 1872–1878.

HARWOOD, HENRIETTA GLENN, Mrs. James Kemp (1833–1885)
Daughter of Judge John Glenn and Henrietta Wilkins Glenn, and sister of William Wilkins Glenn. She was married to naval officer James Kemp Harwood. In July 1862, her eldest child, Henry, was born.

HARWOOD, JAMES KEMP (1824–1895)
Baltimorean; officer in the U.S. Navy; served as purser on Perry's Japan expedition, 1853–1854. Married Henrietta Glenn in 1859. Resigned from the U.S. Navy to join the Confederate naval service in 1861.

HELM, CHARLES JOHN (1817–1868)
Kentuckian, he served as U.S. commercial agent at St. Thomas from 1853 to 1858, when he became consul general at Havana. Resigned in 1861 and became Confederate agent at Havana, where he supervised the shipment of arms to the South. Went to Toronto, Canada, after the war. His wife was Louise A. Whistler.

HETH, HENRY (1825–1899)
U.S. Military Academy, 1847; resigned 1861 and was commissioned a captain in the Confederate army. Promoted to Brigadier General in 1862, he was with Bragg in Kentucky before being transferred to the Army of Northern Virginia.

HEWETT, WILLIAM NATHAN WRIGHTE (b. 1834)
Entered the Royal Navy in 1847 and was promoted to captain in 1862. As commander of the *Rinaldo,* he cruised in American waters during the early 1860s. In 1873 he became Commodore of the Cape of Good Hope, and later commanded Queen Victoria's yacht. He was honored as a Knight Commander of the Bath.

HICKS, THOMAS HOLLIDAY (1798–1865)
Dorchester County, Maryland, politician and American (Know Nothing) Party, governor of Maryland from 1858–1862. A strong unionist, he resisted all attempts to effect the secession of Maryland and followed a course of neutrality. Appointed to the U.S. Senate in 1862, he was elected to the U.S. Senate in 1864.

HILL, AMBROSE POWELL (1825–1865)
U.S. Military Academy, 1847; resigned in 1861 and was commissioned colonel in the Confederate army. Promoted to Brigadier General in 1862, he became a Major General later that year and a Lieutenant General in 1863, serving mainly in Virginia. He was married to a sister of John Hunt Morgan.

HILLEN, EMILY O'DONNELL, Mrs. Solomon Hillen (1818–1888)
Wife of Solomon Hillen (1810–1873), former mayor of Baltimore, she was a daughter of Columbus O'Donnell. The Hillens resided at 62 Franklin Street.

"HILTON" (Baltimore County)
Summer home of the Glenn family, located on a 1,000-acre estate off Rolling Road in Catonsville, Maryland, seven miles west of Baltimore near the Frederick Road. It is now owned in part by the Catonsville Community College.

HINKS, CHARLES D. (c. 1817–1863)
Baltimore flour merchant, and member of the first Baltimore City Board of Police Commissioners.

HOBART, JOHN H.
Episcopal clergyman, became rector of Grace Church in Baltimore, having come from New York in November 1863. In January 1867 he left for a parish in New Jersey.

HOFFMAN, GILBERT L.
Baltimore merchant and partner in Hoffman and Deford, dealers in hides, leather, and oil.

HOFFMAN, LOUISA (1831–1884)
Baltimore social leader, daughter of Samuel and Louisa Gilmor Hoffman; she served as a member of the committee directing the Baltimore Southern Relief Association Fair, 1866. In 1868 she married Alexander Riach.

HOFFMAN, LOUISA AIREY GILMOR, Mrs. Samuel Hoffman (1805–1879)
Baltimore social leader, active in various charities, including the Southern Relief Association Fair.

HOFFMAN, WILLIAM HENRY (1814–1865)
Baltimore merchant and partner of Hoffman, Burneston & Co. dry goods jobbers.

HOLCOMBE, JAMES PHILEMON (1820–1873)
Virginia attorney and author, he served in the Confederate Congress from 1862–1864. Appointed special commissioner to the North American colonies of Great Britain, he joined with Clement Claiborne Clay and Jacob Thompson to work for anti-administration movements in the North. He retired to "Bellvue" in Bedford County, Virginia.

HOLT, JOSEPH (1807–1894)
Kentucky Democratic politician; Postmaster General, then Secretary of War in the Buchanan administration. Appointed Judge Advocate General in 1862, he was responsible for the trials of Lincoln's assassins.

HOOD, JOHN BELL (1831–1879)
U.S. Military Academy, 1853; resigned, 1861. Commissioned a 1st lieutenant in the Confederate army, he became a Brigadier General in 1862 and by 1864 had risen to General in command of the Army of Tennessee. After the war he became a commission merchant in New Orleans.

HOOKER, JOSEPH (1814–1879)
U.S. Military Academy, 1837; Brigadier General of Volunteers, 1861. Commanded the Army of the Potomac from January to June 1863, then went West. At the end of the war he was in command of the Northern Department.

HOPKINS, FRANCIS
New York merchant and partner in Francis Hopkins & Bro., glass manufacturers at 198 Pearl Street. His residence was at Fort Hamilton.

HORN, JOHN WATT (1834–1897)
Prince Georges County, Maryland, resident and Warden of the Maryland Penitentiary. His wife, Elizabeth Wilkins, was related to Henrietta Wilkins Glenn.

HOWARD, ANN HARRISON (1824–1919)
Baltimorean; nicknamed "Nannie"; she was the daughter of James and Catherine Howard and niece of Francis Key Howard. She lived on West Read Street.

HOWARD, BENJAMIN CHEW (1791–1872)
Baltimore politician, son of John Eager Howard, he represented Maryland in Congress as a Democrat from 1829–1833, and 1835–1839, during which time he chaired the Committee on Foreign Relations. A general in the State Militia, he attended the Peace Convention in Washington, D.C. in 1861. He was married to Jane Grant Gilmor, and his residence was "Roslyn" on the Old Court Road near Pikesville in Baltimore County.

HOWARD, CHARLES (1802–1869)
President of the first Baltimore Board of Police Commissioners, he was arrested and sent to Fort Warren in July 1861. A grandson of John Eager Howard and a son-in-law of Francis Scott Key, he took a leading role in civic affairs. His son, Major Charles Howard, served in the Confederate army. He was married to Elizabeth Phoebe Key.

HOWARD, CHARLES (1830–c. 1870s)
Son of Baltimore Police Commissioner Charles Howard and brother of Francis Key Howard, he was a major in the Confederate army and served on the staff of General Arnold Elzey.

HOWARD, EDWARD LLOYD (1837–1881)
Surgeon in the Confederate army from 1861 to 1865 with the rank of major. After the war he edited the *Baltimore Medical Journal* (1870–1881) and was president of the State Board of Health, 1876–1881.

HOWARD, ELIZABETH PHOEBE KEY, Mrs. Charles Howard (1804–1897)
Wife of Baltimore Police Commissioner Charles Howard, she was a daughter of Francis Scott Key and a niece of Roger Brooke Taney.

HOWARD, FRANCIS KEY (1826–1872)
Baltimore attorney and editor, he was the son of Charles and Elizabeth Key Howard and the grandson of Francis Scott Key. He was a partner with William Wilkins Glenn in the *Exchange* and *Gazette* newspapers, retaining interest in the latter until his death. He was married to Lydia Hollingsworth Morris, the sister of Nancy Morris Davis. Howard recounted his prison experiences in *Fourteen Months in American Bastiles* (Baltimore, 1863).

HOWARD, GEORGE
A 1st Lieutenant in Company "K," 1st Virginia Cavalry (Confederate), George Howard was captured September 11, 1861, at the battle of Lewinsville, Virginia. Subsequently exchanged, he was elected 1st Lieutenant of Company "C," 1st Battalion, Maryland Cavalry, on August 4, 1862, and was promoted to captain on August 25, 1863. The designation of this unit was changed to 1st Regiment, Maryland Cavalry on January 19, 1864. Captain Howard was captured again at Pollard's Farm (Hall's Shop), Hanover County, Virginia, on May 27, 1864. Confined at Point Lookout, Maryland, and Fort Delaware, he was exchanged December 3, 1864, gave a Parole of Honor at Manchester, Virginia, April 30, 1865, and took the oath of allegiance from Colonel John Woolley at 230 North Eutaw Street, Baltimore, on May 19, 1865.

HOWARD, GEORGE WILLIAM FREDERICK, 7th Earl of Carlisle (1802–1864)
Member of Parliament, he had been a Privy Councilor in the 1830s. From 1859–1864 he was Lord Lieutenant of Ireland.

HOWARD, JAMES (1832–1910)
Marylander, he served in the U.S. Army from 1857–1861, then in the Confederate army from 1861–1865. In 1884 he was appointed Adjutant General of Maryland.

HOWARD, JANE GILMOR (1827–post-1900)
Daughter of Benjamin Chew and Jane Gilmor Howard, she lived with her parents at "Roslyn" in Baltimore County.

HOWARD, JANE GRANT GILMOR, Mrs. Benjamin Chew Howard (1800–1890)
Daughter of William Gilmor and sister of Robert Gilmor (d. 1875) she married into one of Baltimore's wealthiest families.

HOWARD, OLIVER OTIS (1830–1909)
U.S. Military Academy, 1854; resigned in 1861 to become a colonel in the 3rd Maine regiment. Serving mainly in the East, he rose to the rank of Major General. In 1865 he was placed in charge of Freedman's Bureau and earned the nickname "Christian Soldier." He later became Superintendent of West Point.

HUNT, JESSE (1793–1872)
Baltimore politician and mayor, 1832–1835, he was president of the Eutaw Savings Bank in the 1860s.

HUNTER, DAVID (1802–1886)
U.S. Military Academy, 1822; named Brigadier General of Volunteers in 1861, he served in the West until 1863 when he took over the Department of West Virginia. From February 1865, he served on various court-martial boards, and presided over the commission that tried Lincoln's assassins.

HUNTER, ROBERT MERCER TALIFERRO (1809–1887)
Virginia Democratic Representative, 1837–1843, 1845–1847, he entered the U.S. Senate in 1847 and served until he resigned in 1861. He became Confederate Secretary of State, 1861–1862, then Senator from Virginia, 1862–1865. He served as a Peace Commissioner at Hampton Roads in 1865. In 1877 he became Virginia State Treasurer.

HURLBERT, WILLIAM HENRY (1827–1895)
New York journalist, he resigned from the *New York Times* in 1861 and went South, where he was arrested as a Union spy. He escaped and returned to reporting for the New York *World*. He supported McClellan for the presidency in 1864. From 1876 to 1883 he was editor-in-chief of the New York *World*.

HUTCHINS, SARAH BRIEN, Mrs. Thomas T. Hutchins
Baltimorean, wife of Thomas Talbot Hutchins. There is no record of her arrest in the *Official Records*.

HUTCHINS, THOMAS TALBOT (1830–1890)
Baltimore attorney, member of the House of Delegates from Baltimore County, 1854–1855. He was married to Sarah Brien Hutchins and lived at 132 Park Avenue.

Illustrated London News (England)
Illustrated weekly paper, founded in 1842, published during the 1860s by Sir William Ingram. Charles Mackay was editor from 1848 to 1859; Francis C. Vizitelly worked as an illustrator and war correspondent.

IMBODEN, JOHN DANIEL (1823–1895)
Staunton, Virginia, attorney and organizer of the Staunton Artill-

ery. Appointed Brigadier General in the Confederate army in 1862; served mainly in Virginia and West Virginia.

INGERSOLL, CHARLES (c. 1806–post-1870)
Attorney; pro-Southern Democrat. He lived at 412 Walnut Street in Philadelphia. Authored a play, *Women Rule,* in the late 1860s. He was the son of Charles Jared Ingersoll (1782–1862), the attorney, Congressman, author, and historian under whom William Wilkins Glenn's father, Judge John Glenn, had studied law.

INGERSOLL, EDWARD (1817–1893)
Philadelphia attorney, son of Charles Jared Ingersoll. An authority on constitutional law, he sympathized with the South and was arrested for criticism of the war.

IVES, GORDON—see GORDON-IVES, GORDON MAYNARD

IZARD, ROSETTA ELLA PINCKNEY, Mrs. Ralph Stead Izard (d. 1872)
Resident of Prince Georges Parish, South Carolina, and widow of Ralph Stead Izard of "Weymouth Plantation." She was related by marriage to the Pringle family of "White House Plantation," near Georgetown, South Carolina. One of her daughters married William DeCoursey May of Baltimore.

JACKSON, THOMAS JONATHAN (1824–1863)
U.S. Military Academy, 1846; resigned to teach at Virginia Military Institute. Appointed a colonel in the Confederate army, he was promoted to Major General in 1861 and died as a result of a wound on May 10, 1863.

JAQUESS, JAMES FRAZIER (1819–1898)
A Methodist clergyman, he became a colonel in the 73rd Illinois Volunteers. In 1863 he went South on a peace mission. On a similar mission in 1864, he saw Jefferson Davis and was told that the only acceptable peace terms were complete independence for the Confederacy.

JAMES, THOMAS C. (1824–1888)
Warden of the Baltimore City Jail.

JENKINS, EDWARD F. (1817–1891)
Baltimore hardware and saddle merchant. His home was in Baltimore County near Baldwin on the Harford Road.

JEROME, LEONARD W. (c. 1818–1891)
New York attorney, broker, part owner of the *New York Times,* and president of the Jerome Park Railway Company (1881), in partnership with Edward S. and Eugene W. Jerome. Called the "King of Wall Street," at one time he was reputed to be worth $10,000,000. A founder of the American Jockey Club, his interests included horses, yachts, and music. He married Clara Hall and

moved from Brooklyn to 25 East 26th Street (at Madison Avenue) in 1859. The "Jerome House," a New York landmark, was noted for its small adjoining theater, which seated 600 people. A Unionist during the Civil War, Jerome gave generously to the Southern Relief Fair afterwards. His daughter, Jennie Jerome, was the mother of Sir Winston Churchill.

JOHNSON, REVERDY (1796–1876)
Baltimore attorney; U.S. Senator, 1845–1849, he resigned to enter Zachary Taylor's cabinet. A leading Maryland Whig, he was active in local politics and was an intimate friend as well as a business associate of William Wilkins Glenn's father, Judge John Glenn, and Glenn's uncle, David Maulden Perine. Johnson was a Peace Commissioner in 1861, and was again elected to the U.S. Senate in 1863. He resigned in 1868 to become Minister to England, holding that post until 1869.

JOHNSTON, ALBERT SIDNEY (1803–1862)
U.S. Military Academy, 1826; resigned in 1861 and was made a General in the Confederate army, serving in the West. He died at Shiloh.

JOHNSTON, HENRY ELLIOTT (d. 1884)
Baltimore banker, partner in Johnston Brothers. He was arrested September 24, 1861, and charged with being disloyal and with conveying contraband letters and information to and from the insurrectionary states. He was released from imprisonment on October 8, 1861.

JOHNSTON, JOSEPH EGGLESTON (1807–1891)
U.S. Military Academy, 1829; resigned in 1861 and was named Brigadier General in the Confederate army; appointed General, 1861, in command of the Department of the Potomac; later commanded the Department of the West and the Army of Tennessee. After the war his business activities included railroading and insurance. He was a member of Congress from Virginia, 1879–1881. He was married to Baltimorean Lydia McLane (1822–188?), third daughter of Louis McLane.

JOHNSTON, JOSHUA LEE (1830–1904)
Partner in the Baltimore banking firm of Johnston Brothers.

JOHNSTON BROTHERS & CO. (Baltimore)
Baltimore banking house located at 198 West Baltimore Street. The partners were Joshua Lee Johnston, Thomas D. Johnston, and Henry Elliott Johnston.

JONES, ISAAC DASHIELL (1806–1893)
Somerset County member of the House of Delegates, and owner of considerable land in Somerset and Worcester counties on the Eastern Shore of Maryland.

JUNIOR UNITED SERVICE CLUB (London)

General military club for officers in the army and navy, it was founded in 1827 and in 1953 became a part of the United Service Club. Its quarters were at Charles Street and Waterloo Place, London.

Jura

British screw steamer, built at Dumbarton in 1861. Owned by Fife & Co. of Glasgow, it sailed between that port and Nova Scotia. Her arrival at Cape Race is noted in the Baltimore *Sun* of June 1, 1863.

KANE, GEORGE P. (1820–1878)

President of the Merchants Exchange Company of Baltimore, and Marshall of the Baltimore City Police in 1861. His residence was on the York Road near the first toll gate.

KEAN, CHARLES (1811–1868)

English actor, son of actor Edmund Kean and his wife, Mary Chambers. In 1865 he and his wife Ellen Tree toured the United States.

KEAN, ELLEN TREE (1806–1880)

English Shakespearean actress, married to actor Charles Kean.

KEENE, JOHN HENRY (1836–1914)

Baltimore County attorney and active Democrat from Lauraville near Glencoe, Maryland.

KELLY & PIET (Baltimore)

Baltimore publishing house of Michael J. Kelly and John B. Piet at 174 West Baltimore Street. Also publishers of the *Catholic Mirror.*

KEMBLE, MARY W.

Resident of New York City, she was living at 142 East 18th Street in 1881. She was connected with the New York committee of the Southern Relief Fair.

KENLY, JOHN REESE (1818–1891)

Baltimore attorney, joined the U.S. army in 1861 as a colonel in the Maryland Infantry. Taken prisoner, he was exchanged and soon promoted to Brigadier General of the Maryland Brigade. He was active in western Maryland in 1863, and in 1864 was transferred to the command of the District of the Eastern Shore at Salisbury, Maryland.

KENNEDY, JOHN JAMES

Captain in the Royal Navy, in 1861 he was commander of H.B.M.S. *Desperate*. In command of H.B.M.S. *Challenger,* he was at Hampton Roads in June of 1863.

KENNER, DUNCAN FARRAR (1813–1887)
Louisiana sugar planter, he was a representative in the Confederate Congress and Chairman of the Committee on Ways and Means. He had traveled in England and France, spoke French, and was a close friend of John Slidell. In 1865 he became Minister Plenipotentiary to England and France. After the war he returned to sugar planting and local politics.

KERR, CHARLES GOLDSBOROUGH (1832–1898)
Easton, Maryland, attorney, he had read law in the Baltimore firm of Brown and Brune. In 1858 he was one of the founding partners of the *Daily Exchange*. He married Ella Johnson, daughter of Reverdy Johnson, in 1867 and moved to Baltimore City. In 1879 he became Baltimore City States Attorney.

KEYES, ERASMUS DARWIN (1810–1895)
U.S. Military Academy, 1832; Brigadier General of Volunteers, 1861. He commanded the IV Corps of the Army of the Potomac and resigned in May 1864.

KILBOURN, ELBRIDGE GERRY (d. 1873)
Howard County, Maryland, attorney. Member of the House of Delegates, he was arrested in 1861 and imprisoned in Fort Lafayette and Fort Warren.

KYLE, ADAM BARCLAY (1784–1869)
Baltimore merchant and partner in Dinsmore & Kyle, flour, grocery, and commission merchants. His sons were Adam Barclay Kyle, Jr., and David Kyle. The former was apparently the son killed in the election riot.

LAIRD, JOHN & SONS (England)
Shipbuilders at Birkenhead, England. John Laird was a member of Parliament. The Confederate government's order of several iron-clad rams from this firm contributed to strained relations with the United States.

LASCELLES, CAROLINE GEORGIANA, Mrs. William Lascelles (d. 1881)
Daughter of the 6th Earl of Carlisle, she was married to William S. S. Lascelles, son of the Earl of Harewood and a Member of Parliament. They lived at Bute House in London.

LATROBE, JOHN HAZELHURST BONIVEL (1803–1891)
Baltimore attorney, counsel to the Baltimore and Ohio Railroad, he acted as defense attorney for Police Commissioners Valiant and Young.

LAWLEY, BEILBY RICHARD, 2nd Baron Wenlock (1818–1880)
Member of Parliament from Pontefract, 1851–1852; Lord Lieutenant of East Riding of York, 1864–1880. His seat was "Escrick Park" in York.

LAWLEY, FRANCIS (1825–1901)

English journalist, brother of Lord Wenlock, he had been Gladstone's private secretary in the 1850s. From 1854 to 1863 he was in the U.S. as correspondent for the London *Times*. An author as well as a journalist, he was writing a biography of Judah P. Benjamin at the time of his death.

LAWRENCE, GEORGE ALFRED (1827–1876)

British author and novelist, he is known for *Guy Livingston* (1857) and *Border and Bastile* (1863).

LAWRENCE, SAMUEL BETTS

Officer in the New York State Militia in 1861, he was a captain in 1862, and in 1864, with the rank of lieutenant colonel, was Assistant Adjutant General, Headquarters, 8th Army Corps. He resigned in 1865.

LEAMINGTON (England)

Spa in central Warwick on the Leam River. Popular for its mineral springs, it was the "Royal Leamington Spa" after the 1838 visit by Princess (later Queen) Victoria.

LEARY, THOMAS H. H. (b. 1816)

Baltimorean; cashier of the depository, Custom House. All available evidence points to him as being the brother of City Councilman Cornelius Lawrence Ludlow Leary.

LEBANON SPRINGS (New York)

Thermal springs near the town of New Lebanon in Columbia County, New York.

LEE, FITZHUGH (1835–1905)

U.S. Military Academy, 1856; resigned to join the Confederate army, he was appointed Brigadier General in 1862. In the postwar period he entered Virginia politics and became governor in 1885. He served in the Spanish-American War and retired as a Brigadier General in the U.S. Army. He was a nephew of Robert E. Lee and James M. Mason.

LEE, GEORGE WASHINGTON CUSTIS (1832–1913)

Eldest son of Robert E. Lee; U.S. Military Academy, 1854; resigned; in 1861 he was an aide-de-camp to Jefferson Davis, and was promoted through the ranks to Major General in 1864. He became a professor of engineering at Virginia Military Institute, and then succeeded his father as president of Washington and Lee.

LEE, MARY ANNA CUSTIS, Mrs. Robert Edward Lee (1808–1873)

Descendant of Martha Washington and heiress to "Arlington," where she married Robert E. Lee in 1831.

LEE, MILDRED CHILDE (1846–1905)

Daughter of Robert E. and Mary Custis Lee, she was the youngest of the Lee daughters and, like her sisters, never married.

LEE, ROBERT EDWARD (1807–1870)
U.S. Military Academy, 1829. Married Mary Anna Custis in 1831 and followed a varied career in the army engineers. He was in Baltimore from 1848–1852 to supervise the building of Fort Carroll in the harbor. His sister, Ann Lee, was married in 1826 to Baltimorean William Louis Marshall. Marshall, an attorney and judge, was a former minister and Unionist who became a major and Judge Advocate in the U.S. Army. The Marshalls lived at 29 McColloh Street and their son, Louis Henry Marshall, was a captain in the U.S. Army. Lee resigned from the U.S. Army in 1861 to command Virginia troops; in 1862 he was General of the Confederate army and commander of the Army of Northern Virginia. In the postwar period he became president of Washington College in Lexington, Virginia. Lee's Baltimore connections were many. Samuel H. Tagart (1811–1892), law partner of Isaac Steele, and his wife, Sallie Mifflin Large of Philadelphia, were his hosts during two postwar visits to the city. His first visit, from April 21 to May 1, 1869, was to promote the (Shenandoah) Valley Railroad Co., in which he was associated with Michael G. Harman. At this time he also visited his cousin, Mrs. Samuel George of Ellicott City, and Washington Peter, a cousin of Mrs. Lee, who lived at "Linwood" on Church Road in Ellicott City. Lee visited Baltimore again from July 1 to July 14, 1870, consulting physician Dr. Thomas Hepburn Buckler for diagnosis and treatment. Staying with the Tagarts, he again visited Washington Peter at "Linwood," as well as a cousin, Charles Henry Carter, at "Goodwood," near Ellicott City. Local tradition also says that at some unspecified time Lee visited "Lilburn," the home of a friend, Richard Henry Hazelhurst, and his second wife, Elizabeth Virginia McKim. "Lilburn" was located on College Avenue near St. Paul's Church in Ellicott City, Maryland. Lee's personal correspondence with members of the Glenn family indicate a friendship going back to prewar days and visits to the Glenn estate, "Hilton."

LEE, STEPHEN STATES (1812–1892)
Baltimore iron and coal merchant, he was originally from South Carolina. His home was "Mount Herbert" in Catonsville, Maryland.

LEE, WILLIAM HENRY FITZHUGH ("Rooney") (1837–1891)
Second son of Robert E. Lee, he inherited "White House" plantation from his grandfather Custis. A cavalry officer in the Confederate army, he was appointed Brigadier General in 1862 and rose to Major General by 1864. After the war he became active in Virginia politics.

LEFFERTS, MARSHALL
Colonel of the 7th New York Infantry, his command consisted of

1,050 men who left New York on April 19, 1861, and arrived at Annapolis, Maryland, on April 22nd. In 1863 he commanded the 7th New York City Guards at Frederick, Maryland, and acted as military governor of that city. He and his unit were then sent to New York and were involved in the draft riots.

LEHR, ROBERT (1819–1887)

Baltimore commission merchant, partner in Boniger Brothers and vice-consul of Portugal. He lived on Read Street between Charles and Cathedral streets.

LEMMON, GEORGE (1835–1905)

Baltimorean, son of the owner of Merchant's Shot Works. During the war he served in the Confederate army on the staff of General James Archer. He was captured at Gettysburg and imprisoned at Johnson's Island until his parole in the fall of 1864.

LENOX (Massachusetts)

Town in Berkshire County, near Pittsfield, Massachusetts, some ten miles from Lebanon Springs, New York.

LEONARDTOWN (Maryland)

County seat of St. Marys County in southern Maryland, it is located on Breton Bay off the Potomac River.

LESLIE, WILLIAM 10th Laird of Warthill (c. 1813–1880)

Member of Parliament from Aberdeen, 1861–1866. He also served as a member of the Queen's Bodyguard for Scotland and of the Royal Company of Archers.

LETCHER, JOHN (1813–1884)

Lexington, Virginia, attorney and Democratic politician, he was Governor of Virginia, 1859–1865. He had opposed secession until the President's call for troops after Fort Sumter. At the end of the war he was imprisoned in Old Capitol Prison. In the 1870s he returned to state politics.

LEWIS, MARTIN (d. 1870)

Baltimore stockbroker and consul for Denmark, Norway and Sweden. His residence was 302 West Madison Avenue.

"LEXINGTON" (Baltimore County)

Estate of George Williamson in the 1860s and 1870s, located on the Reisterstown Road near Pikesville, approximately six miles from Baltimore.

LIBBY PRISON (Richmond)

Confederate prison on the James River, formerly a warehouse of Libby & Sons, ship chandlers. Officers were imprisoned there.

LINCOLN, ABRAHAM (1809–1865)

Republican President of the United States, 1861–1865.

LINCOLN, MARY TODD, Mrs. Abraham Lincoln (1818–1882)

Wife of President Lincoln, she came from Kentucky.

LINCOLN, ROBERT TODD (1843–1926)
Son of President Abraham Lincoln, he served on Grant's staff after his 1864 graduation from Harvard.

LOCH FOYLE (Ireland)
Loch on the northern coast of Ireland, serving the port of Derry (Londonderry).

LOMAX, MATTIE VIRGINIA SARAH LINDSAY ("Jenny")
Baltimorean, daughter of Elizabeth Lindsay Lomax, sister of General Lindsay Lunsford Lomax and Mrs. Thomas Green. She is the probable author of *Old Capitol and Its Inmates* (1867).

LOMAX, LUNSFORD LINDSAY (1835–1913)
U.S. Military Academy, 1856; resigning in 1861, he was commissioned in the Virginia State Militia. He was appointed Brigadier General in 1863 and Major General in 1864. Two of his sisters were Virginia Lindsay Lomax and Mrs. Thomas Green.

"LONGLEAT" (England)
Seat of the Marquis of Bath in Warminster, Wiltshire, built 1550 and 1580.

LONGSTREET, JAMES (1821–1904)
U.S. Military Academy, 1842; resigned, 1861, and was commissioned Brigadier General in the Confederate army. Promoted to Major General, he held various commands in the Army of Northern Virginia.

LOVELL, MANSFIELD (1822–1884)
U.S. Military Academy, 1842; resigned and became deputy street commissioner in New York City. Joining the Confederate army in 1861, he rose to the rank of Major General and was commander of New Orleans, which he surrendered to Union forces in April 1862.

LOW, ANDREW (1813–1886)
Savannah, Georgia, banker of English origin, he had been connected with Peabody, Baring & Co. in England. He had gone to Enland in July 1861, on business, and was arrested in November 1861, in Cincinnati, Ohio, on his way home. Two daughters had been left in school in Brighton, England. His wealth, position as a commissioner for the cotton loan in Georgia, and his partnership with Charles Green made him a suspicious character. His second wife, Mary Stiles, was a daughter of William Henry Stiles of Georgia, chargé d'affaires to Austria in 1849.

LOWE, ENOCH LOUIS (1820–1892)
Frederick County, Maryland, attorney and Democratic politician, he was governor from 1851–1854. He supported Buchanan in 1856 and Breckinridge in 1860. During the war he lived in Virginia,

then Georgia, and afterwards moved to New York, where he practiced law.

LYELL, Sir CHARLES (1797–1875)
British botanist, geologist, professor, and author of *The Geological Evidences for the Antiquity of Man* (1863).

LYONS, HENRY J.
New York City commission merchant at 133 Water Street. His home in 1854 was 108 West 20th Street.

LYONS, JAMES (1801–1882)
Richmond attorney and member of the Confederate Congress. In 1862 he was chairman of the commission on Public Buildings. His sister married Henry Wise.

LYONS, RICHARD BICKERTON, Earl Lyons (1817–1887)
British minister to the United States, 1858–1865.

MCCAUSLAND, JOHN (1836–1927)
Graduate of, and professor at, Virginia Military Institute; joined the Confederate army and was active in Virginia and Kentucky. Promoted to Brigadier General, 1864. He participated in the Chambersburg, Pennsylvania raid of July 30, 1864.

MCCLELLAN, GEORGE B. (1826–1885)
U.S. Military Academy, 1846; Major General in command of the Army of the Potomac, then Commander in Chief of the army. Presidential candidate of the Democratic party in 1864.

MCCULLOCH, HUGH (1808–1895)
Comptroller of the Currency, 1863–1865; Secretary of the Treasury, 1865–1869.

MCDOWELL, IRVIN (1818–1885)
U.S. Military Academy, 1838; Brigadier General, 1861; he commanded troops south of the Potomac. Later a Corps commander in the Army of the Potomac and the Army of Virginia. In 1864 he was placed in command of the Department of the Pacific.

MCHENRY, GEORGE
Possibly the brother of James McHenry (1817–1891) of Philadelphia. George McHenry was a Southern sympathizer, while James McHenry favored the North. (See *The Journal of Benjamin Moran,* ed. Sarah Agnes Wallace & Frances Elma Gillespie, University of Chicago Press, 1948.)

MCHENRY, JAMES HOWARD (1820–1888)
Baltimore attorney, grandson of Secretary of War James McHenry, he was raised by his uncle Charles Howard. He had traveled widely in Europe and Latin America. His first wife was Sara Nicholas Cary, daughter of Wilson Miles Cary. He lived at "Sudbrooke," near Pikesville, in Baltimore County.

MCHENRY, RAMSAY (1814–1878)
Harford County, Maryland, attorney, he was a graduate of the University of Virginia. In 1850 he was a delegate from Harford County to the Maryland Constitutional Convention. He never married, and lived at "Monmouth" on Winters Run near Emmorton with his mother, Sophia Hall McHenry. During the war he was imprisoned several times for disloyalty. Both he and his mother are buried at St. Mary's Episcopal Church Cemetery, Emmorton.

MCKAY, CHARLES (1814–1889)
British journalist, he had been with the *Illustrated London News* from 1848 to 1859, lecturing in the U.S. and Canada in 1857 and 1858. From March 1862, to December 1865, he was the New York correspondent of the *London Times,* writing under the alias of C. Smith Montgomery from Staten Island. He was the author of *Life and Liberty in America* (1859).

MCKIM, MARY R. (b. 1838)
Daughter of John S. McKim, "gentleman," of Baltimore. The McKims lived on Belvidere Street near North Avenue.

MCLANE, ALLAN (c. 1820–c. 1890)
Son of Louis McLane of Baltimore, he was a midshipman in the navy during the Mexican War. He was married to Maria C. Bache of Washington, D.C.

MCLANE, JAMES LATIMER (1834–1923)
Baltimore attorney, son of Louis McLane, he had read law under Severn Teackle Wallis. He served in the state legislature in 1879 and was president of the Western Maryland Railroad.

MCLANE, LOUIS (1786–1857)
Delaware attorney, Representative, then U.S. Senator, he was Minister to England from 1829–1831, Secretary of the Treasury, 1831–1833, Secretary of State, 1833–1834, Minister to England, 1845–1846. He was president of the Baltimore and Ohio Railroad from 1837–1847. He was married to Catherine Mary Milligan, daughter of Robert Milligan. His sons were Allan, James Latimer, and Robert M. McLane. His daughter, Lydia, married General Joseph E. Johnston.

MCLANE, ROBERT M. (1815–1898)
Baltimore attorney and son of Louis McLane. Active in the Democratic party; member of the House of Delegates, 1845–1846, he served in Congress from 1847–1851. From 1853 to 1856 he was Minister to China, and from 1857 to 1860 was emissary to Mexico. He was one of Maryland's Peace Commissioners in 1861, and from 1884 to 1885 was Governor of Maryland, resigning to become Minister to France.

MCMAHON, JOHN VAN LEAR (1800–1871)
Cumberland, Maryland, attorney and historian. Moved to Baltimore in 1825 and became a leading Jacksonian Democrat. His partial loss of eyesight caused his retirement in 1857 and in 1863 he moved back to Cumberland.

MCPHAIL, JAMES LAWRENCE (c. 1816–1874)
Baltimore hatter and politician. Appointed Provost Marshall in July 1861. From 1867–1868 he represented the 9th and 10th wards in the Second Branch of the Baltimore City Council.

MCRAE, DUNCAN KIRKLAND (1820–1888)
North Carolina attorney, U.S. Consul to Paris, 1853–1857. He was one of the Confederate Cotton Loan Commissioners and was sent to Europe by Governor Vance to find a market for North Carolina state bonds. He returned home in 1864 to edit the Raleigh, North Carolina, *Confederate.* After the war he practiced law in Memphis, Tennessee.

MACE, ALFRED (c. 1828–1873)
Baltimore City politician; lottery vendor in 1850; from 1859 to 1860 he served in the First Branch of the City Council. In 1863 he was appointed clerk of the Superior Court, while serving as secretary to Mayor John Lee Chapman. He was a charter stockholder in the Union Railroad in 1866.

MADDOX, GEORGE FREDERICK (1826–1871)
Leonardtown, St. Marys County, Maryland attorney. From 1867 to 1871 he was a Democratic state senator from St. Marys County.

MAGNOLIA (Maryland)
Harford County station of the Philadelphia, Wilmington and Baltimore Railroad, 18 miles north of Baltimore.

MAGRAW, HENRY S.
Pennsylvania Democrat with southern and secessionist sympathies, he had formerly been a resident of Maryland. From 1859 to 1861 he had a transportation contract with the U.S. government. After the First Battle of Bull Run, at the request of the family of Colonel James Cameron (Union), Magraw attempted to recover the Colonel's body for burial. He and Kentucky pro-Southern newspaper editor Arnold Harris were arrested by the Confederates as spies and were held until October 1861.

MAGRAW, ROBERT MITCHELL (1811–1866)
Baltimore attorney and iron merchant, he was connected with the firm of Rogers and Magraw. He later became president of the Baltimore and Susquehanna Railroad.

MALET, Sir EDWARD BALDWIN (1837–1908)
British diplomat stationed in Washington, D.C. during the 1860s. Following the war his next post was in Paris.

MALLORY, STEPHEN RUSSELL (1813–1873)
Confederate Secretary of the Navy, 1861–1865, he was a proponent of an ironclad navy. He was arrested in 1865 and imprisoned at Fort Lafayette until 1866. He then retired to Florida.

MALMSBURY, Earl of—see HARRIS, JAMES HOWARD

MANN, AMBROSE DUDLEY (1801–1889)
Virginia attorney and diplomat, he was consul to Bremen, 1842–1849; agent in Hungry, 1849; and agent in Switzerland, 1850. From 1853 to 1856 he was Assistant Secretary of State. Joining the Confederacy, he went to Europe with James Mason and John Slidell. He was in London in 1861, and from 1862 to 1865, in Belgium. After the war he remained in Europe.

MARBLE, MANTON MALONE (1835–1917)
Night editor of the New York *World,* 1860; by 1862 he was editor and publisher. He opposed the Lincoln administration and the suppression of the press, and in 1864 was arrested and accused of publishing a false call to arms.

MARSHALL, CHARLES (1830–1902)
Baltimore attorney in 1861, he had come from Warrenton in Fauquier County, Virginia. A colonel in the Confederate army, he was Lee's aide-de-camp and military secretary.

MARTIN, JAMES L.
Easton, Maryland, attorney.

MARTIN, ROBERT NICOLS (1798–1870)
Western Maryland attorney, from 1845–1851 he was chief judge of the Frederick, Washington and Alleghany circuit. In 1851 he became a Justice of the Maryland Supreme Court and from 1861 to 1867 was a Judge of the Superior Court of Baltimore City. He was also a law professor at the University of Maryland.

MARYLAND INSTITUTE HALL (Baltimore)
Erected in 1851 over the Marsh or Central Market on Baltimore Street, it served as the lecture hall of the Maryland Institute of Mechanic Arts (founded 1849).

MASON, JAMES MURRAY (1798–1871)
Virginia attorney and Congressman, he served in the U.S. Senate, 1847–1861. A Confederate Commissioner to Great Britain and France, he was captured on the British steamship *Trent* on November 8, 1861, and held until January 2, 1862. He was in London at 24 Upper Seymour Street until 1865, and in Canada from 1865 to 1868.

MASON, JOHN THOMPSON (1815–1873)
Hagerstown, Maryland, attorney, he was Collector of the Port of Baltimore, 1857–1861. He had served in Congress as a Democrat,

1841–1843, and from 1851–1857 he was a Judge of the Maryland Court of Appeals.

MATAMORAS (Mexico)
City at the mouth of the Rio Grande opposite Brownsville, Texas.

MAURY, MATTHEW FONTAINE (1806–1873)
Virginia naval officer, resigned from the U.S. Navy in 1861 and joined the Confederate navy. He was in charge of harbor defenses to the fall of 1862 when he was sent to England as a special agent. After the war he promoted the colonization of ex-Confederates in Mexico.

MAXIMILIAN (Ferdinand Maximilian Joseph) (1832–1867)
The ill-fated Emperor of Mexico, his rule was engineered by Napoleon III. Arriving in Mexico in May 1864, he reigned with the support of the French army. When this support was withdrawn in March 1867, he was forced to abdicate and was executed in June 1867.

MAXWELL, JAMES W. (born c. 1835)
Cecil County, Maryland, attorney and member of the House of Delegates. Arrested with other members of the House in 1861.

MAY, HENRY (1816–1866)
Baltimore Democratic Congressman, 1853–1855, 1861–1863. He was arrested by the Federal government in 1861, along with members of the State Legislature.

MEADE, GEORGE GORDON (1815–1872)
U.S. Military Academy, 1835; a Brigadier General of Volunteers, 1861; commanded the Army of the Potomac, 1863–1865.

MEDARY, SAMUEL (1801–1864)
Democratic politician; Governor of Minnesota Territory, 1857–1858; Governor of Kansas Territory, 1858–1860. He became editor of the anti-administration *Crisis* in 1861 and supported Clement Vallandigham and George McClellan.

MEDIA (Pennsylvania)
Town ten miles south of Philadelphia on the Philadelphia and Baltimore Central Railroad. It was noted for its educational institutions, Brook Hall School for ladies and a boys' boarding school.

MEMMINGER, CHRISTOPHER GUSTAVUS (1803–1888)
South Carolina legislator and Confederate Secretary of the Treasury, 1861–1864.

MERCER, RICHARD SPRIGG (1823–1873)
Anne Arundel County, Maryland, gentleman farmer, son of John Mercer and Mary Scott Swann, a sister of Governor Thomas Swann. The Mercers lived at "Cedar Park" on West River. He was married to Emily Coxe of Philadelphia.

MEREDITH, EMMA CLAUDINE (1819–1909)
Daughter of Jonathan Meredith of Baltimore.

MEREDITH, JOHNATHAN (1785–1872)
Baltimore attorney and counsel for the Catoctin and Antietam Iron Furnaces. His residence was 43 Franklin Street. He was married to Hannah Haslett.

MERRICK, WILLIAM MATTHEWS (1818–1889)
Associate Justice of the District of Columbia court, 1854–1863; Judge of the District of Columbia Supreme Court, 1885–1889.

MERRYMAN, JOHN (1824–1881)
Baltimore County farmer; lieutenant of the Baltimore County Horse Guards; in charge of burning railroad bridge approaches north of Baltimore on the orders of Governor Thomas Hicks in April 1861. He was arrested and his case resulted in the famous judicial proceedings *Ex Parte Merryman.* In 1870 he was Treasurer of the State of Maryland, and in 1874 represented Baltimore County in the House of Delegates. His estate, "Hayfields," was two miles north of Cockeysville. He was married to Ann Louisa Gittings.

MEYER, MEYER
Baltimore drygoods merchant at 143 N. Gay Street.

MIDDLETON, HENRY A. (1797–1876)
South Carolina author and owner of "Middleton Place" on the Ashley River west of Charleston. His father was a signer of the Declaration of Independence from South Carolina.

MILES, NELSON APPLETON (1839–1925)
Lieutenant in the Massachusetts 22nd Infantry, he rose to the rank of Brigadier General of Volunteers by 1864; Major General in 1865. He was the jailor of Jefferson Davis at Fortress Monroe.

MILLER, DECATUR HOWARD (1820–1890)
Member of the Baltimore City Council, Second Branch, 1861–1863. He later became a director of the Baltimore and Ohio Railroad and of the Consolidated Coal Company.

MILLER, OLIVER (1824–1892)
Anne Arundel County, Maryland, politician, member of the 1864 Constitutional Convention; member of the House of Delegates, 1865–1867, where he served as speaker. He became Judge of the 5th Judicial Circuit in 1866.

MILLIGAN, GEORGE B.
Baltimore County farmer and politician, he ran unsuccessfully for Congress in 1878. His residence was "Glencairn" off Valley Road in the Brooklandwood area.

MINNIGERODE, CHARLES
Episcopal clergyman, rector of St. Paul's Church in Richmond, Virginia where Jefferson Davis became a communicant in the spring of 1862.

MITCHELL, JOHN K.
Commander in the United States Navy, he resigned in 1861 and became a Commander in the Confederate States Navy; promoted to Captain, 1863. He commanded the James River Squadron, 1864–1865.

MOALE, RICHARD H.
Baltimore attorney, his residence was 60 Franklin Street. He was a member of the Maryland Club.

MONCK, CHARLES STANLEY, 4th Viscount Monck (1819–1894)
Governor General of the Province of Canada and Governor General of British North America, 1861–1866. In 1867 he became the first Governor General of the Dominion of Canada, retiring in 1868.

MONTAGU-STUART-WORTLEY-MACKENZIE, EDWARD MONTAGU STUART, 3rd Baron and 1st Earl Wharncliffe (1827–1899)
Son of Member of Parliament from West Yorkshire, he married Lady Susan Charlotte Lascelles in 1855.

MONTHOLON, C. C. F., Marquis de
Son of General Charles de Montholon, he served as French Minister to Mexico in 1863, Consul General to New York from c. 1863 to 1865, and Minister to the U.S., 1865–1867.

MOREHEAD, CHARLES SLAUGHTER (1802–1868)
Governor of Kentucky, 1855–1859, he was a Unionist and a Peace Commissioner in 1861. He was arrested and confined in Fort Warren, 1861–1862, when he left for Europe, remaining there until 1865.

MORGAN, CHARLTON (d. post-1909)
Younger brother of General John Hunt Morgan and member of Morgan's Raiders.

MORGAN, JOHN HUNT (1825–1864)
Commander of the Confederate Cavalry unit known as Morgan's Raiders, he was a Brigadier General from 1862. Captured in 1863, he escaped from the Ohio State Penitentiary. He was killed near Greenville, Tennessee, in September 1864.

MORRIS, CHARLES MANIGAULT (d. 1895)
Entering the U.S. Navy in 1835, he sailed with Perry to Japan. Resigned, 1861, he joined the Confederate navy, commanding the *Huntress*. He went to Europe to oversee the construction of rams, taking command of the *Florida* in January 1864.

MORRIS, JOHN THOMAS (1827–1912)
Baltimore attorney, partner of Hinkley & Morris. He was a member of the City Council in 1852. From 1862 to 1870 he was a member of the Board of Fire Commissioners. In 1869 he became President of the Board of School Commissioners, serving to 1882.

MORRIS, MOWBRAY (1819–1874)
British barrister, business manager of the *London Times,* 1848–1873. He was married to John Delane's daughter, Emily Delane.

MORRIS, THOMAS JOHN (1837–1912)
Baltimore attorney, he lived at 213 Madison Avenue and was a partner in Hinkley & Morris and a first cousin of John Thomas Morris. In 1879 he became Federal District Judge of the 4th Judicial Circuit and served to 1912. He married Sarah Pinkerton Cushing in 1867.

MORRIS, THOMAS HOLLINGSWORTH (1817–1872)
Attorney; man of letters. Union Club president. He married Mary Johnson, the daughter of Reverdy Johnson.

MORRIS, WILLIAM W. (c. 1801–1865)
U.S. Military Academy, 1820; Colonel, later Brigadier General and Major General, he was a commandant of Fort McHenry, and died there December 11, 1865.

MORRISSEY, JOHN (1831–1878)
New York prizefighter, he gave up fights in the late 1850s to become a New York politician, serving in Congress, 1867–1871.

MOSBY, JOHN SINGLETON (1833–1916)
Confederate cavalry officer and member of the staff of J. E. B. Stuart.

MOWELL, PETER (1806–1869)
Operated an iron works in the Canton area of Baltimore. Died at the family estate of "Glencoe" in Baltimore County.

MUDD, SAMUEL (1833–1883)
Bryantown, Charles County, Maryland, physician who set the broken leg of John Wilkes Booth. He was convicted of conspiracy, imprisoned at Fort Jefferson, and pardoned in 1869.

MUIR, Sir WILLIAM MURE (1818–1885)
British army physician and surgeon. Inspector General, 1861–1873. In 1868 he was named honorary physician to the Queen.

MULFORD, JOHN E.
Captain of the 3rd New York Infantry, appointed May 1861. Stationed at Fort McHenry in 1861. Became Federal agent for the exchange of prisoners. Breveted Brigadier General of Volunteers in July 1864. Mustered out in 1866.

MULLEN, REBECCA WILLIAMSON, Mrs. John Mullen (d. 1898)
Daughter of David and Maria Williamson of Baltimore.

MUNFORD, THOMAS T. (1831–c. 191?)
Graduate of Virginia Military Institute and colonel in the 2nd Virginia Cavalry after Bull Run, he rose to the rank of Brigadier General in 1864.

"MUNTHAM COURT" (England)
Seat of the Marquis of Bath near Worthing, Sussex.

NATIONAL EXPRESS AND TRANSPORTATION COMPANY
Virginia corporation, chartered in 1865, terminated operations in 1919. The corporate officers were largely ex-Confederates. Joseph E. Johnston was president to 1866; Michael Harman was master of transportation. William Wilkins Glenn held stock in the company at the time of his death in 1876.

NEILSON, ALBERT
Owner of "Priestford" in Harford County, Maryland, between Churchville and Poplar Grove. "Mrs. Neilson" of Harford County is probably his wife.

NEILSON, WILLIAM H. (1827–1893)
One of the owners of the *Maryland News Sheet*; from 1863 to May 1864 he published the *Evening Transcript* in Baltimore.

NEVILLE, EDWARD
Captain in the Scots Fusilier Guards, he was commissioned in November 1856. He was a cousin of Francis Lawley. His London address was 5 John Street, Berkeley Square.

NEW YORK HOTEL (New York City)
A large and fashionable hotel on Broadway at the corner of Washington Place.

NEW YORK *Daily News*
New York City newspaper published from 1855.

NEW YORK *Tribune*
New York City daily newspaper, founded in 1841. Horace Greeley was editor.

NORRIS, WILLIAM HENRY (1810–1890)
Baltimore attorney, he became a Colonel and Judge Advocate in the Confederate army. His address was 92 West Monument St. His wife, Mary Norris, was arrested on March 3, 1862, for disloyal correspondence with Zarvona (Richard Thomas).

NORTH, DUDLEY
Lieutenant of the 47th Lancashire Infantry, commissioned October 1861.

NORTH POINT (Baltimore)

Point at the mouth of the Patapsco River where it enters the Chesapeake Bay, c. 12 miles southeast of Baltimore. The site of a battle during the war of 1812, it is now the location of Fort Howard Veterans Hospital.

NORTHEY, FRANCIS VERNON (1836–1879)

Musketry instructor of the 60th Foot, British army, from 1858, he was promoted to Major in 1873, which rank he held until his death.

NORTHROP, LUCIUS BEILINGER (1811–1894)

U.S. Military Academy, 1831; retired 1839. Commissioned Colonel and Commissary General in the Confederate army, he became a Brigadier General in 1864. He was dismissed in February 1865.

Nova Scotian

Wilson & Co., Liverpool, steamer, built in Quebec in 1860, broken up in 1863.

O'CONOR, CHARLES (1804–1884)

New York City attorney and politician, he was a leading peace advocate. He signed the bail bond of Jefferson Davis and served as his senior defense counsel. He was an anti-Tammany political leader in the postwar period. He was also noted for his fine library.

O'DONNELL, COLUMBUS (1797–1873)

Baltimorean; a director of the Baltimore and Ohio Railroad, and president of the First National Bank and the Gas Company (1831–1870). His daughter, Emily, was married to Solomon Hillen.

OLD CAPITOL PRISON (Washington, D.C.)

Federal prison for civilians, it had temporarily housed the Congress after the Capitol was burned by the British in 1814. It was demolished after the war.

ORD, EDWARD OTHO CRESAP (1818–1883)

U.S. Military Academy, 1839; from Cumberland, Maryland. Brigadier General of Volunteers, he was involved in the defense of Washington. From 1862 to 1863 he was with the Army of Tennessee, and was on Grant's staff at Vicksburg. He came East with Grant, remaining in the army after the war.

O'REILLY, MILES—see HALPINE, CHARLES GRAHAM

OULD, ROBERT O. (1820–19?)

Washington, D.C. attorney in 1861, he was an 1842 graduate of William and Mary College and a classmate of William Wilkins Glenn. From 1861 to 1862 he was Confederate Assistant Secretary of War. In July 1862 he was appointed chief of the Confederate Bureau of Exchange with the rank of Colonel.

OWEN, Sir RICHARD (1804–1892)
British naturalist and professor of comparative anatomy at the Royal College of Surgeons.

OXFORD (Pennsylvania)
Junction of the Philadelphia and Baltimore Central Railroad five miles north of the Maryland line.

PAKENHAM, WILLIAM LYGON, 4th Earl of Longford (1819–1887)
From County Longford, Ireland, he rose to the rank of General in the British army before succeeding to his brother's title in 1860. From 1866–1868 he served as Under Secretary of War.

PALMERSTON, VISCOUNT—see TEMPLE, HENRY JOHN, Viscount Palmerston

PATTERSON, ROBERT (1792–1881)
Son of Philadelphia Irish immigrants, he entered the Pennsylvania volunteers as a Major General in 1861, and commanded the Departments of Pennsylvania, Delaware, Maryland, and the District of Columbia. He was mustered out in July 1861.

PEARCE, JAMES ALFRED (1805–1862)
Eastern Shore, Maryland, attorney and politician, he had read law under Judge John Glenn. He was in the House of Representatives as a Whig, 1835–1839 and 1841–1843, and in the U.S. Senate as a Whig from 1843 to 1862.

PEGRAM, HETTY CARY, Mrs. John Pegram (1835–1892)
Daughter of Baltimorean Wilson Miles Cary, during the war she visited Richmond with her sister, Jenny Cary, and her cousin, Constance Cary. There Constance married Burton Norvelle Harrison, and Hetty, a redheaded beauty, married General John Pegram. She was widowed after three weeks of marriage when her husband was killed at Hatcher's Run on February 6, 1865. She returned to Baltimore and remarried after the war.

PEMBERTON, JOHN CLIFFORD (1814–1881)
U.S. Military Academy, 1837; resigned, 1861, and entered the Confederate army, rising to the rank of Major General in 1862 in command of the Departments of South Carolina, Georgia, and Florida. As a Lieutenant General, he was assigned in Mississippi and was involved in the surrender of Vicksburg.

PENDLETON, GEORGE HUNT (1825–1889)
Cincinnati, Ohio, Democratic politician and Congressman, 1857–1865. He ran as McClellan's Vice President in 1864, and was a delegate to the 1866 Loyalist Convention. From 1879–1885 he was in the U.S. Senate.

PERINE, ELIAS GLENN (1829–1922)
Son of David Maulden Perine and Mary Glenn, he was a first cousin of William Wilkins Glenn. He was an attorney after the

war, and in 1865 married Elizabeth Washington of "Mount Vernon," Virginia.

PERINE, ELIZABETH, Mrs. William Buchanan Perine
Daughter of Baltimore Judge Z. Collins Lee, she married William B. Perine in 1861 and was widowed in 1863. William B. Perine was the brother of Elias Glenn Perine.

PERINE, MARY GLENN (1822–1896)
Daughter of David Maulden Perine and Mary Glenn, she was a first cousin of William Wilkins Glenn.

PERRY, BENJAMIN FRANKLIN (1805–1886)
South Carolina attorney, judge, and editor of the *Southern Patriot*. In 1865 he became provisional governor of South Carolina, and in 1866 was a delegate to the National Union Convention.

PETTIGREW, JAMES JOHNSTON (1828–1863)
North Carolina attorney, he was a member of the North Carolina militia, and commanded Castle Pinckney in Charleston harbor. He became a Brigadier General in the Confederate army, and was mortally wounded in 1863 at Falling Waters.

"PETWORTH" (England)
Seat of George Wyndham, Baron Leconfield, in West Sussex. The estate was noted for its fine race horses, beautiful gardens, and luxurious dwelling.

PEYTON, HENRY E.
Colonel in the Confederate army and a member of the staff of Brigadier General John B. Gordon, he was with Lee at Appomattox.

PHILADELPHIA *Age*
Illustrated New Age, a Philadelphia daily started on March 25, 1863 and published until 1874.

PHILLIPS, LEWIS G.
Member of the Grenadier Guards, commissioned, 1859; a captain in the 1860s.

PHILLIPS, Mrs. PHILIP
Resident of New Orleans, imprisoned in Old Capitol Prison in 1861 with her two daughters. Arrested at various times in New Orleans for anti-Federal conduct, to wit : encouraging her children to spit at Federal soldiers, and displaying levity at the funeral of a Union officer.

PHILLIPS, WENDELL (1811–1884)
Massachusetts abolitionist clergyman and author, he was a member of the American Anti-Slavery Society.

PICKETT, JOHN T. (b. 1823)
Kentuckian, graduate of the U.S. Military Academy, and a cousin of General George Edward Pickett. He had served in the Hun-

garian army of Kossuth and was involved in the Cuba liberation movement of Narcissio Lopez. Appointed by Jefferson Davis as Secretary to the Peace Commission in 1861, he entered the Confederate foreign service and served as agent to Mexico, where he had prviously been consul at Vera Cruz (1856–1859). Declared *persona non grata,* he left in 1862. He became chief of staff to General John C. Breckinridge. At the end of the war he was in possession of the Great Seal of the Confederacy and most of the archives of the Confederate State Department, selling those records to the Federal government for $75,000.

PICKETT, GEORGE EDWARD (1825–1875)

U.S. Military Academy, 1846; resigned, 1861, and was commissioned a colonel in the Confederate army. Appointed Brigadier General in 1862, he rose to the rank of Major General in the Army of Northern Virginia. After Gettysburg he was in command of the Department of Virginia and North Carolina.

PIERREPONT, EDWARDS (1817–1892)

New York attorney and judge, he was a member of the Dix-Pierrepont Commission on State Prisoners, appointed in February 1862. In 1869 he became U.S. District Attorney for New York, and from 1875–1876 was Attorney General of the United States.

PIGGOTT, AARON SNOWDEN (1822–1869)

Baltimore chemist, he served as a surgeon in the Confederate army. After the war he was involved in mining in the South.

PINKNEY, CAMPBELL—see WHYTE, CAMPBELL PINKNEY

PISCATAWAY (Maryland)

Town in Prince Georges County, on Piscataway Creek, c. 13 miles south of Washington, D.C.

PITTS, CHARLES H. (1814–1864)

Baltimore City attorney and legislator. Arrested with other members of the House of Delegates in 1861 and imprisoned at Fort Warren.

POINT OF ROCKS (Virginia)

Located at the Potomac River junction of the Baltimore and Ohio Railroad's Main Stem and Metropolitan Branch, 15 miles south of Frederick, Maryland, and 40 miles from Washington, D.C.

POINT LOOKOUT (Maryland)

Site of a Federal prison in St. Marys County in Southern Maryland, where the Potomac River joins the Chesapeake Bay. Established in August 1863 for enlisted men, at its peak it held 20,000 prisoners without barracks.

POLK, LEONIDAS (1806–1864)

U.S. Military Academy, 1827; resigned to enter the Episcopal ministry and became Bishop of Louisiana. A personal friend of Jefferson Davis, he entered the Confederate army in 1861 as a Major General. He served mainly in the West and was killed at Pine Mountain.

POLLOCK, WILLIAM WINDER
Midshipman in the U.S. Navy, 1837; held the rank of Lieutenant from 1851. Joining the Confederate navy in 1863, he was executive officer of the CSS *Huntsville*. Attached to the Savannah Station in 1864, he was temporary commander of the CSS *Macon*. In 1865 he commanded the iron gunboat *Roanoke* of the James River Squadron.

POPE, JOHN (1822–1892)
U.S. Military Academy, 1842; Brigadier General of Volunteers, 1861, he held commands in Missouri and Mississippi. From June to September 1862, he headed the Army of Virginia. Defeated at Second Manassas, he was relieved by McClellan and sent to the Department of the Northwest.

PORTER, HORACE (1837–1921)
U.S. Military Academy, 1860; served in ordnance. A lieutenant colonel and aide-de-camp to General Grant in 1864, he was breveted Brigadier General in 1865. He remained in the army and from 1869–1873 was executive secretary to President Grant.

PRATT, THOMAS G. (1804–1869)
Governor of Maryland, 1845–1848, he was from Upper Marlboro in Prince Georges County. In 1850 he went to the U.S. Senate as a Whig to fill the unexpired term of Reverdy Johnson, and served to 1857. His views on secession led to his arrest and imprisonment in Fortress Monroe in 1861, and when released he was active in support of the Confederacy. He moved to Baltimore in 1864. He was married to Adeline Kent.

PRATT, THOMAS ST. GEORGE (1837–1895)
Maryland attorney and Confederate officer, he was the son of Governor Thomas G. Pratt.

PRESSTMAN, BENJAMIN C. (1812–1883)
Baltimore attorney, member of the 1850 Constitutional Convention, and a Baltimore City judge from 1855 to 1864.

"PRIESTFORD" (Harford County, Maryland)
Crossing of Deer Creek between Churchville and Poplar Grove. Two houses are located at this crossing: one, a stone structure that dates from colonial times and is called "Priest Neal's Mass House" or "Priestford," and the other, a nineteenth-century structure called "Priestford Farm." It is not clear which house belonged to Albert Neilson.

PRINCESS ANNE (Maryland)
County seat of Somerset County on the Eastern Shore of Maryland.

PRINGLE, JOEL ROBERTS POINSETT (1841–1864)
Son of John Julius Pringle and Joan Lynch Pringle of "White House Plantation," Georgetown, South Carolina. He and two brothers were educated in Europe, but returned to fight in the Confederate army.

PRINGLE, JOAN LYNCH, Mrs. John J. Pringle (1816–1896)
Widow of John Julius Izard Pringle (1808–1862) of "White House Plantation," Georgetown, South Carolina. Mrs. Pringle was from New York. John Pringle's mother, Mary Izard, married Joel Roberts Poinsett after the death of her first husband. William Russell visited "White House" in 1861.

PRINGLE, MARY
Daughter of John Julius Pringle and Joan Lynch Pringle. After the war she married Conte Ivan de Francs and moved to France.

RALEIGH CLUB (London)
Social club at 14–16 Regent Street.

RANDOLPH, GEORGE WYTHE (1818–1867)
Virginia attorney, he was a Confederate Peace Commissioner in 1861. A colonel in the Confederate army, he rose to Brigadier General in 1862. From March to November 1862, he was Confederate Secretary of War. In 1864 he went to France for his health.

RANSON, AMBROSE (1831–1919)
Virginian; colonel in the Confederate army. After the war he moved to Baltimore and became a grain merchant. His second wife was Lucy Glenn, sister of William Wilkins Glenn.

RAYMOND, HENRY JARVIS (1820–1869)
New York newspaperman, he had been with the *Tribune, Courier & Enquirer,* and *Harpers* before establishing the *New York Times* in 1851. A Whig in politics, he served in Congress as a Republican from 1865–1867.

READ, CHARLES W. (1840–1890)
Lieutenant in the Confederate navy, he served on the CSS *Florida.* As captain of the CSS *Tacony* he blew up the U.S. Revenue Cutter *Caleb Cushing* in 1863, but was captured off New England in June of that year.

REED, WILLIAM BRADFORD (1806–1876)
Philadelphia attorney, he had been secretary to Joel Roberts Poinsett before being appointed Minister to China in 1857, where he negotiated the Treaty of Tientsin. He was Southern in his

sympathies, and served as an American correspondent for the *London Times.*

REFORM CLUB (London)

Liberal Party club established in 1839, it was located on Pall Mall next to the Traveller's Club.

RHETT, ALFRED

Colonel, Confederate Army. As a lieutenant in charge of an 8-inch columbiad, the red-hot shot fired from his gun is credited with having started many fires in Fort Sumter during the bombardment of April 12–13, 1861. Later in the war he commanded the Confederate garrison on Fort Sumter.

RICHMOND *Times*

Established April 21, 1865, it followed the weekly *Sunday Morning Times* (1863–1864). In 1864 it merged with the *Daily Dispatch.*

RIDGELY, ANDREW STERETT (1822–1877)

Baltimore attorney, his residence was on Read Street. In 1865 he became U.S. District Attorney for Maryland.

RIDGELY, RANDOLPH (d. 1846)

Marylander; U.S. Military Academy, 1842; killed in 1846 during the Mexican War.

Rinaldo, H.B.M.S.

British corvette commanded by Captain William N. Hewett, she was launched in 1860 and carried 17 guns and a crew of 170 men. In January 1862 Confederate Commissioners Mason and Slidell embarked on the *Rinaldo* at Provincetown, Massachusetts en route to England. Later that year she was off Hampton Roads to observe the battle of the *Monitor* and the *Virginia (Merrimac).*

ROBINSON, ALEXANDER C. (1810–1871)

Baltimore physician, he was lecturer in anatomy at the University of Maryland. His residence was at Charles and Saratoga streets.

RODEWALD, HENRY A.

New Orleans commission merchant and member of the firm of Henry Rodewald & Co., Tobacco Brokers. In 1865 he was living at "Star Mount" on the Belair Road in Baltimore County, and in 1868 his address was 7 William Street in New York City.

RONALDS, FANNY, Mrs. Peter Ronalds

American singer, divorced from Peter Ronalds of Boston, she was a protégé of August Belmont and Leonard Jerome.

ROSENCRANS, WILLIAM STARKE (1819–1898)

U.S. Military Academy, 1842; resigned, 1854; entered Ohio Volunteers, 1861. Appointed Brigadier General in the U.S. Army, he was active in West Virginia and Tennessee. He resigned in 1867 and served as Minister to Mexico.

"ROSLYN" (Baltimore County)
Estate of General Benjamin Chew Howard at Reisterstown and Old Court Roads near "Sudbrooke" in the Pikesville area. The property had been in the Howard family for nearly 200 years, but the mansion house is now in ruins.

ROSS, FITZGERALD
Austrian officer, he served in the Confederate army before returning to Europe in April 1864. His "A Visit to the Cities and Camps of the Confederate States" was published in *Blackwood's Edinburgh Magazine.*

RUSSELL, JOHN, 1st Earl Russell (1792–1878)
British Foreign Secretary, 1860–1865, and Prime Minister, 1865–1866.

RUSSELL, WILLIAM HOWARD (1820–1907)
War correspondent for the *London Times,* he was in the U.S., 1861–1862, and wrote several books on his war experiences.

SAINT MAUR, EDWARD ADOLPHUS FERDINAND, Earl St. Maur (1835–1869)
Son of the 12th Duke of Somerset, First Lord of the Admiralty, St. Maur entered the House of Lords in 1863 as Baron Seymour. While visiting the Confederacy he is reputed to have fought in the Seven Days battle around Richmond and with distinguished gallantry at Frayser's Farm. He was later killed and eaten by a tiger in India.

St. Nicholas
Sidewheel steamer, 1200 tons, of the Washington, Alexandria & Georgetown Steam Packet Line, Captain Jacob Kirwan. She was captured in the Potomac by Confederates under the command of Col. R. Thomas, CSA and Captain G. N. Hollins, CSN on June 28, 1861. Her name was changed to *Rappahannock,* and she was sunk while in Confederate service at Fredericksburg, Virginia in April 1862.

SANGSTON, LAWRENCE (1814–1876)
Baltimore hardware and drygoods merchant. Baltimore City member of the House of Delegates in 1861, he was arrested and imprisoned at Fort Warren. He recounted his prison experiences in *The Bastiles of the North* (Baltimore, 1863).

SAINT BARNABAS CHURCH (Baltimore)
Episcopal church, erected in 1859 on the northeast corner of Biddle Street and Argyle Avenue.

SAINT DENIS HOTEL (New York)
Fashionable hotel with 150 rooms, at the corner of Broadway and 11th Street, opposite Grace Church.

SARATOGA SPRINGS (New York)
Popular and fashionable resort and spa 30 miles north of Albany. It is also noted for its racetrack. In the postwar period William Wilkins Glenn had one of his race horses in training here.

SAUNDERSON, LLEWELLYN T. B.
Officer in the 11th Hussars (Prince Albert's Own), commissioned Coronet December 1860.

SCHELL, AUGUSTUS (fl. 1850–1881)
New York City attorney, he signed the bail bond of Jefferson Davis. In 1871 he was Grand Sachem of the Tammany Society. He also served as president of the New York Historical Society.

SCHLEY, WILLIAM LOUIS (1823–1898)
Baltimore attorney, first cousin of Admiral Winfield Scott Schley. He was married to Kate M. Koch of York, Pennsylvania, and lived at 68 North Charles Street.

SCHENCK, ROBERT CUMMING (1809–1890)
Ohio Congressman, 1843–1851; Minister to Brazil, 1851–1853. Brigadier General of Ohio Volunteers, 1861. Appointed Major General, he was assigned to Baltimore in December 1862. He resigned in December 1863, and entered Congress as a radical Republican (1863–1871).

SCHULTZ, ALEXANDER H.
New York City steamboat captain; member of the New York Sanitary Commission, 1849. He was sent to Europe as a diplomatic courier in September 1861, and made repeated trips to England in 1862 and 1864.

SCOTT, OTHO (d. 1864)
Harford County, Maryland, attorney and state senator.

SCOTT, THOMAS PARKIN (1804–1873)
Baltimore attorney, Breckinridge elector in 1860. In 1861 he represented Baltimore in the House of Delegates. He became first Chief Judge of the new Baltimore City Supreme Bench in 1867 and served to 1873.

SCOTT, WINFIELD (1786–1866)
General in Chief of the U.S. Army, he retired in October 1861, and traveled in Europe.

SEDDEN, JAMES ALEXANDER (1815–1880)
Virginia Democratic Congressman and secessionist leader. He was Confederate Secretary of War, November 1862 to 1865.

SELDEN, WILLIAM A.
Norfolk, Virginia, physician, he served as personal physician to Robert E. Lee after the war. His house on Freemason Street still stands.

SEWARD, FREDERICK WILLIAM (1830–1915)
Albany, New York, journalist, and attorney, he was Assistant Secretary of State, 1861–1869, under his father, William Henry Seward.

SEWARD, WILLIAM HENRY (1801–1872)
New York Senator, leading Republican, and Secretary of State, 1861–1869.

SEYMER, ERNEST CLAY (1832–post-1876)
British career diplomat, attaché to the British legation in Washington, D.C. in the early 1860s, he became secretary to the Embassy in Paris, and later Deputy Lieutenant of Berwick and Magistrate for Dorset. In January 1865, he married Gertrude Ker-Seymer and assumed her name in addition to his own.

SEYMOUR, EDWARD ADOLPHUS, 12th Duke of Somerset (1804–1885)
First Lord of the Admiralty, 1859–1866, he was married to Jane Georgiana Sheridan and was the father of Edward Saint Maur.

SEYMOUR, HORATIO (1810–1886)
Democratic governor of New York, 1852–1854, 1863–1865. In 1868 he was nominated for president.

SEYMOUR, LEOPOLD R.
Lieutenant in the Grenadier Guards, commissioned June 1859.

SHEA, GEORGE (1826–1895)
New York City attorney, he served as associate counsel for Jefferson Davis with Charles O'Conor.

SHERIDAN, PHILIP HENRY (1831–1888)
U.S. Military Academy, 1853; served in the Quartermaster's Corps to 1862, when he became a colonel in the cavalry. Rose to the rank of Major General by 1863 and in 1864 was in command of the Middle Military Division.

SHERMAN, WILLIAM TECUMSEH (1820–1891)
U.S. Military Academy, 1840; resigned in 1853 and in 1861 was president of Louisiana State University. He was commissioned a colonel in the U.S. Army, then Brigadier General of Volunteers. He rose to Major General by 1862, was with Grant in the West, and succeeded him as commander of the Division of the Mississippi.

SHERWOOD, ROBERT (b.c. 1839)
Baltimore printer; his father owned Sherwood & Co., job printers at 6 North Gay Street.

SHRYNEK, HENRY S.
Owner of Henry S. Shrynek & Son, Baltimore cabinet, chair, and sofa manufacturers and upholsterers at 6 South Calvert Street.

SINCLAIR, ARTHUR, JR. (d. 1925)
Virginian; his father had resigned from the U.S. Navy in 1861. Entering the Confederate naval service, he served as 4th lientenant aboard the *Alabama*. After the war he wrote *Two Years on the Alabama* (1895).

SINGLETON, JAMES WASHINGTON (1811–1892)
Illinois politician, opposed the Lincoln administration and went to Canada in 1864 to promote peace. Late in the war he tried to work out a scheme to sell Southern goods in the North. From 1879 to 1883 he was in Congress as a Democrat.

SITWELL, HONORIUS SISSON
Captain in the Royal Engineers, commissioned December 1857.

SLIDELL, JOHN (1793–1871)
New Orleans politician and diplomat, he served in the Senate, 1853–1861. He was sent to Europe as Confederate Commissioner to France and arrived in February 1862, after being detained by Federal authorities during the *Trent* affair. He and his family remained in Paris after the war; his two daughters both married Frenchmen. His wife was Mathilde Desolonde (d. 1870).

SMITH, AUSTIN E. (c. 1831–1863)
Son of Virginia governor William Smith; U.S. Navy agent in San Francisco. He was arrested in New York August 2, 1861, and charged with being a secessionist and rebel. He was confined at Fort Lafayette until April 27, 1862, when he was exchanged for Philadelphia merchant William Ayres.

SMITH, EDMUND KIRBY (1824–1893)
U.S. Military Academy, 1845; resigned in 1861 and was commissioned a colonel in the Confederate cavalry. Appointed Brigadier General in 1861, he was a full General by 1864. He campaigned mainly in the West and Trans-Mississippi.

SMITH, GERRIT (1797–1874)
New York Congressman, reformer, philanthropist, and moderate Republican. Signed bail bond of Jefferson Davis.

SMITH, GUSTAVUS WOODSON (1822–1896)
U.S. Military Academy, 1842; resigned, 1854, and became New York City street commissioner, 1858–1861. Declared disloyal by the Federal government, he volunteered his services to the Confederacy and was commissioned a Major General. He was Secretary of War briefly in November 1862, and resigned from the army early in 1863.

SMITH, J. BAYARD H.
Baltimore attorney.

SMITH, SAMUEL W. (1800–1887)
Baltimore merchant, he owned several Pratt Street warehouses, as well as land in Georgia and Alabama and mining interests in Maryland and Michigan. His sons John Donnell Smith (b. 1829) and William H. Smith (b. 1835) both served in the Confederate army. He served on the Second Branch of the City Council in 1868. His residence was 85 Park Avenue.

SMITH, WILLIAM (1797–1887)
Virginia attorney; practiced law in Baltimore with William H. Winder. Returned to Virginia, went into the mail coach service, then politics. Governor of Virginia, 1846 to 1849. Member of Congress at the outbreak of the war. A Confederate general and member of Congress, he became governor of Virginia in 1863 and served to 1865.

SMITH, WILLIAM PRESCOTT (1824–1872)
Baltimorean; master of transportation for the Baltimore and Ohio Railroad.

South
Baltimore newspaper "devoted to the South, Southern Rights, and Secession" (*South,* April 22, 1861), edited and published by Thomas W. Hall. It was suspended September 13, 1861, and reissued by John M. Milles & Co. until February 1862.

Southern Press
Washington, D.C. daily newspaper issued from June 1850 to August 1852.

SPEED, JAMES (1812–1887)
Kentucky legislator; U.S. Attorney General, 1864–1866. He later became Professor of Law at the University of Louisville.

SPOTSWOOD HOTEL (Richmond)
Balconied hotel at Main and 8th streets. Davis stayed there when he arrived in Richmond as President of the Confederacy, and in 1866, while on trial, he was given his former rooms.

STANBERY, HENRY (1803–1881)
Cincinnati, Ohio, attorney. A moderate Republican, he was U.S. Attorney General, 1866–1868.

STANLEY, ARTHUR PENRHYN (1815–1881)
British clergyman and Dean of Westminster Abbey in 1863, he was the author of works on the Holy Land and ecclesiastical history.

STANTON, EDWIN MCMASTERS (1814–1869)
Ohio attorney and U.S. Attorney General, 1860, he became Secretary of War in 1862, serving to 1866.

STARKE, BENJAMIN (1820–1898)
Oregon attorney and Democratic U.S. Senator, 1861–1862. He was a delegate to the Democratic National Conventions in 1864 and 1868.

STEELE, ISAAC NEVETT (1809–1891)
Baltimore attorney, he had served as chargé d'affaires in Venezuela, 1849–1853, and was chairman of the Whig state central committee. His residence was 259 West Madison Avenue.

STEPHENSON, FREDERICK CHARLES ARTHUR (1821–19 ?)
Lieutenant of the Scots Fusilier Guards, commissioned 1854. Companion, Order of the Bath, 1858; Colonel, 1861. He commanded forces in Egypt, 1883–1887.

STERETT, SAMUEL (1833–1879)
Baltimore cotton broker, he joined the Confederate army but was arrested and confined at Fort Delaware for war.

STEUART, RICHARD SPRIGG (1797–1876)
Baltimore physician, he had first practiced law. He graduated from the University of Maryland in 1822. He was head of the Maryland Hospital for the Insane (later Spring Grove Hospital in Catonsville, Maryland). Married to Maria Louisa de Bernabeau (1800–1883), daughter of the Spanish consul to Baltimore. His Anne Arundel County residence was in the vicinity of Birdsville, Maryland, south of All Hallows Church on State Route 2, about nine miles south of Annapolis.

STEVENS, THADDEUS (1792–1868)
Gettysburg, Pennsylvania, attorney and legislator, and owner of the Caledonia Iron Works, he was the leading radical Republican in the House of Representatives.

STILES, ELIZABETH ANNE, Mrs. William Henry Stiles (1810–1867)
Wife of a former chargé d'affaires to Austria (1845–1849), she was the mother of Mrs. Mary Low. The Stileses were from Savannah, Georgia, but had been friends of the Glenns since that family's European trip in 1849.

STIRLING, CHARLES (b. 1834)
Major, British Royal Artillery.

"STOVER LODGE" (England)
Devonshire lodge of the Dukes of Somerset, two miles northwest of Newton Abbot.

STRYKER, AUGUSTUS P. (1830–1891)
Episcopal clergyman, rector of St. Barnabas Church in Baltimore.

STUART, JAMES EWELL BROWN (1833–1864)
U.S. Military Academy, 1854; resigned 1861; commissioned captain in the Confederate cavalry, then Brigadier General (1861). As

Major General, 1862, he was in command of all cavalry for the Army of Northern Virginia.

STUMP, HERMAN (1835–1917)
Harford County, Maryland, attorney, state senator, 1877–1881, and Congressman, 1888. He was a first cousin of Henry W. Archer. His home, "Waverly," was between Emmorton and Belair.

SULLIVAN, FRANKLIN (b. 1815)
Partner in J. Sullivan & Sons, Baltimore general commission merchants, he had been born in Nashville, Tennessee. He was a member of the Maryland Club, and lived at 22 Cathedral Street.

SULTZER, THOMAS D. (1817–1891)
Compositor, connected with the Baltimore *Clipper,* he became a reporter for the Baltimore *Sun* in 1864.

SUSPENSION BRIDGE (Niagara Falls, New York)
Railroad and highway bridge 825 feet long between Canada and the United States, it was built in 1855 across the Niagara River.

SWANN, THOMAS (1806–1883)
Baltimore politician, he was born in Alexandria, Virginia, and moved to Baltimore after his marriage to Elizabeth Gilmor Sherlock. He was president of the Baltimore and Ohio Railroad, 1848–1853. In 1856 he became Mayor of Baltimore as a member of the American (Know Nothing) Party, and served to 1860. He was Union Party governor of Maryland, 1865–1869, and in 1869 was elected to Congress as a Democrat, serving to 1879.

SWEET SPRINGS (West Virginia)
Spa in Monroe County, 17 miles southeast of White Sulphur Springs.

SWINTON, JOHN (1830–1901)
Managing editor of the New York *Tribune,* he later moved to the New York *Sun.*

TANEY, ROGER BROOKE (1777–1864)
Chief Justice of the U.S. Supreme Court, 1836–1864. He was a personal friend of Judge John Glenn, the father of William Wilkins Glenn.

TAYLOR, MILTON N. (b. 1822)
Baltimore City physician.

TAYLOR, RICHARD (1826–1879)
Son of Zachary Taylor and brother-in-law of Jefferson Davis, he was a Louisiana plantation owner and politician. Commissioned Brigadier General in the Confederate army in 1861, he rose to Lieutenant General in 1864. Most of his service was in Louisiana, Mississippi, and Alabama.

TAYLOR, TAZEWELL (1810–1875)
Norfolk, Virginia, attorney, he was aide-de-camp to General Walter Gwynn. After the war he became president of the Norfolk Savings Bank.

TEACKLE, ST. GEORGE WILLIAMSON (1806–1874)
Baltimore attorney, he was born in Accomac County, Virginia.

TEMPLE, HENRY JOHN, Viscount Palmerston (1784–1865)
Liberal Prime Minister of England, 1855–1858, 1859, 1865.

Tennessee, C.S.S.
Steam ram launched in 1864, she was 209 feet long. Involved in the defense of Mobile, where she was captured.

TERRY, ALFRED HOWE (1827–1890)
Entering the Connecticut Volunteers in 1861 as a Colonel, he rose to Brigadier General in 1862. He commanded forces at Hilton Head, 1862–1863, then moved to commands in North Carolina and Virginia.

THACKERAY, WILLIAM MAKEPEACE (1811–1863)
British author, he lived at 2 Palace Green in Kensington. The circumstances of his death on December 23, 1863, are described in the *Dictionary of National Biography.* His two daughters were Anne Isabella, who married Sir Richmond Ritchie, and Harriet Marian, who married Leslie Stephens.

THOMAS, J. HANSON (1813–1881)
Frederick, Maryland, physician, he moved to Baltimore City and continued his practice. He represented Baltimore in the House of Delegates in 1861, and was arrested and imprisoned. His wife was Anna Campbell Gordon.

THOMAS, JOHN HANSON (b. 1841)
Baltimore attorney, son of Dr. J. Hanson Thomas. He was married to Mary Howard Beirne, and lived at 65 McCulloh Street.

THOMAS, JOSEPH (1819–1865)
Baltimore lumber dealer and head of Joseph Thomas & Sons, steam turning and sawing, on Clay Street. He died of self-inflicted gun-shot wounds in Govanstown on April 24, 1865.

THOMAS, PHILIP FRANCIS (1810–1890)
Easton, Maryland, Democratic politician and governor of Maryland, 1848–1851. In 1866 he represented Talbot County in the House of Delegates. Elected to the U.S. Senate in 1867, he was not seated. In 1874 he served in the House of Representatives.

THOMAS, RICHARD, alias "ZARVONA" (183?–1875)
From St. Marys County, Maryland, he had attended West Point but resigned. He had a varied career as a surveyor in California, fought pirates in China, and campaigned with Garibaldi in Italy.

He was captured commandeering the steamboat *St. Nicholas* on orders from the Confederate government. After his imprisonment he lived in France.

THORNTON, Sir EDWARD (1817–1906)
British career diplomat, he was Minister to the United States from 1867 to 1880.

THYNNE, Lady HARRIET BARING (d. 1892)
Widow of Henry Frederick Thynne (1797–1837), 3rd Marquis of Bath, and mother of John Alexander Thynne (4th Marquis) and Henry Frederick Thynne.

THYNNE, HENRY FREDERICK (1832–1904)
Second son of the 3rd Marquis of Bath. He was a Member of Parliament from South Wiltshire, 1859–1885, and from 1875–1888 Treasurer of the Queen's Household.

THYNNE, Lady ULRICA (d. 1916)
Daughter of the 12th Duke of Somerset, she was the wife of Henry Frederick Thynne and the sister of Lord Edward St. Maur.

TOMPKINS, CHRISTOPHER QUARLES (1813–1877)
Richmond, Virginia, resident, he had served in the U.S. Army from 1833–1847. He owned and operated coal mines in Fayette County (West) Virginia, and was married to Ellen Wilkins of Baltimore.

TRAIN, GEORGE FRANCIS (1829–1904)
Merchant shipper, he traveled and lived in Europe, Asia, and Australia. He was jailed in Boston in 1862 for his outspoken Fenian sentiments. Author of *My Life in Many States and in Foreign Lands* (1902).

TRAVELLER'S CLUB (London)
Founded in 1819 and still extant; the necessary qualification for membership was foreign travel. In 1831 it moved to quarters at 106 Pall Mall and has remained there.

TRAVERS, WILLIAM RIGGIN (d. 1887)
New York City banker and stock broker, he graduated from Columbia in 1838. Called the "Stammering Wit of Wall Street" he was Leonard Jerome's cousin and partner. He and Jerome were leaders in establishing the American Jockey Club.

TRENHOLM, GEORGE A. (1806–1876)
South Carolina cotton merchant, he was a partner in Fraser, Trenholm & Co., and from 1864 to 1865 was Confederate Secretary of the Treasury.

TRIMBLE, ISAAC RIDGEWAY (1802–1888)
U.S. Military Academy, 1822; he was responsible for burning bridges north of Baltimore in April 1861. He resigned from the

Army, and was commissioned a colonel by the Confederates. Promoted to Brigadier General in 1861, he rose to Major General by 1863, serving mainly in Virginia. After the war he returned to Baltimore as a consulting engineer.

TROLLOPE, ANTHONY (1815–1882)
British novelist and post office official, he traveled in the United States in 1861 and published *North America* in 1862.

TRUMBULL, LYMAN (1813–1880)
Illinois attorney and judge, he served in the U.S. Senate as a Republican from 1855 to 1873.

TUCKER, JOHN RANDOLPH (1823–1897)
Winchester, Virginia, attorney and Attorney General of Virginia from 1857–1865. He became a professor at Washington College in Lexington in 1870, and served in Congress from 1875–1887.

TURNBULL, ANNA GRAEME SMITH, Mrs. Henry C. Turnbull (d. 1866)
Daughter of Samuel F. Smith of Philadelphia, she was married to Henry C. Turnbull of Baltimore County, and lived at "Auburn" off the York Road. Her two sons were S. Graeme Turnbull and Lawrence Turnbull.

TURNBULL, LAWRENCE (1843–1919)
Son of Anna G. Turnbull, he graduated from Princeton in 1863 and read law under Severn Teackle Wallis. After the war he was an attorney and publisher in Baltimore.

TURNBULL, S. GRAEME (d. 1863)
Eldest son of Anna G. Turnbull of Baltimore County, he served as a member of J. E. B. Stuart's cavalry and was killed in 1863.

TURPIE, DAVID (1828–1909)
Indiana Democrat, attorney, and judge, he was elected to the U.S. Senate after the expulsion of Jesse Bright in 1863.

UNDERWOOD, JOHN CURTISS (1808–1873)
U.S. District Court Judge for Virginia. He presided over the case of Jefferson Davis in 1867.

UNION CLUB OF BALTIMORE
The Union Club of Baltimore, founded in 1863 for the purpose of promoting "unqualified loyalty to the Government of the United States . . . to discountenance all disloyalty to the Government and all attempts to subvert that union . . ." (Union Club *Constitution*, 1863), had its club house at 51 North Charles Street. Joseph N. Bonaparte was the president, and many leading businessmen and attorneys were among its officers and members.

VALIANT, WILLIAM THOMAS (1819–1891)
Partner of William T. Valiant & Co., importers and dealers in

China, glass, and queensware, at 216 West Pratt Street in Baltimore. He became Baltimore Police Commissioner in 1866.

VALLANDIGHAM, CLEMENT LAIRD (1820–1871)
Dayton, Ohio, attorney and Representative from Ohio, 1858–1863. An outspoken anti-administration Democrat, he was banished South but returned to run unsuccessfully for governor of Ohio in 1863. He was a delegate to both the 1864 and 1868 Democratic Conventions.

VANDERBILT, CORNELIUS (1794–1877)
Prominent New York promoter and financier. Signed the bail bond of Jefferson Davis.

VANSANT, JOSHUA (1803–1884)
Born in Kent County, Maryland, he was head of Joshua Vansant & Son, hatters and fur dealers at 109 West Baltimore Street in Baltimore. Active in politics, he was a Breckinridge elector in 1860, and Democratic Mayor of Baltimore, 1871–1875.

VAN VLIET, STEWART (1815–1901)
U.S. Military Academy, 1840; chief quartermaster of the Army of the Potomac, 1861–1862; later in charge of transportation and supplies at New York City.

VIZITELLY, FRANCIS C. (1830–c. 1883)
War correspondent and illustrator for the *Illustrated London News*. He was with the Union army from May 1861, and in 1862 went South with the help of a "Baltimore gentleman." He ran the blockade in January 1864, and returned in June, remaining to May 1865. He was killed while on assignment in Egypt.

VON SCHELIHA, VICTOR
Prussian; Confederate Colonel and chief of staff to General Buckner, he was chief engineer in the Department of the Gulf. He was captured at Island No. 10 in May 1862. Exchanged, he became staff engineer to Generals Polk, Zollicoffer, Crittenden, and MacKall. From January 1864 to the end of the war he was in Mobile erecting extensive fortifications. While there he married a local girl, with his friend Fitzgerald Ross in attendance.

WADDELL, JAMES IREDELL (1824–1886)
Entered the U.S. Navy, 1841; resigned 1862 and was commissioned a lieutenant in the Confederate Navy. He served with the James River Squadron, then went to Paris in 1863. In 1864 he took command of the C.S.S. *Shenandoah* and sailed to Melbourne, Australia, then back through the Pacific, taking prizes until June 1865. He remained in England to the 1870s, then was a captain with the Pacific Mail Lines, and retired to Annapolis, Maryland. His wife was Ann S. Iglehart of Annapolis.

WALKER. REUBEN LINDSAY (1827–1890)
Graduate of Virginia Military Institute, he was a civil engineer until commissioned in the Confederate army in 1861. He was in the artillery with the Army of Northern Virginia, and was promoted to Brigadier General in 1865.

WALLACE, LEWIS (1827–1905)
Indiana attorney, he was commissioned Brigadier General of Volunteers in 1861, rising to Major General in 1862. He commanded the Middle Department with headquarters in Baltimore from 1863 to 1865, and then served on both the courts martial of the Lincoln conspirators and Henry Wirz.

WALLIS, SEVERN TEACKLE (1816–1894)
Baltimore attorney, author, orator, and man of letters. He studied law under William Wirt and Judge John Glenn, the father of William Wilkins Glenn. Urbane, witty, and well traveled, he represented Baltimore City in the House of Delegates in 1861. While serving in this capacity, he authored several of the important reports of the Committee on Federal Relations as well as the Memorial of the Police Commissioners of Baltimore who had been arrested. Wallis was arrested in September 1861 and imprisoned in Forts McHenry, Monroe, Lafayette, and Warren until 1862. A frequent contributor to the editorial pages of the *Exchange* (*Gazette*) newspaper and author of several books on Spain, he was a lifelong friend of the Glenn family and an intimate of William Wilkins Glenn. Throughout his life Wallis retained a passion for political reform and in the postwar years was hailed as one of the brightest luminaries of the Maryland bar.

WALTERS, WILLIAM THOMPSON (1820–1894)
Baltimore merchant; president of the Baltimore & Susquehanna Railroad; he went to Europe in 1861 and remained to 1865. Returning with an extensive collection of art and artifacts, he formed the nucleus of the collection of the Walters Art Gallery in Baltimore.

WAMBERSIE, EUGENE CHARLTON
Baltimore shipping and commission merchant, partner of Wambersie & Son, he came from Savannah, Georgia, in the 1830s.

WARREN, LEANDER (1817–1881)
Commercial editor of the Baltimore *Exchange*.

WASHINGTON, JAMES W. (d. 1865)
Member of the 12th Virginia Cavalry, CSA, he and Herbert Alexander were captured at "Claymount Court" near Winchester, Virginia, in February 1865. General Sheridan ordered reprisals against the farm's owners as an example to others harboring guerrillas.

WASHINGTON, LEWIS WILLIAM (1812–1871)
Virginian, descendant of Bushrod Washington, he spent most of the war period in Europe. His daughter Elizabeth married Elias Glenn Perine, first cousin of William Wilkins Glenn.

WASHINGTON, LUCIUS QUENTIN
Chief clerk of the Confederate State Department, he performed the duties of an assistant Secretary of State. He was involved in intelligence and recruiting activities in 1861, and may have served as a Lieutenant at First Bull Run.

WEBB—see *WILLIAM H. WEBB*

WEBB, CHARLES (1820–1891)
Baltimore manufacturer and politician, he was a supporter of Mayor George Brown. A director of the Baltimore and Ohio Railroad in 1860; in 1878 he became Baltimore City Collector of Taxes.

WEBSTER, EDWIN HANSON (1829–1893)
Harford County, Maryland, attorney, he was elected to the state senate in 1855 as a candidate of the American (Know Nothing) Party and served to 1859; he was a member of Congress from 1859–1865. In 1862–1863 he served as a colonel in the 7th Regiment, Maryland Volunteer Infantry, U.S. Army. In 1865 he was Collector of the Port of Baltimore, serving to 1869.

WEED, THURLOW (1797–1882)
New York politician and journalist, he had been a Whig and supported William Seward in 1860. He was editor of the Albany *Evening Journal* to 1863, when he moved to New York City.

WEEKS, JOHN L. (1822–1888)
Baltimore merchant and partner of Wood, Weeks & Co., steam sugar refiners.

WEITZEL, GODFREY (1835–1884)
U.S. Military Academy, 1855; from December 1861 to 1862 he was in charge of the defenses of Washington, D.C. Promoted to Brigadier General of Volunteers in 1862, he held various commands in the Gulf and in Virginia.

WELLER, JOHN B. (1812–1875)
From Hamilton County, Ohio, he had a political career before moving to California, which he represented in the U.S. Senate from 1851–1857. In 1858 he was elected governor of California as a Democrat, and in 1860 was appointed Minister to Mexico. He was a delegate to the Democratic National Convention in 1864, and in 1867 moved to New Orleans.

WELLES, GIDEON (1802–1878)
Connecticut Republican editor, he was Secretary of the Navy, 1861–1869.

WENLOCK, 2nd Baron—see LAWLEY, BEILBY RICHARD

WEST RIVER (Anne Arundel County, Maryland)
River emptying into the Chesapeake Bay south of Annapolis, it was the location of several popular resorts and was served by a steamboat landing at Galesville. The town of West River was inland on State Route 2.

WETHERED, JOHN (1809–1888)
Baltimore County woolen manufacturer, he was a partner of Wethered Brothers, whose milltown Wetherdsville (Dickeyville) was on Gwynn's Falls. He served in Congress from 1843 to 1845, and was a delegate to the Anti-Registry Law Convention in 1866 and the Constitutional Convention in 1867. He was married to Mary Thomas, daughter of a former governor and president of the Baltimore and Ohio Railroad. He lived at "Ashland" near Catonsville.

WHARNCLIFFE, 1st Earl—see MONTAGU-STUART-WORTLEY-MACKENZIE, EDWARD MONTAGU STUART GRANVILLE

WHITE SULPHUR SPRINGS (West Virginia)
Resort at Greenbrier on Howard's Creek, dating from the late eighteenth century. The spring water was reputedly good for the gout and liver diseases and was sought by Judge John Glenn and William Wilkins Glenn for health as well as recreation. The resort is shown in an 1871 engraving as having a Baltimore Row, where many of the social elite had cottages. Robert E. Lee had a cottage on Carolina Row.

WHITING, WILLIAM HENRY CHASE (1824–1865)
U.S. Military Academy, 1845; resigned, 1861, and was commissioned in the Confederate army. Appointed Brigadier General in 1861 and Major General in 1863, he held various commands in Virginia and North Carolina, and was at one time General Joseph Johnston's chief engineer. He was mortally wounded at Fort Fisher.

WHITTINGHAM, WILLIAM R. (1805–1879)
Protestant Episcopal Bishop of Maryland, and leading Unionist.

WHYTE, CAMPBELL PINKNEY (1828–1903)
Maryland attorney, he was the son of Joseph White, but changed his name to Pinkney in later years. During the war he served in the Confederate army with the 1st Maryland Infantry. He was elected to the Baltimore City Supreme Bench in 1867 and served to 1882, being Chief Judge from 1875–1877. He was the brother of William Pinkney Whyte.

WHYTE, WILLIAM PINKNEY (1824–1908)
Baltimore attorney, he was a graduate of Harvard Law School, and an active Democrat in state politics in the 1850s. In 1868 he

was a delegate to the Democratic National Convention, and was elected to the U.S. Senate in November, resigning in 1869. He ran for governor of Maryland and served from 1871–1874, resigning to reenter the Senate.

WIEGEL, WILLIAM HENRY (d. 1900)
Marylander; officer in the U.S. Army, in 1861 he was a voluntary aide-de-camp to General Butler, and in 1863 was a Captain and an assistant adjutant general. He was appointed assistant Provost Marshal at Baltimore in September 1864 and served to 1865. He was mustered out of service in 1868.

WILKES, CHARLES (1801–1877)
U.S. Navy lieutenant in 1826; commander in 1843; captain in 1855; rear admiral in 1866. From 1838 to 1842 he led an exploring expedition to the Pacific that bears his name. As commander of the *San Jacinto* on November 8, 1861, he removed Confederate commissioners James M. Mason and John Slidell from the British ship *Trent* and precipitated the Union's major diplomatic crisis of the war. He commanded the James River Flotilla in 1862 and later a "Flying Squadron" that sought to destroy Confederate raiders and blockade runners. He is reputed to have been a youthful acquaintance of Slidell, with whom he had a falling out over a mutual romantic interest.

William H. Webb, C.S. Ram
Confederate steam ram serving on the Red and Mississippi Rivers from 1861 to 1865.

WILLIAMS, JAMES (1796–1869)
Tennessee journalist and diplomat, he had been Minister to Turkey from 1858–1860. During the war he wrote for the *London Times* and acted as a Confederate propagandist in Europe. His *The Rise and Fall of the Model Republic* was published in 1863. He remained in Europe after the war.

WILLIAMS, OTHO HOLLAND (1819–1903)
Baltimore merchant, he was connected with William Howell & Sons, wholesale grocers, and later became vice-president of the Farmers and Merchants Bank. His residence was at Park and Madison Avenues.

WILLIAMS, Sir WILLIAM FENWICK (1800–1883)
Colonel Commandant, Royal Artillery, 1864–1883; commander of British forces in Canada, 1859–1865; and Governor of Nova Scotia, 1865–1866. As a general in the Turkish army he had held the city of Kars against the Russians for three months in 1855.

WILLIAMSON, GEORGE W. (fl. 1830–1877)
Owner of "Lexington" in Pikesville, Baltimore County, Maryland. In 1830 he married Mary Boerum of Baltimore.

WILSON, HENRY (1812–1873)
Massachusetts Senator, 1855–1873. In 1861 he commanded the 22nd Massachusetts Volunteers. He was Grant's Vice President, 1873–1875.

WINANS, ROSS (1796–1877)
Baltimore inventor, formerly with the Baltimore and Ohio Railroad, his specialty was steam engines and steam guns. He represented Baltimore in the House of Delegates in 1861 and was a Southern sympathizer.

WINDER, RICHARD BAGLEY
Captain in the Confederate army, he came from Accomac County, Virginia. As Quartermaster of the Andersonville Prison, he was implicated by the Wirz trial. He was arrested August 26, 1865, taken to Old Capitol Prison, and later tried in Richmond. His counsel was William Linn Brown.

WISE, HENRY ALEXANDER (1806–1876)
Virginia Congressman, 1833–1844, he was appointed Minister to Brazil in 1844. In 1856 he became governor of Virginia, serving to 1860. In 1861 he was appointed Brigadier General in the Confederate army, serving in Virginia and the Carolinas.

WITHERS, ROBERT ENOCH (1821–1907)
Officer in the Confederate army in 1861, he commanded a post at Danville, Virginia. He became U.S. Senator from Mississippi in 1875 and served to 1881.

WOLSELEY, GARNET JOSEPH, Viscount Wolseley (1833–1913)
Assistant Quartermaster General in Canada in 1861, he was a contributor to *Blackwood's Edinburgh Magazine*. A colonel in the Royal Horse Guards, he rose to the rank of Field Marshall and Commander in Chief of His Majesty's Forces.

WOOD, BENJAMIN (1820–1900)
Editor and publisher of the New York *Daily News*, 1860–1900, he was a Representative in Congress, 1861–1865, 1881–1883.

WOOD, FERNANDO (1812–1881)
New York Democratic politician, he was a brother of Benjamin Wood. He served in Congress from 1841–1843, was Mayor of New York City, 1855–1858, and 1861–1862. A friend of President Buchanan, he was pro-Southern in his attitudes and a leading peace Democrat.

WOOD, WILLIAM P. (1820–1903)
Superintendent of Old Capitol Prison, Washington, D.C., from 1861–1865, he had been a private in the regular army. A friend of Edwin Stanton, he was known for using his position to advance his personal fortune. In 1865 he became Chief of the U.S. Secret Service.

WOOL, JOHN ELLIS (1784–1869)
Brigadier General in the U.S. Army since 1841, he commanded the Department of the East in 1861, then the Middle Department. He retired in August 1863.

WOOLLEY, JOHN (d. 1873)
Officer in the Indiana cavalry, he was a lieutenant colonel and Provost Marshal of the Middle Department, 1864–1866. He was breveted Brigadier General, and mustered out in 1866.

WORTHINGTON, HENRY GAITHER (1828–1909)
Born in Cumberland, Maryland, he moved West and from 1864–1865 was Republican Representative from Nevada. In 1868 he was appointed Minister to Uruguay and Argentina.

WYNDHAM, GEORGE, 1st Baron Leconfield (1787–1869)
"Adopted heir" of George O'Brien, Lord Egermont, he was created Baron in 1859.

WYNDHAM, PERCY (1835–1911)
Captain in the Coldstream Guards; Member of Parliament from West Cumberland, 1860–1885.

WYNNE, EDWARD WILLIAM L. (1836–1893)
Captain in the Grenadier Guards, commissioned March 1857, he rose to the rank of Major General in the British Army.

YOUNG, JAMES (1816–1872)
Baltimore printer, from 1864 to 1866 he was president of the First Branch of the City Council. In 1866 he was appointed Police Commissioner, but did not serve on the recognized board.

"ZARVONA"—see RICHARD THOMAS

BIBLIOGRAPHICAL ESSAY

The role of Maryland in the Civil War and Reconstruction eras has been largely neglected, mainly because of a lack of extensive manuscript sources. The best secondary source and most detailed account is that found in John Thomas Scharf, *History of Maryland,* vol. 3 (1879; reprint Hatboro, Pa., 1967). Less detailed but more recent popular histories of the period are Matthew Page Andrews, *History of Maryland* (1929; reprint Hatboro, Pa., 1965); and Harold Manakee, *Maryland in the Civil War* (Baltimore, 1961). Jean H. Baker's *The Politics of Continuity, Maryland Political Parties from 1858 to 1870* (Baltimore, 1973) is a scholarly account of politics in Maryland during the war and postwar periods. Each Maryland county has its own history, which proves helpful for local events and personages. The most useful of these has been Scharf's *History of Baltimore City and County* (1881; reprint Baltimore, 1971). Biography, like general history, has been a neglected field in Maryland. Of the Civil War era governors, only Thomas H. Hicks has been the subject of a biography in George Radcliffe's *Governor Thomas H. Hicks of Maryland and the Civil War* (Baltimore, 1901). Frank White's *The Governors of Maryland* (Annapolis, 1970) contains sketches of other governors. Henry Winter Davis and Montgomery Blair are the subjects of somewhat dated biographies. The *Maryland Historical Magazine* includes numerous articles on the Civil War era and prominent Marylanders of the period.

Many of the persons mentioned by William Wilkins Glenn on the national level have been the subject of biographies, and the era of the Civil War and Reconstruction has been explored in countless monographs. Thus the works listed below are only the major sources used in the compilation of the glossary and notes.

General biographical dictionaries provided most of the information on persons mentioned in the Glenn narrative and the reader is referred to them for additional information. Sketches of Americans can be found in the *Dictionary of American Biography* (New York, 1927–1938); *The Biographical Directory of American Congresses* (Washington, 1961); *Appleton's Cyclopedia of American Biography* (New York, 1887–1900); and Mark M. Boatner, *Civil War Dictionary* (New York, 1959).

Biographical information on Englishmen came from the *Dictionary of National Biography* (Oxford, 1921); *Modern English Biography* (London, 1892–1921); *Burke's Landed Gentry* (London, 1894, 1898, 1904); *Burke's Irish Peerage* (London, 1958); and *Burke's Peerage, Baronetage and Knightage* (London, 1868–present). This latter source proved most helpful, as many descendants of Glenn's contemporaries either received titles or married into titled families after the turn of the century. There is no general directory of Members of Parliament, but annual directories for the 1850s and 1860s exist and were consulted. The British army *Registers* for the 1860s were helpful in identifying various officers mentioned by Glenn.

The best general sources for the Civil War, both foreign and domestic, remain *The War of the Rebellion: A Compilation of the Official Records of the Union and Confederate Armies* (*Washington,* 1880–1901); and *The War of the Rebellion: A Compilation of the Official Records of the Union and Confederate Navies* (Washington, 1894–1922). A recent issue, *Civil War Naval Chronology, 1861–1865* (Washington, 1971) has proven a useful guide in both military and naval matters.

Information on persons whose lives have been less well documented has come from the genealogical and biographical files of the Maryland Historical Society, the Maryland Room, and the George Peabody Branch of the Enoch Pratt Library in Baltimore, and the genealogical collections of the National Society, Daughters of the American Revolution, in Washington, D.C. City directories for Baltimore, New York, New Orleans, Philadelphia, Richmond, and Washington, D.C., provided a wealth of information on individuals, businesses, locations, transportation facilities, and civil officials. Contemporary issues of the Baltimore *Sun,* Baltimore *American, Daily Gazette,* and *New York Times* newspapers were consulted for specific events mentioned by Glenn, and the Glenn family papers (MS 1017) at the Maryland Historical Society provided considerable detail on Glenn's associates and family life.

Geographical information contemporary with the Glenn narrative was often difficult to obtain. The Maryland Historical Society has a fine collection of Maryland maps. These, and a series of state atlases from the 1870s, were used to verify local place names, and were at times the only source of information on Marylanders living outside Baltimore City. The George Peabody Branch of the Enoch Pratt Library owns numerous nineteenth-century visitors' guides to Canada, New York City, London, Paris, and Berlin, as well as several guides and gazetteers of Ireland.

INDEX